MW00849636

WALK HUMBLY, SERVE BOLDLY

MODERN QUAKERS AS EVERYDAY PROPHETS

Margery Post Abbott

Inner Light Books
San Francisco, California
2018

WALK HUMBLY, SERVE BOLDLY
MODERN QUAKERS AS
EVERYDAY PROPHETS

© 2018 Margery Post Abbott

All Rights Reserved

Except for brief quotations, no part of this publication may be reproduced, stored in a retrieval system, or transmitted, in any form or by any means, electronic, mechanical, photocopy, recorded, or otherwise, without prior written permission.

Editor: Charles Martin
Copyediting: Kathy McKay
Layout and design: Matt Kelsey

Published by Inner Light Books

San Francisco, California

www.innerlightbooks.com

editor@innerlightbooks.com

Library of Congress Control Number: 2018949552

ISBN 978-0-9998332-6-1 (hardcover)
ISBN 978-0-9998332-7-8 (paperback)
ISBN 978-0-9998332-8-5 (eBook)

Unless otherwise noted, Scripture quotations are from New Revised Standard Version Bible, copyright © 1989 National Council of the Churches of Christ in the United States of America. Used by permission. All rights reserved.

Scripture quotations marked MSG are taken from *THE MESSAGE*, copyright © 1993, 1994, 1995, 1996, 2000, 2001, 2002 by Eugene H. Peterson. Used by permission of NavPress. All rights reserved. Represented by Tyndale House Publishers, Inc.

Excerpts (with some modifications) from the following works by Margery Post Abbott are reproduced with permission from the publishers, as follows:

"Everyday Prophets," James Backhouse Lecture 2016, delivered in Hobart on 4 July 2016 during the annual meeting of the Society. Published by Australia Yearly Meeting of the Religious Society of Friends (Quakers) in Australia.

"Dispatches from a Week of Piano Practice," *Friends Journal* 62, no. 8 (September 2016).

"Multnomah Meeting Procedures relating to Clearness, Support, and Accountability for Friends Who Experience a Call to Ministry Locally or Traveling outside the Region." January 16, 2018. Prepared by Multnomah (Oregon) Monthly Meeting.

The following articles from the e-newsletter *SEEDS* published by Good News Associates, available at http://goodnewsassoc.org/seeds:

"Prophetic Ministry," *SEEDS* (August 2012)
"The Ecosystem of Ministry," *SEEDS* (August 2013)
"Practice and Music," *SEEDS* (February 2015)
"Thoughts on Humility from Africa," *SEEDS* (February 2017)
"Knowing Our Own Demons," *SEEDS* (June 2017)
"Dreams and the Prophetic Life," *SEEDS* (October 2017)

Contents

PREFACE

"I live in the kingdom." Not "as if" but "in." Recently, a criminal justice activist told me of hearing these words spoken to her when she was a new member of the Religious Society of Friends (Quakers). They tore open her heart and overturned her understanding of her place in the world. These words are alive and vital to her decades later, shaping her heart as well as her work with prisoners, victims, attorneys, and prison guards.

This time, as has been true for every era of human history, is plagued by violence. As much as I love to think of my home in Portland, Oregon, as a safe place, no place is immune from eruptions of hatred or desperation. How are we—how am I—to respond if our community is torn apart? How might I act to prevent or lessen violence? How must I act to name what is askew in the world?

Early Friends lived through a brutal civil war that tore England apart and learned that violence could not bring about the kingdom they sought. The discovery that the kingdom of God is within set the course of Quakerism. Now, over three hundred years later, Friends continue to rely on the Inward Guide that inspired the Hebraic prophets and points the way to living justly and nonviolently.

Today, individuals like myself who were raised on secular anti-war and other protest movements have also learned their limits. We long to regain that certainty and power that our spiritual ancestors knew. Recently, Brian Drayton of New England Yearly Meeting wrote a letter to Friends that evokes the passion of our spiritual ancestors (see appendix B).

This longing is apparent to me in many ways. For example, when I organized a workshop titled "Listening in the Midst of Conflict," almost twice the expected number of participants showed up.

Afterwards, several commented on the need for additional time considering this topic. They were responding to the increasingly toxic political atmosphere following the election of Donald Trump. Friends at the workshop expressed a strong desire to shift away from the loud voices and "fake news." Such interactions in community have worked on my soul and reset my sense of what it means to live out God's kingdom here on earth.

The Prophetic Stream

Bill Taber was a Conservative Friend[1] who articulated the Christian dimension of Quakerism while remaining welcoming to many perspectives. Taber described the prophetic task as beginning with discovering and interpreting the law (the new covenant), work that was Jesus' task. As Jesus' friends, we are to carry on the prophetic work. In so doing, we are to show the way to live out the new creation, the kingdom of God. We offer an example of how to walk with God even when we are conflicted and fail to live up to our ideals. We help make the Inward Guide and Monitor available through prayer and intercession and by living our passion truly. As we help others make themselves available to the Spirit, we are called to lead people to the foot of the cross. Bill's understanding of prophetic ministry encompasses much of what we do when we speak, act, or pray in accord with God working through us.[2]

Are Friends still part of the "prophetic stream," as Bill challenged us to be?[3] This question became alive for me when I gathered as part of the School of the Spirit's Way of Ministry program in 2008–2009. There, twenty-odd Friends continued an active conversation begun four years prior at a retreat led by Bill focused on prophetic ministry. The program pointed to the biblical prophets for inspiration, particularly Jeremiah, and Bill drew from Quaker experience. The Way of Ministry program pushed our growing edges and made us all uncomfortable. In a talk soon after the program concluded, Bill pointed to the everyday process of being a Friend and described how the prophetic stream is integral to our path and relevant to our daily lives (see appendix C).

Everyday Prophets

Every people has its prophets. Some are truth-tellers, and others claim to know the future. Prophets have often been men. I visualize them as predicting doom, living isolated in caves, and appearing only to issue proclamations. In contrast, a radical tenet of Quakers—perhaps the central teaching—is that *all* people have the capacity to directly hear the divine voice offering guidance for our lives and words to share. If we learn to listen daily for this guidance, it becomes visible in a way of life characterized by simplicity, peace, integrity, community, and equality.

I describe Friends as "everyday prophets," a people who seek to pay attention to the nudges and visions of the Spirit on a daily (or even minute-by-minute) basis, to live in accord with the guidance they receive, and to help others know this Inward Teacher and Holy Guide. A few everyday prophets may receive bold visions and be called to witness publicly against injustice or seek in other ways to make more visible the city of God on earth—the kingdom that my friend recognized. Sometimes I refer to this subset of Quakers as 'public Friends,' the term early Quakers used for those who spoke to large groups or were visible agents of social change. Any of us, but especially those led to a public witness, face the traps of ego, fear, uncertainty, or other temptations. Without time apart from the broader culture, regular spiritual practice, and the support of a prophetic community that understands that truth of adherence to holy guidance is visible in the way its members live, the message of public Friends can be distorted or lost.

This book explores the modern Quaker experience of the prophetic stance, drawing on the stories of numerous individuals from around the world and from the various branches of Friends. Friends have no monopoly on prophetic ministry by any means. My hope is that this exploration of the ways the early Quakers' distinctive understanding has taken shape today will be of value to others as well as to Quakers. Many more volumes could be written on this topic, but my hope is that this will open conversations and perhaps be of support to individuals and meetings.

Many thanks to Charles Martin for having enough faith in me to commit to making this book a reality and to Kathy McKay for her guidance in editing. I am grateful to the many Friends who read all or parts of the manuscript and engaged me to consider this issue more fully. I will only name a few of these people, as I will inevitably miss some if I attempt a full list. In particular, my anchor committee, Julie Ann Peyton, Darren Kenworthy, Nancy Richard, and, more recently, Dan Rosensen, met with me faithfully on behalf of Multnomah Monthly Meeting of Friends, which has formally released me for my ministry of writing and teaching. Rachel Cunliffe and Darren Kenworthy also have been extremely helpful as the other two members of my writers' group. Kathy Hyzy also helped nurture this work. A peer group composed of Ken Jacobsen, Emma Churchman, and Allison Randall has also done much to sustain me and to help shape this volume. Nonetheless, any mistakes are mine.

INTRODUCTION

In the seventeenth and eighteenth centuries, the medieval worldview shifted towards the scientific, rational emphasis of the Enlightenment. Quakers arose at the same time Newton was doing experiments that helped define the scientific era. This era was also one of great disruption in England, ranging from civil war to plague to the Great Fire of London. Quakers of that time nurtured the prophetic voices among them, resulting in an influence well beyond their numbers and position in society.

The twenty-first century appears to be one of those turning points in history when humanity faces significant choices. Bleak options are presented passionately. The waters will rise and flood many communities and even nations. Enemies, often in the name of religion, will destroy much that we value, including icons of culture and opportunities for freedom. Choices are named in apocryphal terms. Hatred is voiced in public spaces.

Rather than slipping into violence in words and deeds and a constriction of possibilities for much of the world, my hope is that humanity can embrace the new yet very ancient vision that acknowledges that we are only as safe as the most vulnerable among us. I hope that we will be able to ensure that nourishment and water are available not only for all people but also for all living creatures. Can humanity replace the contemporary emphasis on entitlement with an ethic of responsibility?

My hope is that those of us who hold this vision of a world free of war and full of concern for each person's well-being, whether or not we are Quaker, will be involved in naming a new vision for humanity that defines this age. Today, voices can be heard that bemoan the limits of the Enlightenment perspective, with its mix of hope in rational thinking and the "brotherhood of man." Others call us to a harsh, punitive approach for self-protection. What ideals do we turn to in order to address the needs that confront all life on this globe? One task of the prophets among us is to make visible the new creation. Eileen Flanagan, a Quaker writer and activist, leads workshops titled "We Were Made for This Moment" to encourage others to find their calling and live it boldly.

This book aims to encourage the growth of the prophetic witness and a new statement of the vision that Friends made so compelling in their early years. My emphasis is not so much on prescribing the vision as it is on exploring how we might create the conditions that support individual and community witness to a way of being that might better sustain life and spirit.

On Being Prophets

So, what is a prophet? One straightforward definition I find very helpful comes from *Harper's Bible Dictionary*, which names a prophet as a "person who serves as a channel of communication between the human and divine worlds." *Harper's* notes that the Christian tradition has more often seen the prophet as predicting the future but that generally, in the biblical context, the prophets are viewed as "moral and ethical innovators."[1]

The prophets of the Hebrew Scriptures are often held up as the primary examples of moral and ethical innovators. Isaiah and Jeremiah had long, complex stories of faith. Daniel and Ezekiel had amazing visions. Jonah ran away from God's call to prophesy to the people of Nineveh. Then Jonah railed at God for sparing the city after they repented, complaining, *"I knew that you are a gracious God and merciful"* (Jonah 4:2). Micah left us with the indelible words, *What does the Lord require of you but to do justice, and to love kindness, and to walk humbly with your God?* (Micah 6:8), words that are often echoed in the writings of Friends over the centuries.

These prophets were often angry at the injustice and wrongheadedness of those around them, but more importantly, they did not just spout anger, they mourned deeply. They mourned when their people suffered. They mourned when their people turned away from God. They were very much a part of their community, and the vision they carried was that of the covenant between the Hebrew people and Yahweh. They inspired more than they condemned, and above all they offered hope in the face of apparent hopelessness. They reiterated the call to the generous peace of shalom, to caring for the widows and orphans, to hospitality, and to worshipping a merciful, just God. They extended the love of God to the lost.

Jews, Muslims, and others consider Jesus a great prophet. Christians often speak of one of the offices (functions) of Christ as that of a prophet, along with those of teacher, king, etc. The gift of prophecy is spelled out by Paul in 1 Corinthians 12, along with faith, healing, wisdom, speaking in tongues, and other spiritual gifts that together are part of the body of Christ. Specifically, *those who prophesy are to speak to other people for their upbuilding, encouragement and consolation* (1 Corinthians 14:3). The prophet also holds a people to account and reproves individuals who thrive on injustice so that the secrets of their hearts might be revealed and they might come to worship God.

There are strictures on the prophet as well:

> *Let two or three prophets speak, and let the others weigh what is said. If a revelation is made to someone else sitting nearby, let the first person be silent. For you can all prophesy one by one, so that all may learn and all be encouraged. And the spirits of the prophets are subject to the prophets, for God is a God not of disorder, but of peace.* (1 Corinthians 14:29–33)

3

The idea of prophecy excites some people and disturbs others. 'Prophetic ministry, ''prophecy,' and similar terms are used with some frequency and little consistency. Yet it is my sense that words can point to an awareness and activity that invigorates communities and calls them to compassion.

This book offers a glimpse of how prophetic ministry thrives among contemporary Friends. It shows some of the ways Friends nurture the imperative to witness to a life grounded in love rather than fear. I focus on Quakers because this is my faith community. Friends persist in proclaiming the prophetic voice as integral to the community and believe that faith is meaningless if not embodied in action.

In the early decades of the Religious Society of Friends, even their form of worship—believing that any person present might be called to speak in worship, that the sacraments must be experienced inwardly, and that the Holy Spirit communicates with individuals who listen deeply—was seen as enough of a threat to the state that the English Parliament adopted a law banning it. The consequences of claiming to speak for God can be severe even today, although they rarely involve imprisonment.

The Friends ways of worship and ways of living in the world grow in power when grounded in daily and sometimes minute-by-minute attention to the motion towards justice, towards the voice of the Spirit in the heart, and when this is allowed to guide every word and action. I have come to see Friends as a band of everyday prophets who are called to evoke a vision of the new creation in ways large and small and to speak the truth of how we have all fallen short of this vision as well as to raise up those who walk in love.

Implicit in this concept of prophetic ministry is a prophetic community that carries a vision of a just world, respects the equality of all people before God, and replaces violence with empathy and deep caring. Such a community nurtures awareness of the divine presence. It fosters awareness of the ways to distinguish between the voice that is holy and the many other voices that are not—those that pull individuals into greed, hostility, and destructive words or actions. Such a community finds ways to continually revitalize its faithfulness to the prophetic calling through small actions as well as large.

In many ways, it is redundant to speak about prophetic ministry among Friends. Quakers hold a tradition that claims ministry in its many dimensions, but traditionally they have seen the vocal ministry that arises during worship on Sunday morning as Truth, spoken in response to internal prompting by the Spirit of God. They believe that all their actions are to be oriented to the divine source, just as was true of the prophets of old. Yet in using the term 'prophetic ministry,' I recognize that today the spoken messages given in worship at times rise out of an individual speaking to a political cause or personal concern without reaching deeper. Vocal ministry may at times be a teaching ministry or a personal reflection by an individual wrestling with particular dilemmas. Such vocal ministry may be edifying for the group gathered, but it may not reach far into the core of life. Similarly, much Quaker action in the world may be fine social justice work or service to the community or a way of gathering people to Christ. None of these are necessarily wrong, but neither are they necessarily prophetic.

I see prophecy as both a terrifying calling that should be held in awe and as an everyday occurrence that is integral to being a Friend. An element of prophetic vision and proclamation among Friends has put them in the forefront of those condemning injustice and at times has subjected them to the wrath of those in power. Nonetheless, Friends are humans who get caught up in the limits and lures of the secular culture, fall short of what they hope to embody, and need to reflect anew on the prophetic vision in each generation.

Why Friends?

The explicitly prophetic dimension of early Quaker practice and theology is still teaching us and also provides a helpful model of prophetic ministry that remains relevant in the twenty-first century. George Fox, founder of the Religious Society of Friends, addressed his fellow seventeenth-century worshippers as prophets. They certainly saw themselves as people led by the Holy Spirit and speaking as God gave them utterance. They were inspired by the Light of Christ to declare that the kingdom of God is in us and among us now as well as coming in the future. They boldly described that kingdom even as they sought to live it out. Friends identified with the Hebrew prophets who had no qualms about naming the consequences of people's actions. They also followed Paul's admonition in 1 Corinthians 12 to prophets to build up the church. Beginning with Fox's vision on Pendle Hill of a "great people to be gathered," Quakers viewed their dreams and visions, along with their sense of daily guidance, when rightly ordered, as coming from a divine source.

Friends worship, practices, and testimonies grew from the Judeo-Christian tradition and are solidly Christian in the eyes of the overwhelming majority of modern Quakers, yet today they are flavored by Buddhist, nontheistic, and other perspectives from around the globe.

Friends Today

Friends stretch across the continents in the twenty-first century and encompass a range of beliefs from fundamentalist Christian to nontheistic. They may worship in expectant silence with no program and with an invitation for anyone to speak out of the silence in response to the movement of the Spirit. Or, their worship may be organized as an essentially generic Protestant church service, with a programmed set of hymns, Bible readings, and a prepared message from a pastor. The variations in belief and practice are substantial between these two extremes. These disparate Friends are both my source of understanding and my primary audience, but I hope this exploration will be of use to anyone who wishes to build relationships in the face of antagonism and be part of an extended community that seeks to bring the new creation to life.

I am very aware that I speak from the liberal, minority tradition of unprogrammed Friends and that many of the respondents to my queries for this book are also part of that tradition. I am thankful for those evangelical Friends who have been willing to be part of this project and have shared their perspective. If an evangelical Friend had written this book, the perspective would be quite different. I only hope that I have treated all my correspondents' words with respect and have offered to the reader a sense of the wide and sometimes divergent perspectives of modern Quakers scattered across the globe.

The website of the West Richmond Friends Church provides the perspective of a Friends church that is at once decidedly Christian and very aware of its Quaker identity. I offer their words as a kind of "median" statement of modern Quaker identity:

> Friends (or Quakers) are a Protestant Christian group which began over 350 years ago. Our name comes from a passage in the Bible, John 15:14, where Jesus says, You are my friends if you do what I command you. . . .
>
> In an increasingly busy and stressed-out world, Quakers practice a religious life which is direct, simple, and in touch with the Holy Spirit.

We believe:

- God speaks to the hearts and minds of every person, in every walk of life
- Every moment and every occasion can be a time of special closeness with God
- In telling the truth at all times, no matter what the cost
- God knows what is best for the church, and that God can lead ordinary people and provide concrete guidance for our decisions
- Jesus came to bring peace to the world
- Worshiping together in spiritual unity is more important than agreeing to things on paper
- Every person is called to be a minister
- Our outward lives should line up with our inward feelings and convictions

Friends have no written creed. Our services do not include any physical sacraments. We don't decide church business by majority rule. We welcome people from many different backgrounds.[2]

I offer this statement to help those not well acquainted with Quakers today to better understand some of the practices I mention. Throughout this book, the reader will find variations in forms of worship, beliefs, and how Friends view the prophetic ministry. I do not attempt to reconcile all of these variations because I find the variety and ambiguity valuable as a reminder that there is no one person or elite authorized to define Quakerism for all Friends. We are left short of certainty, suspended in paradox, and called to listen humbly.[3]

Availability of the Spirit to All

One of the biblical passages often cited by Friends describes the day of Pentecost, when *suddenly from heaven there came a sound like the rush of a violent wind* (Acts 2:3). The house where the disciples were staying was filled with this sound. All the disciples were filled with the Holy Spirit and began to speak in other languages, amazing all those who were near. Peter then addressed the crowd with the words of the prophet Joel:

> *"In the last days it will be, God declares,*
> *that I will pour out my Spirit upon all flesh,*
> *and your sons and your daughters shall*
> *prophesy,*
> *and your young men shall see visions,*
> *and your old men shall dream dreams.*
> *Even upon my slaves, both men and women,*
> *in those days I will pour out my Spirit;*
> *and they shall prophesy."* (Acts 2:17–18)

George Fox addressed groups of Friends, particularly those who traveled in the ministry, as "Prophets," and he clearly believed that speaking the words given by God was part of their purpose in life. Among the early Quakers, the role of prophet was available to young as well as old and to women as well as men in a time when women were proclaimed by some to have "no more soul than a goose."4

Fox's revelation was that each person is capable of directly hearing God's words and then sharing those messages with others. These earliest Friends constantly encouraged others to pay attention to the Light of Christ within their own souls and to be transformed by this power. In this transformation, they would find the path of obedience to the cross of Christ and would be able to live faithfully in accord with divine direction. The Hebrew prophets spoke mainly to the people of Israel. The early Quakers spoke a similar message derived from both the Hebrew and Christian Testaments (the terms I prefer to use for the Old and New Testaments of the Bible), but they believed the message was available to all people, even those who had never heard of Jesus.

Radical Witness

Quaker ministers in the past often felt called to go forth and proclaim God's word to the world, yet their message was as much in their actions as in their words. They warned of the doom that would befall people if they did not change their ways and were willing to risk all they valued as they challenged the injustice they encountered around them and called people to live in God's kingdom here on earth.

Fox was such a prophet, and Friends grew rapidly in the early years. Yet he was often attacked and beaten or thrown into prison for the words he spoke. His social superiors, including judges, would become irate at some of his practices, such as his refusal to respectfully doff his hat to them.

Women were equally bold. Mary Fisher, a servant, was convinced of the truth of Friends ways and became known as a minister. She knew divine power was leading her, and she was called to travel across Europe in 1657–1658, including across battle lines, in order to visit the sultan in Adrianople to tell him of the transforming work of Christ. Fisher and the sultan apparently conversed with mutual respect, enough so that the sultan offered her safe passage home across the battle lines. She courteously but firmly rejected his offer, believing God's protection was sufficient, and made her way safely back to England. She, like so many others, was focused on faithful attention to the Spirit, not on any particular goal or outcome.

Another group of Quakers, Mary Dyer, Marmaduke Stephenson, William Leddra, and William Robinson, each felt God leading them to Massachusetts to protest the persecution of anyone who did not adhere to the dictates of Puritan leadership regarding worship and other matters. After being variously whipped, imprisoned, and exiled, all four were hanged in Boston Common between 1659 and 1661. Although other women were burned at the stake in Massachusetts, Mary Dyer was the only woman hanged in that colony.

These Quakers wrote letters from prison in the days before they were hanged, speaking of the love of God that upheld them and offering encouragement to others who might be called to bear witness against the harsh condemnation and restrictions of the Massachusetts Bay Colony or to follow other seemingly impossible callings that might fill their hearts. Marmaduke Stephenson wrote the following shortly before his death:

> Now mind well and consider what I say. The true, unfeigned love to God doth not break the love from one another, but it breaks the bands of wickedness, as strife, debate, anger and envy that have lodged in the mind against another. When these things are destroyed in men and women, then comes the love of God about in them and increase one to another. And this I witness, and the Lord bears me testimony to what I speak, that my love is dearer and nearer to those in relation to me than it was before.[5]

Everyday Prophets

Quakers also raised up the words of Joel from Acts 2, quoted above: *"That I will pour out my Spirit upon all flesh, and your sons and your daughters shall prophesy."* This concept was central to their understanding of how they were to worship. To worship, they did not need a special, consecrated space, nor did they need a specially designated individual to tell them what God might want them to know. They gathered in homes, in fields, and even in taverns, as well as in meetinghouses—in any space they could find. All present, women and men, children and adults, then settled into an attitude of silent listening with the expectation that the Holy Spirit might give anyone words meant for the whole gathering to hear.

Thus, in their fundamental joint act—that of worship—Friends expected to hear prophetic messages and believed that any person present might hear and speak the word of God. All who responded to the transforming work of the Inward Light within the human heart were among the prophets. This attitude of worship, they felt, could be carried with them into the world each day, and they urged one another to constantly and prayerfully listen for divine guidance in every action and in every word.

Making Sense of the Tensions

These different perspectives lead me to describe the prophetic ministry among Friends in two ways that reinforce each other and at times blend together. I use the term 'everyday prophet' to describe all those individuals (and this goes well beyond the Quaker community) who listen for the Holy Spirit to shape them and guide them on a daily basis. This is an incarnational faith in its fullest sense, a faith that the Inward Guide is ever present. The consequences of such faith are visible in word and deed and can be described by the fruits of the Spirit as listed in Galatians 5:22 (peace kindness, gentleness, patience, self-discipline, joy, and love).

Everyday prophets are people who are faithful to the path of truth and love and whose lives project hope and a passion for justice. This path is at the core of Quaker worship and spiritual discipline.

Such everyday prophets may experience a life-shattering transformation. They may, for a time, be called to serve the Quaker world and/or the wider world in a highly visible way, bringing a message of hope as well as of warning. I sometimes refer to those individuals called to a radical witness as 'public Friends.' Their strength lies not in their uniqueness but rather in the everyday nature of their faithfulness. When an individual is called to such a visible ministry, it is crucial that they maintain a daily spiritual practice and be transparent in their work, sharing their hopes and their fears, their failures and their joys, with a community of equals. As such, they are integral to the band of everyday prophets who happen to call themselves Friends.

Quaker tradition nurtures everyday prophetic ministry as Friends gather to listen for guidance in regular times of worship and in daily or hourly times of silent inward attention in a living room, beside a lake, or in the midst of a busy office. Everyday prophets may have a ministry to a small group of individuals or be filled with a sense of call to build up the community around them. They may find themselves working in prisons or in war-torn nations, teaching nonviolent communication and trauma healing, or being a witness simply by their presence. They may speak quiet words of hope to a few despairing individuals, or they may travel to mission fields in foreign lands. Their work may change many lives or one.

In their daily and even minute-to-minute listening for inward guidance, they may experience "baptism by the Spirit" again and again as they are brought more fully into obedience to the Inward Guide. They learn to "take up the cross daily," letting go the demands of the ego even if they do not know that phrase. Gradually, the impulses to greed, to revenge, or other damaging behaviors and the attraction to the lure of popular culture become weaker and weaker in the face of the drawings of the Eternal.

These Friends are also part of what at its best might be called a prophetic community—a community that recognizes that each person must attend to the Inward Teacher and follow that guidance. This group believes that the Spirit can be sensed in the worshipping community and that the business of the group can reflect this divine voice in relation to concerns large or small. This does not mean that there is a holy plan for the color of the meetinghouse carpet, but it is imperative that we listen to and respect one another and seek what the Spirit is saying through each voice in the room. We seek to find the way forward that is right for the whole body, not to accomplish certain agendas or attempt to reach compromises that mollify those who are dissatisfied with a decision. Together, Friends work to make real the city of God on earth, both individually and jointly.

This is our tradition.

Context for the Conversation

In this book, I lay out some possible answers to the question of what constitutes prophetic ministry. My answers have benefitted from the generous responses of many Quakers who shared their experiences and understanding of Friends' calling with me. I spent much time with their reflections and often found their words opened new insights and challenged my assumptions. I am grateful for their honesty and vulnerability.

As part of my research for this book, I posed queries by email to many Friends from around the world and from our varied branches to gain their perspective on this topic. Although I did not conduct a systematic selection, I contacted Friends in leadership positions, either with Quaker organizations or as individuals asked to travel and speak among Friends. I asked each of them about their experience of prophetic ministry in their own lives or in those of people they know, and I asked why they would name particular actions as prophetic. I then asked them about what might help prepare people for prophetic ministry, how it has been supported in their community, and any obstacles they have identified.

The responses of these many Friends are incorporated throughout this book and did much to expand, refine, and illustrate my perspective. My intent is to open a wider conversation through this book rather than provide a sociological study.

In the following pages, I describe my understanding of the prophetic witness among Friends today—not so much by detailing the specific peace and justice actions that meetings or individuals might take but by identifying what underpins the distinctive witness of modern Quakers.

This book has seven sections, each with a brief introduction followed by several chapters. Each chapter ends with a set of queries that can be used for individual exploration and journal writing or worshipful group conversation.

In my own reflections, I largely confine my answers to the Judeo-Christian tradition as this is where the roots of Quakerism lie, despite the fact that some Friends today see their faith as separate from these roots. Although the language used by a Buddhist Friend, for instance, may be quite different from mine, I find strong commonalities in the values and practices of my yoga practice and among Buddhist Friends I come in contact with through workshops and in my travels.

The Shape of This Book

In this book, I lay out one vision of what a prophetic community might look like among Friends, recognizing fully how often we fall short and how our visions differ. Yet I have hope that by reaching far we might at least in part demonstrate what it means to live in the city of God.

The opening section, titled The Prophetic Voice: Walking with God, begins with reflections on the inward listening for God's presence that underpins Quaker worship and all prophetic work. It then considers the prophet as the voice of the deepest hopes of the community as well as its conscience. In the process, this section explains the primary work of prophetic ministry as shaping and being shaped by an alternative community that is attentive to the well-being of the weak. Such a community sets its sights on being able to act out of a spirit of abundance even in times of scarcity, walking humbly and serving boldly.

The second section, The Prophetic Community: The Hopes of a People, explores the vision of a just and merciful future that underpins the prophetic calling, including the nature of peace, the grief that opens the heart to compassion, and the dreams that at times expand the imagination. It ends with a return to the listening attitude that is so important to Friends.

The section titled Individual Recognition of the Prophetic Call addresses individual calls and the personal sense of calling and transformation that characterizes the prophetic ministry. This is followed by the section Learning the Territory, an exploration of how some Friends come to a fuller sense of their own inner life and the pressures they experience that lead them towards, or away from, their walk with God. As I share the stories I've gathered, the emphasis shifts back and forth between individual action and community action. Both are essential dimensions of the prophetic dynamic.

Being Part of the Whole is the section in which I consider the various ways that prophetic ministry is rooted in interdependence and relationship to one another and to all that is holy. Essential to this relationship is the responsibility of the community to nurture its members, including those who bring difficult messages that articulate how the group has fallen short of its vision of the city of God.

Every person I've encountered who sets out on this path finds themselves encountering resistance, whether their own fears or those of the community around them. In the section titled Headwinds, I describe the forces that can batter the soul and complicate the way. Any of us can easily be led into weedy byways and end up taking small steps that by themselves are not wrong but can in some circumstances amount to a false path. Learning to know the voice of the Inward Guide as an expert sailor learns the tides and winds is a lifelong task.

The final section, Making Space for the Prophets among Us, brings together the themes explored in earlier sections and offers one vision of how we might be more faithful individually and as a community. This section considers how we might better learn the territory we are called to traverse and find ways to identify as early as possible the actions and thoughts that are stumbling blocks. In addition, learning how to still the mind and come to walk humbly with God is integral to becoming what I refer to as a "band of everyday prophets" who share what we have learned about how we might be faithful to our vision of the city of God brought to life on this planet.

THE PROPHETIC VOICE:
WALKING WITH GOD

The following section on the prophetic voice is comprised of four chapters. The starting point for prophetic ministry comes in LEARNING TO LISTEN beneath the words and sort out the voice of the ego from the motion of the Spirit. In worship, there is space to listen for the Light to show us the way, be it through a gentle nudge or deep quaking.

The words SCARCITY AND ABUNDANCE conjure up the disparity that is prevalent throughout human history between those who have enough food and other material goods and those who struggle to find enough to stop the aching pangs of hunger. I have always lived amid a culture of physical abundance, yet I can see how often people hold tight to belongings as though they did not have enough to meet their needs, much less their desires. Stories abound in many cultures of people who have little yet share what they do have. Proposals to close borders and build walls reflect a sense of scarcity writ large. The greatest challenge to coming generations may be to find a path to live on this planet with a spirit of generosity to all people, not to mention to the multitude of other life forms that surround us.

My spiritual ancestors, the generations of Friends who preceded me, valued Jesus' Sermon on the Mount and the way he lived out that central message. WALKING HUMBLY with God has been a defining statement since the days of Micah almost three thousand years ago. Can we be neither arrogant nor filled with a sense of worthlessness but instead know that there is an Inward Guide we can follow with confidence? When walking this way, side by side with justice and mercy, SERVING BOLDLY becomes natural and marks our calling.

CHAPTER 1
LEARNING TO LISTEN

Some people say that children naturally hear the voice of the Light echoing in their inner ear. If I had this awareness as a child, it was drilled out of me during a time that predates my memory. Or perhaps it would be more accurate to say, since I was raised going to Quaker meeting, that I was aware at some level of this possibility. However, it never occurred to me that I might hear the words of the Inward Light echoing in me or might ever be expected to speak in worship. I don't recall ever hearing either of my parents speak in meeting, but I do recall being embarrassed when a cousin spoke occasionally.

The first time I felt unmistakable words inside me that I was supposed to speak aloud during worship, I tried to rise and share them. The feeling was intense in my whole body. I was shaking. I may even have lifted myself up a few inches above my chair. But the force of fear within me was too firm. It kept me pinned down no matter how I struggled to stand. At last, I gave up. Almost immediately, someone stood behind me and spoke the words that had been inside me. I was totally bewildered. I could not make sense of what had just happened. It certainly could not be explained rationally.

A few years after my initial call to speak in meeting for worship, I was again aware of that which is beyond all comprehension yet immediate and real. This time, it was a flood of unconditional love that filled me and released my grief over my father's death. Interwoven in that experience of total acceptance and welcoming was a strong call to speak when I am given words—in other words, a call to vocal ministry. I was not to speak that day. I was simply to be present in that moment to the olio of grief and of being held in total affirmation and joy.

By gathering in expectant silence, Friends gently teach one another what it means to listen to the depth of the soul, to the voice of all that is holy. This ability to listen is central to the calling of prophetic ministry. Without listening and being able to sort out the guidance of the Spirit from the needs of the ego or the expectations of family and of the world, how can anyone speak prophetically?

The certainty of being embraced in the Eternal stays with me decades later, even though it rarely is a conscious feeling. The immediacy of my experience compelled me to seek out others who might aid in the process of bringing my head and heart into alignment. These included a small group of Quakers who sat with me regularly for a couple of years as I tried to find language to share this experience. I also turned to the journals and other writings of early Friends who knew this overwhelming abundance of love even as their lives were turned on end. Gradually, I became embedded in a wider and wider circle as I sought to be faithful to this calling.

Integral to my call to ministry is the knowledge that I must be open to the full range of ways in which Friends today live out our common faith. This book is part of that calling because I bring together what are at times jarringly different perspectives as I seek to be faithful to the words of Friends of our varied branches in these pages. I suspect many people will find some of what is shared hard to accept or even listen to.

Yet this is the condition of the world. More and more people inhabit this finite globe, and we often are at odds in language, in custom, in belief—in many of the specifics of our lives. Friends have always claimed that the Seed of God is in every heart and that what many Friends know as the Light of Christ is accessible to every human being who is open to it, even those who know nothing of Jesus. Today we disagree on how to name that Seed, even as we agree on the reality of the divine spark in everyone. As a people, do we accept that every heart can be filled with divine love and that the kingdom of God can be lived out in this world as well as in some future heaven? How do we live out the new creation among ourselves so we might more truly be examples as we go forth around this world?

The most penetrating message from my Quaker spiritual ancestors is the intermeshing of worship grounded in community with our daily actions and the words we speak. The power of their words arose out of their attention to the Spirit and their willingness to follow the Inward Guide even when what they were asked to speak was difficult and what they were compelled do seemed impossible. As they walked humbly with God, they learned that their own skills and knowledge were valuable but were not sufficient.

These Quakers came to speak boldly to the world about the nature of the new creation, the city of God on earth. They encouraged all they met to listen for the Inward Teacher and to make this guidance evident in all they did. In this way, they were living and speaking much as the Hebrew prophets did. Some of us bemoan this loss today; others claim the prophetic heritage. Still others do not use this language and wonder what it is all about. Thus, I attempt to explore and articulate the Friends prophetic tradition in contemporary practice.

Speaking God's Word

Several individuals I contacted for this study responded by asking me how prophetic ministry is different from the vocal ministry Friends are used to hearing and offering during meeting for worship, where anyone may stand and speak into the silence. My basic response is that ideally they are one and the same. The standard set for us by our spiritual ancestors is the expectation that we will be guided by the Inward Teacher and given words to speak. Ministry in our meetings today is a mixed experience.

Even in the most liberal Friends meetings, however, there are those who see vocal ministry as prophetic. Roger Sturge (Britain Yearly Meeting) speaks of times he would identify his vocal ministry as prophetic:

> I am inclined to recognize any truly inspired ministry—that which one can truly say "I was a channel" rather than "I said"—as in the prophetic tradition. In this wider sense, I can say that I find myself in meeting speaking words coming from a deep place that seems to be beyond my consciousness and my person. When that happens, I often cannot recall the words afterwards. . . .
>
> The only example I can give was an occasion, I think during the first Gulf War. One Sunday I was sitting as an elder on what passes for the facing bench in our meeting. I found myself on my knees praying for forgiveness. The effect on me was astonishment; I don't know what effect it had on the meeting. Embarrassment, perhaps?[1]

Roger's concluding words—his awareness that many in the meeting might have been embarrassed to see him on his knees—might bring a laugh of recognition for some. For others, it might be an indicator of the contrasting expectations of worship that exist within the Quaker world.

The Spirit among Us

Joe Snyder (North Pacific Yearly Meeting), a Friend from an unprogrammed meeting, writes:

> Most of the Friends I know who have been used as ministers share similar experiences. One of the more common of these experiences involves wrestling with a message in meeting,

---

[1] All quotations that do not have citations are from personal communications to the author between the years 2015 and 2017.

being uncertain or timid or resistant, only to have another stand up and deliver the message.

As noted above, I have had the experience that Joe describes here. I knew I had a message but could not give it, only to hear someone else speak nearly every word. How does one explain this except as the work of the Spirit, which acts in every heart if we will only listen?

Joe goes on to describe the reactions similar situations can bring:

> Sometimes that brings a sigh of relief: "Ah, she was meant to give that message. It is well I remained silent." Sometimes it hammers home my unfaithfulness: "I was meant to give that message; God had to go to the bench [to find someone else to speak] on account of my timidity." One hopes to learn from these experiences. It is a work in progress.

In contrast, the discipline of silence can be an unexpected teacher in the movement of the Spirit, as Shannon Harbke (Alaska Friends Conference) discovered:

> I was fed up and disgusted with the sound of my own voice running on continually. As a high school teacher, my mouth was always moving! UGH! Anyway, I decided that the simplest (!) way was to speak only the truth, and then only when no one else spoke it. For the next two years I was mostly silent, and discovered, to my great amazement, that almost always my profound thoughts that I was burning to share were soon spoken by someone else if I just kept my mouth shut.

This awareness of the Teacher that is beyond any one human's control comes in many ways, but it often comes through being willing to stop constantly verbalizing and doing and instead take the time to feel for something that exists beyond our everyday senses yet has unexpected power and consequences in our lives. A healthy prophetic community nurtures the awareness of this power and teaches its members how to recognize its work.

The Risk of Speaking

Ann Janes's (Britain Yearly Meeting) discussion of the prophetic nature of ministry starts with her acknowledgment that while most unprogrammed Friends know something of the nudge to speak during worship, few are called to speak to the wider community. She adds:

> My own experience suggests that words or actions, perceived as a personal call to ministry from 'God' (I realize I have not used this word so far) in areas which break new ground, or open up new perspectives, however limited, for the community served, involve a degree of struggle. Voicing the prescient word involves taking a risk—the risk being that I am not saying the right thing or have mistimed or misjudged it or, worst of all, have misperceived the call. In a faith community such as mine . . . the onus tends to be on the individual to ask for support in discernment. This can feel a tougher barrier than the ministry itself for the diffident, reserved or independent individualist!

Some Friends meetings, particularly unprogrammed ones, have in recent years been nurturing the ministry by offering clearness committees in which members of the community help individuals discern calls to the ministry. They also encourage care or spiritual accountability groups to support the ministry once a call has been publicly acknowledged. Many programmed and some unprogrammed Friends still use the old tradition of the recording process that offers those who are called to ministry the opportunity to study and work with a mentor.

These tools for nurturing ministry are discussed further elsewhere in this volume, but they have been powerful aids for numerous Friends. Although not generally used for vocal ministry in one's home meeting, these tools are useful both for testing that one has correctly heard the Guide and for aiding one in going forward and living out a broader ministry with the support of the community. Most often, a broader calling has its seeds in the vocal ministry of weekly worship, where skills of discernment are developed and the individual learns to take risks amid familiar listeners.

Our Varied Forms of Worship

It is not hard to draw Friends from different branches into a debate about worship. I was raised with the clear understanding that only spontaneous messages arising out of the silence could be considered true ministry. There was no question that any individual who felt called to speak out of the silence had to submit to the discipline of silent listening for the word of God in the midst of the gathered community. I was rather horrified to discover, soon after graduating from college, that there were Quakers who worshipped with prepared sermons and bulletins and an order of service that included hymns. Wasn't the formal order of worship something George Fox protested against? Certainly I was taught that true worship arises out of the silence.

Keith Barton of Berkeley Friends Church in the Western Association of Friends offers an alternative perspective:

> Spoken ministry, however powerful or inspired, is not particularly adequate to the needs of most people these days. This has something to do with why relatively few people

go to Quaker meetings or churches. Aside from the rather Spartan liturgy and spare effects of Friends, the spoken ministry is frequently neither powerful nor inspired, and moreover, it is typically brief.

Now for those of us who may like it that way, it works to a greater or lesser degree; but what many people seem to need is a more coherent framework for religious ideas that goes beyond a few sentences or perhaps a couple of paragraphs spoken in earnest. Many people need a sermon or something like a sermon. The question for Friends is whether a prepared sermon can be inspired or prophetic. My own experience is, yes, it can. In fact, it can originate from the same level of expectant waiting that generates a spontaneous spoken message.

Teaching messages are vital. There is certainly a place for longer prepared messages—I can't deny that, given how many talks I have given at my own meeting and elsewhere at times other than Sunday morning. These I work on carefully and prayerfully. A strong element in my prepared messages is that of teaching. At times, I hope they provide inspiration and arise from the same Spirit that can be so palpable in worship. But I differ with Keith in that I believe—that I *know*—that something happens in the expectant silence of worship that is not the same as providing a "framework for religious ideas." When we let go of intellectual control and still what some call the "monkey mind," the Light can pry open the corners of the heart and show opportunities for transformation. Listening into the silence, it is possible to hear holy guidance outside anything rational thinking might affect. I, for one, would not wish to lose this dimension, this direct demonstration of the law that is written on the heart (Jeremiah 31:33).

Even so, many old stories describe how the spoken word can trigger transformation. Ann Wilson spoke words in the early 1700s to lazy, young Samuel Bownas (a man she had just met) that propelled him into the ministry. In a story even more dramatic, Stephen Grellet was moved to enter an empty hall and then, in the silence, was led to speak despite the apparent absence of any audience.[1] Only years later did he learn that a man who was sitting outside had heard every word and was cut to the core. Because of Grellet's words spoken faithfully, that man's life was remade. One thing all such stories hold in common is the faithfulness of the speakers in listening and only speaking when the Spirit prodded them.

I am so used to this movement from the Guide happening out of the silence that I have to be reminded by people such as Keith that most people expect a more structured time of worship. Peggy Parsons (now Morrison) wrote a helpful article soon after giving the keynote talk at the unprogrammed, liberal North Pacific Yearly Meeting. As a pastor in Northwest Yearly Meeting, she had to respond to many skeptics about the foundation of her preaching, and she did so in this article.

> I am aware that there are many non-Quaker preachers who also consider their call to be message bearing. But all of us, when we are honest, know when we have presented a sermon and when we have borne a message. . . . I consider my job as a preacher/message bearer to have five parts. The first requires me to live my life in a state receptive to the Divine. I, myself, must be fertile soil. . . . When I am receptive—messages arrive. It is essential that I recognize and accept the messages. . . . The third step is to discern who the message is for, and when it is to be given. . . . After discerning the recipient, I must hold the message. The gestation time for messages varies from seconds to months. It is not always comfortable to hold a message. I do not like all of them. Some of them scare me. Some of them are so wonderful that it is all I can do to not share

them before the appointed hour. . . . The final step is to transmit the message. It is my job to get the message back out and through me and to the recipients. This requires my free will and obedience.[2]

I have come to learn that the form does not govern whether or not the Spirit is present in the words spoken during worship. But I also recognize that the prepared messages offered by the pastor from the pulpit have different parameters than the words offered out of the expectant silence.

Most obviously, modern standards for length strongly dictate that words spoken out of the silence last a few minutes at most and that they arise out of individual experience, unlike in centuries past when messages might last an hour or more and be heavily laced with biblical passages. Verbal prayer may be included, but this has dropped in frequency. Occasionally an individual may sing or ask the group to sing.

A pastor's message is longer, often twenty minutes or more. These messages may be for teaching, exhortation, or inspiration. A time of vocal prayer is often included, along with hymn singing and Bible reading. Thus, in duration and in the components, these "programmed" messages may be closer to those of the early Quakers in some respects. Numerous meetings in the United States and elsewhere hold "semi-programmed worship," which may include one or two hymns, sometimes a Bible reading, and then a five-minute reflection by someone in the community or a visitor. The variations are many.

All of this is a long way of saying that the most important dynamic of the Friends meeting for worship is paying attention to the Spirit, not the particular form in which this is done. No community is immune from straying from this goal of listening for the Inward Teacher and falling back on reliance on a comfortable *form of religion while denying its power* (2 Timothy 3:5).

When Is the Spirit Truly Present?

Meetings and churches around the world face similar problems of discerning when the ministry offered during worship is truly Spirit-led and when elders of the meeting should intervene. Zablon Malenge (Nairobi Yearly Meeting) reports of his experience in the local unprogrammed worship:

> Yes, I have personally witnessed someone else carrying out prophetic ministry in my meeting. This friend was in a habit of ministering every Sunday for between 10–15 minutes and it was always about God's creation, environmental degradation, and bad politics in Kenya. Members raised a concern in a business meeting. . . . so after all had been said I guided the meeting to understand all ministry was supposed to be spiritually led and therefore prophetic. We had no reason to judge this member but we asked him to search his soul himself and that which he ministers so that the Spirit which prompts him to minister can recognize the groaning Spirit in others against his ministry.

Friends communities have long considered it well-ordered eldering to ask an individual to search their own soul to see if their messages are from the Inward Teacher or are from an ego-driven place. This is a very different approach from the common perception that to 'elder' someone means to tell them that their behavior is wrong and that they have to change. When done well, eldering helps the individual be more aware of divine leadings and is a tool for deepening the spiritual life of the whole community.

Some see prophetic ministry as a process whereby the individual is simply a vessel for the divine word to flow through. At times the query is posed, "Does the water taste too much of the pipes?" In other words, has the message been changed excessively by individual concerns and ego-driven demands? Yet Jewish scholar Abraham Heschel notes that the prophet is a person, not a microphone; the prophetic message as given is a combination of grace with individual temperament and personality.

Many pitfalls arise as we take on the risks of ministry, be it speaking in worship or confronting the evils that too often surround us. I cherish having a companion that travels inwardly with me as I explore what I am called to do. My anchor committee does just that—it gives me an anchor in the community and calls me back to the ultimate anchor in God.

Queries for Reflection and/or Discussion

1. Is the vocal ministry or message offered in your meeting or church prophetic? Should it be? How do you recognize this?

2. If the ministry were more prophetic, what might that mean for the community as a whole?

3. Do you experience sitting in the silence during meeting for worship as different from silent meditation or prayer? If so, could you describe some of the differences?

4. Have you offered vocal ministry that you would consider prophetic? What was that like for you? How did others respond?

CHAPTER 2
SCARCITY AND ABUNDANCE

Shalom. Peace to you. This conventional Jewish greeting, when considered in depth, encompasses a stance towards the world grounded in justice. To restore, to heal, to make reparations, and to reward others are all embraced in this word. Shalom is the path of an abundant faith, hope for the world, and generosity to those around us. It offers sharp contrast to a way of life based on scarcity, which encourages hoarding, theft, and exclusion. The gift of manna from God to the Israelites described in the book of Exodus is one example of this divine abundance; God caused the manna to fall on the Israelites and nourish them each day. They were instructed to gather only as much as each of them needed, and when they tried to stash some away, it rotted. They had to live in trust that this manna, their main source of food, would be there each day (Exodus 16:21). In the story of Jesus, this sufficiency and abundance for those who trust comes when Jesus feeds the crowd of five thousand with just five loaves and two fish.

I live in a beautiful city near the ocean and surrounded by mountains, and I have a loving husband and many deep friendships. We have more than enough money to be able to give much away without feeling pinched. This comfort protects me. Ironically, living amid this abundance, I catch myself clinging to it and resisting anything that threatens it. This inner sense of scarcity was part of my childhood, where my very middle-class mother convinced me early on that we were poor despite the obvious comforts that surrounded us. There was never enough for us to meet her unspoken aspirations. Thus, I know in my gut that scarcity and abundance, which are physical realities, can be a state of mind in terms of the presence or absence of "enough."

This inherited mindset of scarcity interferes with my standing side by side with the many in this city who do not have the basics of enough food, safety from random gang violence, or even a heated space with a roof to protect them from the rain. I give away much, but I am not able to follow Jesus' instructions to the young man of wealth that he give away *all* he had to the poor. Nor have I felt a call to take that final step.

At Quaker business meetings, all those in the community are invited to join in making the basic decisions about their common needs and direction through listening for the guidance of the Spirit. The presiding clerk will at times signify the decision by asking if "Friends are comfortable." This is taken to mean, "Are Friends at ease with this decision?" For many routine actions, this is appropriate. But it sets up assumptions that may hinder our ability to really hear in times when the divine guidance presses us to take radical action out of an inner knowledge of God's abundance. To act justly may be far from comfortable.

Justice and God's Reign

Shalom, as used in the Hebrew Testament, is most importantly about action and is central to a system of trust and mutual agreement. At the foundation of a shalom community is the understanding that if I do you harm I will repay you and make you whole, even if my actions were unintentional. Such actions form the basis of a system of justice that George Fox spoke of as taking away the occasion for war. Anthony Prete shares another dimension of shalom that reveals more about the formation of a just society.

> As a noun, Shalom has the basic meaning of 'sufficiency.' Again, the context is concrete. The sufficiency involves food, shelter, clothing, land, or work. It also includes the feeling of being satisfied because one's legitimate desires have been met. . . . Who among us is not aware, as we look around the world [today], that even in the face of abundance, sufficiency is in short supply?

Justice and compassion are core to many civic institutions as well as religions. In many venues, these are secular values, but in many religious traditions, these values are dimensions of all that is holy and reflect the nature of the divine as well as hopes for how the human community might live together. Concrete actions of care for others, not just being comfortable and being nice to each other, are the basis of lasting peace.

Friends have always held that the city of God is not only for the distant future or for after death but can be realized on earth among us today. Jean Zaru (Ramallah Friends Meeting) writes of her understanding of the reign of God:

> Jesus distilled from the long experience of his people in violent and nonviolent resistance a way of opposing evil without becoming evil in the process. . . .
>
> WHERE is God's reign?
>
> Wherever domination is overcome, wherever people are freed, wherever the soul is fed, wherever God's reality is known.
>
> WHEN is God's reign?
>
> God's reign is whenever people turn away from worshiping power, wealth and fame. It is when we insist on creating a society of equals.
>
> WHAT is God's reign?
>
> God's reign is the transformation of the Domination System into a nonviolent, humane, ecologically sustainable, livable environment, which enables people to grow and live well.
>
> The reign of God cannot just be "inner" or "outer"; it must be both or it is neither.[1]

This awareness of a world in which concern for others moves individuals to justice opens possibilities of a way of engaging the world rather than clutching tightly to that which is "mine." Living in the city of God calls us to speak out when we see bullies harassing a child in the schoolyard or non-Muslims intimidating a Muslim woman on the bus.

To act can be costly. In 2017 in Portland, Oregon, a man harassed two young Muslim women on a train. He then stabbed to death two men who tried to intervene and badly wounded a third before leaving the train. One can only surmise what might have happened to the women if these men had not acted, but this tragedy points to the need both to act and to find ways to prevent such violence.

There is a way of living that respects civil authority yet speaks up when police use unnecessary violence when arresting a black man, stands with immigrants being deported, and responds to any of the infinite examples of injustice in the world. Friends are not immune from harsh or blind behavior, but we do carry this ideal. Not all are called to act in violent circumstances, and I doubt I could do what those two men on the bus did. Yet we hold to the hope that we might look within for the city of God so that it might become visible to others by our actions, even when to act is costly.

Living in Scarcity

Friends have a testimony of simplicity. At one point, this was interpreted to mean we could only wear dull clothes of a certain style and could not decorate our homes or play the piano. These practices were supposed to keep our attention on God. To my modern eyes, this feels like an imposed scarcity. I long for an internal sense of abundance and a visibly welcoming space to live in that invites others on the journey. I view simplicity as a paring away of the unnecessary so that there is room for the heart to grow.

Scarcity can be an internal emotional state, a lack of hope. We live in a country and on a globe where there is still an abundance of the essentials of life, yet there is much pressure to identify "more" as the route to satisfaction. No matter how much one has, there is always the possibility of more, the idea that an increase in things will somehow replace fear, self-hatred, absent love, and missing hugs. I find that learning to step away from these fears is a dual process whereby I first notice the psychological violence around me and then turn my attention away from the angry, ugly voices. This makes space for me to smile, to see humor, to really notice the people I encounter, and then to take small steps to reach out and cut through the aloneness and prejudice that swirl around us.

Despite our ethic of simplicity, most Friends live very comfortably. We support our meeting but generally keep a tight rein on its finances. David Zarembka (Baltimore Yearly Meeting) offers an example of ways in which some meetings function from a mentality of scarcity and a desire for control.

> In the 1990s I was involved with three prophetic ministries. . . . In all three cases, the women needed financial support for their ministry since they planned to do it full-time.

His story starts out positively in that two of these individuals found support to do the work they were called to undertake even though their meeting did not directly fund them. This has been my meeting's approach—to support a person with a call to ministry by finding outside donors rather than directly funding individuals for more than minor expenses.

In the case David cites, the community was not content to rejoice in the work being done. The financial sense of scarcity was underpinned by a harsher emotional scarcity. He continues with his story:

> This did not stop members of the meeting from complaining—as they came from a position of scarcity (a common American trait that belies our immense wealth). They felt that the funds donated for the release would come out of the same funds that were donated to the meeting

so that the meeting would financially suffer. That there was no evidence for this assertion did not stop people from saying it. . . . Those naysayers also said that these released Friends were a "hireling ministry," which mostly indicated how little they understood of the early Quaker objections to a "hireling ministry."

The naysayers were only a few at the beginning and never people who ever gave any financial support to the ministry. But each business meeting where the ministry would be brought up—and approval was always for only one or two years—these detractors would raise these and other objections. Other meeting members, including strong supporters of one released Friend, became disheartened; of course, so did the released Friend. Finally, there was no unity in the meeting . . . and the release was terminated.

It is painful to hear of the ways we can back away from supporting one another. This is also a reality we must face, however, if we are to undertake an expansive witness to the world.

There are infinite tales of how we trip one another up and hold tight, whether to money, to emotions, or to preconceived notions. The journey we are on asks us to constantly be alert to the voices we hear within our being and to notice when we have stepped outside the path.

Rachel Cunliffe (North Pacific Yearly Meeting) has strongly felt the internal dimension of scarcity. She wrote about her experience of attempting to consolidate her books and files into a smaller space:

I feel overwhelmed by the task of sifting and winnowing. . . . Here is the history of many great ideas, unfinished projects, false starts. Why can't I let go? . . . Because I am afraid! These are my contingency plans against

> forgetfulness, lost opportunities, previous glories. I do not trust myself to be open to God's will. And I do not trust God not to abandon me with an empty mind and no remembrance of what has driven my passion. . . . and so I operate from a sense of scarcity. . . . My sense of my own scarcity effectively bars me from seeking the abundance of God's love. The notion that I do not have to do to be loved is *entirely* foreign.

I share Rachel's fears, and at times they arise strongly in me. It is very hard not to pin my identity on the books I have authored and on my public self. It is very important for me to have people around me who knew me and loved me before the public persona was even a possibility or dream and to recall in moments of fear the overwhelming joy of God's arms around me. Rachel also knows that scarcity is not the way:

> Today I heard a man mention he had been goal setting for the year. Silently, I lamented my own lack of direction. In my prayer and meditation, I brought this concern to God, who laughed. I realized my goal is to take every opportunity to love, to pay attention and to build peace in all my relationships including with Him and myself. That's all. That's all. *Si*mplicity and integrity leading to abundance.

I love Rachel's encounter with God who laughs— laughs at our foolish worries but, much more, laughs with us in delight.

God Invites

Anthony Prete's reflections on shalom include other dimensions. One of these is that the opposite of shalom, of peace, is not war; it is chaos, the chaos that existed before creation. Prete writes, "Biblical chaos is the condition that existed before creation. And biblical creation is the taming of chaos so that abundance can abound and shalom can blossom."[2] What I like most about this concept is his observation that biblical creation was not an order from God but rather an invitation: *"Let there be light."* Prete expands on this, saying:

> God conquers chaos by sharing power.
>
> The second [observation] is that God invites this creation to be abundantly self-sustaining—and it accepts.[3]

Yet God does not take control. Horrible things happen and people cry to God to fix what is wrong, but the solutions are left to humanity. People lament these horrors and seek a just God who will prevent them. In contrast, Prete sees lament as an audacious form of prayer. "The lament gives voice to pain, abuse, isolation, and oppression. . . . [Laments] are a way of doing the work of justice so we can come to peace."[4] Yet laments also bring our great needs before God. Laments may need to come from the hearts of those of us who are comfortable. We may need to be the voice of others who have nothing and are desperate, and to do this we need to know them and feel true compassion.

We may not agree as to whether there is a God who makes all things right or whether we are the only hands that God has or about any of the other ways we experience the holy, but we come from a tradition that honors the need to correct injustice and reject the mindset of scarcity and a tight control of resources or behavior. We are invited to act; we are not forced to act. We are called to live out of a sense of abundance that spills across the community and the world. And we will all experience times when other individuals or the community as a whole gets trapped in the mentality of scarcity. This seems inevitable, yet the only response is to find ways to call each other back to the way of shalom.

Abundant Forgiveness

Cornelius Ambiah (Nairobi Yearly Meeting) writes of the reality of God's abundant love filling him and preparing the whole community:

> A time I felt I was offering a prophetic ministry was during a forum where I had an opportunity to share on forgiveness. It was a beautiful experience just to feel the presence of God very much alive, real, and present.
>
> Yes! For prophetic ministry to be a reality, the person sharing must have faith that whatever they intend to share is a message from God and they are just vessels being used to deliver the message; prepare the message in accordance with God's will and believe that the Lord will accomplish the rest.

I am excited by my own meeting's support of a young woman with a music ministry that challenges those who reject gay or trans individuals. Yet the community may resist even when justice cries out for action. Esther Mombo (Highland Yearly Meeting) offers a practical example of how she responds with a spirit of abundance when the community does not act.

> I say that if women are called to the ministry, they should be allowed in. Sometimes there is no money for them . . . so my social engagement is to look for funding to help pay for their tuition, whether it is my own time that I commit myself to anonymously pay . . . to support them.
>
> So there are three ways [to support women called to the ministry].
>
> One is to encourage the women when they say they are not able by saying, "No. You are able. If God is leading you to this ministry, you better take it."
>
> Two is to challenge the systems that deny them to participate, so that if the pastor is not willing to sign the papers to bear testimony for them, then I will say "why?" Sometimes they

will say it is because they are single mothers, so I say single mothers need to study, widows need to study, separated people need to study, because those are the things that exclude women, especially those who are single, etc. So I challenge that.

Third is to be practically involved in raising funding for them to study.

We as humans are quite good at justifying our own self-protective ways of being. Comfortable ways of thinking and living hold a powerful sway over most of us, individually and communally. Esther's frustration led her to take immediate action on her own. She was not willing for the women called to ministry to suffer further and lose their dreams. She also kept working to break through the comfort, to change hearts and behaviors. Esther's example presses me to do more, to not be bogged down in confusion or a sense of inadequacy. She is only the latest in a long line of spiritual ancestors who live out of the power that is present when we trust the Guide. She is one of many examples of how we may grow and change over the years when such generosity is made visible and the beneficial consequences of acting out of this spirit of abundance become evident even to the doubters.

Queries for Reflection and/or Discussion

1. What triggers a sense of internal scarcity within you?

2. How do you respond when life becomes hard for you in relation to finances, poor health, severe weather, or other conditions that make life feel tenuous or elicit fear? How do you respond to the people around you, both those who are close to you and those who are strangers?

3. Can you share a story of a time when you felt despair in the midst of stress or chaos? Who or what is with you to tell you that you are able to face whatever comes?

4. What opens your heart to abundance and generosity? How have you or might you sustain this feeling in times of danger or poverty?

CHAPTER 3
WALKING HUMBLY

In the face of the infinite, the only sane posture is that of humility. That much I know, despite my scientific training and attachment to rational thinking.

No matter how we name the Inward Guide, for this to be a true Guide, the words that resonate most deeply in my heart are those from Micah 6:8 that call us *to do justice, and to love kindness, and to walk humbly with your God*. These words, along with the call from John 4 to know that God is to be worshipped *in spirit and truth*, also summarize for me much of what I read in the writings of early Friends as well as the central message I take from the Bible. All this is part of what I explore in this book.

This Inward Teacher can show us how to live dependent on infinite Love knowing that we are no better (and no worse) than others around us. We have no special right to wealth or privilege, no special claim to think that everything we have to say, even in worship, has merit, and no basis in our lives for hatred or greed. At the same time, when we have spent time in discernment and know the motion of the Spirit in our lives, we have the responsibility to speak what we know boldly.

The lives of other Friends also tell me that transformation in some manner is central to all of us, even if it is a point of serious contention. Turning, awakening, being transformed, being cognizant that we cannot do it all on our own without an Inward Teacher—these are all part of who we are. Among the most widely quoted of early Quaker writings are these words by Isaac Penington:

> Give over thine own willing; give over thine own running; give over thine own desiring to know or to be any thing, and sink down to the seed which God sows in the heart, and let that

grow in thee, and be in thee, and breathe in thee, and act in thee, and thou shalt find by sweet experience that the Lord knows that, and loves and owns that, and will lead it to the inheritance of life, which is his portion.[1]

The various branches of Friends hear these words differently. The breadth of meaning encompasses knowing the one true Guide as the Spirit of Jesus Christ and knowing that there is a force of love and truth in the world that can guide every individual no matter what their beliefs or religious tradition. Without question, Jesus Christ was Penington's Guide, yet he measured following the Guide by the evidence of a person's actions and words and believed that salvation was possible for those who knew nothing of Jesus. Today, I too often encounter people who assess others either by what they believe about Jesus or by their behavior as if they were separate criteria.

Walking humbly, for me, means
- to be grounded, without pretence;
- to be fertile soil for the growth of the Spirit among us as humus is for our gardens;
- to know that I am no better than others;
- to know that I am no less worthy than others;
- to live with an undivided heart;
- to be teachable;
- to be open to the unexpected;
- to walk with God; and
- to listen and follow.

The Nature of Humility

The day I wrote the above paragraphs, October 14, 2015, John Muhanji, Friends United Meeting Mission Director in Kenya, posted the following on Facebook:

Why is humility a strong Quaker value? Humility is the true key to success. Successful people lose their way at times, as some

43

Quakers did in the past. They often embrace and overindulge from the fruits of success. Humility halts this arrogance and self-indulging trap. Humble people share the credit and wealth, remaining focused and hungry to continue the journey of success. Share what you have to promote the ministry of Christ.

The message and awareness of the living presence of Jesus that has shaped Quakerism from the start keeps swirling around the call to walk humbly and the message that the weak and meek will be raised up. The challenging passage known as the Beatitudes (Matthew 5:1–12; Luke 6:20–23), and in fact the entire Sermon on the Mount, calls out to us to forget about amassing celebrity and fame, to stop chasing after wealth and status, and to end our part in the violence of the world.

Jesus specifically acknowledges humility as crucial for all those who would follow him. After telling the crowd to listen to the words of the scribes and Pharisees but not to follow their actions for they do not practice what they teach, Jesus tells the crowd, *"All who exalt themselves will be humbled, and all who humble themselves will be exalted"* (Matthew 23:12). Jesus repeats this message twice more in Luke.

I like the gentle humor of Bruce J. Malina, who writes, "Humility is a socially acknowledged claim to neutrality in the competition of life."[2] This invitation to be at odds with the rules that govern public discourse and human striving is one more piece of the upside-downness of the way, whether one follows the Christian path or the Buddhist path or that of many other ways that point to compassion, truth, and justice. Being on such a path underpins the true prophetic voice.

It's Not about Us

Mary Lord (Baltimore Yearly Meeting) is one of several of my correspondents who spoke to the centrality of humility in their understanding of the prophetic ministry:

> Essentials of prophetic calling are humility, obedience, and submission to the Divine. What comes from the ministry is not about us; it is only powerful when the Divine is speaking or acting through us. It is not our power or knowledge that can best change the world but the power that flows from us. Often, we do not know what has been most important or what has happened or why we needed to do or say what we did. Courage is also useful because it is such a march into the unknown, and sometimes I have been in physical or spiritual danger.

Mary, who has worked in Africa as well as in North America, is well known for her stance for nonviolence and reconciliation. She has a fine laugh that dismisses attempts to elevate her above others and a calm surety of being grounded in holy guidance.

Seth Hinshaw (North Carolina Yearly Meeting [Conservative]) studied and wrote much about Friends, including these thoughts about the balance between assertion and humility.

> A great religious experience gave early Quaker ministers great assurance and confidence. Consequently, they made bold and strong assertions . . . comparable to the boldness of the apostles in the early church (Acts 3). This aspect of ministry however was not without serious difficulty. How can this kind of boldness be balanced with proper humility and an awareness of human fallibility? The prophet must not speak in a tone of uncertainty, nor from an insecure position.

Neither must he lose sight of his own inability to comprehend all truth, and his own inability to express it inerrantly. The mere claim that one has been divinely led to make certain statements requires a bit of honest inquiry. In early Friends meetings when some ill-informed person made statements out of harmony with Truth as Friends understood it, he was not dealt with during the meeting for worship, but afterward in a private and gracious manner.[3]

Chutzpah Tempered

Speaking boldly is an easily asserted characteristic of prophets. Aren't they the ones called to shout from the mountaintops? Don't they speak with the authority of God? I like the way Becky Thomas Ankeny (Sierra-Cascades Yearly Meeting of Friends) assures us of the strength of the prophetic voice and of our right to name what needs naming and claim our place among God's children:

If I were asked for two words to summarize the habits of the heart American citizens need in response to twenty-first-century conditions, I would choose chutzpah and humility. By chutzpah I mean knowing that I have a voice that needs to be heard and the right to speak it.

I also value her tempering of chutzpah with humility:

By humility I mean accepting the fact that my truth is always partial and may not be true at all, so I need to listen with openness and respect, especially to "the other," as much as I need to speak my own voice with clarity and conviction.

Boldness and arrogance can be too easily confused when they tumble together. Arrogance forgets the worth of other beings and asserts a unique place in knowing what is right and wrong. Holy boldness has the confidence of divine prompting that comes when we know that we are not the source of all knowledge or right answers and that our inner ears get stuffed up from time to time. Holy boldness comes as we take up the cross and know that we are part of the sorrows of the world as well as heirs to joy and delight. While we are each unique and uniquely valued, no one of us has the right to ignore the needs and well-being of the myriad other souls on this planet or treat them as less than human.

Self-Proclamation

"There are no self-appointed prophets. Those who think they are, aren't." These words of Lloyd Lee Wilson (North Carolina Year Meeting [Conservative]) are sharp and clear. Debbie Humphreys (New England Yearly Meeting) has a similar view:

> My sense of prophetic ministry is that as soon as you self-proclaim you've lost it. Prophetic ministry—bringing forth the eternal story as resonant in the now—is about 'being' in the right place—which has to be about deep humility. And part of the deep humility for me is trying to always hold that I might be mistaken.

Paul Buckley (Ohio Valley Yearly Meeting) offers a gentler, more expansive statement:

> Most Friends today would be wary of naming any experience as prophetic ministry. We don't think of our lives as the lives of saints. We certainly have experiences others would name as prophetic ministry, but we don't feel we can or should claim that name for ourselves. It feels proud. It feels self-righteous.

The modern condition sometimes seems miles away from early Quakers who unselfconsciously attributed their words to God. Today, the self-awareness of the prophet can be a strange, touchy thing. It requires that we be able to listen to the Inward Light and be able to recognize that Spirit amid the multitude of demands on us and voices that sound within. To stay within that point of awareness is a substantial gift. As Debbie Humphries notes, as soon as you see yourself in this role, it disappears.

Our spiritual heritage is one that is wary of self-proclamation even as it encourages us to listen for the movement of the Spirit and to follow it. Again and again we are brought into this paradox, a place that is hard to hold. These same ancestors felt that true recognition of the prophetic gift could only arise in community. Over the centuries that Friends have formally recognized and minuted the gift of prophetic ministry in their midst, the process is normally initiated by the elders, not by the individual concerned.

To Be Humble Enough to Step Down

Esther Mombo (Highland Yearly Meeting) offers the advice that we be willing to test a call to ministry or leadership and, if appropriate, say, "No, it is not from God for me to do this, even leadership." She expands on this as follows:

> To be humble enough to step down. I am speaking from a context where many people may not step down until they die. There are too many who stay too long. To be humble enough to say I think so and so can do that better than I, so that I am not the one who knows it all.
>
> Prophetic ministry is shared ministry. That is why there were many prophets. Even today there are many prophets that come in our midst.
>
> It takes humility to acknowledge that I am not the only one who can do it and to be able to raise the others as well into the ministry rather than to be the "lone ranger," as we say here. I don't believe the prophetic minister is the lone ranger. It is a shared ministry, either by

couples or by meetings or by friends. But it is a humbling experience, it is not one you grab.

Esther adds the wonderful dimension that prophetic ministry gives one permission to argue with God.

> It is one ministry where you question God. When you read of the prophets, most of them say, "Why me?" But I also believe that God does give us the strength to go on in that ministry. It is one where we have to be aware that God can move even stones. This is where we need to be aware that God doesn't even need you but can use stones, trees.

"Why me?" is a question I often ask myself, especially when I am preparing to speak and my nerves take over. But Esther also reminds us of the strength we will be given, a reality I have learned to trust. For me, it means stepping into the place of fear and knowing that fear is often a guidepost showing what I most need to say.

It's All about How You Relate to People

Moses Bigirimana (Kibimba Yearly Meeting), who lived through the terrible violence in Burundi, reflects at length on the nature of humility.

> Humility is all about behavior—how you relate to people, how you communicate to people, the social status you are giving yourself, the way you are treating other people. More precisely, it is the way you understand that even other people are important: they have a place, they can do something. You are somehow equal to other people so there is room for other people in your attitudes. You don't undermine them; you give them chances to do things; you seek to understand them.

49

It is so easy to confuse humility with humiliation and see it as a sign of weakness. Instead, Moses notes that humility has dimensions of self-discipline.

> Humility does not mean cowardliness but to express yourself and to have room for the other ideas, have room for more understanding. Also, the way you express yourself, both in writing and in speaking, you control your own words so as not to wound others. Avoid attacks, but just make yourself understood and use modest language. Maybe your appearance, the kind of clothes you are putting on, can make a difference, not dressing extravagantly. That is how I understand humility. But spiritually speaking, humility is just to recognize and abide with the inner voice of the Holy Spirit, just accept what he is telling you to do in all parts of your life.

These are powerful words from a man deeply affected by the turmoil his nation has faced and the trauma that results from such violence. He knew beyond doubt the painful consequences of arrogance and the need to stand up to the harshness that reality can throw into any of our lives.

Speaking Out against Wrongdoing

I asked Moses Bigirimana about how the stance of humility functions when a person has to say that something is very wrong and assert that with enough authority to make his or her voice heard. This is his response:

> One thing to do is not to be passive; don't just let whatever is happening happen. You must address that but in a very bright manner, in being simple. Not confronting others, but seeking to understand what is going on, that is number one. Then, after understanding, give your own insight as to what may be the way out and create a better space to communicate, communicating humbly, without attacking.

50

Moses's approach is a good counter to the tendency of so many to avoid confrontation at all costs. He is clear that stepping forward when things go wrong is crucial. If we can step forward with clarity but without hostility, new ways can open. By clarifying a situation, it is possible to learn some of the complexities of the situation and gain insight into the true issues to be resolved.

> Yet whenever you want to talk about a sensitive thing, the other person may be looking at it as an attack. (Yes, I have experienced this several times). But you just keep on. You don't just persist—if doing that particular thing is not right, or if you are not the right person, you just find another one to do it. It may not work for you, but if you find someone else it may work. It is a matter of assessing the situation and seeing how it is.

Two things stand out for me in this last paragraph. The first is the need to be aware that people are naturally defensive, and if you are perceived as attacking them they will not hear what you have to say. Thus, it is important to step back and consider alternative approaches. Second, you need to be aware that you might not be the right person to speak up in a particular circumstance. This can be hard to admit.

All of this tells me the prophetic voice may often be very gentle and unobtrusive. It is concerned with bringing the community more into alignment with God's way, not with making someone's reputation or giving in to the person who shouts the loudest or debates most effectively.

Queries for Reflection and/or Discussion

1. Have you encountered someone who was convinced they had a prophetic message? What was that encounter like for you? Was his or her concern authentic? How did you respond?

2. What does humility look like in your experience? How is it part of the prophetic ministry? What allows you (or reminds you) to practice humility in your interactions with others? What hinders you in this practice?

3. Have you encountered situations in which you or others you know have continued to do work or take on leadership beyond what seems consistent with the guidance of the Light? How did you become aware of this? What actions did you take?

CHAPTER 4
SERVING BOLDLY

To serve boldly, at least for me, means to offer words *and* actions that name truth firmly and with clarity. At times, this means stepping in and doing what we can to stop injustice. It has nothing to do with loudness of voice or self-aggrandizement or the level of drama involved. To speak boldly is to be aligned with the Spirit, to know that holy center where we might faithfully take up the cross we have been given, and act out of divine strength rather than our own.

In this context, I find it helpful to consider the work of the majority of everyday prophets alongside the more visible work of those Friends called to public witness. Everyday prophets include all those who listen for truth each day and respond faithfully to the Guide even in small things. A few of these everyday prophets are called onto a broader stage and are led to more visibly address societal issues, speak to problems within the Religious Society of Friends, or offer a vision of hope. As noted earlier, I refer to these Friends called to public witness as 'radical prophets' or as 'public Friends.'

The Still, Small Voice of the Everyday Prophet

Many are the traps we can fall into. Even with the best spiritual discipline and intent, almost any of us can offer words that spring from what Thomas Merton calls 'the false self'—that place where the ego serves its own immediate needs and the words of the Spirit get lost.[1] Although the following story is not about an attempted grand, prophetic pronouncement, Julie Peyton (Sierra-Cascades Yearly Meeting of Friends) shares a clear example of how her ego emerged and derailed her unexpectedly at a Coalition of Christian Colleges meeting. Julie's story grew from an experience she had as a youth when her efforts to stop an injustice (told in chapter 29) left her vigilant to find errors in others. This second experience brought home

53

to her that she had learned the wrong lesson. In the episode recounted below, the quiet, prophetic words of one person marked an important turning point in Julie's life and let her see the centrality of vulnerability and relationship.

The event that changed me occurred some twenty years after my teenage encounter, during a workshop offered by the Coalition of Christian Colleges. I had begun to read about Quakers and was hoping to meet Howard Macy from George Fox University.

The guest speaker for the weekend began listing the things to do to be faithful, starting with #1: go deeply into your own field, know it well, be an expert. As was typical of me, I was taking notes, listening for what might be useful and for good questions to ask. His list grew longer and longer. Somewhere around #12, he told us to read widely, to know what other people are doing in their fields.

At this point I put my pen down, because I had him. I knew exactly what I was going to ask when he finished, and mine was the first hand raised. I asked him how realistic it was to be expected to go deeply in our own fields and also read widely in others' areas. Given all the tasks on his list, where were we supposed to find time?

He mumbled around in reply, saying these were, of course, mere suggestions and no one could do them all, etc., etc. You could feel it in the room, you could see it in the eyes of everyone that this talk had been a colossal waste of our time. I had done my job well: I had been calm, strong, invulnerable, correct, clear. I sat back, proud of having nailed this charlatan.

Then Macy, the Quaker, spoke, quietly, gently. He reminded us that teaching is a difficult vocation. The rest of what he said didn't matter. What mattered, what struck me between the eyes and went directly to my heart, was that he got choked up. His vulnerability was the most powerful event at the conference, and his words cracked something open in me, not just in me but in all of us. The room became very still as we allowed Macy to bring us back to a community of teachers who grieve because the work is greater than we can accomplish.

And with a new-found humility, I thought to myself, "That's what Quakers do. I want to be like that."

P.S. I wonder, if my snarkiness actually helped the situation by allowing Macy to speak into that tense, uncomfortable space my question created. (Good prophet/bad prophet?)

P.P.S.: What I said was true; it's the attitude I so deeply regret. In other words, there seems to be a way to be prophetic that is different from the words of the prophet.

The prophetic ministry can be evident in such small, everyday moments, and the lessons of self-knowledge can be painful. In so many ways, if we can be alert to the truth in a given situation and name it, there is opportunity for transformation. Julie experienced such a turning of her life, and she still carries with her, years later, the image of one professor speaking quietly and reminding all present of their commonality and of the pain we cause or ease.

Confronting Injustice

Soon after the start of the twenty-first century, I was part of a group of Friends, both evangelical and liberal, who were actively lobbying our congressional delegation. Our concern was to encourage a just solution to the Israeli-Palestinian tensions. The particular issue is not important here, however; what I want to raise up here is our behavior. In the midst of a lively and informed discussion of the issues with a sympathetic, high-level staff person, suddenly a member of our delegation stood up and loudly berated the staff person, furious that he could not promise what she wanted. His immediate response was a mix of anger and pain. When she would not stop her tirade, another member of the delegation escorted her into the hall. Everyone in the room, including the congressional staff-person, agreed with the substance of what the delegate had said. The manner in which she spoke, however, came close to alienating a key ally.

Adam Curle, a British Friend who participated in peace and reconciliation work for many years, wrote in his book *True Justice* about how some Friends seem to respond to the Quaker phrase "Speak truth to power."

> I think to some Friends this suggests marching into the office of the president, the local mayor, or whosoever it may be, and issuing a ringing denunciation of his policies. If a relative stranger had done this to any of the presidents or prime ministers I have known, s/he might have been treated with cold courtesy or hot anger, but the message, because of the manner of the delivery, would have been unheard.[2]

In contrast, Micah Bales (Friends of Jesus Fellowship), in a blog post on holy anger, articulates his view that anger is inherent in the prophetic voice.

> It has never been clearer to me that there are times to bind up a whip of cords and chase out the moneychangers. Real love refuses to allow injustice to stand. If "loving" the oppressor means assuming the best about their motivations, I don't. If "loving" them means treating them with gentleness, allowing them to continue doing evil unchallenged, I can't.
>
> Real love gets furious in the presence of oppression. Real love sees that the only way to freedom—for all of us, regardless of our station in life—is to work for justice for the widow and the orphan, the foreigner and the poor, those who are most marginalized in our society. We

will be judged based on how we treat the least of these.[3]

Love does get furious in the presence of oppression. Love weeps with those who are suffering. Love knows that we are ultimately part of the injustice and that we cannot hold ourselves apart from this fact. Love knows that our strength is in God. This is what the Lamb's War was all about. In the seventeenth century, Friends used this term to name their way of confronting evil wherever they encountered it, but they always knew that violence, hatred, and other tools of evil do not defeat evil.

In John 2:15, Jesus overturned tables and otherwise disrupted people's greedy activities. Early Friends recognized that forceful, impartial action is sometimes needed to disrupt violence or other harmful behaviors, and they saw this as a task of the magistrates. Anger can quickly get out of control and be damaging in various ways, even as it energizes us to protect the vulnerable from harm. Such contradictions seem to be an inescapable dimension of prophetic work, a topic explored in more depth in chapter 19.

Another Way: Relationships and Patience

The variety of situations found in large meetings can help prepare those called to a radical, public ministry to deal with the multiple pressures they might encounter. The internal discipline required to face truly violent situations takes years of practice and self-knowledge. Such work starts at home and then is tested in community, and at times the fruits can be invaluable in the public arena. In *True Justice*, Adam Curle (Britain Yearly Meeting) wrote of what he learned through his experience as a mediator in Nigeria, Southeast Asia, and numerous other places around the world experiencing violent conflict:

> For my part I would never presume to criticize people caught up in a situation I do not share with them for the way they are responding to

that situation. How could I, for example, preach to the oppressed of Latin America or Southern Africa? Nevertheless, I explain that I do not believe in the use of violence as either practical or moral; my job is to help people who can see no alternative to [using] violence to find a substitute. What this may mean in practice . . . is to ask a question, although probably not as bluntly as this: why not try talking rather than shooting? The reply, not infrequently is: we would like to but . . . The task is then to analyse the nature of the "buts" and to see if they cannot be eliminated.[4]

Finding a way to build relationships and trust is a theme that arises again and again among those who have been visible presences witnessing for nonviolence and justice in revolutionary situations. Another British Friend, John Lampen, shares out of his experience as a mediator in Northern Ireland and other political hot spots:

As friendship and trust grow, so does honest speaking. It becomes possible to speak out critically, but this should only form a small part of the total relationship. George Mitchell, the American mediator of the Good Friday Agreement in Ireland, told how the turning point came when at last he stopped being nice with the delegates and lost his temper with them. His burst of anger was not calculated, but it succeeded because of the trust and respect they already had for him.[5]

John also notes the danger to the work when the relationship grows close, so close that the mediator loses the ability to be impartial. Impartiality is a key ingredient in the Quaker ability to serve and in the reputation of Friends as effective mediators. John says one of the criteria he uses in his work is being able to say the same thing to all parties in a negotiation. This work is often slow and hard. Major change takes time and often requires confrontation of some sort. But years of experience have shown how quickly violence can escalate, particularly when rumors and misperceptions are rampant. The ability to quickly step in and defuse tensions can be critical, and this can be dependent on the trust the individual has built. This advice applies to small communities as well as nations.

A Different Kind of Boldness

How might we better serve boldly? So often, being bold gets tangled up with aggression and anger. Such attacks often contribute to adversarial situations and cut off the possibility of problem-solving and developing relationships. These are dimensions of living boldly that speak to me.

- Start in prayer.
- Do Truth—live in that life and power that takes away the occasion of war.
- Be passionate; act out of the courage that comes with faithfulness to the Spirit.
- Act with clarity—see beneath the words.
- Seek a just peace.
- Empower others—don't just assume what they want and need.
- Listen with respect for the Divine spark in each heart.
- Be accurate and speak truthfully.
- Be transparent.
- Be willing to have your words and actions tested.
- Know when anger energizes you to act and when it is pressing towards destruction.
- Be kind rather than nice.
- Act with the confidence that comes of knowing the Inward Guide.
- Stop thinking you have to defend yourself or apologize for being faithful.
- Live in a state of teachable assurance.
- Always be grounded in compassion.

- Know deep joy.
- Constantly pray for guidance.

Speaking up. Being bold. These are among the hardest actions for me. I do not talk easily, and I strongly dislike anything that might call attention to myself. Thus, to be bold enough to step forward without being invited by others is a critical spiritual discipline for me. How can I notice when I should be doing this? I too often notice well after the fact and am then embarrassed. Can I find ways to make amends for when I am wrongly silent? These are important aspects of this spiritual discipline in my life.

Liberal Friends often joke about being introverts, so I am clearly not alone in my need to practice being bolder. For others, the challenge may be more along the lines of recognizing when their speaking firmly slides over into hostility towards others or gets tied up in anger and becomes destructive. This is all part of staying in touch with the Inward Teacher, which can keep our lives in balance so we may better build up our communities and find ways to strengthen them rather than berate them.

Being a Friend often calls us into living amid paradoxes. We are asked not only to walk humbly and serve boldly but also to take personal responsibility even as we live out of God's grace. A challenge for us today is to define a clear group identity for ourselves as Friends and at the same time be radically inclusive. Many more such paradoxes exist. When we, as human beings, set such issues up in opposition to each other, they polarize us and cause us to reject one another or even demonize each other. Grace abounds when we can recognize the paradox as such rather than assuming the worst or projecting our fears onto those with different beliefs.

This brings me back to discernment, the skill of being able to recognize what is truly damaging and needs to be changed and sort that out from what is simply uncomfortable or outside our experience. George Fox was adamant about the need to know our own inner state so that we can see when we are the problem; today we would talk about the need to avoid projecting our own fears and other problems onto the situation around us. Fear is the strongest inner headwind in my life, and it often interferes with my ability to act. It is up to each person to be able to name what is true for them and find ways to warn themselves when such winds arise.

I raise one caution regarding the way Friends sometimes lightly use the phrase "way will open" as if expecting that, in being called to take action, everything will go smoothly. At the spiritual level, that may be true when we are clear as to a leading. However, we may find ourselves at odds with our meeting community or others we expect to support us. Such a situation opens up possibilities for testing to see if the leading is true, but it may also mean that we have touched on an uncomfortable issue that requires others (or us) to change. In that case, patience and gentle persistence may be needed. Certainly, when working in the world, perhaps against those who are doing violence, resistance and an angry response may well be firm signs of being on track. Being aware of and exploring our own responses to such headwinds is an important part of prophetic ministry.

Queries for Reflection and/or Discussion

1. Does Adam Curle's discussion of ways we might better act in potentially confrontational situations speak to me? Have I experienced such situations in my immediate family, in my community, or in the world? How did I respond? How might I have better responded?

2. What does it mean to me to act boldly? What emotions help me to speak out? When have my emotions made a situation worse?

3. How do I respond to the concept of serving boldly as a spiritual discipline? Is serving boldly part of my life? How have I learned to grow in this discipline? What are examples of this?

THE PROPHETIC COMMUNITY: THE HOPES OF A PEOPLE

The following section on the prophetic community is comprised of five chapters. The prophet Habakkuk, when the people were faced with invasion by a foreign power, was told by God to begin WRITING THE VISION, to make the message of hope so plain that someone running past could read it (Habakkuk 2:2). If even one person names the possibility of a just society, a way of being with others in a community of respect and integrity, space suddenly opens for others to shout yes, this is what we want.

The U.S. government has named a type of nuclear missile Peacekeepers. Friends have always asserted that a world without violence cannot be created by violent means. Commitment to nonviolence means we need to find the paths to A GENEROUS PEACE.

The northern European dimensions of American culture have few traditions that involve visible mourning and lamentation. Many American Quakers think that, in the face of tragedy, a stiff upper lip prevails over wailing and lamentation. How might we better enfold GRIEF: THE MISSING DIMENSION into living out the prophetic calling?

The prophetic minister is called to listen beyond the rationalizations of his or her culture and to recognize and trust the voice of the Spirit. DREAMS: SEEING WHAT MIGHT BE help shape the prophetic vision and free our hearts to see beyond the rigidity, materialism, and self-centeredness of our culture.

MAKING THE SPACE TO HEAR can take conscious intention. Listening for the unseen Guide requires us to make space in the midst of our busy schedules and the pressure to achieve in visible ways. It also asks that we not be wrapped in fear so that the Holy may penetrate our lives.

63

CHAPTER 5
WRITING THE VISION

My high school teachers decided for some reason that I had to take advanced Latin. This wasn't terrible in and of itself, but the course met at the only time biology was offered, and my dream was to be a scientist. No one supported my dream, even though for days I sat in the hall during class in protest. In college, a professor told me I shouldn't major in chemistry because I was only going to have children and was wasting his time. This rebuff fueled years of my work for women's rights. In a world where people are shot for having the wrong skin color, my hurts are minor, but they are also indicative of how pervasive injustice can be. No young person should be treated as a stereotype. No person should be rejected based on some arbitrary prejudice.

My activism also grew out of the vision carried by my faith community that we are all loved by God. The nineteenth-century Quaker Lucretia Mott was my hero for her work not only in women's rights but also to end slavery and the mistreatment of African Americans. I don't know if I would have had her courage to walk down the street hand in hand with a black friend at a time when people were threatening to burn her house. I do know how important her vision of another way of being has been in shaping my life.

Vision is one of those lovely words that have different meanings and thus many layers of understanding. It can refer to our physical eyesight, but more often I use it to point to a deeper capacity, the capacity to see beneath the surface and open new possibilities. A vision might be a specific image, a dream, or a well-seasoned description of a better way society might function. The breadth of justice can be made visible even in small actions, as Lucretia Mott showed simply by being open in her friendships.

The power of a vision arises from its lived reality. The power of a vision may come as well from what it stirs in the hearts of others. A vision projects a new way of being. When it lays out the parameters of the new creation, it offers both hope and signposts on the way. When people cry out against the injustice embedded in their society in a manner that frees other hearts, they can simultaneously fulfill the yearning of those who have been harmed and affirm the reality of their pain. Such a vision leads away from revenge or other violence and towards hope for all.

To Write the Vision

Prophecy includes clear seeing—seeing with the eyes of God, as some would say. When we see clearly, we have the responsibility to speak, to act on what we hear within the deepest corner of our being. Prophetic ministry arises from that part of us immersed in the juncture with all that is holy. The Hebrew prophet Habakkuk reported:

> *Then the Lord answered me and said:*
> *Write the vision;*
> > *make it plain on tablets,*
> > *so that a runner may read it.*
> *For there is still a vision for the appointed time;*
> > *it speaks of the end, and does not lie.*
> *If it seems to tarry, wait for it.* (Habakkuk 2:2)

Habakkuk, like many prophets in the Hebrew Testament, wrote in a time of war when his people were under the threat of exile. His words are framed around unanswerable questions: "Why does evil go unpunished?" and "Why does God use the more wicked to punish the less wicked?" His worldview is totally different from mine. I do not see God as actively controlling human actions nor as punishing individuals' wrong behavior. I find that there are plenty of natural consequences to bad behavior that are sufficient punishments in and of themselves. We have learned that illness is a result of disease, not of divine retribution.

At the core of Habakkuk's story is the strong awareness of the prophet. The prophet recognizes when the innocent are being harmed, when people are gathering up wealth in a self-centered way, and when children are without food and cities are being plundered. These are signs that something is totally awry in human behavior. In such times, individuals need to stand on the watchtower and write the vision. They need to name the consequences of evil behavior and call the nation to rejoice in God, in the potential for beauty, justice, and mercy even when *the fig tree does not blossom, and no fruit is on the vines.* (Habakkuk 3:17). In such a place, with such trust in God guiding us, we find our strength and the seeds of the shining city on a hill that will welcome all with an open heart.

Overwhelmingly Caught Up

The narratives we tell about our society often omit large segments of the community or assume that those without power are happy in their roles. Breaking open these assumptions can be painful. Proposing a new narrative, a new vision, takes imagination and courage. Ann Janes (Britain Yearly Meeting) writes about attending the 1986 Swarthmore Lecture given by the Quaker Women's Group titled "Bringing the Invisible into the Light":

> I had an overwhelming sense of being caught up in something profoundly significant and relevant to me personally as well as to the Society of Friends of which I was a newish member. I did not name it 'prophetic' but I knew we were receiving deeply challenging ministry, and this spoke very personally to me at a time of great difficulty.

The women of the Quaker Women's Group raised their voices in 1986 in a new and powerful way. Those invited to give the Swarthmore Lecture had been almost exclusively male for the seventy-five years or so the lecture had been offered. To have a woman speak was significant. To have several women jointly prepare the speech and the book that accompanied it was a radical, communal expression of a society in which women were fully visible and their full capacity utilized.

Ann knew patience is needed for hearts to change and for real transformation of society to happen, yet she also knew she had to be involved in seeking equality for all women from then on.

If we are paying attention, each of us might have such a moment, a moment when we know that acting with others is crucial to our own integrity and our own walk with God.

Energizing and Imaging

'We are the ones to do it!'" This is how David Thomas, a young missionary from Northwest Yearly Meeting, summed up a visioning session held by leaders of Rwandan Friends. David viewed this awareness as a major step in a decade-long process in which Rwandan Friends were becoming less reliant on North American financing and the dependency that implied.

David described to me his role as a catalyst, using his prophetic gift for the benefit of the community. He held onto that hope even though he experienced rejection along the way by those who preferred the known, the comfortable. Having a vision, even one that resonates with the deepest hope of the people, may initially be rejected when the price of change is high.

Rwandan Friends faced the challenge of envisioning how to support the church without a steady stream of money from North Americans. Where would salaries come from? How could they finance the building where they worshipped and where they taught their children? These basic questions were made more intense by the difficulties of a nation recovering from

massive genocide that not only took lives and
disrupted the economy but also destroyed trust.
Neighbors saw neighbors committing unbelievable
horrors. Most lost family and friends to the chaos.
How is it possible to rebuild hope out of such ashes?
David writes:

> We took time in silence to listen to God, then
> we shared the images, Scriptures, and ideas
> together. Over a period of two days a vision
> emerged of a holy, transforming people on a
> hill shining Christ's light throughout the
> nation. We would get there by being disciples
> of Jesus and through prayer.

This vision that was first expressed in 1999 continues
to bear fruit. Work on healing trauma has been a
central work of Friends throughout the Great Lakes
region of Rwanda, Burundi, and the Democratic
Republic of the Congo. Friends also work in the
refugee camps of the Congo, teaching women to sew
and to earn a living when they have no other support
structure and their families are scattered if not
destroyed. Their vision incorporates generosity and
reaching out to those who have nothing.

Sustaining and expanding the scope of the vision are
times of gathering such as the 2013 Peace Conference
for Young Friends that was held in venues in Rwanda,
the Congo, and Burundi with several speakers in
common. Central African Friends conceived of this
gathering as a journey. In this manner, they were able
to build a common vision of their work for nonviolence
and engage many local Friends who could not readily
cross national borders. The stated intent of the
conference was:

> To come to an understanding of the role of
> each of the three countries in the violence of
> the past and the present. . . . The "journey"
> theme suggests journeying toward greater
> understanding of the complex problems of the
> region. . . . There are no easy answers to the
> problems of violence in central Africa and the

participants must come with a spirit of openness and with a willingness to listen to God and to one another.

The other meaning of "journeying" will be the unusual geographic feature of the conference, with its four different venues in the three countries. The days of travel between each segment of the conference will provide a chance to "digest" the learning from the previous location and to think ahead to the learning that will take place at the next part of the conference.[1]

The prophetic imagination sets us on a journey. It thrives on the paradox of connection with tradition and embrace of discontinuity, according to Walter Brueggemann, a scholar of the Hebrew prophets. He starts his discussion of prophecy with the mystery and sense of all that is beyond human comprehension: "First, energy comes from the embrace of the inscrutable darkness." Then, "There is a wondrous statement of a new reality that must surely emerge."[2]

It takes imagination, as the young people of Central Africa know, to see beyond the immediacy of the crisis and bleakness of the day, whatever that might be. It takes even greater imagination to recognize the source of numbing fear and oppression and to visualize alternatives. Yet, when we can be open to the creativity of the Spirit, this is where the true hope lies.

Brueggemann also identifies the "alternative community" as an essential carrier of visions. Such a community is set apart enough from the society around it to be able to see and name cruelty, self-centeredness, greed, or other evils as they arise. The alternative community is the breeding ground for prophets.

One Person's Vision for the Whole

For some Friends, the vision they are given may be specifically about their own part in living out a much larger task. Marcelle Martin (Philadelphia Yearly Meeting), who teaches regularly at Pendle Hill, a Quaker community outside Philadelphia, was given such a vision.

> In the vision, I was seeing Earth from a cosmic perspective. I knew that humanity was facing an impending catastrophe. In "heavenly" realms, this was known far in advance, and a whole cadre of souls was being born with the specific purpose of helping humanity to make a necessary shift of consciousness that would advert the catastrophe. I was one of those souls.

Marcelle's task was to teach skeptical Friends of the power of prayer and the work of the Eternal in addressing the overwhelming problems of the world. In her vision,

> We took hands around the circle, and I said, "Let us pray."
>
> However, nothing happened in this circle. People did not believe in the effectiveness of prayer. I felt the intellectual skepticism of the people around me and began to fear. I did not know how this group was going to learn to pray. And I was afraid, because I knew . . . this group had a necessary role to play in averting the catastrophe that was impending. They could only play their role if they could pray. My fear caused me to forget how to pray.
>
> So I spoke to God. "Dear God, I don't know how to pray. Teach us how to pray." . . . Divine power flowed around our circle. Our hearts opened together as one heart, in childlike trust of a powerful God of Love.
>
> A child in the group then remembered . . . a dream of a rebellious adolescent who received

the news that in spite of their rebellion, they would nonetheless inherit the Father's kingdom.

Marcelle notes that dream expert Jeremy Taylor advised her that it was perhaps *because of* the adolescent's rebellion that he or she would inherit the kingdom of God.

The power of the prophetic vision grows from the intersection of human experience, the tradition carried by the alternative community, and our connection with all that is eternal and beyond our human understanding. Early Friends were certain that the kingdom of God is within and constantly urged others to turn inward and wait on God. This advice is similar to Marcelle's message that we should turn to the Spirit in prayer and be open to the guidance it offers.

Doxology or Ideology? Song or Theory?

The great Song of the Sea (Exodus 15:1–18) and Song of Miriam (Exodus 15:21) are the most eloquent, liberating, and liberated songs in Israel. The last energizing reality is a doxology in which the singers focus on this free one and in the act of the song appropriate the freedom of God as their own freedom.[3]

Songs and images touch a part of my being that words cannot penetrate. Even so, I had to do some research and pondering before the above words of Brueggemann made much if any sense to me. Merriam-Webster defines doxology as an "expression of praise to God" that is usually liturgical.[4] Okay. Music activates a different part of the brain than spoken words, and some people who have lost the ability to speak or understand speech can communicate by song. Incorporating a vision of freedom into music and dance speaks to me of integrating this freedom into the body, which holds on to the tune and the beat. In the same way, nursery tunes still arise in my head sixty years after I first heard them as a child or a song triggers tears and emotional memories.

Brueggemann identifies the alternative community described in the book of Jeremiah as people who "saw how surely fatal everything that the kings called life was." He notes that "numb people do not discern or fear death. Conversely, despairing people do not anticipate or receive newness."[5]

Brueggemann argues that doxology redefines social perception by nullifying the official state version of events, expressing freedom of movement, and setting loyalty to God above obedience to the state.[6] This is dense language. I would restate it by saying that songs of praise and vision transform fear into energy and are essential to justice. These are things that those of us who have been on marches for peace and justice know in our bones.

Ironically, I find an echo of this argument in the early Quaker objection to singing in church. These Friends were not objecting to the music and song so much as to church, and ultimately state, control of what was sung and when. So, they objected to programmed song but not to song rising from the Spirit during worship. The exodus from ancient Egypt is not as far away as it seems.

A Vision of the World To Be Begins Now

Ann Janes (Britain Yearly Meeting) finds "nowness" integral to the vision. The vision is not realized in a future millennium far in the distance, nor does it come in an instant without our participation. Realizing the vision is our responsibility, yet at the same time it is only possible through God who is present among us.

> Prophetic ministry has to speak for its time and also give a pointer towards a new way of seeing or being. . . . the message to be given has to touch me deeply and activate some latent or

hidden energy within that needs release. At the same time, I have to have a sense that this is both needed and likely to be heard by at least a few.

Chris Densmore of Philadelphia Yearly Meeting describes a work of art created two centuries ago that made visible the ancient image of the lion lying down with the lamb juxtaposed with an image of William Penn signing a respectful treaty with the Lenape, a Delaware people.

> One of the few icons of Quakerism is Edward Hicks's painting(s) of the peaceable kingdom based on the verses in Isaiah about the time when the lion shall lie down with the lamb. Quakers at their best live as members of the peaceable kingdom and as if the Sermon on the Mount is its law. This is a prophetic vision of the world, not as we know it to be by listening to the evening news about war and violence but as [the] world we see before us as revealed by the Spirit, not as utopian dream but a lived reality.

Isaiah 11:1–9 offers perhaps the most widely known vision of the peaceable realm. Friends have long cherished this vision. Many paintings of the scene of the lion lying with the lamb were created by Edward Hicks in the late eighteenth century and were often hung on the walls in Friends' homes.

In the Isaiah passage, Jesse, the father of King David, is set forth as the father of a new generation, of a new branch of Israel that would grow and blossom. This Hebrew vision has been adopted by Christians who see it as the foretelling of the coming of Jesus, but I believe it speaks to all humans who yearn for peace.

> *A green Shoot will sprout from Jesse's stump,*
> *from his roots a budding Branch.*
> *The life-giving Spirit of GOD will hover over*

him,
the Spirit that brings wisdom and
understanding. . . .
He won't judge by appearances,
  he won't decide on the basis of hearsay.
He'll judge the needy by what is right,
  render decisions on earth's poor with justice.
  . . .
Each morning he'll pull on sturdy work clothes
and boots,
  and build righteousness and faithfulness in
  the land.
The wolf will romp with the lamb,
  the leopard sleep with the kid.
Calf and lion will eat from the same trough,
  and a little child will tend them. . . .
Neither animal nor human will hurt or kill
  on my holy mountain.
The whole earth will be brimming with
knowing God-Alive,
  a living knowledge of God ocean-deep, ocean-
  wide. (Isaiah 11:1–9 MSG)

The lived reality of Isaiah's words is an essential dimension of the vision Friends carry into the world. We are called to be actively transforming our homes, our communities, and our nations into places where people actually live in simplicity and interact without violence. Hicks's paintings of the peaceable kingdom have spoken to Friends for several hundred years, but they raise the question for me of whether we need a fresh symbol for the twenty-first century. What new image can speak without words of generosity, equality, and so much else we hold as central in the midst of new challenges?

Queries for Reflection and/or Discussion

1. How might you articulate the vision that your community holds in trust for the world? What might it mean to enter the darkness that Walter Brueggemann mentions? Is this essential to the emergence of a new vision? If so, in what way?

2. What helps sustain the vision of the new creation and the kingdom of God among us from generation to generation? How are you part of this chain of remembrance?

3. What obstacles do you find to naming and living out such visions?

4. What do we need to do to reach greater unity in our communities on the vision we hold for the new creation? How can we better use song and other media to express the visions we hold?

CHAPTER 6
A GENEROUS PEACE

Let justice roll down like waters. (Amos 5:24)

They shall beat their swords into plowshares.
(Isaiah 2:4)

*What does the Lord require of you
but to do justice, and to love kindness,
and to walk humbly with your God?* (Micah
6:8)

These phrases are familiar to most Friends, even those who have never opened a Bible. The call to justice rings clear as well to people of many other faith backgrounds. Such words evoke the peaceable kingdom where every person's basic needs are met and no person or group satisfies their lust for power or their greed at the expense of those who have little. Weapons of war will not be needed, and the materials that once constituted weapons can be reformed into tools for feeding the community.

Despite the often confusing messages of the Hebrew Testament—the calls for vengeance, the pronouncements of judgment, the awful slaughter—our spiritual ancestors lifted up the thread of the divine promise that the peaceable kingdom is attainable. In fact, in the words of William Dewsbury, "The Kingdom of God is within you."[1] This we can know for certain, in our bones and listening for the voice of the Guide, rather than dismissing the kingdom as a distant hope that will arrive miraculously in some future time or only after our death.

The immediate reality of the new creation is a vision that the Religious Society of Friends has carried since its inception. The Friends conviction is that this new creation will grow in our inward beings and become increasingly visible in our outward actions. Quaker meetings have been an important vehicle for nurturing this vision and making space for individual prophetic ministry.

Yet, because they are not immune to the human condition, meetings periodically fail in their support of this vision and even seem to lose track of it, resulting in tension between what the group understands and can affirm and what an individual knows deep in his or her being. This tension is evident throughout these chapters. Even a Friend as eminent as John Woolman encountered resistance within the meeting community to his strong, clear callings. Woolman believed that engaging with his community was part of his calling, part of bringing other Friends to see the evils of slavery.

The vision is there for most of us, even if only dimly understood. Today, the centrality of the peaceable kingdom is affirmed again and again by Friends such as Jean Zaru (Ramallah Friends Meeting), who wrote the following when her son was protesting against the Israeli military governor and she convinced him to take tea and cakes to the governor in response to the governor's demands for meetings:

> To be a follower of Jesus is not to be relieved of the responsibility to think and act. What we know for sure is that in the complicated demands of any situation, we must respond to our neighbors, all of them, not in proportion to how we judge them worthy. They are our brothers, our sisters and God's children, all of them—the military governor, the sixteen year old protester, and his terrified mother. We are asked by Christ to let the matter of cost be of least importance. My son and I finally agreed that in our situation no one can set rules for us to follow, but what we can do is to testify to the Spirit of God who leads us and gives us the needed guidance for every new situation.[2]

"Many People Risked Their Lives"

One of the most vivid moments in my high school years was when my tenth-grade English teacher met with our high school Quaker group. He spoke out of the depth of his conviction that not only is war wrong but that we cannot and should not be compelled to fight. He had refused to register for the draft during the Korean War and, as a result, spent five years in a federal penitentiary.

In North America and Europe over the last half century, Friends have lived largely without fear of death, or even imprisonment, as a consequence of our faith. There have been periods when some were jailed or beaten, such as during the civil rights movement in the United States or anti-war activities. Our awareness of the potential risk was intensified when Tom Fox, a Quaker, was taken hostage and later killed in Iraq, where he had been witnessing to the horrible treatment of Iraqi civilians.

In other parts of the world, almost every life has been touched by violence, and families and meetings have been torn apart. Living out the vision of the peaceable kingdom in those circumstances is mostly beyond my comprehension. Moses Bigirimana of Burundi (Kibimba Yearly Meeting) speaks to some of what he and others faced during the genocide in Central Africa and its aftermath.

> Where there is war, Quakers should just voice out and have a say. Again, Quakers should not participate in violence. We have experiences in Burundi where Quakers did everything to not participate in the killings. Many people risked their lives just by refusing to participate in violence.
>
> Now, Quakers have tried everything to be examples after the war—some worked in trauma healing and reconciliation seminars, trying to bring together people who are no longer talking together, no longer living

together, who are no longer really communicating with each other. Trying to reconcile people—Friends have done that.

To act in circumstances in which most people are severely traumatized and fear almost everyone around them takes great strength and commitment. Knowing the Spirit's guidance and being able to be aware of it when the world we know is crumbling and pulverizing our homes, our bodies, and our hearts is truly knowing the power of God. To speak out against what is happening and not take up a gun or a knife against someone who is brandishing such a weapon is truly a prophetic witness.

"Whatever They Have Given Me"

It is very easy to say "I didn't have the opportunity" or "I would have done this if . . ." Esther Mombo (Highland Yearly Meeting), who overcame many obstacles in gaining an education and a place of respect as an academic vice chancellor at St. Paul's University outside Nairobi, has little patience with the idea of waiting for the right circumstances. Excuses are not part of her vocabulary. She has done much to empower other women and to challenge the structures that would keep them from participating fully in the ministry.

> Where I have spoken boldly about it is at the yearly meetings. I'm surprised I have not been kicked out of speaking at yearly meetings. But I have been asked to be a guest speaker. The yearly meetings in this country [Kenya] are interesting. They give you four days of expounding Scripture every morning. So you have a whole hour each day with a thousand people listening to you. So I have used that. The yearly meeting always gives me a theme and a reading—I never choose the theme or the reading—I wish I would, but I don't. They choose. But I have ensured that whatever theme they have given me, I have inculcated in

79

it issues of social justice, issues of gender justice, issues of equity justice.

We each have a path in this world. Each path is unique, and each has the potential to grate against the fabric of the community that surrounds us. Part of my work is to build relationships among individuals and meetings in different branches of Quakerism, which can lead to objections such as "They are not really Quakers!" or "We cannot be yoked with sinners." At this point in my life, I cannot be true to the deepest calling in my heart without doing this work. As I have persisted, I have found many companions along the way, just as Esther does in the yearly meetings that invite her to speak even though she challenges them to turn to a broader vision.

When Others Charge Us to Act

Sometimes we may have little choice about stepping forward and speaking with a prophetic voice. Circumstances, be they a particular role we hold or events in the world around us, give us the opportunity. The sense of calling may be more external than internal. Linda Chidsey (former clerk of New York Yearly Meeting) describes being thrust into the public arena.

> After the events of September 11 . . . I was soon catapulted into the role of speaking on behalf of the yearly meeting in a far more public forum than I had ever anticipated or experienced before. The yearly meeting body sent me forth, upheld me, and held me accountable in the most remarkable of ways and I found myself asked to speak, bear witness, and testify in a variety of venues.

As Linda recounts her experience, two things strike me. One is the sense of support and accountability she felt from the body—the yearly meeting—that was putting such demands on her. The second was the way in which her role grew as she accepted the challenge of the ministry.

In contrast, John and Diana Lampen (Britain Yearly Meeting) have often felt cut loose and on their own, even though they have done work under the care of a Quaker group. Although they received practical help, the spiritual dimension was ignored. It seemed to be assumed that if they had a calling, they did not need local care and accountability.

Their work in Eastern Europe came under the care of a related Quaker body as well as of a local host school. These groups handled the finances and provided administrative support, but they offered little help with planning and evaluation. John and Diana found that the arrangements required an expertise that could only come from experience in the field:

> We valued [the] trust in us, but we suspect we were not often in their minds except on the days when we sent in our proposals or reports. They saw the work as "Diana and John following their leadings, and we're glad to back them" rather than adopting it as their own— though they certainly see their work as an expression of Quaker concern for peace and were glad for us to add an international dimension.

This contrast is alive and real in many corners of the Quaker world. No one has tracked this, but it is likely that many more people have had John and Diana's experience than Linda's. One of the challenges for our meetings today is to find better ways to stand with those who are carrying out a concern, even if the community has not taken the work up as its own ministry.

As one who has long had a ministry recognized by my community, I am acutely aware of the need to engage this question of how to care for those Friends who experience a strong leading. Occasionally the entire community may take the concern up as its own and a large number of people become involved, but I don't expect that to happen often. That is not always the problem and often not what prophetic ministers need. The increasing use of clearness and spiritual care or accountability groups is frequently an excellent way to respond. As we grow more skilled in this process, we become more capable of nurturing and sending forth individuals who are acutely aware of injustice and have a calling to speak boldly.

Finding Wider Community

I was not born when the Japanese internment occurred during World War II, and I was in college in the 1960s during the civil rights movement and the start of the anti-Vietnam war protests. In the 2010s, the peaceful witness of Native Americans against a major oil pipeline on the Standing Rock Indian Reservation in North Dakota became a significant symbol of injustice for me.

For a delegation of Quakers from New England, the witness at Standing Rock revealed both the great dangers that lie ahead related to climate change and the bold faithfulness that is being called forth:

> Once again we are invited, through faith-fulness, to the quiet yet profound voice of Truth that whispers in our hearts and gives us courage and power to walk boldly in uncertain times. When we give ourselves over to it, we know we too can enter into this Kingdom where our hearts are clarified in purpose, where we cling less to the illusory safety of our culture, where we feel more closely the security and Love of God.[3]

I am thankful and amazed by every person who can see such a reality when it presents itself and acts on it. Every generation has its horrors. The city of God seems far distant. As long as there are human beings, it seems, there will be prejudice, greed, and violence.

We cannot hide from these even if we live far from any town. Gold miners, loggers who clear-cut forests, and others whose actions have damaging consequences reach into every corner of the globe. Yet individual witness never ceases to present a glimpse of the new creation and point to hope.

The Complex Dance of Individual and Community

The lure of grand actions is strong. Martin Luther King Jr.'s "I Have a Dream" speech is well known and still feted over fifty years after it was given. Most of us, I think, feel at least slightly that pull to fame, that desire to do something lasting that is recognized widely. Yet large moments are shored up by thousands of points of witness that few will ever know of or recall. Prophetic witness—speaking boldly in the face of injustice or taking corrective action—is often quiet, without much drama, and part of the larger fabric of our lives.

In 1990, a group of white Friends in Wichita, Kansas, including Dorlan Bales (Great Plains and Mid America Yearly Meetings), purchased and moved into an apartment building in a low-income African American community to learn and build relationships with their neighbors. They could not ignore the poverty and systemic racism they saw around them.

A few years later, the group, which called itself Friends of Jesus, came to unity that gays and lesbians are not necessarily sinful. As a result, Evangelical Friends Church—Mid_America Yearly Meeting ended its formal recognition of the ministry of Dorlan Bales and Dorothy Craven. Dorlan describes the faith behind the Friends of Jesus in its call to be a multiracial faith community that accepted homosexual people.

> Having been judged by a church body that violated its own procedural ideals, my understanding of the role of prophetic ministry was broadened. The world's civil rulers and corporate leaders are not the only, perhaps not

the primary, people who need to hear God's call to justice for all. Faith communities, too, need to hear the Spirit's call to love.

As Dorlan learned, being judged and found unacceptable by one's own faith community can spur one to work harder against the injustice that others face. Because Dorlan and Dorothy were disciplined for Friends of Jesus' support of equality for gays and lesbians, Dorlan's call to love his neighbor was strengthened.

Prophetic ministry is not primarily a charity, making sure that individuals receive care on a case-by-case basis, though that is a good thing. Prophets ever since Moses (let my people go!) have called on the powerful to be mindful of God's love for the multitudes who have little power and experience all the consequences of poverty. The importance of ordinary people holding the powerful accountable to a God who is just as well as merciful is the basis on which Friends of Jesus member Laura Dungan created, with my support, Sunflower Community Action soon after the community moved into the apartment building. This multi-issue, multiracial group grew to give national leadership on issues like worker justice, access to the polls, and immigration reform.

Dorlan's broadened understanding of justice led him in two ways. One was to not just act charitably but also to work to change the structures that perpetuate poverty and alienation, holding the powerful to account. The other was to constantly be mindful of God's love and to act out of that awareness despite the loss of trust and the resultant grief he experienced.

I've seen the frustration of individuals because my meeting in Portland took a decade or more to accept the rights of gays and lesbians to marry and be full members of the community. Like Dorlan, I've seen the celebration when the community said yes and encouraged our state to do the same. The prophetic gift seems to thrive in some way in this interplay.

Queries for Reflection and/or Discussion

1. How do we retain our grounding in awareness of divine love as we address painful issues of poverty, abuse, and corruption? What does it mean to hold the powerful accountable before God?

2. Have you ever experienced being chastised or censored by your community? If so, what was your response? If your calling still remained within you, how did you go about acting on it?

3. Have there been times when your sense of what constitutes justice was expanded? How did this happen?

CHAPTER 7
GRIEF: THE MISSING DIMENSION

Strong emotions, expressed freely, scare me. So what was I doing at the Way of Ministry program at Pendle Hill retreat center, where people were taking up a lamentation, wailing over the ills of the world, and then singing, dancing, and crying out their joy? This was not something I had expected. Lamentation speaks to me of being amid a people who have lost everything and are in the midst of chaos, such as a woman crying out over the body of her dead child. I don't think of it as appropriate for a group of well-fed, comfortable, healthy people gathered in a warm place on a winter night.

What does such a crying out, in such unlikely circumstances, do? Does it do more than cause some of us to shut off our emotional receptors in self-protection? Is it cathartic? I suspect so. But it also seems to open some people's hearts to empathize with those who are suffering and help fuel their commitment to feed the hungry—spiritually and emotionally as well as physically. Scholar Walter Brueggemann writes:

> Compassion constitutes a radical form of criticism, for it announces that the hurt is to be taken seriously, that the hurt is not to be accepted as normal and natural but is an abnormal and unacceptable condition for humanness.[1]

Naming and grieving the hurts they see around them is a central aspect of the role of the prophet. In so doing, the prophetic voice has the responsibility to move people to compassion rather than to let hurts stew into a mass of bitterness and desire for violence and revenge.

Lamentation

In 1662, Mary Howgill wrote *The Vision of the Lord of Hosts*. In this tract, she described a vision she had had of the ruin that was to come upon England and its people if they did not change their ways. She was intensely aware of the injustices of English society, injustices inherent in the class system, and of the ties between the church and the state. Her response to the prospect of destruction raining down was a great sorrow.

> Then did sorrow seize on my heart, and great grief upon my soul, and a great weight upon my body, which caused my lips to quiver, and my belly to tremble, and a Cry ran through me, *O Lord, what wilt thou do with this Land, or with thy People therein, unto whom thou hast so largely manifested thy Name?*[2]

Brueggemann argues that grieving is essential to the prophet. The prophet must act out of compassion, bringing a message of divine mercy as well as a call to mend. Brueggemann believes that correction of injustice must be rooted in sorrow for what is wrong—not hatred of the enemy—and hope for a new way of being. He states that "the real criticism [of an unjust society] begins in the capacity to grieve because that is the most visceral announcement that things are not right."[3]

The Hebrew word *za'ak*, 'to cry out,' Brueggemann notes, describes both a moan of misery and an official filing of a legal complaint. So, it not only fulfills an emotional need but is an essential step in creating a remedy.

The Cross of Joy

In Christianity, the ultimate symbol of grief and the wrongness of the world is the cross. The cross is the topic of a section of my book *To Be Broken and*

Tender, largely because I found the concept alienating and contrary to my faith and to my understanding of the world. Delving into early Quaker writings gave this symbol life. I began to understand how seventeenth-century Friends such as Margaret Fell knew the cross was essential. I translate their phrase "taking up the cross" as conveying the profound shift from being self-centered to being Spirit-led; it means being healed inwardly. Again and again, Fell and others instruct Friends to let go of the demands of the ego so that it is possible to listen for the guidance of the Inward Light. Given how hard it was for me to come to terms with the concept of 'the cross,' I was not at all surprised when people told me they loved my book but came to a stop when they encountered the section on the cross. They imagined it to be about punitive self-sacrifice or total, literal belief in many Christian doctrines that liberal Friends today cannot accept.

To top this off, the first time I heard Bill Taber speak about the "cross of joy" I was definitely shocked and totally disoriented. For Bill, this experience was of awareness "of the radiant love of God: patient, tender, uplifting, and healing."[4] He found that much was being asked of him, not as a sacrifice or in pain but in the spirit of joyous acceptance of whatever comes. In this place, one can be totally present, alive, and at peace. This all sounds quite similar to the Buddhist concept of nonattachment. I still have trouble engaging the language that Bill uses, but I am intrigued by his conviction that the cross of joy "frees people to be more alive, creative, and vital."[5] I do know those moments when all is right, when I am doing what I have been called to do. This may occur when I travel in the ministry or in simple acts at home when I recognize that I have attended to that gentle nudge on the soul.

Taking up the cross means letting the old self die, not being dominated by fear, and not being swallowed by a sense of inadequacy and guilt or the feeling that I can do it all. These are at the heart of taking up the cross, the cross that is the path to the joy that arises from faithfulness. Wondering about the paradox that is the cross of joy and stepping outside the culture I live in, the one that so often shapes my thoughts and actions, break open my complacency and certainty, leaving room for God to work. It is so easy to think that the latest crisis is the worst ever experienced or otherwise disastrous and to be blinded to the ways in which my actions have contributed to injustice or the perpetration of empire. Somewhere in all this I catch glimpses of what Bill Taber knew so innately in his soul.

Strengthening the Bond of Community

In the twentieth century, Ramallah was a crossroads of much violence and injustice. I was deeply shaken when I met Israelis and Palestinians there who had lost their children and individuals who had lost their livelihood. I encountered children who showed clear signs of the trauma of violent incursions, such as from seeing a neighbor shot for simply stepping out on her own balcony to hang clothes to dry. Grief and faith both permeated their lives and spilled out when they told their stories.

Friends have been in Ramallah since the late nineteenth century, when they started a school for girls and established a meeting there. The school has thrived and now includes boys, and it is the only school offering international baccalaureate degrees in Palestine today. Only a few Quakers are still in Ramallah. Each of them must face the nearly constant tension between their commitment to nonviolence, the losses, and the realities of the violence that surrounds them. Jean Zaru (Ramallah Friends Meeting), a lifelong Friend and resident of Ramallah, writes:

> Times of grief and anguish can strengthen our bonds. Now we need each other as never before, we need to treat each other well, to cherish and care for and support each other to become the community we imagine. Our

solidarity must go deeper than we have ever known before. Solidarity means strengthening our practice of direct democracy, our openness and communication with each other, our willingness to bring everyone to the table and network with like-minded people.[6]

We know grief in many ways, even when our lives are sheltered from the violence that sweeps through lands such as Palestine. Nancy Richard, in her book *A Small, Steadying Sail of Love*, writes these simple words:

> This also is true:
> it may be possible
> to meet
> in a place of tenderness
> with a person
> whose troubles trouble you.[7]

Suffering in Itself Does Not Teach

The ability to grieve and to express grief is one of the qualities of the prophetic ministry that I brought up earlier in this section. Many ways in which people point to the cross of Christ come across as inducing guilt and imply that in following Jesus we will somehow learn from suffering, especially Jesus' suffering, or otherwise be saved from suffering if we only believe hard enough. Yet some experience a mysteriously transformative dimension of grief and an intertwining between joy and suffering. Anne Morrow Lindbergh, writing after the kidnapping and murder of her young son in 1932, expressed it this way:

> I do not believe that sheer suffering teaches. If suffering taught, all the world would be wise, since everyone suffers. To suffering must be added mourning, understanding, patience, love, openness, and the willingness to remain vulnerable. All these and other factors combined, if the circumstances are right, can teach and can lead to rebirth.[8]

Hostility, blaming others for actions that may have begun within ourselves . . . we try to escape pain and suffering in so many ways. We easily forget that one function of pain is to tell us that something is wrong and that action is needed to remedy what is wrong. Some of the most intense physical pain I ever experienced was due to appendicitis, a pain that would not stop until the damaged appendix was removed. If all I had done was to take pain medication, the pain might have eased, but my appendix would have deteriorated and burst, with severe damage to my health.

Thus, one function of the prophet is to name the underlying damage that needs to be repaired in order for the pain to end—or perhaps to become the germ of a new thing, a new way of being in the world. Sometimes there is no immediate solution to the suffering of an individual or a community. In that case, all we may be able to do is stand with those whose lives have been filled with trouble, bear witness to the wrong that has been perpetrated, and simply hold their pain in prayer. The advice I hear from early Friends is to go deep, to focus on the city of God in our midst. There is great value in having people skilled in the inward life who can identify ways to sustain relationships or alleviate the pain so it can be eased. Even more needed at times is the ability to sustain hope, to name it, and to make it real even when hope seems impossible.

Queries for Reflection and/or Discussion

1. What role does grief play in your life? Does it help you or prevent you from speaking the prophetic word?

2. Walter Brueggemann states that the Hebrew word *za'ak* describes both a moan of misery and an official filing of a legal complaint. What might he mean by this? How does this affect your understanding of the work of the prophet?

3. Has grief been associated with what you have been called to say or do? How has that modified or strengthened the message you were called to offer?

4. Do you find meaning in Bill Taber's concept of the 'cross of joy"? What does it mean to you?

5. Anna Morrow Lindbergh points to actions she sees as integral to knowing a new way of being and to learning compassion through one's grief. Do these speak to you in any way? How might you identify the skills that assist in this kind of healing?

CHAPTER 8
DREAMS: SEEING WHAT MIGHT BE

When I was in Kenya for the 2012 World Conference of Friends, I asked a variety of people about prophetic ministry. As I spoke with one Kenyan woman, I realized she and I were speaking at cross-purposes. When I asked her what prophetic ministry meant in her church, she replied: "Prophets will foretell events, saying, 'Oh, I dreamed.' Or, 'I was doing works.' Or, 'I dreamt I was dancing.'" In her mind, prophets were not to be taken seriously. She concluded, "The leaders always discourage such things in the church." This is certainly a very different understanding than I have and a good example of how widely varied our understandings of words can be.

Yet dreams and visions have always been part of the Friends way of being open to the Eternal Teacher. Almost every Friend knows about George Fox's vision of a great people to be gathered. This prediction of what was to come has sustained and inspired many over the centuries. Fox described it as follows:

> As we went I spied a great high hill called Pendle Hill, and I went on the top of it with much ado, it was so steep; but I was moved of the Lord to go atop it; and when I came atop it I saw Lancashire Sea; and there atop of the hill I was moved to sound the day of the Lord and the Lord let me see a-top of the hill in what places he had a great people to be gathered.[1]

The February 2013 issue of the Quaker publication *What Canst Thou Say?* focused on the subject of prophetic ministry among Friends. Some Friends who submitted essays described specific foretellings of events. Others felt they were given a distinct vision or heard clear voices in their heads. Such glimpses of the future or visions may appear to come from specific individuals who have died; in other cases, the source is experienced as divine or perhaps even beyond comprehension. A few contributors were brought into an all-embracing awareness of the oneness of all, even in the midst of very everyday doing. Some of the experiences offered were intensely personal and held in the heart. Other Friends had heard clear messages to be shared with the world. These essays make evident the wide variation that exists in how we hear and interpret the images, words, or unarticulated nudges that come to us.

Early Quakers and Dreams

It is not unusual to find reports of dreams or visions (early Quakers often did not distinguish between the two) in the journals of Friends who traveled in the ministry. Such prominent friends as Mary Penington and John Woolman reported on dreams in their memoirs, not always commenting on the meaning. In the earliest years, visions and dreams were seen as prophetic, carrying weight similar to the biblical prophets. That understanding quickly faded as the seventeenth century progressed, but it was not totally lost until the nineteenth century. Dreams were also viewed as an important way for Friends, especially women, to influence the world around them. Second Day Morning Meeting, the body that oversaw Quaker publications beginning in 1672, allowed many dreams to be published, indicating that influential Quakers acknowledged the importance of dreams and the potential they had to convey divine guidance.

In the eighteenth century, it became popular for Friends to copy down reports of others' spiritual dreams, and by the end of the century some were keeping "vision books." Carla Gerona, the author of a scholarly book on Quaker dreaming whose work informs this chapter, reports that

> Quakers publicized and recorded their dreams
> to resolve these larger community concerns
> [e.g., slavery]. These visionary experiences
> carried authority because Quakers collectively

thought that dreams channeled divine intimations.[2]

Gerona reports that Quakers used dreams as a way to criticize government and the Anglican Church. As they became more involved in settling North America, "Their dreams acted like maps that allowed them to bring their unique universalist vision of Christianity to faraway places."[3] Gerona adds that they also used dreams to lay out order in meetings and to advocate for major change in society such as pacifism, the abolition of slavery, and even total racial equality.

On the Balance Point

Even today, the Quaker reliance on the Spirit can place us on the edge—on the balance point between the world we live in now and the world to come, between imaging the future and fantasizing, between assurance and arrogance, between mental health and delusion, and between truth and wishful thinking.

Having no firm rule book, no neat hierarchy or appointed final authority such as the pope, we as Friends are dependent on paying attention to the Spirit and possessing enough self-knowledge to be able to recognize the voice of the Light with some assurance. If that assurance is not tempered by humility, our disagreements turn into fights over territory and the community can be broken.

When we keep naming what we hold most dear and holding up our vision of the new creation using the idioms of our day and age, the words become more vital and carry more life. This is an ongoing process as each generation and each community of Friends is asked to do this for ourselves, but not in isolation.

I think of mental health as one's ability to function in the world even when many of the world's values seem alien and destructive. We come from a long tradition of compassion for the mentally ill. This is for good reason, as there is often a thin line between the behavior of Quakers and what the world may consider delusional. Similarly, sorting out the real truth of a situation and naming it may strike others as delusional, especially when a major factor is the guidance of the Inward Teacher.

Friends do not take an easy path. Choosing to be out of conformity with the world can have many consequences and rarely leads to riches and ease. Even within the wider community of Friends, one body of Friends often seems to be out of conformity with what others hold most central. All of this requires us to hold one another in patient, loving prayer before God.

Sorting Out Delusions

In 1685, Mary Ellwood and Margery Clipsham published *The Spirit That Works Abomination and Its Abominable Work Discovered*. The authors included many warnings about how people might be led astray, even in the subtitle of their work:

> As a Warning to all who profess to walk in the
> Light of the Lord, that they keep close in Spirit
> to the Lord, and listen not to that adulterated
> Spirit, which labours to draw from the way of
> Truth, lest they be destroyed by it.

To emphasize their point, they added biblical admonitions such as this from Jeremiah 14:14:

> The Prophets prophesie Lyes in my Name: I
> sent them not, neither have I commanded
> them, neither spake unto them: They Prophecy
> unto you a false Vision, and Divination, and a
> thing of nought, and the deceit of their Hearts.

Thus, from the early days of the movement, Friends have faced the challenge of figuring out who is speaking truth and who is not. This seemed to be the case in biblical times, and it likely is so in any society that gives individuals the right to speak truth verified largely by an invisible power. Discernment becomes even harder when the individual condemns the actions of community members and leaders, pressing them to live in a new way.

In today's world, this remains a concern. Darren Kenworthy (North Pacific Yearly Meeting) puts it this way:

> Wanting to know how things will change, believing we know, pretending to have special knowledge about how things will change, are all grave and terrible temptations that can seriously impair our clarity. Traditions of spiritual seeking of great diversity take pains to call into question the wisdom of being preoccupied by the temptation to presume foreknowledge.

Dreams have been important in my spiritual life, particularly in developing a language for speaking of the Giver of Life and Breath. For many years, when I could not find words I would be given vivid images in my dreams. By describing these images, I could convey to others something of the way the Guide was reshaping me inside. But along with these rich images, I also would have vivid, sometimes distressing dreams that would wake me in the night. As I spent time with the complex of dreams that filled my nights, I came to learn that many of them were ways that my head and heart were sorting out my past. Such dreams were meant only for me and had no significance for others. Yet I could have read some of them as portents or used them to threaten others with dire consequences if they did not act in a certain way.

Anyone who has paid much attention to dreams knows how difficult and fascinating dream interpretation can be. Many people (even in the seventeenth century) have developed dictionaries purporting to tell the meaning of dream images. It is clear that dream images reflect an individual's culture to some degree. They may reflect what has been happening during the day, distant childhood memories, paintings or television images, or world events. The potential for many interpretations of dream images is always present; the meanings are rarely absolute.

Quaker ministers in the past seem to have done an initial sorting of dreams themselves and then tested out their understanding of the dreams that seemed significant with the larger community. Once vetted, such dreams might be part of a minister's message or otherwise shared verbally, and those that reverberated as true were circulated in writing.

In deciphering dreams as well as in the case of any significant decision, the criteria included testing with the community and with the Bible, a clear inward sense of peace or rightness, and what has been called "moral purity," which I might name consistency of ends and means with Jesus' teachings. In many ways, early Quakers were saying that the Light would not contradict itself by approving nonviolence one day and violence the next. And, as importantly, what we are advocating should be visible in all of our doings and words.

Seeing Before Others Are Ready

Karen Putney (Southeastern Yearly Meeting) described the feeling of being out of step that comes when a person or group sees something that the rest of society seems blind to.

> Years ago I was sitting in a meeting at Friends Committee on National Legislation. . . . we were all feeling rather discouraged with how horrifyingly wrong things seemed to be and feeling uncertainty: how could we be so out of step when 'everyone' else seemed to see the matter so differently. We were just puzzled at how differently we seemed to see things yet just so certain that we were on the 'right' path.
>
> Then a young person spoke up, basically positing that this must be what being prophetic is. "You see something clearly, you declare it

and are out of step." She felt that being prophetic explained how Friends witness often seemed to be ahead of its time. That that's what prophetic is: seeing how things should or could be and declaring it, often before others can see or be ready for it.

Friends have relatively few outward absolutes. We have no fixed creed that assures us we believe the right things. We do not turn to priests who tell us with authority what biblical passages mean. We rely heavily on discernment, both by the individual and by the community, a discernment that relies heavily on sense and feeling as well as behavior. Dreams are part of the prophetic life but, like so much else, they do not fit into neat categories. Dreams are not reliable indicators of truth or of what the future might foretell, yet they may offer invaluable insights into actions we might take and inspire the community to move towards change and to live in hope.

Queries for Reflection and/or Discussion

1. Have you experienced dreams that seemed prophetic? If so, how did you determine this? How did you share the dream or vision?

2. What is your response when you hear others speak of dreams and name the significance of these dreams for the community?

CHAPTER 9
MAKING THE SPACE TO HEAR

Being listened to in the depths of the soul is an amazing experience. It has changed me and helped make concrete the shifts in my assumptions about myself, moving me out of my tendency to deny my own worth. Even more, the listening hearts of others have made it possible for me to say yes in unexpected ways.

"I Am Only a Boy"

Listening and being listened to beneath the words and beyond the limits of our expectations can open the soul to prophetic ministry. The way of the prophet is not a path many would choose. Jeremiah, for instance, protests God's call to speak out, stating firmly that he was too young, but God quickly rebuked him. God made no bones about the need to listen and to follow:

> *"Do not say, 'I am only a boy'; for you shall go to all to whom I send you, and you shall speak whatever I command you. Do not be afraid of them, for I am with you to deliver you."* (Jeremiah 1:7–8)

I came back to these words again and again as I struggled to accept that I was supposed to speak in worship. And then again, as I found myself asked to speak to larger groups and to travel widely among Friends, "Why me?" echoed often in my head. Constantly, through inward guidance and the words of friends, the reply was "Be not afraid."

Now I have come to see how these words lay out two essential dimensions of prophecy. First, and above all, is faithfulness to the movement of the Spirit. If a person is attempting to speak out of their intellectual knowledge only, or because of some ego-driven purpose, or from a desire to please others, that person quickly risks falling into the category of "false prophet." To be true to a calling requires attention to both the world around us and to the guidance of the Spirit echoing inwardly. It is frightening to say yes to such a call. It is easy to teeter between feelings of inadequacy and arrogance. Often the fate of the prophet is to be an outsider, reviled by the establishment and sometimes by everyone. There is good reason to fear faithfulness to such a call.

Walter Brueggemann's book *The Prophetic Imagination* assigns responsibility for the prophetic ministry squarely in the hands of alternative communities that can step back critically from the dominant culture and be communities that acknowledge pain and can articulate hope. He views the prophet as one who offers a critique of society, mourns the ways it falls short, and energizes those who might be changed in themselves and act to change society by providing an alternative vision of the way we might live. He contrasts the oppression of the pharaohs' rule with the expansiveness and justice of God's way.

One piece of my work at the moment is to identify ways we might understand and recognize the prophets among us within the Quaker community. Brueggemann tells us first that prophecy is an engagement of "the religion of God's freedom with the politics of human justice" and then asserts that

> criticism is not carping and denouncing. It is asserting that false claims to authority and power cannot keep their promises, which they could not in the face of the free God.[1]

The Space to Be Heard

I have a soft voice and often lack the will to persist and insert myself loudly into a conversation, even among friends. Others often talk over me and don't even realize I want to speak. I end up feeling invisible, separate from those around me, even if they are close friends. If I feel this, even in my position of being comfortable, well-off, and generally respected, how much more difficult must it be to live in a condition where no one ever hears you or takes your perspectives and your needs seriously?

How often does our culture encourage us to dismiss the voices of outsiders, be they someone new to the community, someone whose heritage is different from ours, or someone whose accent or vocabulary is unusual? Governing authorities may make some space for constituents savvy enough to approach them in an accepted manner, but too few decisions that matter take the voices of ordinary individuals into account unless they can unite and show there are enough of them to affect elections.

Actions to give aid to the impoverished all too often are on the government's terms; those in power may bristle with distrust and offer little that is relevant to the people receiving the aid. The media are notorious for their focus on those with 'star power,' wealth, or positions of authority. Attempts to speak with ordinary people yield mixed results at best. Entertainment value and selling air time or print space are the priority. In most churches, people tend to hear the pastor, not those in the pews. Truly, listening is rarely valued in North American culture and is probably devalued in many other cultures as well.

Friends seek to be grounded in listening to the Eternal as well as to the people we encounter day to day. Kathleen Wooten (New England Yearly Meeting) describes the way an unexpected, unknown voice can change a group and help it discern what is right:

> In a particularly challenging moment, a small group charged with ministry and counsel work was trying to discern how they would go forward . . . at a time where there was not much clarity. Suddenly a new attender . . . said, "I have no idea what we are to do. But I feel in this moment an amorphous yes that we are

supposed to attend to. I do not know where this comes from—but I have deep trust that the rest will be given after we say yes!"

The whole meeting shifted at that moment. Clearness was discovered not in the details but in the willingness to move forward, to become unstuck, to shift to a sense of possibility and wondering what might be next.

What I've been considering in terms of this wider definition of "prophecy" is not the message itself—but the space in which it can be heard, where it can be shared, and how it can be received. . . . [T]hat young man opened the space for God to be present to us again. [We became aware] of an alternate possibility, a moment where we could accept the newness of Love breaking in as we said yes in covenant community—and not just any community but the community called together by God into the work in hope and Love.

Awareness of the dynamics of listening can be made evident in committee meetings or full business meetings by an attentive clerk who draws out words needing to be spoken and the places where decisions are needed. Yet many of us also benefit from individuals who can sit one on one and create space without always jumping in to propose solutions or share the details of their own experience. Such people are able to hold the silence in such a way that change can occur.

A Ministry of Being

I doubt I am unusual in visualizing prophetic ministry as active, as involving heroic actions that range from preaching the Gospel in lands hostile to Christianity to physically standing in front of a bulldozer to protest ways of oppression and violence.

Respondents to my questions reminded me of another way. Our presence alone may be enough if we are truly centered in attention to the Inward Teacher and remain faithful to its holy nudges. Such nudges may lead us to simply be present among a group that is facing harsh challenges or even to be a steadying presence in our home meeting. This was enacted by Avis Crowe and Dyckman W. Vermilye, who felt a call to travel to Cape Town, South Africa, and spend time with the local Quaker meeting and in the segregated townships. They went in the 1980s without any sense of what they were to do other than to accompany those who lived there. Before going, they did not see themselves as ministers and were uncomfortable with the term. Yet that was the most apt way to describe their role. Their model was Henri Nouwen's book *Gracias!*, in which he writes:

> A "pastoral presence" is more important than any plan or project. This conviction has grown out of the observation that, more than anything else, people want you to share their lives. More and more, a desire grows in me simply to walk around, greet people, enter their homes, sit on their doorsteps—play ball—and be known as someone who wants to live with them. It is a privilege to have the time and the freedom to practice this simple ministry of presence.[2]

Avis and Dyckman described getting to know people and playing with children. They also accompanied adults in practical ways, such as helping them set up bank accounts for organizations so that they could receive grants. Dyckman found this ministry incredibly difficult. He was clear he could not take the lead but only walk alongside and help when asked. People questioned their lack of agenda. Helping people get to know and trust one another, listening to those with whom they disagreed and occasionally speaking out, were not activities that fit in a neat plan. Their everyday work, however, helped build relationships that would be necessary for peaceful resolution as political change came to South Africa.

This kind of ministry can occur in many venues, and Friends have a particular discipline and practice that make this a natural way of witnessing to the work of the Spirit that is separate from activism and engagement in large-scale projects to encourage change. Linda Chidsey (New York Yearly Meeting) speaks of the ministry of presence this way:

> My understanding of the prophetic has shifted even more from that of witnessing and speaking to one of "being." I want to say that again. One can be prophetic in her/his mode of being. Of course, this doesn't mean I never speak out or take action; rather, I've experienced what I call a "proportional shift" toward the contemplative.

The presence of a single individual who knows at the core of their being what the Inward Teacher is asking of them can engage the hearts of others in brief encounters and even the hearts of people who only hear of their witness.

The Prophetic Stream

Many Friends cherish the idea of being part of "the prophetic stream" as Bill Taber (Ohio Yearly Meeting) calls it. At the 2008–2009 Way of Ministry program, Friends continued an active conversation begun four years prior at a retreat led by Bill focused on prophetic ministry. The Way of Ministry pushed our growing edges and often made us all uncomfortable.

Bill's work points to the everyday process of being a Friend, and he names the prophetic stream as integral to our path. He summarizes the lives of the prophets through four key concepts: justice, knowledge of God, faithful covenant love, and walking with God. His biblical and early Quaker examples bring these concepts alive.[3]

Being Prophets

The prophetic tradition remains active among us today. During the year-long Way of Ministry program, talking about prophecy started to sound normal to me, even though it was not part of my vocabulary at the onset. We learned that prophets aren't just lonely voices crying in the desert about a disastrous future; they are representative voices. At times they seek to throw down evil systems, but they are also people who build and plant a vision of a more just life. These are the notes I took in one of the sessions.

> Who is a prophet? An individual formed by God. God breaks in and calls us, meets our resistance, and then fills each heart with trust, love, passion, and sympathy.

> What is the task of the prophet? To impassion the people with an understanding of the Holy. The prophet is not asked to say "everything's okay" but to note what is awry and to voice the grief and pain of that disjuncture. At the same time, the prophet is called to voice the hunger and thirst for a better world and to offer a glimpse of what wholeness looks and feels like, asking others to join in making this possible.

> How is the prophet formed? Through deepening levels of faithfulness, trust, and surrender through which each individual comes to her or his authentic self. This formation occurs in a context of accountability and corporate care that is aligned with the divine way.

> Feeling different or even marginalized within a basically supportive community is not unusual. This may prompt us to ask whether what we are expecting from the community is an unattainable ideal, whether God is working in us in a way that leads to new insights or strength, or whether there is a way we might help the community to grow.

Bill began one talk on prophetic ministry (see appendix C) by affirming Howard Brinton's assertion that true ministry is prophetic at its root, "arising spontaneously and unpredictably under a sense of Divine urgency."[4] Bill said:

> Even though the context of a given message may be categorized as "teaching ministry" or "pastoral ministry" (giving comfort or inspiration at times like birth, funerals, marriages, etc.) or speaking to the condition of one or more people in the meeting, all such ministry is prophetic if it arises from a Divine "inward motion" in the speaker. This use of the word prophetic goes beyond the common understanding that prophecy is only about foretelling the future. Instead, it assumes that prophecy is really about God's yearning for us to shape up now, in the present time![5]

Friends are part of the prophetic stream when we are willing to set aside time in our lives to listen in order to make space for the Inward Teacher to make itself known. When we can make space to examine our own motives and come to recognize the voice within that treasures compassion and truth and to see the divine motion in our everyday actions, we make more space for the radical prophets to come forward and offer a witness to the world.

Queries for Reflection and/or Discussion

1. How do you make time in your day for listening beyond words and into that space in your heart where the Spirit is at work? What is that experience like for you?

2. Can you recognize when you are caught up in the sometimes overwhelming demands for activism and the desire to help make a more just world? Is it helpful to step back and refocus on the work that is yours to do?

3. What keeps you from listening inwardly on a regular basis? How might you set aside more time to listen?

INDIVIDUAL RECOGNITION
OF THE PROPHETIC CALL

The following section on recognition of the prophetic call is comprised of seven chapters that describe some of the groundwork that prepares individuals for God's call and offer examples of how the call has been recognized.

I have experienced a PRESENCE, a force of compassion, truth, and righteousness that seems to be independent of culture or faith tradition. The ability to sense this force, this Presence, enlivens the ministry. Becoming aware of the reality of love is the first step to BECOMING OPEN TO MINISTRY.

Our spiritual ancestors' lives were changed by their sense of divine grace; they experienced TRANSFORMATION (AGAIN AND AGAIN). Early Quakers described the intensity of change as the refiner's fire that melts away the dross, leaving behind the pure metal. Quaker meetings for worship provide a place both to listen deeply for the guidance of the Spirit and to offer to the community WORDS GIVEN by that Spirit.

Faithful response to the divine nudges on the soul allows each of us to find the particular service that is ours to give. This may be quiet and mostly out of sight, or it may be something larger that the community helps to grow by NAMING THE MINISTRY.

It is easy to set ministers on a pedestal and elevate them in a hierarchy. Friends are radical in saying IT'S WHAT WE DO—it's what all of us do, ideally all the time. Ministry is about service to the world, to the people we consider our enemies, and to our closest friends. Ministry can be rather mundane, very public, or even dangerous. This service, which some name DILIGENCE IN THE LORD'S SERVICE, is basic to being a Friend. May each of us recognize this in our lives and find language to help it come alive.

CHAPTER 10
PRESENCE

Many stories, ancient and modern, tell of children who from an early age feel the touch of something holy protecting them or guiding them. They sense an unmistakable quality of love, of being uplifted, of an otherness that can protect the soul in dangerous situations or fill the heart with awe. Some people experience a nudge or are otherwise convicted that they must step forward and act. Many people have no sense of the mystical until much later in life, however, and some never have such a feeling. As I learned in midlife, this sensation can absolutely convince one of the presence of God and can change one's life in amazing ways. In and of itself, the mystical experience is not the same as the prophetic call. It is an experience of connecting to the divine, whereas the prophetic call is a leading to take up certain actions or to offer words—there is motion involved as well as active guidance.

Recognizing the whisper that pierces the soul, the words of another that shake the core of one's being, and also being a witness to injustice large or small that requires a response—such things are at the core of prophetic ministry. The call comes in many ways but always involves a turning, a shift away from a comfortable, self-centered life to one centered in the Eternal. It may come at a low point for someone mired in addiction, callousness, or greed. It cuts through arrogance and convicts the soul of all that is not in line with the holy.

Quaker history, like the Bible and many traditions worldwide, is full of stories of unlikely people being called into ministry. Children, women, men—all can experience this force of compassion in their lives that lifts them away from the ordinary patterns of life.

Living in this world is a demanding task for many of us. It can take all our energy and attention just to get through the day, to earn enough to nourish our bodies and those of our families, much less to pay attention to the Spirit. The press of the here and now is real and demanding. We may hardly recognize when our lives have slipped into constant activity that has little to do with the values we hold most dear. Yet, even in the rush of obligations, the deepest hope of our hearts might slip through. Dorsey Green (North Pacific Yearly Meeting) calls attention to the times we may be doing God's work without any awareness of calling or even conscious decision-making.

> I actually suspect that many people are called and act on that call without recognizing it for what it is. I think most of us need to pay a lot more attention and listen for divine direction. The world is so busy and fast that I certainly can go a long time before I realize I'm not listening or grounded.

I know I need practice and external reminders to help me remember to still my mind enough to let go of the constant internal commentary and my tendency to pronounce judgment on everything, especially my own behavior. The constant inner chatter leaves little room for the Guide to get a word in edgewise. Some people actively yearn for that spiritual guide and a sense of holy direction for their lives. Having spent over half my life with no inkling that I might even be aware of the Spirit's presence in my life, I can affirm how unexpected a divine calling is for some of us.

How do we become open to the ministry that might be ours to live out? Transformation of mind, body, and soul is part of the turning—the metanoia—that opens the heart to service to a community or the world. Entering into that place where the way becomes clearer and Truth is the touchstone is humbling and empowering. Such is the place where the Light becomes more visible and actively illumines the path.

Friends hold the conviction that guidance is possible, guidance that fulfills more than our own personal wants and needs. This guidance counters the pull of commercial television or the secret personas lurking on the internet or twisted political games; it is consistent with the hope that others will find joy and a healthy, engaged life. In the vision handed down to us, we are encouraged to focus on what is most holy, what we value most, and allow this to order our lives. We know that this guidance comes with a voice in the heart, but it is affirmed in the best of our faith community, in trusted spiritual writings, in our behavior, and in an inward sense of peace and rightness.

Within the faith community, we have the opportunity to empower others by naming ministry when we see it. Members of the community who have known the transforming call and have recognized the voice of the holy in their own life can offer a great service by supporting others when they encounter what can sometimes be an overwhelming force of love. Such experiences of God's presence may be gentle or may come like lightning. No matter what form it takes, the call is to what some have called "diligence in the Lord's service."

Queries for Reflection and/or Discussion

1. Have you ever experienced the presence of God/Spirit/Oneness? What did that feel like? What made you say that was a holy moment?

2. How has this encounter with the Spirit changed the ways in which you engage with the world? How has it opened your heart?

CHAPTER 11
BECOMING OPEN TO MINISTRY

A man of Tarsus named Saul, *still breathing threats and murder against the disciples of the Lord*, was approaching Damascus when *suddenly a light from heaven flashed around him*. Falling to the ground, Saul heard a voice asking, *"Saul, Saul, why do you persecute me?"* For three days, Saul was without sight and did not eat or drink (Acts 9: 1–9).

In unanticipated moments, a person may be changed without conscious volition. Saul, who became known as Paul after this experience, became a central figure in the spread of the Gospel of Jesus. For Saul and others, there seems to be no warning. God's call comes, and one's life is changed in a moment. Skills once used for harsh or even self-aggrandizing purposes might suddenly find a place in creating a just society.

But often a call to prophetic ministry is subtle or at times a nudge so gentle it is easily missed. Even clear moments of calling are often the start of an ongoing process. Transformation may take hard, ongoing work. Learning what a calling is actually about in terms of action may take a period of testing and of tiny actions to learn what comes next.

For most of us, this means that the more we prepare ourselves to listen to our own hearts, to the world around us, and above all to that still small voice, the more we are able to act faithfully when the time comes to move.

Awareness of the World around Us

Anthony Manousos (Pacific Yearly Meeting) reminds us of our shared commitment to notice those caught up in injustice:

I have been involved one way or another with "prophetic witness" for over 20 years. . . . I feel closest to God when I am doing this work, particularly with others who feel a similar commitment. [I visited] a Muslim who was unjustly imprisoned by ICE [U.S. Immigration and Customs Enforcement] at Terminal Island in Long Beach. As I went to visit him, I walked by a statue of Japanese fishermen who were placed in internment camps during World War II, and I felt as if I were walking in the footsteps of Friends who had been in solidarity with these internees. Later, when this Muslim was released I had the opportunity to pray with him.

It is very easy to walk by a statue of fishermen and not ever notice that this piece of art is recalling the misery of so many Americans of Japanese heritage who were forced to give up their homes, their livelihood, and their lands during World War II. Many of us have stepped around a mentally ill person sleeping on a sidewalk. The hurry of life conceals so many injustices and gives us reason to keep our eyes averted.

Often it is the prodding of others, or a direct encounter with someone who has been treated in a way that makes us wince, that presses us to say, "No, that is not how humans should treat one another!" I often go this far. To go the next step, to act to change what we see, is often too much. Change, even small change, can feel debilitating or threatening. Too few have the courage to step forward.

Recognizing God Walking Alongside

The way to recognizing and naming a ministry is not always simple or obvious, as Carla Coleman (Northwest Yearly Meeting) has found.

Through the years I kept experiencing glimpses of His presence. . . . It took a few personal tragedies and when I turned thirty I began the slow journey of surrendering my life to my Savior. . . [Now,] when I sense God's heart, and if I'm aligned with Him, I know when something goes against God's loving heart. Naturally, that only happens if I am centered in Him.

Carla has long been aware of the condition of people she has encountered. She has also occasionally intervened in conflict, even when—especially when—no one else was willing. What was missing, that she only recognized in retrospect, was the inward transformation that heals wounds of the heart and opens space for forgiveness. As she learned to rely on divine accompaniment and found the Love that encompassed her as well as the world, she found new freedom and the ability to act out of that Love. As this happened, she became able to accept the call to prophetic ministry.

Nurturance and Recognition by the Community

Some people are fortunate enough to be part of an engaged community that pays attention to those present, including the young people, and calls them to pay attention to their spiritual life and listening for the Inward Teacher. Such communities may see the Eternal at work in a person's life well before the individual has any awareness of a calling. Arthur Roberts (Northwest Yearly Meeting) caught the attention of others in his meeting while still a teenager. He was guided into the work that allowed his gift of ministry to flourish then and that continued as he approached the later years of his life. As he put it,

> When I was just a teenager, local elders sensed God's call upon me and nurtured that gift, as did the yearly meeting in recording my gift of ministry. For me, a support group provides helpful fellowship and also capacity for discernment that prevents the self-deception that can so subtly tempt gifted individuals.

One of the regular complaints I hear, at least in unprogrammed meetings, is that we are poor in nurturing each other's spiritual gifts and that we are especially poor in training our young people. My guess is that some of the problem stems from a lack of self-confidence as well as our not appointing people specifically to nurture the spiritual life of our meetings. The Bible is central for Arthur, but many Friends rely on other resources for primary guidance.

When there is a pastor or appointed elders, responsibility for this work often lies with them. In unprogrammed meetings, though, this work is left more to chance. Is there an individual or small group that has strong personal spiritual practices and is seeking to encourage this in others? Are there some who are good at working with young people and helping them find their way? Sharing responsibilities in these meetings has many advantages, and I find those advantages compelling. But there is also the challenge of mutual spiritual care and the naming of ministries that we need to integrate into our communities if we wish to grow the prophetic ministry in our midst.

Love of God and Love of Persons

How do we recognize divine love? Is it manifested in our human relationships? Some Friends have encountered this love of God for us in the love they experience for another human being. Darren Kenworthy (North Pacific Yearly Meeting) tells how his love for his fiancée made divine love more real:

> In her company, I began to glimpse what it would mean to approach a relationship between two people as a covenant with God as the third party. This was a prophetic experience in its own right. My experience of love was transformed. We were engaged less than a year later. For me, marriage and child-rearing comprise a prophetic ministry in that

we continually live into our changed understanding of love.

In contrast, Hal Wright (Intermountain Yearly Meeting) finds that loving God is very different from our human relationships.

> I learned what loving God is in centering prayer. It is not a feeling like loving someone; God is incomprehensible and one can have no direct sense of a separate entity. Loving God is the yearning and intention to be present and open. And in the openness I learned that love is not an emotion; it's an action. This for me is the link between inner spirituality and working for social justice. The result of centering prayer is an integrated, centered life.

Intentionally making space to pay attention to the needs of the soul; learning the taste and feel of love in our own lives; and being willing to open the doors of the heart to the reality of compassion for oneself and for others, be they friends or strangers—such inward actions are among the disciplines that prepare the way for prophetic ministry.

Articulating God's Work in Our Lives

How often do we notice within ourselves a real concern for the poor when we read about the huge number of children who go hungry in this country? How often do we burn with fury at thoughtless killings and attacks on civilians by our government, by individuals, or by small groups of fanatics? Then, how often do we let our feelings of sympathy and pain recede or our fury burn out, only to go about our ordinary business, as Dorsey Green mentioned in the previous chapter?

Dorlan Bales, cofounder of the Friends of Jesus Community in Wichita, Kansas, speaks below to the inherent calling of anyone who truly is a follower of Jesus—something I would extend to all traditions that hold compassion as essential. The challenge then becomes how and when we are willing to voice this concern, stepping forward to take concrete steps to address oppression. Stepping forward is often an individual act. But the presence of a community that recognizes this calling and is willing to test it and support it when it is time to act is invaluable. Dorlan describes the prophetic call as follows:

> 1. A prophetic call means blessing the poor and powerless the way Jesus did and being taught by prophets who came before and after him.
>
> 2. [The] willingness to speak well-considered truth in love to those who oppress can be costly, whether they have worldly power or are part of the family and religious communities upon whom we rely.
>
> 3. A community of prophets to support one another, test leadings, and take action together is essential to an extended prophetic ministry.
>
> 4. A prophet's sense of her or his limitations is important lest temptations to pride or despair be too great. God's calling to do justice and love mercy is an impossible task, humanly speaking. It is comforting to know that prophetic fellowships are small but important links in a long chain of faithful people who are the world's light, salt, and yeast.

Becoming open to prophetic ministry is at once intensely individual and fully communal. It may or may not involve a group of people agreeing to act in concert. The call to ministry is most often, at least initially, a personal calling. Yet the presence of even one individual with such a calling tests the community. Are we open to taking the time and energy and possibly the financial responsibility to support this individual? Is the sense of calling infectious among us? Do we empower others to accept that the niggling in the heart they feel may be a prod to action?

Queries for Reflection and/or Discussion

1. What does it mean to you to be open to ministry? Are you open to this in your own life? How have you seen this openness (or closedness) in those around you?

2. What allows you to listen better for the work of the Spirit within? How do you help others pay attention to the Inward Guide?

3. Do Dorlan Bales's suggested prerequisites for prophetic ministry resonate with you? How have you experienced this in your own life? How might you help empower your community to be open to the prophetic ministry among you?

CHAPTER 12
TRANSFORMATION (AGAIN AND AGAIN)

Writing this chapter, which is on a topic I often teach and have written about extensively, I find myself bumping into an awareness of people's conflicting responses to the prophetic call. Emotions, intellect, and soul rub up against each other uncomfortably until an internal shift occurs. A person reaches a new point of reconciliation between self and God in a way that brings to mind the old Quaker saying, "Live up to the measure of Light thou hast and thou wilt be given more." Another distinctive way Quakers talk about this is in terms of growing into perfection—perfect faithfulness to the Light of Christ, completion, and wholeness. Yet as we grow, this place of perfection shifts and we are transformed yet again as another dark place in the soul is lit up and made clean.

I use the word 'transformation' to mean a shift in orientation from being centered in self to being centered in the ultimate source of love and truth. Many call this conversion and link it to an individual's acceptance of Jesus. Others tie it to the conviction that they are to work for justice. Still others experience a moment in which they see they are linked to all life. My definition expands to include all these and ties us to those early Friends who lived in faithfulness to the Light.

Transformation is not just an instantaneous, one-time event, although some of us experience sharp moments of turning that are unmistakable. Early Friends mentioned in their journals decisions as simple as not to play cards or dance as critical turning points.

'Conviction' was also an important word for early Friends. In the Light of Christ a person was convicted of sin (which may only have been their love of dancing), but most importantly, the Light would show them the way to live in the Truth. These early Friends were quite harsh towards others who did not believe humans could live free of sin, and they often accused Puritans of "preaching up sin." This transformation was a process of taking up the cross of Christ, of knowing Christ more fully within and following the guidance of that Inward Teacher.

Today, in the more liberal tradition of Friends, inward transformation is not an explicit priority, yet it is not unusual for me to learn of individuals who have had strong transforming mystical experiences but have rarely spoken of them until they hear my story. More often, in the liberal branches of Friends, we focus on how we live. Are we pacifists? Do we care for the environment? How do we eat? We are much shyer about sharing that dimension of the Spirit at work within. In the evangelical traditions of Friends, conversion is an important marker. In whichever way it comes, as a single moment of transition or a gradual shift, it is an expected part of the religious life and is testified to by many as the beginning of their spiritual journey.

Minute by Minute or Like Lightning

The immediate awareness of the presence of God comes in many ways, sometimes when we are alone and sometimes in community. For a few it comes sharply, like a lightning bolt. One's whole life is suddenly turned on end.

Yet, based on my years of teaching and talking with people about their spiritual lives and their ministries, I am pretty well convinced that most transformation comes slowly and looks more like a series of nudges or taps on the shoulder than a drastic change. This is true for many who become aware of their calling to prophetic ministry. For example, Paul Buckley (Ohio Valley Yearly Meeting) writes:

> What does prophetic ministry look like in my own life? . . . As often as I remember, when faced with a choice, I take a breath and

inwardly pray, "Okay, now what?" It's not a lot, but it runs contrary to the messages to exalt personal preference and individual freedom with which we are constantly bombarded. This is not reserved for "big, important stuff"; it is a minute-by-minute exercise in intention and humility that opens the possibility for each moment to be an opportunity for prophetic witness. This doesn't mean I will hit a home run—often enough it's a foul ball. Still more frequently I strike out, but then the next opportunity is there and I can start again.

Paul's counterpoint to the American dream of heroism reflects his view of prophetic ministry as something we all have the capacity for in some measure. This sense that each of us is able to bring divine love and wisdom into our everyday lives is a peculiarity of Quaker spirituality. It informs how we worship and how we make decisions together and run our institutions. Concurrent with this vision of the everyday prophets is the responsibility of the whole community to seek to embody this.

Varied Ways of Conversion

Jaime Tabingo (Philippine Evangelical Friends Church) writes of conversion in terms of accepting Jesus Christ. Here, he speaks of the changes that are essential for the person who is called to the prophetic ministry. For early Friends, the Word was Christ, as described in the opening chapter of John, in contrast to the usual Protestant usage in which the Word is the Bible. Jaime knows the prophetic ministry as a ministry of bringing people to Christ and thus to salvation, and he includes seminary training as a prerequisite to prophetic ministry, something our spiritual ancestors avidly rejected. Yet we agree that in experiencing this calling, lives are changed in ways evident in their work, and Friends are fortified by the training they receive.

> If this prophetic ministry refers to the preaching and teaching of the Word, the prerequisites are that the person (a) must have experienced the new birth; (b) give evidence of a changed life; (c) be actively involved in the Christian ministry; (d) have received formal training in Bible school or seminary; (e) experience joy in serving the Lord; and (f) must be convinced that the Lord has given him or her the gift of prophetic ministry.

Jaime's words are echoed by many North American Friends. For example, Norval Hadley (Evangelical Friends Church Southwest) writes, "I'm sure the prerequisite for prophetic ministry is first of all to be fully yielded to Christ and filled with the Holy Spirit, who guides us into all truth, and then to seek the Lord and wait on Him for the leading of the Spirit for that ministry." That sense of waiting for guidance and even the expectation of transformation—of conversion of the heart—is common across the Quaker spectrum despite contrasting and seemingly conflicting theologies.

Jean Zaru (Ramallah Friends Meeting) writes of the ongoing change in the human heart when the Spirit of Christ works amid the suffering and pain of venues and communities that have been torn apart by aggression and hatred. Immersion in the reality of such places calls up seemingly impossible questions whose answers are beyond conventional human solutions:

> We are called to conversion, to be converted to the struggle of women and men everywhere who have no way to escape the unending fatigue of their labor and the daily denial of their human rights and human worth. We must let our hearts be moved by the anguish and suffering of our sisters and brothers throughout the world. How can we bear the pain, and where do we look for hope? Is there anything we can do to solve the political chaos

and crisis in the world? Is there anything we can do to stop wars of all kinds?[1]

Zaru and other Friends around the world see the turning point as occurring when one accepts one's responsibility to lift up the poor and suffering, to end violence, and to live simply.

What these lives tell me is that conversion in some manner is central to all Friends, even though it is a point of serious contention. Turning, awakening, being transformed, and recognizing that we cannot do it all on our own without a higher power are all part of who we are. Among the early Quaker writings I cherish are Isaac Penington's words:

> Know what it is that is to walk in the path of life, and indeed is alone capable of walking therein. It is that which groans, and which mourns; that which is begotten of God in thee. The path of life is for the seed of life. The true knowledge of the way, with the walking in the way, is reserved for God's child—for God's traveller.[2]

Some Friends hear in these words a knowing that the one true Guide is Christ Jesus. Others recognize that there is a force of love and truth in the world that can guide every individual, no matter what their beliefs or religious tradition. Penington would say both these things are true. Without question, Christ was his Guide, yet he measured following the Guide by the evidence of a person's actions and words.

Various traditions of Friends hold out their own ways of assessing faithfulness, and at times we are rigid to the point of condemning all those who don't hold the same understanding. I accept a range of beliefs about the name of God even as I know Jesus Christ has a particular place in shaping Quakerism, but I find lives that reflect justice, kindness, peace, generosity, and humility more telling than the particular words we use.

The Refiner's Fire

Friends have given us many stories over the centuries about the power of transformation. It is another one of the paradoxes of faith that we encounter this searing pain of transformation at the same moment that we may know great joy for that which is being born within. Grief, loss, and joy were all bound up in the encounter with the Infinite that completely turned my life in a new direction and opened up my soul. It has been very comforting and reassuring to hear of others who have had similar experiences.

Dorothy Selebwa (Nairobi Yearly Meeting) was struck in the heart in the middle of the night with words prompting her to change her life:

> One early morning at 3 o'clock, I heard a voice calling, "Dorothy, do you see those widows and orphans?" I kept quiet. It came a second time. I kept quiet. Then a third time. This time I shouted, "*Yes!*" As soon as I said yes, my eyes opened and what did I see? Women and children in tattered clothes.

As Dorothy went into a ministry with widows and orphans, the voice said, "Take care of them." A few years later she expanded her work, which now cares for over fifty children. Dorothy's ministry has, empowered school dropouts and widows and otherwise supported families.

Emma Condori Mamani (Holiness Friends Yearly Meeting) is a young Bolivian Friend who has known the Holy Spirit working through pastors when they offer a message on Sunday morning.

> Often a Quaker pastor does not speak her/his own thoughts and perceptions about the faith community's condition before the sight of God. God, through the Holy Spirit, gives the messages to them. Many times when I was attending a worship service . . . I felt the message came to my heart like lightning with

lots of thunder. Experiencing those messages in that way made me feel that I was in the presence of God during that worship meeting. The message spoke to my soul.

Emma had a calling to empower the young people in Bolivia. Here she speaks of the start of her work to help Bolivian youth establish their own structures nationwide to connect with each other and to find the spiritual nurture they needed.

I remember a time when I offered a prophetic ministry in Bolivia. . . . God let me see the suffering of the people of God in that yearly meeting.

The lack of patience and understanding for each other was causing harm to this large faith community. At that time, adult Friends were facing many trials in their spiritual lives and in society . . . and hardly could think about providing any spiritual nourishment for younger Friends. They acted as if the youths were a separate group that was a burden for them. At this yearly meeting, it seemed to me that there were two groups of people of God, each . . . viewing life differently. The younger generation was seeking to experience the love of God and to do the will of God

. . . Younger Friends wanted to gain more knowledge about their Quaker heritage, Quaker teachings, and Christian life at an academic level. All this knowledge would help them be grounded in their faith in the world but not of the world.

In 1647, George Fox reports in his journal that a transforming fire appeared in his soul, cleansing him so that he might follow God.

Then after this there did a pure fire appear in me; . . . and then the spiritual discerning came into me, by which I did discern my own thoughts, groans and sighs, and what it was that did veil me, and what it was that did open me.

And that which could not abide in the patience nor endure the fire, in the Light I found to be the groans of the flesh (that could not give up to the will of God), which had veiled me, and that could not be patient in all trials, troubles and anguishes and perplexities, and could not give up self to die by the Cross, the power of God.[3]

Fox was reporting on one of those intense moments of clarity, a turning point, but this was only one point in what may have been a long period of searching beforehand and of deep interior work afterwards in order that the promise might be fulfilled.[4]

Today we might speak of the recognition within ourselves that each of us has the capacity to do great harm to other human beings and to the earth. In this recognition comes the humility to address the wrongs done by others without being blinded by our own arrogance and sense of superiority. In this humility we might truly be part of that ocean of love that sweeps over the ocean of darkness.

Taking Up the Cross: The Pain

Yrma Hilarión Escobar (National Evangelical Friends Church of Bolivia) serves as a Sunday school teacher and worship leader in Santa Cruz. She was torn apart by the pain of her mother's dying.

I found myself unprepared to live through this experience [of my mother's leukemia]. I felt a deep emptiness in my heart. . . . I almost couldn't bear the death of my brother, who'd recently passed away, and now this other hard truth—the sickness that was maybe going to kill my mother.

But the hard times were my opportunity to draw closer to the Lord, to let his word come alive in me. I suffered to be able to understand that God, our Lord, was beside me, and that he was allowing to happen all that we were living through. Little by little, my faith gained some hope.[5]

I recognize in Yrma's words the transforming power of deep grief and pain because my own life changed dramatically in such a time. It was only as I mourned that I first experienced the all-embracing love of God. The loneliness that had always been so strong in me was magnified by my father's dying. Yrma describes her mother's ability to focus on gratitude and notes how aggravating she found it that her mother was at peace with her impending death. Yrma adds:

> For me, this was another blow. I was still praying for healing. But I understood that what interested our Lord was that my mother would give herself over to his will, that she be able to accept whatever he might decide to do with her life.[6]

These times of great sorrow and agony can open up the heart and make more vivid for some the reality of Jesus' grief in the garden of Gethsemane. To take up the cross, as early Friends advocated, is no easy task. The cross is a heavy thing, and to carry it requires one to give up ordinary expectations and lift someone else's burden.

To take up the cross does not often mean we risk physical death. It may not result in any form of outward suffering. What it does ask of each of us is the willingness to let go of what seems most dear to our being. The loss of someone we dearly love may bring this to the fore. Yet the loss may be a goal related to personal success, or it may be releasing a focus on wealth or something else that is valued in our culture. At another level, it may mean giving up an inward image of oneself that is blocking one's relationship with all that is holy. This may be pride, or it may be a sense of worthlessness. It can be just as hard to accept that one is loved as it is to come to terms with the reality that one's needs and desires are not the most important thing in one's life.

Taking Up the Cross: The Power

Against all rationality, the letting go of something dear, of releasing the need to control one's life, and of admitting personal powerlessness can be the point of transition into strength. In 1660, Margaret Fell spoke of the cross of Christ as the power of God. She knew that by standing in this place of the cross, agreeing as Jesus did in the Garden of Gethsemane that *thy will be done*, one can embody the city of God and make it a reality.

I have recognized this in others. One example is Rachel Cunliffe (North Pacific Yearly Meeting), who has devoted her life to witnessing to the horrors of the death penalty. She has compassion for all people involved in this process: the victim's family, the prosecutors, the murderer, the executioner. She describes her ministry as follows:

> My work has been in the context of a compassionate listening project with people entangled in the death penalty. . . . Currently, I consult with defense attorneys on capital cases to try to develop opportunities for restorative justice capacity building. This frequently brings me in contact with the survivors of people who have been murdered with opportunities to help them achieve a measure of restorative justice alongside criminal justice processes.
>
> During one evolution of the listening project, I was very involved in advocacy and activism around the death penalty specifically. That was when Multnomah Friends Meeting took my ministry under its care. Since then, my focus has been more on building peace and reconciliation among those who have been affected by a murder. This is not to say that I

believe that they must reconcile with each other, but, much in the vein of Murder Victims Families for Reconciliation, I believe that we must all face our histories and come to some kind of reconciliation with them if we are to reclaim our lives from the past and live in the present.

There are infinite variations of listening and turning inherent in the concept of taking up the cross. The lives of many people like Rachel witness to another way of being, one in which we pay attention to the needs of others and to the Light that points to justice and reveals our part in it.

The idea of taking up the cross is sometimes used to claim that we need to suffer as Christ did in order to become more like him. The early Quakers did not use suffering as their measure. Instead, they used obedience. To take up the cross is to listen to the divine call, not to our personal, immediate desires. When it means we have to give up whatever is most appealing to us at the moment or have to let go of our personal comforts, there may be times of suffering. But that is not the point. As so many have attested, this place of faithfulness not only leads to greater freedom, compassion, and equity but also to surprising joy and a sense of rightness deep within.

Living into the Message

Change is rarely a one-time event, even if we've experienced a blinding moment of newness. Thus, our spiritual ancestors wrote of "many baptisms"—the ongoing shifting and growing we experience as new pockets of darkness become obvious within and we take steps to make them visible and transform them into something that helps us or others grow.

Jan Hoffman (New England Yearly Meeting) experienced transformation through the process of acting on a calling. She felt God call her to accept an invitation to offer three talks to New York Yearly Meeting and just as clearly call her to tell the yearly meeting to repent. She resisted speaking this message in the first two talks but discovered that the pain of her own unfaithfulness required her to experience in herself the inner work she was asking Friends in New York Yearly Meeting to do. Note that New England and New York Yearly Meetings are on the more liberal end of the Quaker spectrum and that Friends in these yearly meetings express their spiritual experience in a wide range of ways. Jan writes:

> I began the third talk by confessing my own unfaithfulness in the second and my need to repent of this unfaithfulness—which I then did. I described some of my own inner work both alone and with elders who had enabled this change, with God's grace and guidance. Then I spoke the message God had given me for New York Yearly Meeting: "Repent." In this grace, a message I had spoken the second day in anger—"I'm tired of hearing about your differences and your diversity"—was transformed in the third talk through my repentance and reconnection to God's love into "It's time to stop talking and start praying." Thus God led me through my own need to repent before I could speak that message to the yearly meeting.

Jan's description of living the message she was to give to the yearly meeting calls up the sense of integrity that is central to this internal change. The message could only be released as something inside her shifted and was brought in line with the words she felt called to give. No true message that is given, be it in worship or on the streets or in daily interactions, holds any weight unless it reflects the work of the Spirit on the condition of the speaker. As Jan showed, the process of offering words or other ministry can, if divinely oriented, be the instrument of transformation.

Everyday prophets learn to recognize when the Inward Light is directing their life, opening possibilities or perhaps calling them to radical witness. The calling may come slowly or dramatically, but the ongoing prophetic work is often dependent on regular attention to one's inward state and learning to recognize and follow the Inward Guide.

Queries for Reflection and/or Discussion

1. What is your experience of being transformed? How did you recognize the Spirit at work within you? Have you known "the struggle of women and men everywhere" that Jean Zaru knew or the "new birth" that Jaime Tabingo described? How is this knowing visible in your life?

2. Was your transformation accompanied by a sense of newness or healing in some way? Did you experience the Refiner's fire that sears out that which is counter to love or did you feel gentle nudges on your heart? How did these inward forces move you closer to wholeness?

3. What helps you remember to listen inwardly? How do you distinguish your own emotional needs and desires and the pressure that comes from others from the voice of all that is holy?

CHAPTER 13
WORDS GIVEN

In the United States, we are trained to think that public speaking is for show, for entertainment, or for winning (often an election). Group discourse becomes a free-for-all in which people speak loudly but listen very little to one another. We expect individuals who are worth hearing to have a particular charismatic gift, training in public speaking, expertise, and/or the support of media consultants. Even in churches, we expect the pastor to have a seminary degree, and charismatic preachers who draw hundreds and thousands of people to megachurches get much media attention.

The Quaker perspective is almost a hidden option. Any person can be called to speak in open worship. In unprogrammed meetings and in many Friends churches that have periods of open worship, every person is encouraged to listen for God's message. We seek as well to listen in the midst of our jobs, while caring for children, and in the ordinary rhythm of things. We listen for the Spirit as it stirs the heart and as it guides the people around us. We hold up the ideal of testing and discerning which messages we hear are truly of God, which of these messages are for the individual alone, and which are to be shared further and acted on in the world.

The Bible is full of stories of prophets, beginning with Moses, whose first reaction to God's presence and the call to ministry was to say no. Many biblical figures forgot to listen at all. Others listened but then didn't act, often with disastrous consequences. In Isaiah's case, he was willing to serve but felt himself inadequate to the task. Then a seraph touched his lips with a burning coal to purify them before he was sent out to speak for God—not exactly a reassuring or pleasant experience. Jeremiah protested that he was only a boy and not adequate to preach. For this, he was rebuked by God and told he would be given words to speak.

Hearing and Sorting

Quaker history is full of stories of traveling ministers who visited community after community with the commitment to speak only when prompted by the Holy Spirit. Many of these traveling ministers recorded a time when people filled the building expecting to hear the traveler and the minister sat mute; no words arose out of the deep center.

At times, early ministers recorded in their journals that they were given a clear sense that those present were not open to the message—that they had come for entertainment or to have their own wishes affirmed. This was not the purpose of the minister's work. The call to remain silent was often painful for the minister and undoubtedly left those who came to hear him or her quite disappointed. This practice occasionally occurs today in Friends churches in which the pastor normally speaks weekly. I know several pastors who have found on a Sunday morning in the midst of the worship service that the message they had prepared was not to be given. Most often, they tell the congregation this and ask everyone to settle into an extended period of expectant silent worship.

This process of listening and sorting and then speaking and acting is inherent in all Quaker worship and discernment. Early Friends were more in sympathy with the oral tradition and dependence on the direct encounter with the Light of Christ as the Word, the Inward Guide, than they were with the Protestant focus on the Bible as the Word. Friends quickly became dependent on passing down their faith through the personal journals of ministers—their stories of obedience, struggle, and faithfulness—rather than primarily through creeds and systematic theological texts.

I find it much easier and safer to offer an academic treatise than to speak in open worship. Preparing a talk in advance (even if it is not an academic work) is reassuring. I can hone the words and determine how best to convey an idea or pick the best story to tell the tale. I know that such messages that are prepared in advance can be every bit as inspired by the Spirit as a spontaneous message that arises out of the silence. Paying attention to what is holy and how to convey it is not confined to any time, place, or people. Each congregation and each individual has its own expectations, its own temptations to slide into self-will, arrogance, and the desire to please.

Thus, the trap I can easily fall into is the desire to show how well-educated I am and how well I know a particular subject, be it the ways of early Quakers or the fine points of Quaker practice. I find it very difficult to speak without the mental and emotional crutches provided by quoting others (living or long gone) and being able to reference respected tomes. I am part of the unprogrammed tradition, so I do not use these crutches much when speaking during worship, but I do get pulled into overreliance on them when I lead workshops or give public talks.

My strong reticence leads to different temptations in open worship. There, I am overly picky, perhaps even harsh, in judging what is of the Spirit and what is not when I sense that I am supposed to speak. I test and test again to see if the words really are Spirit-led. I wait until I feel a strong vibration within. I wait to see if anyone else happens to be offering the message so I don't have to. My process of discernment is at one extreme, and I often do not speak words that I should.

Tests for Discernment

I teach often about spiritual discernment. I believe it is an essential skill. In most Friends churches, discernment is tied up tightly with knowledge of the Bible, and the perspectives of the pastors, elders, and clerks carry much heavier weight than in many unprogrammed meetings. At one end of the spectrum, some evangelical Friends have asserted that only the pastor, and perhaps the clerk, can truly discern God's will for the congregation. Yet another extreme in some unprogrammed meetings leaves discernment solely in individual hands and resists any idea of testing in the wider community or using any external guidance. Many of us who are not at one of these two extremes often draw on the words and example of seventeenth-century Quakers, who point to a more moderate way.

Hugh Barbour, an important twentieth-century Quaker scholar, identified five "tests" used by seventeenth-century Friends to discern the source of a leading: patience, moral purity, consistency with others, consistency with the Bible, and inward unity. Despite all the reading of early Friends' writings that I have done, I can still look at this list rather blankly and wonder what it means in practice. However, I have understood in part some of the tests. Certainly, discernment is not based on a list with yes or no answers.

Patience is the most accessible of these tests, both as one of the "fruits of the spirit" listed in Galatians 5:22–23 and in the meaning it was often given by George Fox and others: if you are not willing for others to test your leading, it is unlikely to be from God. This testing might be done with respected individuals in the community, living or dead. Testing a leading for consistency with the group and with the Bible was essential to discernment for early Friends. They were certain that the Bible must be read in the Spirit and found the new covenant most vivid in Jesus' words, especially the Sermon on the Mount.

Early Friends often spoke of moral purity as the willingness to take up the cross and follow in Jesus' steps. One way to translate this into modern concepts is to think of taking up the cross as letting go of self-will and not being egotistical. To early Friends, taking up the cross meant being willing to give up everything in obedience to the divine calling, taking seriously the Sermon on the Mount. For this reason, a person's life was to be of a whole. Unless a person's life and words matched, belief alone was meaningless.

Inward unity is sometimes spoken of today in terms of peace on a very deep, personal level. A calling might lead into a situation in which it is right to be afraid, yet at the center of one's being is a solid peace. Evidence from the past and from today makes it clear that grounding in God's peace makes it possible to act in ways that seem beyond one's capacity with a joy and a certainty in the work that can't be shaken and with behavior in accord with the fruit of the Spirit.

Above all, the process of discernment takes self-knowledge and honing of the inward senses. I love the words of Isaac Penington, who tells us to turn inward as we seek all that gives life and the Life that sustains our beings:

> Life gives [the soul] a feeling, a light, a tasting, an hearing, a smelling, of the heavenly things, by which sense it is able to discern and distinguish them from the earthly. And from this Measure of Life the capacity increases, the senses grow stronger; it sees more, feels more, tastes more, hears more, smells more. Now when the senses are grown up to strength, . . . doubtings and disputes in the mind fly away and the soul lives in the certain demonstration and fresh sense and power of life.[1]

Penington does not hesitate to remind us that patience and letting go of control are essential to enter into this Life:

> In that which is begotten of God there is not a hastiness or suddenness to determine; but a silent waiting on the Lord in subjection, till the life speak, and make things manifest.[2]

137

None of us is immune from the possibility of losing all sense of direction or feeling that God is absent, which often happens when we most deeply desire divine assurance. Penington offers only one way to respond.

> When the life is at any time lost, the only way of recovery is by retiring to the invisible, and keeping there, and growing up there; and not coming forth in the visible further than the life leads, nor staying there any longer than the life stays.[3]

Much has been written about spiritual discernment, and I will not repeat it here. I also do not want to convey the idea that discernment is always a lengthy process, leaving no option for quick action. As one gains experience and self-awareness, at times only a brief stop and internal check is needed to note a yes or a caution. When that caution sign arises, taking the time to reflect and explore further can be invaluable.

Speaking So Others Might Hear

On the person-to-person level, this can be stated as a question: "What obligation does the prophetic minister have to speak in a way that others can hear the message?" When I lead discussions on the nature of unprogrammed meeting for worship, I do so aware that worship is a time for learning to hear and follow the Voice of the Light; sometimes we do it well, and sometimes we totally miss the mark. It is not unusual to encounter those who object to the language or content of messages spoken during worship or for individuals to declare that a message was inappropriate and not Spirit-led. One response I give is to encourage people to let words that do not speak to them simply go by, accepting that the message might be true and right for someone else. I have experienced numerous times when that is true. Another response is to remind people that many of us use different words to express similar concepts. A negative reaction in the listener might be an encouragement to honor the many ways we speak of God or it might be a sign that healing is needed in the listener's heart. At times, a person will stand and speak in a way that everyone present can see is not appropriate. In extreme instances, someone will stand and, gently but firmly, stop the speaker. More often, it is right for two members of the Worship and Ministry Committee to sit with the individual, at a later date, and nurture their ability to discern when they are being prompted by the Spirit. All this is part of the work of the prophetic community in growing everyday prophets.

Accompaniment

Elders, companions, peer groups, support committees, spiritual friends, spiritual accountability groups—these are among the ways we name the people who aid the minister in discernment and ask them the hard questions. Because of the open nature of Friends worship and the expectation that individuals may be called into prophetic work, a healthy Quaker community uses many tools for the encouragement of those among them.

Support and accountability come in multiple forms. Jan Hoffman (New England Yearly Meeting) reports on the spontaneous appearance of an elder who balanced out the carefully selected individuals gathered to help her speak to New York Yearly Meeting.

> In addition to these elders chosen by me, God sent an additional elder. I received a letter from Carol, a woman from New York Yearly Meeting I knew only slightly, who said she was led to come to New York Yearly Meeting that year specifically to elder for me.
>
> A week before New York Yearly Meeting sessions began, Carol sent me a letter ("It came on me in worship today to write you a letter").
>
> . . . She addressed matters from spiritual realities to the rhythm of the day at Silver Bay [where the sessions would be held] and to the tradition and expectation of New York Friends

to "bring a beach towel if you want to swim."
This grounded me in the realities surrounding
the release of my message and made me feel
more at ease with an unfamiliar place.

Just as in the case of travel in the ministry, the process
of accompanying an individual with a prophetic call
can be full of surprises. Sometimes the individual with
the ministry is asked by a group to offer a talk or
workshop; other times, the individual feels called to
travel to a particular venue. Similarly, the minister
may carefully name others he or she wants to have as
support, the meeting may name these individuals, or,
as in Jan's case, an elder may unexpectedly appear.

Do Not Be Passive

While it is easy to portray the Quakers as sitting
quietly in the silence to the degree that it becomes a
parody about doing nothing, one theme echoes across
all the various traditions among Friends: living one's
faith is essential.

In some Friends churches, evangelism is central. Their
mission is to bring people to Christ, and their focus is
on the salvation of souls. Coming to Christ is also
about bringing peace and healing to their
communities, especially in countries that have been
torn apart by waves of violence.

Moses Bigirimana (Kibimba Yearly Meeting) spoke to
me passionately about the call to action he felt was
central. He described Quakerism as a practical faith,
not one that allows people to hide from the problems
of the world and comfort one another.

Quakers have to be practical, rather than
theoretical. If nothing is done, for sure this
world will continue to suffer further damages.
Friends all over should be able to speak up so
that people may be aware of the problems
surrounding us and be active in trying to bring
some solutions to these problems. This is what

I understand by being a prophet. Wherever Quakers are, we should be noticed and speak out, we should do something. Not to be passive. It is not like that.

The tension between solace and action seems to be inherent in any group that nourishes the prophetic dimension of faith. Religion is for many a place of comfort. One hopes to find solace in the church, a place to be apart from the chaos and violence of the world and to be nourished. That is all essential. Yet the call to radical witness often stirs up the immediate community when it has become self-satisfied as well as names the injustice in the world. Then follows the choice to remain closeted and secure or to live into the power that obedience to the Light asks of us.

Queries for Reflection and/or Discussion

1. What is your experience with discernment? How do you know when you are truly led to speak or to act? What tells you that a decision is right or wrong for you?

3. Have you ever asked for support and accountability from other individuals or through a clearness process? How did that happen? What was that experience like?

4, Have you ever been an elder or been asked to provide support and/or to hold someone accountable? What was that like?

CHAPTER 14
NAMING THE MINISTRY

Naming has always conveyed a certain power among humankind. Sometimes that power is seen as magical. It confers the ability to affect other people's lives, for good or for ill. Naming lets us recognize an item, an individual, or a skill, and it gives us the ability to talk about it, evaluate it, and shape it. Who thinks about the thousands of endangered or extinct species that have never been named?

The Nature of the Naming

When we name our children, we place upon them our hopes for their future. We might choose names that evoke places we love, such as "Forest," or name a child after a favorite relative or a public figure. Such naming carries with it the expectation that the child will in some way live into the beauty, heroism, or conviction of the name.

The process among Friends of naming someone as a minister has long been considered a recognition of the individual's ordination by God; we as humans can only name what God has done. The church does not have the power to invest individuals with ministerial functions or to confer holy orders upon someone. Early Quakers were also unusual in not requiring seminary training for preachers or pastors This is entwined with the belief that ordination and outward signs such as physical water or bread and wine are not essential for the congregation to experience the sacraments of baptism, marriage, and communion.

Friends, especially in unprogrammed meetings where anyone may speak out of the silence, are quite ambivalent about any action that separates out or holds up one individual. Their reaction makes visible some of the ways in which naming can be fraught with emotional baggage. The Quaker community where I worship is willing to formally recognize a ministry, but it is not willing to identify anyone as a minister. Another way to put this is that we support individuals in the work that they are doing—be it attempts to end the death penalty, offer end-of-life care, work for equality for gays and lesbians, or writing and teaching—and affirm that this is work led by the Spirit. We support such work in a variety of ways and expect that this recognition needs to be renewed regularly.

In contrast, Friends churches recognize individuals as having a gift of vocal ministry and value them for speaking during worship, whether in the form of prepared or spontaneous messages. This naming is often given for a lifetime and is not connected to any particular work that the individual may feel led to do. My use of the term "prophetic ministry" applies to both these practices.

What does it mean when someone is named as having a prophetic ministry? How do we know when someone has a prophetic ministry? What makes this visible? Diane Randall (New England Yearly Meeting) lays out three succinct criteria that all need to be present:

- listening deeply and constantly to God;
- waiting for divine guidance and acting with courage and confidence; and
- practicing humility, obedience, and patience.

Diane notes another important dimension: "Being called a 'prophet' (which is quite unusual among Friends today) or being named as having a ministry carries a huge weight." She finds that "public naming connotes a recognition by the community that carries expectations, and our expectations within the Religious Society of Friends can be heavy." I have also found this to be true; many Friends carry an image of a Quakerism that is heroic in its stance for justice, a vision that is fueled by stories of past successes but often forgets the struggles and failures that came first.

Formal Naming of Ministry

David Thomas (Northwest Yearly Meeting) speaks to the importance of being recorded as a minister and also his wish that Friends would formally recognize the prophetic ministry.

> Northwest Yearly Meeting recorded me as a pastor. I do show gifts of leadership, a sensitivity to the Spirit, and a love for sharing God's word, but I am much more of a prophet than a pastor. In my American Evangelical Friends circles, it seems we do not talk very much about the prophetic ministry, and we do not have a category to label leaders who express prophetic giftings.

The recorded ministers I know greatly value not only the formal naming but also the ongoing support and accountability when it is there. Some yearly meetings provide a place for recorded ministers to speak freely with their peers about their experiences and faithfulness to God, be it in their home meeting or church or when they feel called to travel.

The expectation that words spoken during worship will be given by the Spirit rather than through formal biblical exegesis or other ways focused on human learning and skill is not uniform today. Recognition of ministers was initially grounded in the expectation that individuals can hear the divine Word directly—a dimension of the prophetic ministry. The early Quaker expectation that Christ has come already to the world as well as will be coming more fully at some point in the future changed the nature of worship from an interim practice of waiting for Christ, which is prevalent in most Christian churches, to a time of expectant listening for current guidance and a hope of transformation that will bring the new creation to life.

Reluctance to Call It Prophetic Ministry

David Thomas mentioned above the reluctance to name 'prophetic ministry' among evangelical Friends. As a liberal Friend, I do not use this term much outside of the context of writing this book. I certainly never use it about myself. It is not part of my self-image. Others would have to say whether it is part of my calling.

Ashley Wilcox (Freedom Friends Church), who has been part of what Friends call a 'semi-programmed meeting,' describes her reaction to being told publicly by a teacher that she was called to a prophetic ministry. She immediately rejected his characterization of her gift as prophetic.

> When I was doing the School the Spirit program On Being a Spiritual Nurturer, we had visiting teachers at each residency. The core teachers told us that [a particular visiting teacher] had a gift for naming gifts in others. Sure enough, that was one of the things we focused on during the time he was with us.
>
> After some icebreakers, [the visiting teacher] asked people to name their gifts at random. I held back, as I often do in group settings. People shared their gifts: hospitality, prayer, teaching. Finally, I said, "telling the truth." [The teacher] spun around and looked directly at me, "You mean, prophecy?" I said, "I didn't say that!" But he would not let it go. He asked why I was reluctant to claim the gift of prophecy, and my friend Jane chimed in, "You know they kill prophets, right?"

Discomfort with Callings

In the responses to the questions I asked various Friends when writing this book, I noticed that many resist accepting a calling and wait until the meeting comes to accept it before letting go of their discomfort.

Marcelle Martin (Philadelphia Yearly Meeting) wrote of her early experiences offering vocal ministry that discomfited some in her liberal, unprogrammed meeting:

> Later, I started attending the nearest Quaker meeting. Eventually, after some resistance, I began to offer vocal ministry. Sometimes I spoke of mystical experiences, and one day someone let me know that a couple members of the meeting were uncomfortable with these messages. This made me question whether or not I belonged among Quakers. I had felt very drawn to them after a weekend workshop at Pendle Hill and after reading about George Fox.
>
> Now I wondered if Quakerism was still a community that supported those with mystical experience and a prophetic call. I stopped attending meeting for worship. And then I had a dream—or perhaps it was a vision.
>
> The vision showed me participating in a traveling ministry. I had not yet heard about the traditional Quaker traveling ministry, in which people usually traveled in pairs. . . . I felt called to go back to meeting . . . and was moved to stand in vocal ministry and tell the vision I'd had. There was a powerful response. One of the elders in the meeting quoted Scripture, "Your sons and daughters will prophesy, your old men will dream dreams, your young men will see visions."

It is not only the liberal meetings that are uncomfortable with prophetic ministry. Some evangelical Friends churches object to women preaching. The example below is from Kenya, but in the United States, too, some churches are reluctant to have women in any leadership positions other than working with children. Margaret Namikoye Musalia of Nairobi Yearly Meeting, which is in the programmed tradition, writes:

At times I felt a prophetic ministry when I preached or prayed for something and people opposed it. Then after a year or so people started talking about how Pastor Margaret said this. Sometimes I didn't remember but they reminded me—e.g., counseling a couple without knowing what was hurting them. I just spoke a word of wisdom.

At times I felt I had delivered something heavy on my heart. Afterwards, my heart was lighter, had released the burden. But I didn't sit down and plan to say certain words. God brings the message for me to speak at the right time, right place, and to the right people—a burden that I did not understand.

In response to my query, "What was that like for you?" she responded:

It was like lightning or a push like a woman in labour pains—when a child is ready to come out. The mother must have the strength and breath to push out powerfully. The experience was overwhelming and sometimes not clear until it [was] repeated.

Margaret named it a prophetic ministry "because nobody could see what I was seeing or feeling" and noted the consequences, which could have included silencing or rejection by her church.

In the past half century or so, Friends in the United States as well as in Africa and South America have struggled with ongoing questions related to recognizing true ministry. In Marcelle Martin's case, the resistance was around prophetic ministry and mysticism rather than around gender, which has been a central issue in Friends churches. In liberal meetings, some people are sensitive to the harm done by institutional Christianity over the centuries or dismiss the reality of mystical experiences.

Naming is not always a simple action. The refusal to name a ministry can be devastating for the individual who feels called to a particular work. Strength, clarity, and the patience to remain true to a calling and invite others to welcome it are sometimes necessary.

Queries for Reflection and/or Discussion

1. Why did you (or might you) name your own calling a form of everyday ministry?

2. What might the consequences of this naming be for you or for those around you?

CHAPTER 15
IT'S WHAT WE DO

Our heritage is grounded in the expectation that each individual will hear, speak, and act out of the leadings of the Spirit, certainly in worship and then in carrying worship with them into daily life. Ben Richmond (Indiana Yearly Meeting) states this succinctly:

> I have sometimes been accused of committing prophetic ministry. That has always been problematic to me. On the one hand, I appreciate what is clearly meant as an affirmation, though it usually sounds a bit uncomfortable and "apart setting." In my view, if people speak in ministry and it is not prophecy—in the sense of speaking words that God wants these people at this time to hear—why, they "should be silent." (Isn't that how George Fox interpreted the 1 Corinthians 14:30, 34 prohibition?) And therefore, the fact that a certain person's ministry is "prophetic" should not be something unusual or worthy of comment. It is simply what we do.

Paul Buckley (Ohio Valley Yearly Meeting) offers a contrasting insight to the conversation about how we live as Friends, which he incorporates into his own story:

> When I was young, I read the lives of the saints. Invariably, the story was of a man or woman who wasted [their] youth in the pursuit of something worldly—money most often, as I remember it—but eventually faced an overwhelming crisis that turned them to God. Not a few of these stories ended with martyrdom and glory in heaven.
>
> These books were written for a teenage audience, and their purpose was to inspire young people to lives of devotion and good works. At least for me, they failed. Although I could identify with the wasted youth part, the

crises were beyond anything I had experienced, and, to be honest, the transformations were unappealing. More than that, each newly minted saint was extraordinary, and I knew myself to be ordinary. It was like reading superhero comic books—undoubtedly entertaining but not providing realistic career options.

After putting this in the context of John Woolman throwing stones at a bird and Elias Hicks's love of dancing, Paul goes on to say:

Most Friends today would be wary of naming any experience as prophetic ministry. We don't think of our lives as the lives of saints. We certainly have experiences others would name as prophetic ministry, but we don't feel we can or should claim that name for ourselves. It feels proud. It feels self-righteous.

To me, it is essential we not separate prophetic ministry as something that happens episodically or only to certain individuals. Within our tradition, I believe true prophetic ministry is an attitude toward life that produces a renewed state of being. It is the belief we can act at all times under divine guidance. When we are in this condition, every aspect of our lives has the potential to be ministry and each act, however small, can be prophetic.

Paul adds that being in this state of accord isn't hit-a-home-run perfection. Borrowing from the words of a contemporary Quaker song, he says it's living up to the Light that you have and, when you do, more will be given you.[1] It is both now here and still coming—a state of communion with the divine we can live in and continuously grow into.

Paul describes prophetic ministry in his own life as follows:

[It is] a series of ordinary, everyday events, rooted in the sure knowledge the Inward Light is always present and always ready to guide me. As such, it is not an all-or-nothing gift, not something peculiarly bestowed on some, but not on others; nor a bolt-from-the-blue special occasion but a capacity we each have in some measure. . . . [It is] what we do now and work to get better at later. Even for a natural slugger, the difference between home runs and strikeouts is day-by-day batting practice to develop talent and hone skills. Just as with any ability, each time we start where we are and build on it. If I strike out, there will be another [time] at bat coming.

Paul then emphasizes the importance of being part of a community. Prophetic ministry, no matter how ordinary, is not a solitary exercise.

Everything I've said so far portrays prophetic ministry as a solitary exercise. It would seem to be a route to isolated personal perfection, and I'm sure that's possible. There is a long history of hermits who withdraw from the world into an austere divine communion. If that is your calling, you have no choice but to follow, but it's not mine. I'm not that independent. I need a community to help me along the way. Patience does not come naturally, humility is harder, and a supportive congregation bears me up when I fall.

Like Paul, I see the calling of Friends as one of paying attention to the guidance of the Inward Light on a daily or even minute-by-minute basis, knowing we all fall short. By focusing on the everyday nature of the prophetic task, I hope to demystify it and to elevate this attitude of following the guidance of the Inward Light as central to the meeting community rather than as the work of a very few individuals who are somehow chosen to be special.

Run-of-the-Mill Prophetic Ministry

Although it is very easy to assume that the call to prophetic ministry is something grand—a clear vision from God about what needs to happen, instructions on what to say, a conviction that one has to speak to the whole community or to the world—I believe this is the exception, not the defining case. More often the prophetic call comes quietly and leads us in gentle ways. Similarly, Paul Buckley concludes:

> The grand crisis is a reality in some lives. And perhaps the early Friends were right. Maybe we will each face a dramatic day of visitation when we are required to choose between good and evil. If it happens, I hope I am ready, but I'm not going to put my life on hold waiting for it. I think if I did, it would be unfaithful to my calling. Life is a day-by-day, minute-by-minute process—full of perfectly ordinary events, but each one an opportunity to ask, "Okay, now what?"

By considering the prophetic ministry an ordinary consequence of listening for the Spirit of Truth as often as possible in all we do, space opens up for this way of being to be part of our life journey. The awareness of God, for me, is an awareness of the value of all life, knowing that we are just a small part of life and not the center of attention as our ego tempts us to believe. Considering this as part of a journey makes it easier to accept setbacks and mistakes and to notice growth and newness, whether our journey is one of radical witness or of loving care for our neighbors.

A Lifelong Journey

Mary Lord (Baltimore Yearly Meeting) is a well-known peace activist. Her calling began in college when she was involved in civil rights work and active in the Methodist Student Movement. She notes that she was radicalized by actions against the Vietnam war, against poverty, and for women's rights as well as the experience of "working in federal buildings that some radical group decided to bomb."

Through all these decades of engagement, Mary found that "calls to prophetic ministry do not come as isolated episodes. It has been a life journey that becomes a way of living." She explains:

> This is a life journey of being shaped, molded, healed, broken, and healed until one is taken over willingly (always we are asked to consent) to the Divine Will.

Some of us find the Spirit calls us to act out of a place of weakness and resistance. In contrast, Mary's call coincided with her natural gifts and inclinations, a calling that has been part of her life for fifty years. For Mary,

> The Divine builds on our gifts. I had a natural interest in public affairs, peace, and justice and a gift of public speaking. Paths were opened. Paths were closed. Other paths were opened as I gained knowledge, skills, and experience that would allow me to be useful. Sometimes, I think we are sent, and sometimes I think we are the one available to be used although someone else might have had more to offer if they had been willing or paying attention.
>
> Sometimes we are the ones to get things started and wake up those whose calling it really is to do the work. It is dangerous to be proud of the calling because this is not the work of ego; it is the surrender of ego to what is higher. When ego tries to lead the calling it is more apt to fail because the work is not led by God and is vulnerable to destructive forces.

This describes what I visualize when I think about everyday prophets: someone listening and paying attention to where he or she might be called and stepping forward, whether it be to hold someone's hand, as so many of us do, or to mediate a civil war, as Adam Curle did. Mary's calling is evident in much she has done and in her patience and willingness to continue despite obstacles, be they others' prejudice or the fact that she might have misheard. Like so many of the people who responded to my queries, a supportive community is part of the foundation that upholds her. Mary describes it this way:

> Prophetic ministry is by definition mystical. The mystic needs the grounding community to discern what is of God, what is of self, and what is something else. I could be an activist and I could give ministry, but I did not become prophetic until I became grounded in a faith community. I cannot sustain my calling without that foundation. It is difficult for me because I have moved a lot and need to reestablish the ground in new communities.

Mary and I both can attest to the difference it makes in our lives to have a supportive community that stands with us even when they do not understand what we are talking about. My community has pushed me to speak and listened to my stumbling. They have asked hard questions, and sometimes I have had to do much research and self-searching in order to respond. We all grow in the process. They recall me to prayer and on occasion chastise me. They share their spiritual practices and their doubts. And they pay attention to where the Spirit is calling them.

Grumpiness or a Ministry?

Choice. That is always what we face—the choice to reach for our own comfort or to reach out to our neighbor. Ron and Pam Ferguson (New Association of Friends) recount such a choice that they brought to the attention of a Friend.

> Not long after we arrived in Winchester, an elderly (and chronically grumpy) Quaker woman was hospitalized in a double room in the town's old hospital. Her elderly roommate

was terminally ill, in considerable distress, and apparently had no family or friends accompanying her in her final days of life. Each time we visited our grumpy Friend, she would complain vehemently about the noise the roommate made at night, preventing her from sleeping. She even asked to be moved to another room but was told the hospital was full.

During one of her tirades, I acted (with considerable fear) on a clear leading from the Spirit to ask her to consider the possibility that God had placed her in that room at that time for the purpose of ministry to a dying woman who had no loved ones caring for her. I suggested that she might have been put there to pray whenever her roommate cried out in the night and perhaps to ensure that the woman would not be alone at the moment of her death. To my surprise, our Friend calmed down, said, "I hadn't really thought of that," and agreed to pray for her roommate instead of criticize her. Until the roommate died, we never heard another complaint.

I'm sure I'm not the only one who has experienced a similar situation. When I'm feeling miserable, even for good cause, it is hard to recognize that a choice is possible. Yet such small choices are part of our day-to-day encounter with the world. Our challenge is to be able to see that this is so and to acknowledge the tug towards generosity and caring.

I started this book by noting that the meaning of shalom, which I so often translate as 'peace,' carries in it this connotation of generosity and abundance. I am regularly brought up short by the contrast to the culture of "I've got mine, you have to deserve getting yours" (and I might fight you for it). Ron and Pam are among those who cultivate a countercultural sharing out of scarcity and in that sharing come to experience abundance for the giver as well as for those who receive. Surely this is integral to the city of God.

"The Pieces Weren't Coming Together!"

Everyone I know has experienced times when, even with the clearest of callings and the best of intentions, it seems impossible to go ahead with a project. At such times, my challenge is to find a way to "sink down to the Seed" as many early Friends advised or otherwise seek out that Light which points out my errors, knowing that it will show me a new way.

I find this regular attention to where the Life rises up to be similar to the creative process of the artist because it will not flow easily if one is taking an intellectual approach or trying to reason one's way out of a jam. Ashley Wilcox (Freedom Friends Church) tells such a story about a block that became a catalyst for a new approach.

> I have given big, prophetic messages in meeting for worship, but I think the act of naming something on a smaller scale can be just as powerful.
>
> A few years ago, I was on a committee that was struggling. Everyone on the committee believed in the ministry we were trying to do, but there had been a number of roadblocks along the way. The members of the committee lived at a distance, and it was hard to find times to meet. On the day of one of our meetings . . . I learned that about half of the committee members were not going to be able to make it to the meeting. I was disappointed and asked about a particular Friend I had hoped to see. The convener said that the Friend had tried to find a way to come, but "the pieces were not coming together." In that moment, I had clarity: the pieces were not coming together—not just for the Friend who could not come but for the committee as a whole. During our meeting, I was able to name that. It was

hard and painful, but it helped us come to the conclusion that it was time to lay the committee down so that the ministry could go forward in a different way.

I read this story as illustrative of the difference between actions that we want to make happen and a truly prophetic work. This is a regular problem with Quaker peace and social concerns committees. Too often the work of the group is focused on a project that everyone thinks is a good thing to do and may well very much need doing, but the waiting on the Light seems to be missing.

Sometimes the pieces never seem to come together, yet individuals or the group continue to feel the need to act. Discernment does not always lead to a clear answer. Perhaps years later the puzzle pieces make sense and we know we acted rightly or wrongly. Or not.

Queries for Reflection and/or Discussion

1. When have you experienced the pieces not coming together? What was that like for you? How was your life changed? How did you share this with others? How did they help you go forward?

2. What does it feel like to consider the prospect of prophetic ministry as a process of small, daily steps and regular seeking for guidance rather than a more spectacular, numinous event?

3. How do you bring the experience of worship into your decision-making and into each group of people you engage with?

CHAPTER 16
DILIGENCE IN THE LORD'S SERVICE

Given the complexity and variety among Friends globally, it would take me aback if we all expressed the heart of our faith and action in the same way. The seemingly infinite array of human words and practices on this planet argues that each of us encounters the exigencies of daily life and the mystery of human existence and inspiration in a unique manner.

I am one of the minority of Friends who do not hold that belief in the unique, essential, saving nature of Jesus' death and resurrection is at the core of being a Quaker. I am not an orthodox Christian but have found much in the Quaker understanding of the Christian way that speaks to my experience and faith. I have known a conversion of heart and soul in a way that echoes the early Quaker experience of the Refiner's fire and the baptism of the Spirit. The call to take up the cross daily speaks to my condition as I sort through the demands of the ego and the guidance of the Inward Teacher. I have spoken in worship about the immediacy of divine communion. Speaking of "diligence in the Lord's service" is not my language, but my heart knows what this is.

Diligence in the Lord's Service

I believe the words of Zablon Malenge (Nairobi Yearly Meeting) articulate a sense of calling and obedience that many Friends could affirm wholeheartedly:

> Prerequisites for prophetic ministry to me are integrity, uprightness, simplicity, persevering, servanthood, and diligence in the Lord's service. To me, this is the way of the cross and that is the purpose of prophetic ministry. Yes, I believe those are the qualities and values observed before I was nominated as presiding clerk of Friends Church in Kenya. My support

comes from both the Lord and the people I serve.

I would add the following prerequisites for prophetic ministry: simplicity, patience, constancy, humility, nonviolence, faithfulness, and forbearance towards others. Constancy and steadiness are important, as is interior attention to the work of the Inward Guide and to the steady searching out of one's own actions and words that lead to greed and hypocrisy, underpin hatred or revenge, or otherwise contribute to the seeds of war.

The phrase "diligence in the Lord's service" brings to mind Jesus' difficult admonition in Luke 14:26 about the need to hate one's mother and father in order to follow him. Placing obedience to the Light above personal comfort, above normal chores and work responsibilities, and even above the demands of family is the example we have from our spiritual ancestors. Many ministers left behind their families, even small children, for weeks and months at a time when the Spirit called them to travel. Women ministers left children at home knowing they were ill and might die soon, yet at least one of these women reported that the ill child encouraged her to leave. This prioritization of duties was shocking two thousand years ago and three hundred and fifty years ago, and it still seems harsh to many today. It raises many questions about what a true calling is and how much prophetic ministry demands of us. From some, over the centuries, the ministry has asked everything.

God Knitting Our Hearts Together

Although the phrase 'diligence in the Lord's service' sounds harsh to me, the idea of God knitting our hearts together is just the opposite. Bringing together the community in common purpose and attention to well-being as well as service—that is the image I find in the following reflections by David Thomas

159

(Northwest Yearly Meeting and Evangelical Friends Church—Rwanda):

> I thrive on being able to see the big picture, and a good vision inspires me. I see my prophetic gift in being able to see the organization I am a part of with an eye to what it needs to grow forward into the future. . . . I could see that we as a church organization did not have a clear sense of vision, of the direction God wanted us to head in.
>
> I asked permission . . . for a special retreat to seek God, to listen to him to discern his vision for us as the Friends Church in Rwanda. . . . It was a time when God really knit our hearts together with our Rwandan leaders. . . . Over a period of two days, out of times of silence and then sharing together, a vision emerged of a holy, transforming people on a hill shining Christ's light throughout the nation. We would get there by being disciples of Jesus and through prayer. The only phrase that our current Yearly Meeting superintendent (Augustine Simparinka) shared that whole day was *Nitwe tubikora!*, which means, "We are the ones to do it!" This vision is still a strong guiding vision among our leaders and in our churches today.

David adds:

> There are now a majority of strong Rwandan leaders in the Friends Church who believe that God can work through them to build his church in Rwanda. They demonstrate a strong faith and courage in God through their leadership and actions. This sense of ownership and deep trust in God is what he can use to build his church.

David has the gift of naming the vision that will give hope to the community, a community that suffered in ways I cannot even imagine during the genocide that swept their country. Part of the task of the prophet is to be a voice for the community so that it might see itself better and find renewal through the lens of the holy.

Saying No and Regretting It

It is not unusual to find stories of people who find the call to ministry totally outside their idea of what is possible. Some of these stories end there—"This is not something I can do!" Other times, as in the case of C. Wess Daniels (Sierra-Cascades Yearly Meeting of Friends), saying no is not an end point but rather a point where life shifts and one's entire perspective is reoriented to a new way of being. Here, Wess tells of learning that saying no was a big mistake:

> I had a "No" like this that I said to God's face once. When I was first called into ministry I flat out said to God, "No way, no how." I felt kind of bad because of my attitude. (After all, my parents taught me to talk respectfully to my elders. If God wasn't one of my elders, who was?)
>
> So I back tracked a little and said, "Okay God, ... So here's the deal. You are going to have to make me want to be a pastor, actually make me desire it and see how I fit with it. Because there's no way on earth I'm doing something I don't want to do like that." . . .
>
> But you know how the story ends, or you can assume the ending. It didn't take too long to learn that if I held onto my no, I was going to prevent a lot of things happening that I would later regret.[1]

Wess then considers the 'no' that arises in the context of improvisational theater. In improv, 'no' is a block to action. It stops the entire flow of the theatrical performance. It eliminates possibility after possibility. Improv depends on being able to 'go with the flow'—to react and adapt to changing circumstances and to allow something creative and unexpected to be formed. He sees John the Baptist blocking the movement of the Spirit when he first refuses to baptize Jesus. But then he relents and agrees to what Jesus asks of him. Wess describes the consequences this way:

> The way of the kingdom of God is not through no, it is through a yes. We don't become disciples of Jesus by saying no to him.
>
> Jesus' line that [John the Baptist] must do this to "fulfill all righteousness" . . . is actually a clue for us not just in thinking about improv, but how the kingdom of God itself works. Jesus demonstrates that obedience to God is not about "blocking"—as John may have thought—but about "Building" on what is already there.
> . . .
> Jesus' building upon John's call to turn towards God is what creates the beloved community where all are welcomed and forgiven.[2]

We each face in our own way the possibility that we might be called to build on Jesus' work among us. Taking action often feels to me like improv, and I thank Wess for bringing these concepts together.

Initially, All Were Part of the Church

Being part of a community offers many choices related to facing or hiding from disagreement and from people whose ways may feel alien. The larger the group, the more the potential for diversity, yet in a small community slight differences can be intensified and explode if not recognized as a natural part of human interaction. Finding the patience and generosity to continue to engage even when we harm each other, as humans inevitably do, is not always simple and sometimes does not seem possible.

Moses Bigirimana (Kibimba Yearly Meeting) is one of the many Burundian Friends who chose to engage in the hopeful yet dangerous and sorrow-filled work of reconciliation. He organized one of the country's first seminars on reconciliation in 1997.

> It was at a terrible time when it was still a big risk just to get out and say something. To get people to come to seminars on reconciliation, talking of reconciliation was like you were mad, because people were so angry with one another. . . .
>
> We went by familiarity, by friendship. In our context, the problem was between ethnic groups, and I had some friends from the other tribe, other than mine, so we paired together. We tried to organize together, and I invited those from the other tribe to join me in organizing that particular seminar in order to convince others to come and join us. It was a time when I had just come from Woodbrooke, from the Responding to Conflict program. I used what I got there at Woodbrooke to organize the training. Finally we organized a big seminar on peace and reconciliation.
>
> That was the beginning, and it went on and on and reached many people. It is very big now and is an independent organization, not part of the Friends Church now.

The possibility of reconciliation with neighbors who have betrayed you in the worst and most final of ways is almost beyond comprehension. Moses and so many others have taken this massive risk, knowing that this work is at the core of faithful obedience to God. Yet his story offers a caution to us all because it ended with tensions between several organizations.

Doing prophetic work does not leave us immune to the frailties that arise and can trip up any of us at any time. *Where two or three are gathered* holds the potential that the Spirit is with us and at the same time the potential that egos will be bumped and bruised. Honest disagreements can be seen in uncharitable ways. Regarding the seminars on reconciliation, Moses says, "But initially, all were part of the church." I hear this as a statement of both failure and of hope, for if the church is true, the connection will always be there and can be renewed.

Does Belief Matter?

For those of us in the more liberal, unprogrammed Friends meetings, it can be more difficult to speak of a deep calling or a sense of divine presence in our lives than for Friends who belong to churches where it is usual to think of God as acting in human affairs. The dynamics of this involve many factors, from our rejection of the term 'God' to our natural reticence about what is most precious to us. This latter is the case in communities where there is a focus on action and engagement without sharing about the spiritual dimensions of what we do. Reticence occurs in churches as well as meetings when the individual feels his or her experience and beliefs do not mesh with those of the community.

Mary Lord (Baltimore Yearly Meeting) speaks in a way that reflects my experience.

> I found it essential to have a strong faith (by which I mean a set of beliefs and an intellectual understanding of the Divine as humans have understood the Divine) and a spiritual practice. . . .
> Sometimes liberal Friends say it doesn't matter what we believe and use this as an excuse for spiritual laziness and sloppy thinking. Other kinds of Friends can be so rigid in articles of faith and practice they are mortally afraid to consider change.

More than a focus on "right belief," however it might be defined by one's community, Mary places primary importance on self-awareness and knowing what one actually believes.

> My experience is that it is important that I know what I believe because that shapes my interpretation of experience and new

164

information. Self-awareness of our beliefs also for me at least makes it clearer when I need to adjust or even radically change my beliefs. Spiritual practice also needs a combination of stability and capacity to change what has become dry.

Life tests each of us over the years. When we are immersed in the hard places of life, we may learn that something that once seemed central to our belief and being is no longer crucial. In paying attention to the inner life and reaching to notice the movement of the Spirit, there is space. Here we might find stronger, richer, and sometimes more lightly held (though no less deeply cherished) images of the Eternal and of our place in living out the infinite love and hope that are at the heart of our common faith.

Queries for Reflection and/or Discussion

1. How do you respond to the phrase "diligent in service to the Lord?" What do you believe this phrase means? What language might you use to convey this message?

2. How have you been "diligent in service to the Lord?" Could you describe this work and how it is in service to God and to the world? How does it reflect your core faith and understanding of the work of love in your heart?

LEARNING THE TERRITORY

The three chapters in this section are about listening for God. We can't do it without QUIETING THE MIND. Learning to still the constant chatter that so many of us experience when we are preoccupied with the matters of the world rarely seems to happen instantaneously. Yet as we come to still the mind, space opens for us to hear the movement of the Spirit and to come to recognize the different internal voices that compete to guide our lives.

The Persian poet Rumi likened the mind to a guest house where a wide variety of emotions, desires, and fears arrive at all hours of the day and night, uninvited and often not eager to leave. I equate some of these guests with the demons that appear in the gospels. KNOWING OUR OWN DEMONS is part of discernment as we learn the territory of our own spiritual and emotional being.

Some of these demons have complex natures. Anger is just one of these. When we are caught up in an anger driven by fear, hostility, or other such emotions, we risk becoming JUST ANOTHER ANGRY GUY who is marching "against" and perhaps tossing ugly words around and otherwise rousing up hatred. Yet anger grounded in compassion, anger at injustice, may be a source of energy and commitment. May we each come to know the difference between anger that comes out of fear and anger that is grounded in the Spirit.

CHAPTER 17
QUIETING THE MIND

Relying on the Light for guidance is a dicey thing. It feels threatening to those who want simple, definable, or yes/no answers. It is not a readily reproducible experiment that always leads to the same result. I have needed practice to learn when I am following the True Guide and when I am flitting after a whim, reacting to my dislike of someone, or giving in to unrecognized anger or the desire to put myself forward as an expert. The ways I can get distracted or misled seem infinite. Sitting for an hour in expectant silence every Sunday is invaluable, as are journal writing, daily meditation, and hiking on Mount Hood. These practices have shown me much about my own patterns of behavior and the impulses that push me to action or inaction.

Knowing the dimensions of my own inward state has made it more possible for me to recognize the gentle nudges on my heart that come from that Inward Teacher that is beyond my own willing, beyond my willfulness. Learning the sounds that ring in the inward ear—the taste of fear, the smell of anger, the laughter of delight—takes time and attention for some of us.

As a reminder to take time apart and to hone the skill of going deep, I offer this extended meditation on practice. In this case, I use the example of piano practice, something I took up when I was in my sixties. Paul Buckley, whose reflections on the everyday nature of prophetic ministry I've cited in earlier chapters, uses baseball as his model. I encourage you to find the image, the practice that you can feel in your bones, to help you learn better your own heart and your own stumbling points.

I recently had a piano lesson, the third week that I had spent largely on Bach's two-part inventions. It is a reach for me to play these at all, much less master them. Full of scales and other basic exercises, they still

167

are lovely to play and hear even as I stumble, seeking to find the music in them. I often find myself asking, "What is the difference between exercises and music?" Externally, one sounds rote, but the other links to something inside me and lifts me. The query is in how to move from the one to the other. Underlying this is a sense of the way in which the experience and vision of our spiritual ancestors can point the way for us to find the holy Life and Power that can fill us today.

Such day-to-day exercises help me relate to prophetic ministry and to speaking of the movement of the Spirit, the music that can't be heard by physical ears. At the piano, I notice that I extend notes in sequences Bach wrote as evenly paced and that I provide pauses when none are marked but that echo the sound I hear in my head. Trying to find the next note and fumbling around does not evoke music, but this erratic testing is part of the way; similarly, in learning to listen, my mind might be jittery, impatient, and far from the stillness I seek, and discernment seems impossible.

Playing the piano has an obvious component of practice and discipline. Training helps my fingers reach the notes. When I attempt to make use of both hands together, I feel like new neurons have to form in my head to make this possible. One hand can play easily, freely, and with assurance, but when I try to match it with the other, all falls apart and I fumble again.

My analytical mind regularly scans the music, noticing repeated phrases, full-octave jumps, and other such patterns. When I memorize a piece, I no longer have to think about what note comes next, allowing the music to better emerge. Memorization means I have spent enough time with a piece to allow it to take its own shape within me and to fill my head, even when I am miles from the instrument. In the same way, my awareness of Spirit grows as I learn to focus my mind on that still point in the soul and to gently bring it back each time it wanders.

Some people have a genius for improvisation. That is not my gift. My mind and being seem to need the guidance that comes from playing what someone else wrote, first in a way similar to what they might have intended and then making it more and more my own. Thus, I have learned to speak of the inbreaking of God into my life and to help others name that experience, which is always there, always unique, and always part of one whole through time and space.

How else might I apply this playing the piano to listening for the word of God, to the Light, be it gentle or harsh, as I become more alert to noticing and responding? My initial answer seems to be that they aren't related. My mind says that the process of composing, the creative process, is what ministry is about—listening to the deepest core of one's being and beyond and feeling something new rising up. Yet, so often, isn't the act of prophetic ministry an act of repeating a message that has been told again and again but repeating it in one's own voice for one's own time and place? So the stumbling fingers at the piano are part of it, as well as the slightly shifted beat.

Each pianist has his or her own understanding of what is loud or soft—pianissimo or forte. When I lead workshops, it takes several tries to gain any kind of fluency. Gaining the basic vocabulary and concepts was all I could work on at Multnomah Monthly Meeting or in the Way of the Spirit program. I was reaching for something more by the time I was co-leading a session at Pendle Hill, but I was still tripping over my own limitations and the strong feelings that push me around.

I seek to integrate the lessons from the past, be they the lessons of spiritual ancestors or great musicians. The Bartók lesson books titled *Mikrokosmos* indicate the number of seconds it should take to play a piece. When I time myself, I'm usually at half speed, even when I think I have mastered the piece. This is very discouraging. It is a sign of how much I have to learn and of how much I have to train my body to function within the demands of the music.

Some of this description makes the discipline sound rote—and very distant from the open, freeing feeling I associate with the Holy. I can feel caught in that practicing, that almost mechanical dimension of learning a skill. Obviously, I will never be a concert pianist—it is clear that they have an amazing freedom within the discipline and have gained an innate feel for the instrument that I don't have.

The yoga discipline I follow certainly teaches the value of a body that is both strong and flexible so that it may hold the movement of the energy flow and spirit in the interior spaces. Quaker discipline has always had a strand of spending extended time in contemplation— learning to clear the mind of all the ordinary musings and focusing it on biblical passages or the stories of ministers or simply emptying it and listening. Yoga practitioners urge daily practice, but Friends don't have an explicitly physical dimension beyond old meetinghouse benches that passively provide an impetus to sit up straight, similar to the yoga expectation that allows the chi, the energy, to move freely.

Early Quakers also had disciplines that involved giving up distractions, such as not overeating or overdrinking. The time they spent in prison did all kinds of things to the body that I can't imagine— enforced fasting, sleeping in impossible circumstances, or going for long periods without much sleep. They dealt with much that was ugly and foul and still turned their minds and hearts to God and found joy in the filth and stench and hardship. This is a very different discipline from piano or yoga practice, yet it is also very much the same.

I find I do need teachers, both for my attempts at playing the piano and in matters of the soul. One opening from my piano teacher was an invitation to expand my concept of composing and creating beauty.

She encouraged me to explore the truth the composer is showing me and what is true for me in the music. That's not so much about getting it right as it is about discovery. This echoes within me and parallels the advice I give when teaching discernment.

We each need a community around us, even just one other person, who knows something of the work of the Spirit and can listen beneath the world's chaos that can engulf us. Such guides, including our spiritual ancestors, confirm the reality that hope and love are at work despite apparent darkness. Their way opens possibilities, broad pathways that can teach us, yet we are each to listen with all our being to find the Life that is within and to learn the particular way that is ours to take.

Queries for Reflection and/or Discussion

1. How do you practice listening for the voice of the Holy? Do you long for more time attending to the Spirit within? What might make this more possible?

2. Where do you find joy in the everyday rhythm of your life?

3. What helps you sustain your spiritual practices during times of dryness or discouragement? How do you find your way when you are lost?

CHAPTER 18
KNOWING OUR OWN DEMONS

Those who know Muriel "Mickey" Edgerton of Philadelphia Yearly Meeting may have at times encountered something of her sharp tongue. We all also have reason to know the depth of caring that can burst through her demeanor even when she is most caught up in pressing for us to live up to her vision of what Quakers might be. She describes herself this way:

> I have a vision of how Quakerism *can be* and *has been* practiced, and my judgmental personality type interferes badly with my ability to participate lovingly and wisely with Friends at my meeting and probably everywhere else!! . . . [My] opportunities to share the Good News with others have been mostly in my encounters with hospice patients and their families and with my hospice colleagues.
>
> So I have no doubt that God is using me just the way I am, flaws and all, in witnessing to and modeling Jesus' teachings of how to do kingdom living. I know that is what my life is "supposed" to be about, and I am doing that the best I can, and mostly that makes my heart sing. When I get involved in something that makes my heart sink, I am pretty sure that is a sign that I'm *not* supposed to be doing that.

As Mickey notes, self-knowledge can be painful, yet my experience with Mickey has made clear her gifts in nurturing the ministry of others. I for one am sure I drive people nuts with how little I talk. Many probably see me as aloof because of this. Since I easily go into defensive mode, I can seem even pricklier and push people further away. I have whole baskets full of fears—demons, if you will—that mostly sit on an interior back shelf these days, but they can tumble onto the floor and make a real mess at unexpected times, making it hard for me to recall what I do right. We each have our own ways of being in this world that make it difficult for us to love and be loved, just as we each have qualities that burst through gloriously when given the chance.

Recently, I was able to sit quietly with someone in agony. I was able to listen to his pain without jumping in or offering false comfort. Focusing on divine Love allows me to engage with others honestly and stop projecting my problems onto them or attempting to fix that which I can't change. I cherish these moments when I can drop the pretense of competence, which is so often a kind of armor to keep others at a distance. Such moments help open the door to humility and right relationship. Here, I neither lord it over others thinking I have all the answers nor cower with a sense of worthlessness. Here is the point where hurts can meld into deep caring and anger can morph into a powerful energy and passion. The unique blend of contradictory feelings that is in each of us is transformed as we stand still in the Light. In attending to this Inward Light, we move close to the new creation.

George Fox was quite aware of the contradictory, confusing, and sometimes ugly impulses that any of us may experience. In his journal, he writes about it this way:

> Yet I was under great temptations sometimes, and my inward sufferings were heavy; but I could find none to open my condition to but the Lord alone, unto whom I cried night and day. . . . And I cried to the Lord, saying, "Why should I be thus, seeing I was never addicted to commit those evils?"[1]

Since I am skilled at imagining the multitude of things that can go wrong, I am especially good at seeing the things I can do to make any situation worse. Such imaginings often leave me frozen and silent when I should be reaching out. It was very helpful to me to discover that an essential lesson of the Light is not just that it makes you more conscious of your own flaws—being aware of the wrongs you might do can make you less judgmental of others. My awareness of my own weaknesses also somehow transforms them, pointing the way to living more fully and experiencing healing as well as greater awareness of how to address the needs of the world. Fox put it this way:

> And the Lord answered that it was needful I should have a sense of all conditions, how else should I speak to all conditions; and in this I saw the infinite love of God. I saw also that there was an ocean of darkness and death, but an infinite ocean of light and love, which flowed over the ocean of darkness. And in that also I saw the infinite love of God; and I had great openings.[2]

Blindness to our own condition can sneak up on us and really mess things up. Discernment is not possible without an honest understanding of our own impulses and tendencies. Ministry can easily be turned into something damaging, even with the best of intentions, if we do not pay attention to who we are and the forces that press us to act or not act. A recent example of this happened during an early morning Bible study class. The group listened as two participants went deeply but gently into painful memories of the civil rights era. Then a third person burst in with a passionate statement that threw us all off balance. This passion was a kind of preaching and could have been helpful under other circumstances, but the moment called for something that ministered to our souls. Fortunately, we were able to refocus our attention to recreate the space so that the initial exploration could find its own conclusion.

Conflicting Awareness

As might be expected, self-knowledge is not enough. Perhaps some people can will themselves to change in significant ways, but my personality is such that as

174

soon as I try to push myself hard in one direction, something inside me fights back, digs in its heels, and clings to familiar patterns. I might crack jokes about not looking at that white bear (or any other particular item), knowing that such instructions inevitably lead to our turning our attention to the bear. Paul's oft-quoted words address this:

> *I obviously need help! I realize that I don't have what it takes. I can will it, but I can't do it. I decide to do good, but I don't really do it; I decide not to do bad, but then I do it anyway. My decisions, such as they are, don't result in actions. Something has gone wrong deep within me and gets the better of me every time.* (Romans 7:18–20 MSG)

The apostle Paul sees this struggle as part of the human condition; we are trapped in sin, separated from God, and unable to do what we know is right. He names the freedom he found in Christ to overcome this power of sin and resistance. Modern-day Americans might explain this in psychological terms, but Paul's experience is real for many people.

As I learned to trust in the Spirit and stopped attempting to tightly control everything around me, something shifted within. Supportive people are invaluable in this process, as is coming to find the humor in my efforts. Slowly, I am more able to enjoy my own foolishness as something to let drop away rather than cling to.

This shift, this change, has been for me a long, slow process. Even after years of being an occasional public speaker, I have not consistently found my voice. At times, I am able to bring my heart, mind, and voice into unison with what the Spirit is asking of me, yet I also find that other times, if I don't write out every word, some niggling fear deep within leads me to drop important pieces. I see others speak with verve and confidence and wish I could do the same.

How often do we confuse ourselves by comparing what we are doing with what others have accomplished and then list all the ways we fall short? I am especially good at doing this when I am first learning something. I see vividly how well the task is done by those who have been practicing for years and see myself as inadequate. Each of us has our own story of falling into the trap that the apostle Paul bemoans of being unable to live up to our own hopes and ideals and thus feeling paralyzed.

Mental Health and Prophecy

Allison Randall (New England Yearly Meeting) asks whether a real prophet knows he or she is a prophet. "Who makes the judgment call as to who is a prophet?" Allison wonders at those who claim they are prophets even though no one listens to them, "yet they insist they know the Truth, that Truth has been revealed to them." Her concern grows out of encountering individuals who are mentally ill.

Prophets are sometimes known for their odd behavior: walking naked as a sign; fasting; speaking out of unusual, vivid, and sometimes incomprehensible visions; and more. Just as with the mystic, the line between the prophet and the mentally ill can be fine and hard to define. Psychologists sometimes label mystical or prophetic visions "delusional" or "psychotic." Jennifer Elam spoke with many Friends as she looked at that wavering line between mysticism and mental health. She writes:

> Mysticism in my life involves a current of energy that connects that of God in me to that of God not in me. Mystical experience is part of a committed way of life. It is opening my soul and holding in it the creative space that existed before God created the universe. It is co-creation with God in that space.[3]

Jennifer continues, "Einstein declared that true science, true art, and true religion come from the same place."[4] She argues that mysticism offers a glimpse into that space. I suggest that prophetic ministry also taps into that space, giving the energy and direction to speak and act to help bring the city of God into reality on earth.

I find that mysticism and prophetic ministry are both about being in that deep space with God. The mystic enters for a time that holy space, often encountering vivid images or visions, while the prophetic becomes a visible link connecting the holy with the community and the world by offering forth words or actions he or she has been given. I name the place of mental health as one where relationships can grow, not break, and where individuals retain a sense of their true self. Jennifer notes,

> The language around obedience, giving up ego, being selfless is very confusing and has caused harm to many people. . . . Living in the presence of God requires a strong sense of our uniqueness, a strong sense of our truest identity, a confidence in the power of that creation ability we have when we are connected to God.[5]

Jennifer finds that mystical openings can be healing, but for some they are quite disorienting and uncomfortable. Because of this, she advocates the need for "accompaniers" to walk with those whose path is that of the mystic. Such accompaniment, for her, is not about believing or disbelieving but about

> honoring their unique experiences while knowing clearly our own limits so that we might be well grounded while doing such work and not be afraid. It is important to be clear that God would not, for instance, ask someone to harm themselves or others.[6]

Jennifer's words about self-harm may not apply to the prophet, much as I want them to. The examples that raise this question include Friend Norman Morrison, who, along with several Buddhist monks, set himself on fire in protest of the Vietnam War. In the past, I think of the four Friends who returned again and again to the Massachusetts Bay Colony despite warnings and were eventually hanged. These early Friends took action knowing that they would be punished harshly by the authorities or that they would be at risk of drowning during ocean crossings. They acted in assurance both that God would protect their souls and that they were divinely called to witness to evil. I believe this applied only to putting themselves at risk, not others, so that may be an important demarcation along with their willingness to test their leadings with their companions.

Whether we name them elders or companions, people who are well grounded and sensitive to the movement of the Spirit can be invaluable as they walk alongside both the mystics and the prophets among us, a subject covered in more depth in chapter 23.

The earliest Quakers were sympathetic with those who might be labeled as mentally ill. The behavior of Friends was often outside the norm of their day, and they understood much about being ostracized. After all, they went around proclaiming that God had spoken to them directly and motivated their actions at a time when people either relied on the direction of priests or appealed to the Bible for inspiration. Their experiences led to pioneering work in the treatment and care of the mentally ill, an early example being the York Retreat in England. Such work in and of itself might well be considered prophetic witness.

Among the people who worked with Jennifer was a man who, after describing a deep mystical experience during worship, stated "My purpose in life has changed from improving the City of Man to upholding and bringing forth the City of God." Perhaps this is the point where the mystic becomes the prophet, or perhaps you could say that mystical experience blends into prophetic experience.

After describing how the changes in his life were driving his wife nuts because he no longer was concerned about work and earning money, this unnamed man gained the insight that he needed to "look for an edge of reality, a grounding for the fantastic." He eventually concluded, "I am suspicious of a mysticism which disdains the affairs of daily life."[7]

Being Intentional

Do I know what might make me burst out in frustration? What might make me yell at another person? What might make me become overly shy and unwilling to speak up when I have much to say? These are the kinds of questions that can be helpful as we are called to step forward to make a public statement or move into social justice action.

Paul Buckley (Ohio Valley Yearly Meeting) is quite explicit about the importance of self-knowledge and honesty about our own condition:

> We need to know our own demons. Being intentional—remembering to ask—is a struggle. Finding the humility to wait for an answer is even harder. For much of my life, I have been encouraged to make decisions and was rewarded for it. Taking the time for real discernment can feel like an excuse for procrastination, and sometimes it is. My personal temptation is to act more than to wait.

For Paul, the struggle is to "not run ahead of the Guide," in the words of Isaac Penington. He thinks he knows what is needed, so the discipline of waiting for the holy yes is a hard one for him. I'm the opposite in that I can often find myself half paralyzed and unwilling to act. It constantly amazes me how many wonderful excuses I can find for not doing something that is uncomfortable or that stretches me, even when I know that this is where I am being led. This is a strong contrast to the impulse to speak quickly, without reflection, that is endemic in our culture.

We each have the capacity to look inside, to watch how we react in different situations, and to be intentional about how we interact with other people and the issues we choose to engage with. Do I want to be part of every cause? Do certain people infuriate me, even when they don't intend to? Do I get trapped in a sense of unworthiness if someone questions me? Do I want everyone to hop on my bandwagon immediately? What are the demons that push me into unhealthy conflict?

My short list of what to do when the demons fill my head starts with noticing what is happening and how I feel. Then I try to spend some time identifying the underpinnings by asking myself why I feel this way. What assumptions am I making about the people and situation around me? Is love motivating me, or is it fear? Are there other questions I should be asking? Am I breathing?

It may take a minute or it may take days to sort out how these "demons" are pushing their agenda. Yet at times they bring a helpful perspective, as Ken Jacobsen suggests later in this chapter when he speaks of the guest house within. Mostly, these demons are familiar, and they may be easily welcomed and put in an appropriate place. At times, they are indicators of serious, deep-seated problems and are prods to obtain help.

George Fox wrote the following advice to Friends:

> Whatever you are addicted to, the Tempter will come in that thing. When he can trouble you, then he gets advantage over you, and then you are gone. Stand still in that which is pure, after you see yourselves; and then mercy comes in. After you see your thoughts, and the temptations, do not think, but submit. Then the Power comes.

> Stand still in that which shows and discovers; and there does strength immediately come. Stand still in the light, and submit to it, and the other will be hushed and gone. Then contentment comes. When temptations and troubles appear, sink down in that which is pure, and all will be hushed and will fly away. Your strength is to stand still, after you see yourselves.
>
> Stand still in that power which brings peace.[8]

Fox was far from the only early Friend to advise "standing still" or "going deep" when you feel you are lost or in a jam. It is just the opposite of the impulse to do and do and do without relief. When the choice in front of me is to face some painful emotion or clean the kitchen floor, the floor gets really clean and I fall prey to the temptation to ignore the cause of my anxiety. Fox advises that temptations lure us regularly, but unless we slow down enough to recognize that a given temptation to act is for selfish reasons, we cannot find peace. It is in the stillness that we can let the Inward Teacher show us how to avoid being trapped by temptation and instead know the power that comes bringing peace.

The Guest House

While writing this book, I was a member of a small peer group accompanying Ken Jacobsen (Ohio Yearly Meeting) as he mourned the death of his wife Katharine. Ken shared with us poems describing the guests that had arrived during the night. He was referring to the writing of Jalāl ad-Dīn Muhammad Rūmī, the thirteenth-century Persian Muslim poet who knew well the visitors, such as joy, sorrow, or shame, that can fill the "house" of any of us.[9]

Ken expanded on these words as he grieved the death of his wife Katharine. In the example below, Ken describes each of his "guests" as they appeared or reappeared. Ken writes:

The Only Rule Is Love

my friend,
if you're thinking of coming to my guest house,
the only rule is love; . . .

last week grief came, with a lot of baggage,
she sleeps late, when she wakes I hear her crying upstairs,
and I make her a little breakfast;
she doesn't eat much or say much,
sometimes we cry together in the kitchen—
the only rule is love;

the other night, anger came,
barged in without knocking;
he needed a room to himself
where he could shout for a while at God and the world,
he felt better in the morning, so I sent him off
with some food in his pack;
he doesn't know his schedule, but I think he may be back—
the only rule is love;

humor came for a bit,
trying to get me to laugh,
raucous, slapstick, witty, off-color humor,
sometimes it's funny, sometimes not,
I don't blame him for trying,
this morning he took off his clown-nose
and headed down the road,
he said to call him when I would like another laugh,
or even a smile;
I thanked him—
the only rule is love;

my friend,
whoever you may be,

182

you can come too,
I'll try to make room among the others,
they are not always the easiest guests,
I'm not always the easiest host,
especially since my wife died
and I have to manage things by myself—
you'll have put up with my cooking
and my (far from perfect) housekeeping,
but come if you want, if you need a place to stay
on this healing journey—
the only rule is love.[10]

Ken's poems offer an invaluable map of his inward landscape. That landscape is different for each of us. It can change with the seasons or as new plants are tended or weeds are allowed to grow freely. This landscape is where, somehow, body, mind, heart, and soul all intersect. All have the capacity to inform our being, and when they are in balance, we may perhaps be more fully whole and complete as individuals.

As we become more whole, we not only are more at peace within, we also have the capacity to bring this centeredness into engagement with the people around us. We then engage with others we meet face to face— those who are angry, those who are depressed, those who make visible all those demons we face within. Our meetings are such guest houses where anyone may enter. One challenge for all of us is to explore how we might better welcome all of the community into our lives.

Conflict as Part of Life

Friends have varied opinions about how we should address differences. Given the heavily middle-class orientation of Friends in the United States, George Lakey (Philadelphia Yearly Meeting) offers a perspective on building a new society that is uncomfortable for many of us. In an interview for *Peace News*, he told Milan Rai:

Middle-class pacifism has a very strong interest in the common ground, in reconciliation. For example the Fellowship of Reconciliation, it's built into the title. "Let's find a way to come together," that's very strongly the concern. So that is hugely a value in the middle class, harmony and common ground.

The trouble with this approach is that: "only harmony" is really insanity. "Only harmony" is death. So there also needs to be conflict. So the nonviolent revolutionary tradition is one in which the emphasis is not on harmony, it's on conflict. We have to have polarisation.[11]

In this interview, Lakey lifted up Dr. Martin Luther King Jr. as a person who was responsible for raising much conflict.

King said: peace is about conflict. Because peace is a concept that includes justice. And you can't have justice without conflict. You have to struggle, you have to polarise the situation in order to get something done. So that is a very major distinction.[12]

The example of King makes me aware of how complicated this all is and how easily I slip into assumptions, such as thinking about the fact that someone who brings conflict is loud and angry and insulting and harsh. In contrast, I think of King as forthright and speaking truth boldly in a way that engages the full heart. He set himself up not as separate but as grieving for our nation as well as for the blacks who have suffered such injustice, and he held a vision for us all. Grief was part of the power of his message, which others felt deeply. Some were threatened by his message and responded with violence.

Each of us needs to determine whether and when we are willing to speak Truth, how we recognize a broader truth than "your truth and my truth," and how we speak it. I would argue that radical prophetic ministry should emphasize naming injustice truthfully rather than polarizing people. This world is full of contrasts and different ways of living. I believe that our deeper call is to name the paradoxes and live into them rather than to press people into polar opposites where so often our egos can leave us stuck and unable to change.

Growing in the Capacity to Be Different

Since I can only start where I am, I have to acknowledge how hard it is for me to stand out, particularly when it means saying that I disagree with someone else or think what they are doing might lead to bad consequences. Others might find they want so hard to be recognized as different and unique that they put themselves in awkward positions that have little to do with who they truly are or how they want to engage with the world.

No matter what our reactions and ways of being are, we will inevitably come into conflict with others. Elise Boulding encourages to start learning new ways of naming our differences without being either defensive or on attack. She notes that "differences should not be considered an attack on family wholeness, but rather an affirmation of the individuality of each member of the whole."[13]

Boulding argues that we can start participating in what she calls "conflict maturing" within our families and then take this learning into larger and larger communities. She recognizes that this process can be hardest within the family (or a tight-knit community), especially in ones where there is a strong sense of closeness and a feeling that one knows the other thoroughly. Disagreement can seem doubly painful in such cases. She describes our tendency to see pain as something to be avoided and notes that pain can also be a sign of growth:

> The more we are faithful to our togetherness and our separateness, which is what the inherent contradictions of the family Tao ensure, the more pain we may feel. . . . It is seeing pain as a signal of growth that makes the conflict maturing process possible.[14]

For Boulding, the loving family is the central metaphor of the new creation, and in her studies she finds this to be widely true for how the world names love.

> We love one another beyond reason and beyond design, at the far side of hurt and anger, because there is an order of loving in the Creation of which we are a part.[15]

In the family, we gain much of our foundational learning that may serve us well in the world or that may need to be approached afresh, perhaps with the help of God's arms around us, as I experienced. The call to be part of this new creation comes with new awareness of the centrality of repairing and building relationships, be they with those closest to us or with those we might think of as our enemies.

Queries for Reflection and/or Discussion

1. What guests tend to enter regularly into your guest house? How do you welcome them (or not)? Have you found a way to keep them from controlling your actions or damaging your relationships with others? Have any become valuable guests in some way?

2. Is there some behavior that throws you off-center? What triggers it? How does it cause you to forget to listen for the Inward Light?

3. How do particular actions or words help you open up a new way of responding rather than pull you into old habits or unhealthy ways of being?

4. How does your meeting or church help those among you who are carrying with them past harms to find a place where they can grow into a fuller life, one grounded in love rather than fear?

CHAPTER 19
JUST ANOTHER ANGRY GUY

After the invasion of Iraq, I was so furious I couldn't talk politics at all. I couldn't believe what a horrible mistake had been made and, on top of it all, that the White House considered it a positive event and twisted the truth to convince the nation its actions were right. Ironically, in the midst of this extended period, I was serving on the executive committee, and eventually as presiding clerk, of the national Quaker lobby, Friends Committee on National Legislation. I had to find ways I could work to strengthen the witness of that organization without getting bound up in my own stuff.

Lots of angry people share this globe. Some are responding to careless or addicted parents, some have inherited centuries-long memories of injustice and violence, and some have been treated miserably by "the system." Work is still needed to make visible what I know in my bones—that the prophet's face can reflect the full range of humanity. Neither gender nor age nor social class determines who may be called to radical witness; anger is not a prerequisite, only the ability to hear and follow the voice of the Light.

Anger

In the early twenty-first century, anger and lies fill the political process, becoming so intense they drive people away and leave them frustrated by the pettiness, self-seeking, and greed that fuel the anger. Recently, a friend who works in the school system commented on the resentments of the Vietnam era that still are present. She finds at times clear lines between those who fought during that war and those who did not that are acted out in ways damaging to the school. I have felt some of this tension in places where I have worked and have no doubt of the power of this bitterness to surface years after events if we do not bring it out into the open and find resolution.

188

Patience Schenck is one of many Friends who bemoan the reality that "we have come a long way from those thundering early Friends." She asks, "Why don't we shake all the country for ten miles around?"[1] In answering her own question, she notes how often we are overwhelmed by the sheer volume of needs that call out to us and the guilt that can paralyze us. Her Pendle Hill pamphlet titled *Answering the Call to Heal the World* focuses on the process of discerning the call to address the larger injustices in the world.

Just the wording of Schenck's 's statement and the title of her pamphlet open up for me the differences between the noisy anger that is emotionally overcharged and bent on retribution and the strong, clear energy of anger that points out evil-doing but seeks to heal the world. Another way of saying this is to note that when anger is based in fear, it can easily control us and become destructive, spreading indignation, bitterness, and shame. Anger grounded in love is energizing and is expressed with generosity as well as patience, self-control, and kindness.

Rachel Cunliffe (North Pacific Yearly Meeting) teaches on topics including conflict resolution, crimes against humanity, and the death penalty. She identifies two very different dimensions of the way people understand anger: anger from love and anger from fear.

For example, I've been scared and then angry when someone in the right-hand lane decides to make a left turn in front of me. Parents can become furious when a child defies them. Rachel knows personally young men who have been imprisoned for serious crimes or forced to go through detox. For these young men, fear is the primary emotion and anger is the secondary emotion. Fear leaves them feeling like victims. Anger makes them feel big and important. Fear-based anger quickly becomes desperate and can grow to become hateful. It is often inarticulate, out of control, and ineffective. Such anger leads to bad decisions and impulsive behavior.

In contrast, love-based anger is often expressed in terms of indignation—indignation at promises broken or laws that put black men in jail at a much higher rate than men with lighter complexions. Rachel finds that anger grounded in love and a passion for justice and mercy can be regenerative and renewing.

Individuals who are confronted by angry people acting out of fear can become indignant and feel falsely accused. Those who encounter love-based fear may feel ashamed because of the harm they have done in triggering this anger. It is the duty of those who carry this anger to manage the shame so that it becomes a pathway for belonging to the community once again and does not remain a stigmatizing shame.

I find Rachel's distinctions quite helpful in broadening my sense of the place of anger in community and in defining how we might respond.

Stirring Up Drama

Numerous meetings have been torn apart by strong emotions and angry exchanges. At times, these experiences can be traced to one individual, but sometimes the stress is widespread. Other times, such anger is expressed as a prophetic message aimed at the meeting community in some way. The challenge of sorting out personal anger from a Spirit-led critique of ways in which the community has lost its way is one of the hardest things a meeting can face.

Looking back on a time when her meeting was filled with distrust and hostility, Allison Randall, an elder in New England Yearly Meeting, reflects on how she experienced this painful time.

> You will doubtless see a lot of cynicism here.
> Since a narcissist split our meeting in two,
> maybe nine years back, by proclaiming

untruths about individuals in the meeting and being a very good dramatic actor, and then quit our meeting because we didn't feel called to do all the things that he had determined we should do, then joined another meeting and threw himself into becoming well-known among Quakers, I have become cynical about the gullibility of Quakers.

If someone very good at lying, stroking people's egos, if he thinks it can advance him in some way, attaching himself to people he feels can help him on his way, and doing a lot of self-promotion, if such a person can become respected among Quakers, what does that say about us? About our ability to recognize Truth? Falsity? True prophets? False prophets?

The whole business scares me.

Allison's tiny meeting did not have a solid discipline or the resources for considering the accusations that were made or for reacting to someone who seemed to be bullying the community or otherwise acting out their own personal drama. When such is done under the guise of correcting what is wrong with the community, it makes a huge difference if there are people who can meet with the angry individual calmly and with open minds. In such interactions, the meeting should convey to the person the message that it is not appropriate to intimidate or lie about others. Second, the meeting should listen humbly to determine whether the community is doing something that needs to be changed and/or whether assistance should be given to the individual.

The Words We Use

Even seemingly tiny actions, such as referring to others in thoughtless ways, can contribute to the expansion of fear, resentment, and desire for power into mass violence. In the extreme, this can lead to genocide, as it did in central Africa in the 1990s. No one was safe from the killings. Those who survived carry with them the concern to determine what caused this catastrophe and how such horrors might be prevented.

The roots of the violence may go back, in part, to simple actions and inattention to the damaging effects of the words we use to speak of other people. Here, Moses Bigirimana (Kibimba Yearly Meeting) speaks of the effects of calling your neighbor a frog or a snake and how that can become twisted. He begins by reflecting on encountering known killers today and recognizing the potential for evil in every human being.

> What is amazing, I see that today, we meet, we talk with such men. It is being patient. Sometimes we wait. We just forgive him. We just have courage to do it, to run reconciliation programs, etc., because it happens. No perfect person exists. As long as you let the devil use you, you can be a bad person.
>
> In the context of Burundi, Hutus cannot blame Tutsis and Tutsis cannot blame Hutus. To do so you are just a partisan, because we know them being devils, but we also know them being wonderful people. This is from both sides. Not totally one side. The devil and the Holy Spirit—we are to be careful about and not let the devil become your master. If you do that you will do horrible things. I know that someone can be a good person, but if he lets the devil use him, he can be a bad person. We have examples right in front of us.

When we dehumanize other people, we open pathways to violence. Moses lived through a time when simple words blinded too many to the reality of what they were doing.

> We start saying, "My son, Hutus are bad" or "Tutsis are bad," and then it becomes "My son, don't marry a Hutu" or "Don't marry a Tutsi." Like that it comes through, and then you know that Hutus are snakes or you know that Tutsis

are awful frogs. The image of the human being you are translating into evil, into the image of a snake or a frog. Because if they are animals, who is to condemn you if you kill a snake? Who will blame you if you crush a frog? It has started just as a small thing.

It is too easy for those of us in America to think we are immune from such things. I pray that we never reach the point where genocide becomes a reality. However, here in Oregon, as in so many other places, we have experienced young men shooting their schoolmates and other similar tragedies. Then there are the people who believe that violence will change the world in a way they think will be better.

The social media has made it easy to anonymously scatter derogatory comments far and wide without taking responsibility. On the internet, we don't even see face to face the hurt we have caused, much less take ownership of the damage caused by ugly words. Finding ways to cut off streams of hatred and bullying is perhaps one task of the everyday prophet. The task can require creativity at times and good computer etiquette at other times, as well as being grounded and in a place where courage brushes away fear.

Acting to Stop Patterns of Harassment

During the early months following the election of Donald Trump as U.S. president, many people came forward posting advice on ways we might expose actions of harassment that all too often remain private and unchallenged. More people became aware of seeing, on the streets, on buses, in schools, and in other public spaces, people being challenged. They might be subject to threats because they had dark skin or wore a hijab or be subject to intimidation for any of the many reasons people harass those without power. The American Friends Service Committee encouraged anyone who witnessed such acts to intervene. They suggested:

DO
Make your presence as a witness known.
Take cues from the individual being harassed.
Keep both of you safe.

DON'T
Call the police.
Escalate the situation.
Do nothing.[2]

This is only one small way people can take their faith into the world. Acting justly does not have to be on a grand scale; it has infinite everyday dimensions. Such practical advice makes it much easier to find the courage to act. It takes away the excuse, "I didn't know what to do, what would help." The need for such witnesses has existed for centuries or even millennia. The only things that seem to have changed are the awareness of urgency and of the importance of individuals who are not intimidated by harsh language or mockery.

Resisting Lies, Becoming Truth-Tellers

The earliest Quakers called themselves Friends of Truth. Strict honesty in business became an early mark of a Friend, as did setting a single price for goods. Early Quakers were committed to honesty, but they also used the word 'Truth' as an alternative word for 'Gospel.' As historian Rosemary Moore puts it, "Their mission was 'to declare the truth.'"[3]

The Friends tradition of truth-telling and integrity seems an important way to make a witness in today's world. In the seventeenth century, one of the most visible Quaker witnesses was the use of the singular 'thee' when speaking to an individual of any social status. Since 'you' was used at the time to refer to social superiors, whether one or many, using 'thee' was subversive of the social hierarchy. I keep searching for a similar simple yet powerful witness for today. In the meantime, one task we have is to counter falsehoods wherever they appear.

Jean Zaru of Ramallah Friends Meeting in Palestine wrote the following well before "false news" and "alternative facts" became dominant issues in North American politics in the 2016 elections.

> We can never know how painful the daily newspaper can be to those who find themselves in it with no way to defend themselves to the great faceless population out there that is using it to judge them. Do we silently accept this? It is vitally important too to insist on a prophetic ministry in today's threatened world, to expose the lies and myths that have been created mainly by the powerful to cover up the pain and grief of our world. This ministry should resist the monopoly of knowledge and the power exercised by the dominant. It should struggle to forge a new discourse, one that includes critique from the margins.
>
> Therefore, it is essential that all engaged in a prophetic ministry should make contact in each place with the dispossessed, the prisoners, the immigrants, the refugees and the downtrodden. Spaces must be created for such people to share their stories of grief, to express their anger and hope.

Alongside raising up truth, Jean reminds us of the value of resistance to unjust systems. Such resistance, she tells us, can be about coming forward, being visible when society tries to make us invisible. If we accept such systems without speaking up, we have lost the possibility of transforming them to be more inclusive and compassionate.

But, it is also important to remember the need for renewal, for times apart from the struggle and the passion. Part of prophetic ministry is to take time for what early Friends called "retirement": time apart when we can renew our links with all that is holy and be steadied in our words and actions.

Steadiness

If the prophet speaks and acts based on the power of the Infinite, then that same power is holding him or her with steadfast support. Margaret Namikoye Musalia of Nairobi Yearly Meeting writes of the role the church provides in this support:

> The church . . . nurtures people who have this prophetic ministry. This ministry can be misinterpreted [as] false or truth. But the true prophetic ministry will be firm. It's never angered.

What I hear her saying is that people who hear the ministry may react quite differently to the same words, some getting behind it with enthusiasm, others disagreeing or even stating that it is a false ministry. In the face of this reality, a person with a true ministry will remain steady and not be tossed around by his or her own temper or uncertainty.

Being Energized

Anger at injustice is real and cannot be belittled. The question for me becomes one of how the anger is made manifest. Is it a source of energy in actively challenging and transforming the situation or is it a flailing about that inflicts damage and may well increase the problem? Micah Bales (Friends of Jesus Fellowship) might disagree with me. He wrote the following in his blog:

> I told [a friend] about what I witnessed, how furious I was, how wrong the men at City Realty were, and how we had to fight back. My friend was clearly concerned about the way I was talking. "What about 'that of God' in the real estate investors?" he asked me. "Aren't we called to love them, too?"

This question surprised me. I had just described a grave injustice occurring—evictions, dispossessions, the livelihood of ordinary folks being gobbled up to line the pockets of a few crafty men—and my friend's first reaction was to talk about "loving" these perpetrators of structural violence

Of course, as a follower of Jesus Christ, I am called to love my enemies. But that does not mean I do not have enemies, nor that I need to be nice to those who plot evil and eat up my people as if they were bread. Jesus knew how to call a fox a fox. He knew a den of vipers when he saw one. I looked into the face of evildoers yesterday, and I am not going to sugar-coat what I saw. I am not going to play nice with those who steal from orphans and widows.[4]

I agree with Micah on the need to call out dangerous, hateful, or otherwise evil actions. My sense is that Quakers too often misunderstand a key part of "answering that of God in everyone" by thinking it means being nice. I read it somewhat differently. It is a statement of hope and a call to live out the Sermon on the Mount, but this call might be buried deeply in some hearts. The "answering" is a process of listening for that divine spark and seeking to draw it out to where it begins to guide the actions of the person we are engaging. It may involve naming that which is not of God in someone's actions. The real challenge may be to find how to speak so that our words strike deep and make possible a turning towards the Light.

Micah continues:

Anger is a gift from God. It is an alarm bell, alerting us to the presence of conditions that we should not accept. Before we can even consider how to speak tenderly to those who are taking advantage of our people, we must first know that wrong really is wrong. We must hear the wake-up call of anger, letting us know that this kind of behavior is unacceptable. We have to feel in our bones that dispossessing the poor is evil, that pushing families out of their homes for profit is a despicable business.

For a middle class person like me, it is easy for me to treat this kind of injustice as an abstraction, but I cannot do that anymore. Holy anger has woken me up. This struggle is real, and I have to be a part of it.[5]

I also agree with much said here. It is right to be angry at oppression. Anger is an alarm bell, as Micah says. And I am one of those middle-class people who have been taught to suppress anger at all costs. Passive-aggressive behavior is not the stance of the prophetic minster. But neither is uncontrolled fury, the desire to hurt others, or revenge.

Lashing out, however, is all too often a sign of impotence, and it easily triggers an increasingly visceral response from the oppressor without making the oppression visible, much less stopping it or rousing others to change their ways and stand against evil. Too often, anger pushes us to take up the very behavior we would condemn.

As Micah says, the call for us is to avoid getting tangled in our emotional fervor. Instead, may we know the hand of God's presence and be transformed so that we may speak out with conviction and stand up in the face of injustice.

Compassion for the Angry Prophet

Over the years, I have come to respect the fact that many (or all) of us need safe places to let loose our anger or other powerful emotions that can build within us, to express them in a way that will not harm others or damage the community. In so doing, we need people who can call us back to the truth and compassion that we seek. Anthony Manousos (Pacific Yearly Meeting) writes of one such incident:

> A few years ago, when my wife passed away of cancer, I was asked to clerk the pastoral care and the peace committee at the same time. This was very unusual, but [clerking these two committees concurrently] helped me to see that often behind people's strong political and social concerns there are psychological or physical wounds or suffering.
>
> Realizing that helped [me] to respond more compassionately when prophetic concerns came up and some Friends responded with more heat than light. Often it was because of some personal issue. I realized how important it is to not let our concern for issues get in the way of love.

One caution this raises in me is to note that it can be tempting to "diagnose" the mental health of others in our community. There is enough psychological knowledge floating around to make it easy to say "he is bipolar" or "she is depressed" with no basis in anything other than our own assumptions. This tendency needs to be resisted. Can we take care to recognize the difference between stating reasons that help us understand others, being patronizing, and labeling people in demeaning ways? At times, suggesting that someone may benefit from professional advice is needed, but with much gentleness. Our gifts are as a spiritual community, and, as such, we can seek ways to help each other stay grounded.

Knowing the Winds of the Spirit

Strong emotions can toss any of us around, just as winds can whip the sails of a boat and threaten to throw it on the rocks. The first thing the sailor has to do as the storm arises is to make sure he or she knows where the wind is coming from and how the seas are moving. The sailor must then look to adjust the sails, often taking some sails down or reefing them in so that the wind will not overpower the craft. Such skills are honed by the experience, sometimes terrifying, of being out in a storm and knowing when to run for a safe harbor, if possible.

There are many situations in which uncontrolled emotions may gain immediate attention but are ultimately destructive. Firm knowledge of a situation, perseverance, preparation both spiritual and practical—and finding adequate support—can be determining factors in work aimed at ending injustice or violence.

Anger has its place in prophetic work. The challenge to some who carry a prophetic ministry is to see any anger that arises within for what it truly is and be able to note when it is leading them counter to the Guide. It is a gift to be able to move with the energy of the anger without being consumed by it and ultimately allowing it to negate the movement towards justice. Often, the best course is to step aside and let the anger subside and then move forward with patient faithfulness to name what is wrong and to act on that which we are truly led to change.

Queries for Reflection and/or Discussion

1. Have you experienced righteous anger or been with others who have? What was the source of this anger, and how was it expressed? What actions were taken, and how were they received?

2. Has anger played a part in decision-making in your church or meeting? How was it received, and how did people respond? What was the source of the anger, and how did it affect the community?

3. How should Friends respond to anger when it arises in the community? How might we best sort out the prophetic message from personal emotions and motives?

BEING PART OF THE WHOLE

The following section on community (meeting or church) is comprised of six chapters. For two millennia, Christianity has raised up the body, the body of Christ, as a central image of the church. Today, we have a new way of talking about how all life is interrelated. This section opens with an exploration of MINISTRY AS PART OF A HEALTHY ECOSYSTEM.

DISCERNMENT IN COMMUNITY is one of the distinctive ways of Friends. Sorting out the different emotions and pressures on our lives, communally as well as individually, is essential to knowing and responding to the Light.

As a community, we have the responsibility of WALKING WITH ONE ANOTHER, be it in pain, in confusion, or in celebration. We also carry a vision of the world handed down from our spiritual ancestors that is still vibrant and alive today if we tend the fires.

As a community, we also have the tender responsibility of paying attention to each other's calling. Can we remind ourselves that we are each BEING HELD TO ACCOUNT by that Inward Guide and still have the discipline to know we can't fix it all and to let others live with integrity?

Even at our best, it is not unusual for individuals to be at odds. What happens WHEN THE COMMUNITY RESISTS? The prophet can often feel alone, as if carrying a huge weight that needs multiple hands and backs to lift. Reconciliation and forgiveness can do much to weave us together. SILENCE IN THE COMMUNITY is central to our way of being. Expectant silence in worship can be life-giving. Silence can also be deadening or damaging to relationships. May we grow in our knowledge of ways to nurture the silence that sustains and empowers us.

CHAPTER 20
MINISTRY AS PART OF A HEALTHY ECOSYSTEM

How, in a secular age, do we describe our faith community? My impulse is to look for more fluid, dynamic ways of conceptualizing how we relate to one another and offer the Spirit-led service often named as ministry. Ecological concepts offer another language and unexpected perspectives on the world and our place in it.

In the Bible, Paul makes repeated use of the image of the body of Christ to explain what he means by community, but I turn more towards the concept of the ecosystem. No metaphor fully matches the reality we face, so I find it helpful to have more than one way to articulate what I hope for. Each of these images tells us we are not alone and that our actions affect others, just as their actions affect us.

What if we step back and consider each community in which we live or worship as an ecosystem whose health and resilience is shaped by the spirituality of its members? A healthy human ecosystem is one in which many individuals are willing to minister to the community and to cherish their interdependence despite the painful demands it may place on them. No one is totally isolated.

Our awareness of the larger forces shaping our world (the shifting climate, for example), is important. Are the winds and rains damaging or valuable? How might we respond? What message, what warning might we have for those in other ecosystems? Just as scientists are learning that the melting of ice in Greenland has global repercussions, what can we see in our Quaker ecosystem that has ramifications for the spiritual and physical well-being of this globe we inhabit?

Balance Point: A State of Equilibrium

Ecology—the science of how we and all other living things co-exist on this planet—is a subject that humanity is only beginning to grasp. Even at our most optimistic, we can only say we have small glimpses of it. The creation is full of beauty, of wonder, of marvel that stretches our imagination. Creation is also full of dangers and has its own complex balance of life and death. Change is a constant, yet change is terrifying to many. Ecosystems may find an equilibrium that lasts for a time, but then something shifts and adaptation is needed. Several words can be used to reflect the condition in which two or many different forces carry similar weight. I especially like the third definition of balance in the 1996 unabridged Webster's dictionary: "mental steadiness of emotional stability; habit of calm behavior, judgment, etc."

Many see creation as part of a divine plan with the establishment of humanity at its center. In Genesis 1:28, God tells Adam and Eve to *"be fruitful and multiply, and fill the earth and subdue it."* In this recounting, humanity—made in the image of God—is to have dominion over the earth and all its creatures. As we attempt to respond to the increasing disruption of the balance of nature, which is due in significant part to the actions of humanity, it is hard not to condemn the Genesis story as destructive. I seek to find another way to read this account of how humanity thousands of years ago made sense of their place on this globe. I am certain that a literal reading of this verse as licensing humans to blindly consume the resources of the globe and to misuse creation for our own pleasure is not what is intended. That reading is inconsistent with much else in the Bible.

Here I touch on only a fraction of the images and dimensions of thought that arise from considering ourselves part of an ecosystem. In an ecosystem, each individual is dependent on others; individuals interact with each other. Ecosystems depend on light and water to thrive. When the balance is disrupted, as by flooding, excessive heat, or the loss of key species, the whole is upset and perhaps torn apart. The complexity and resilience of life on this planet is wonderful to contemplate, but human actions are stressing the ability of many species to thrive.

Ecosystems are not static, rigid, or completely isolated. The system is part of a cycle in which a substance that is viewed as waste one moment becomes freely incorporated into fresh soil and nourishes plants and the multitude of creatures that inhabit each bit of ground. There is a give and take of nutrients and other dimensions of life, some within the system and some from adjacent areas.

Mount St. Helens is easy to see from Portland, and I watched daily from my office for years as it repeatedly exploded in huge clouds of ash and steam. It seemed impossible that anything would survive. The 1980 eruption took over one thousand feet off the top of the mountain. Hot ash and snowmelt wiped out large sections of the valleys leading away from the mountain. Yet, in the thirty-plus years since then, the forests on the slopes of Mount St. Helens are reforming and elk walk the slopes. Seeds buried in the ash survived and have sprouted. In human terms, thirty years is a long time, but this eruption is a reminder that the cycle of renewal takes time and often happens out of sight. Such images remind me of the value of patience. The silence of meeting for worship can work quietly on our hearts and minds in ways not visible for months or years.

Living Water at the Heart of Ministry

Ecosystems may be healthy or unhealthy. Water is essential to human life as well as to so much else of creation. There is the water of life that nourishes the soul as well as the liquid water that sustains the body. In the Pacific Northwest, many in the Quaker world are engaged, open, and caring across traditions that have renounced each other. These individuals seek forgiveness for the ways in which we inadvertently hurt one another and focus on the benefit to the whole rather than on our personal wounds. Yet too many of us rage or spread fear, knocking communities out of balance just as the pine beetles destroy trees and leave them vulnerable to fire. Living Water is an essential image to return to again and again.

The nature of our interactions affects us at a level it is hard to imagine, perhaps even at the level of the cells of our body. Ministry is grounded in compassion: love for one another, for this planet we share, and for the Eternal. Early Friends sensed the weight their words carried and took great care in how they spoke about and towards each other. Today we have tools and language that allow us to see new dimensions of our impacts.

A Healthy Ecosystem

Ecology, "the concept and the reality of an interwoven universe we increasingly experience and confirm with body, heart, and mind," in the words of Ken Jacobsen (Ohio Yearly Meeting), is appropriate for our day and age. In many ways, shifts in the climate are shaking our confidence and assurance that life will continue as it always has. Nonetheless, the use of ecological concepts might help shift our hearts and actions, giving us ways to reconceptualize our relationships with one another in community as well as our relationship to the natural world.

Various Friends have offered glimpses throughout this book of what our meetings might look like when they are attuned to the heart of creation, leading us to care for the whole of the world around us, both locally and globally. Here is what I offer as a starting point.

- A healthy ecosystem is always in a transitional state, responding to shifts in weather patterns, natural disasters, migrations, etc. Thus, we might regularly ask, How can we create human institutions that change and adapt as conditions around them change yet retain at the core that which gives life?

- Many processes of ecosystems are resilient in the face of change, in response to internal or external stress. I am fascinated to watch the forests of Mount Hood regenerate—although not always on a human timescale—after fires pass across the landscape.

- Deep beneath the surface, scientists have come to learn, are interconnections; the roots of trees and fungi weave together in surprising ways. Science and spirituality both act to reveal unexpected dimensions of human capabilities.

- Climax forests, like human communities, are mosaics and consist of multiple stages. All are needed. Dying leaves, trunks of trees, and creatures of all sorts, when allowed to rot naturally, provide whole new generations with nutrients. The nursery logs in rain forests are a visible symbol of this renewal and rebirth that sustains natural communities.

- The natural world is not free of pain and horror. Our spiritual ancestors developed what Rosemary Moore calls "a theology of suffering"[1] in response to their experience. They regularly faced imprisonment, loss of homes, and other penalties as a consequence of worshipping outside the state-sanctioned church. Our challenge, like theirs, is to recognize and articulate our relationship with God, with each other, and with the world that acknowledges the pain and danger of life as well as the beauty and joy and that embraces the fullness of humanity's condition.

- Isolated ecological systems can preserve unique conditions and eventually be of value to the whole when massive damage is done elsewhere. Some Quakers consider Conservative Friends an example of such a community. If this is so, what have they

206

preserved for us? How might we be strengthened by their example? What is the cost?

- Unhealthy systems have toxic by-products. Can we recognize toxic relationships among us and name them as such? How might we develop ways to neutralize the toxins, especially to protect the vulnerable but also to nurture the everyday prophets, creating a place among us to sustain those called to radical witness?

- Just as in the human body, each participant in an ecosystem or a meeting has its role to play; if we act faithfully, we contribute to the health of the system.

As I work with these concepts and see what applies to the reality of our lives, I better appreciate the metaphor of the body. Modern science describes the complexity of the human body as a living system—an ecology of its own, if you will—bringing into the picture the crucial work of veins and arteries, of nerves and organs, of bacteria and enzymes. The wonder of this multitude of layers and interdependence rivals the natural ecosystems of our forests and deserts.

The Body of Christ

Many Friends around the world cherish the sense of being part of the body of Christ. Since it is such a well-known image, I will only note the connections between all the parts and their mutual dependence to varying degrees. Joe Snyder (North Pacific Yearly Meeting) writes of his understanding of the community as the body of Christ as described in Corinthians, recognizing that prophetic ministry is given to the community, not *to* the individual but *through* the individual:

Paul talks about the church as the body of Christ, and that image/metaphor has been an important part of my faith understanding. Prophecy is an important gift for the development and growth of the body. The gift may not be given to everyone, but prophetic words are given to everyone, to the body as a whole, to make it fit and join it together in growth and unity. Growth is not always easy, and the words may not be easy to hear. If they are authentic, though, they will move the body into greater unity and maturity despite, or perhaps because of, any discomfort they bring.

Seeing our communities as a single body makes it simple to lift up the ways in which each of us plays a unique role in sensing and responding to the world around us. Every participant has the responsibility to inform the whole of what he or she experiences, be it the signs of pain that, when addressed, can heal or the delights of the warm aromas that tell us of the foods that sustain the whole. At the same time, I find it easy to see this metaphor as sustaining a hierarchy—I simply think about the little finger responding to the brain.

Our bodies also can be thrown out of balance and harbor deadly toxins. As Joe reminds us, some of our organs, most notably our livers, have significant overcapacity, which means that it is possible to drink excessive amounts of alcohol for years before the system collapses, possibly fatally. Science articulates what our spiritual ancestors knew intuitively, that our daily words and actions are as important as our long-term objectives. It is as easy to go astray in multiple small ways as it is to misread the big picture.

Just as there are advantages and limitations to using the human body as a metaphor for our meetings, there are also limitations to the metaphor of an ecological system. All too often people look at the natural world and come to easy conclusions, such as "survival of the fittest," that justify a damaging action they wish to take. A major challenge for all of us is to raise up the awareness that even the pride of lions, deadly as they are to their prey, is dependent on the weakest of the animals around them. When their prey disappears, so do they.

Another aspect of the natural world that is contrary to all that my faith tells me relates to how we treat the weakest of those around us. For the lion, the very young, the old, and the ill in a herd of elands are the best prey. At one level, we can see that removing the weak allows the remainder of the herd to thrive. Yet that voice within, the Guide to all that is holy, speaks of the centrality of protecting the weak and allowing them to thrive, and we all gain from such compassion. Any one of us might be that weak, ill eland trailing behind its herd, its community.

The Ecosystem of Ministry

So, how might we link more clearly the concepts of ecosystems and prophetic ministry? It is easy to think about nature in terms of the raw and sometimes violent nature of the food chain—eat or be eaten is the message of many classic television documentaries about the wild. What if we focus instead on natural systems as places where balance is essential in maintaining the systems? Humanity is only beginning to grasp the interrelationships that are essential in the natural world. The actions of one affect the lives of others, a perspective that can apply to the spiritual community as well as the physical world.

Jan Hoffman (New England Yearly Meeting) is one of several of my respondents who place their ministry firmly within the worshipping community around them. She describes this as the "ecosystem of ministry." I read her statement in light of a broad concept of ecosystems that includes the complex interactions of physical matter and spiritual and physical energy as well as the interplay of information and communication. Some meetings recognize individual gifts and then provide active support as well as accountability. Doing so sets a context that nourishes and strengthens individuals amid the sometimes frightening and lonely practice of listening to and acting on the motions of the Spirit in the heart. Jan offers this experience:

For me, there is a whole ecosystem of ministry of which the actual speaker is just a part. For instance, Mount Toby Meeting extended its own Sunday worship to join (spiritually) with Friends in the final worship at the 2005 Friends United Meeting Triennial that I was leading. I discovered later that at some point in that worship at Mount Toby, someone rose to say, "Jan is speaking at this very moment—hold on firmly." I believe that was indeed the moment I did begin offering the message I was given. All this matters.

Jan's awareness of the ecosystem of ministry "begins with the felt awareness of Life already present within." It is a grace; it is unearned. It is about "life seeking life." Ministry "simply makes God more visible."

Jan asserts that corporate worship provides an opportunity to practice seeking this Life together; in this process, the expectation of tension between individual and corporate needs and leadings is foundational.

Passing of the Seasons

Every meeting goes through its own cycle, from the planting of the seed and the formation of a stable community through fat years and lean years and the time to be laid down. This waxing and waning applies to how we receive those among us who experience a call to ministry. Robert Greenleaf says in *Servant Leadership* that we get the prophets we deserve—those that we will give room to—not necessarily the prophets we need to hear:

> The variable that marks some periods as barren and some as rich in prophetic vision is in the interest, the level of seeking, the responsiveness of the hearers. The variable is not in the presence or absence or the relative quality and force of the prophetic voices.

Prophets grow in stature as people respond to their message. . . .

It is *seekers*, then, who make prophets.[2]

I am aware of at least some of the fluctuations among unprogrammed Friends over the decades I have worshipped among them. Resistance to spiritual, and particularly Christian, language in many meetings has at times been pronounced. Some resistance came with the waves of social justice activists. Some was the result of the cautiousness around speaking about belief arising from the reunion of meetings that had once split over these issues. Some resulted from conscious tenderness towards new participants who were fleeing other faith communities' use of the concepts of hellfire and damnation and salvation as hammers to mandate conformity or who were disillusioned by encounters with hypocritical individuals. There is thus good reason for much of this resistance.

Learning to Fly

South of Mount Hood in Oregon, a group of scientists gathers every fall on Bonney Butte to count the hawks, eagles, and other raptors as they fly south for the winter. I've taken the heavily rutted dirt road to Bonney Butte several times during this annual count and have been able to sit in the blind where hawks are briefly captured and banded and then let free again unharmed. To capture the hawks, a pigeon (dressed in leather "armor" to protect it) is placed outside the blind. Passing hawks see it and dive down in hopes of a quick meal. Sitting in the blind, I learned that not all hawks catch the pigeon. Young birds, in particular, can be pretty bad at it. It takes them a while to gain the skills essential to feeding themselves. Foolishly, I had assumed that they just "knew" how to capture prey. I have since learned that spiritual muscles need training, too, which is a process that resonates viscerally with my experience of learning to play the piano.

The Bible offers lovely images of divine presence that give a sense of growth and imply that we are initially helpless and need someone to help guard us and nurture us as we learn. In Psalm 131:2, the soul is seen as a weaned child with its mother. Jesus offers the image of the mother hen and her chicks in Luke 13:34. In Isaiah 40:31, those who rely on God shall mount up with wings like an eagle. In all these images, there is a blend of dependence and growing independence, of coming to know that which is essential to life in the very bones of our bodies so that our wings may lift us into flight.

Native Species

My spiritual native species is among Quakers. One of my challenges has been to recognize that this "species" is much broader than I was taught as a child. Part of my ministry is to engage with evangelical Friends. We arose out of the same basic ecosystem but now inhabit adjacent valleys and struggle to cross those boundaries. As we engage with each other, we find more resources that help us all thrive and enlarge our sense of what our ecosystems look like. Our connection with God expands across not only our Quaker ecosystems but also the entire human biosphere. Lloyd Lee Wilson (North Carolina Yearly Meeting [Conservative]) speaks of the relationship of the minister to the community in a way that sounds much like a species in its native environment.

> True prophets of necessity must be and feel an integral part of the worshiping community they are called to address. Their ministry is expressed in the first person, 'we,' rather than the second person, 'you.'
>
> The work of the prophet is carried out in a "covenant triangle" consisting of God, the faith community, and the prophet. Each of these actors is in an ongoing dialogue with each of the others concerning the prophetic task.

Prophets should not expect to be respected and accepted for their work—it's just not in the job description.

Prophetic ministry takes a long time. Don't expect quick results from being faithful in this work.

Native species do not necessarily have an easy time thriving. An ecological system contains many competing plants and animals that have adapted to each other to varying degrees. Adaptation usually involves pushing and pulling—tensions reflecting the wide-ranging needs of many individuals. The intrusion of new species, brought by humans or blown on the winds, can seriously upset the balance of a given ecosystem and damage many of its components.

In our separate Quaker ecosystems, prophetic ministry sometimes looks quite different. These differences can be growing points in the complexity of discernment. We have in our separate valleys incorporated alien species, such as the pastoral system and resistance to accepting Jesus as Savior. Over the decades, such intrusions have become integrated into our communities. When we interact, those of us from different valleys see more clearly the invasive species in the midst of other valleys and may better assess what is life-giving and what is destroying the native habitat in those other valleys. In coming together, we have found renewal as we have engaged with what we once saw only as harmful.

Wild Weeds, Neglect, and Ignorance

Wild weeds can sprout and thrive when local communities fail individuals. We are tempted more than we would hope by vivid but toxic blooms—the attractions of the culture around us. But when there is a solid core, an interweaving of deep roots is evident in unexpected moments.

Margaret Namikoye Musalia (Nairobi Yearly Meeting) states, "I am what I am because of this great Evangelist who taught me and empowered me for the ministry." She values the aid she was given in bringing to fruition the lessons she found in Scripture and heard from God's Spirit. She then notes her place in the church through preaching and prayer, emphasizing the need to stand firm.

Margaret then succinctly lists some of the qualities detrimental to a healthy spiritual ecosystem: "There is no teaching. There is no nurturing. There is no caring. There is no spiritual support." She cites certain traits as inherently toxic, such as dismissing others because they don't fit our image of what a Quaker should be. I see times in my own meeting when back-biting or criticism of what is said in worship starts to fester. When that goes unchecked, the atmosphere can be poisoned. Such toxic behavior can stifle vital leadings, especially from new and tender ministers.

When an ecosystem is out of balance, the forest can turn deadly. Without experience in finding sustenance or safe places for refuge, most young cannot thrive. So it is in our communities. People are needed who can hold the space that allows others to see God at work in our midst. Such people can affirm those who are testing their voice or are newly learning to discern the guidance of the Inward Teacher.

Margaret also notes times when the stream of Living Water is flowing weakly or has dried up completely. Without this Living Water, the community cannot thrive. Margaret closes by claiming the prophetic ministry that grows out of the healthy Quaker ecosystem:

> But I believe the Quakers had this prophetic ministry of making peace, loving people equally, sharing materials, finances and spiritual. Those who got the word, God spoke to them. Speak the truth and you have to affirm

your Yes is Yes and No is No. This was surely prophetic ministry all over the world.

In this, she voices a challenge to all of us in a world where truth and accuracy seem valued less and less.

The Kudzu of the Soul

One of the things humans have enabled is the spread of plants and animals into virtually every corner of the globe. As this happens, creatures that are benign in their native habitat become aggressive and splash widely across landscapes where the plants and creatures that kept them in balance are missing. An attractive houseplant or would-be pet goes wild, leaving little room for native species that once thrived. Stopping this process can seem impossible, just as it seems impossible to shift humanity away from the appeal of aggression and desire for control at the expense of those with less power. Jan Wood (Sierra-Cascades Yearly Meeting of Friends) writes:

> Changing a culture seems as impossible as trying to catch a cloud. Yet cultures are constantly changing. We have all seen this happen before our very eyes. As Americans, we have cultivated a garden where violence . . . has become part and parcel of our worldview. We have made all other lives and futures dispensable when violence suits our aims. And this part of our culture is destroying our souls, our relationships, our communities, and our nation from the inside out. It is the kudzu of our souls.[3]

I recall the dismay expressed when people realized that kudzu, which was introduced to the American South to stabilize soil, was able to spread and take over the landscape. People felt a sense of helplessness as this vine spread and spread. I experience some of this same sensation when I listen to people I know talk about their helplessness in the face of American militarism and the materialistic fervor of our culture. Yet Jan feels a hope and a direction:

> There is something deep that is calling God's people to the prophetic; a place of voluntary standing with and repenting for a deeply corrupted American culture. It isn't enough to just try to be better than the culture. Deep compassion and broken hearts compel us to call out to God on behalf of our culture. . . . Let us simply stop. Stop inwardly justifying our own choices and sink into the broken-heartedness that is called for. The list of what everyone else should and must do goes silent. In that space, we can feel a deep wellspring of repentance. A broken and contrite heart that simply collapses before God and cries out: "Oh God, forgive us!"[4]

Jan concludes: "May it begin with us." In the face of despair, may we come to know the brokenness that is the path to new life and be something other than agents of hopelessness. May we live this new creation into being—free of poisons and out-of-control, destructive weeds—through divine guidance.

A Fragile Community: Finding Resilience

Established ecosystems are resilient, able to recover from many pressures and disruptions. Yet there is a potential fragility to the environment when it is in the process of becoming or it is disturbed beyond a certain point.

I've watched the area around Mount St. Helens as mosses, brambles, insects, and wildflowers have returned following the eruption in 1980 that seemed so devastating nothing could ever thrive again. There is a pattern to succession as the hardiest plants become established first. Fireweed and other hardy specimens provide nourishment and habitat for seeds buried in the ash or carried in by birds. A new ecosystem is evolving with a different mix of trees and animals than was there before, a reminder that our human systems shift as well and that interdependence aids the new to arise.

Alternatively, we can easily see the breaking point for well-established ecosystems in the Appalachians, where mountaintop mining of coal is prevalent. Huge machinery slices through plants, soil, and rock, churning it up in ways that bring toxic chemicals and metals to the surface, contaminating streams and aquifers. The debris is pushed into valleys, cutting off streams and changing the entire landscape faster than it can recover. Such is true of our human communities when we ignore the soul.

Kathleen Wooten (New England Yearly Meeting) speaks to what the fragility of newness might look like in our meeting communities.

> Now I stand at a very new edge. . . . this call to intervisitation is ministry. . . . The call to visit [other meetings] in worship, to experience together that always-new breaking in of God . . . and to name it [is] to enable God to knit us back together. In relationship with each other, listening, acting as called—so many new edges, and our community is so fragile, so brittle, so unable to hold the powerful love that needs to be poured in. Poured into, and over, and around and through us all.

Resilience in our communities—the ability to recover following disturbance—is measured by the degree we can love one another and be vehicles for the infinite love that is beyond all human comprehension. Kathleen continues:

> We need to be the community we long to see in the world. The gifts, the Way—it has all been given to us. It has been laid upon the hearts of so many in our monthly meetings. They know it too. We all just think we are alone in being able to see it.

The idea that each of us only *thinks* we are alone and capable of being self-sufficient pokes at my tendency to go it alone. I may just have a self-centered habit of forgetting how much wisdom is present in others, something that is easy to do when someone doesn't totally agree with me. The prophet stands in an odd place, both dependent on the wisdom of the community yet at times mandated to call the community to account. Love has to be integral to this evolving relationship or else our words become damaging rather than life-giving.

The Hebrew people carried the tradition and knowledge of God's steadfast love, *hesed*, which is an act of compassion, not a romantic notion. God calls the nation to welcome the stranger with love and treat him or her as part of the community. Marriage and family are often used as metaphors to describe loving relationships that are characterized by a sense of responsibility, caring, and loving-kindness. First John 4:8 states firmly, *He who does not love does not know God, for God is love.*

The Individual in the Environment

Not surprisingly, very different concepts speak to different individuals. Some on the more liberal or radical end of the Quaker spectrum see God present and active in all aspects of the world we live in and see ourselves as part of the ongoing web of life. Mary Gilbert (New England Yearly Meeting), who has been dedicated to the work of Quaker Earthcare Witness, offers a vivid image of this way of seeing the place of the individual in community:

> Think of a mushroom. The largest life form on earth happens to be an underground filament-style fungus occupying many square miles, and I don't know how deep it goes. It's also the weightiest life form. But the mushroom you may see briefly on the surface is just the "fruiting body" of the fungus. It's not even necessary to the organism's survival or

thriving. I, as me, Mary Gilbert, am like a mushroom. I'm a living part of the Earth but really a temporary fruiting body with a short time span. Analogously, I am also the whole filamentous organism out of sight below the ground. I am Mary Gilbert, who is a temporary organization of molecules that are flowing through my form as I am born, grow, do things, and then die. My real nature is that I am a fragment of how the Earth is manifesting at this moment. . . . So, the planet is my real body.

This is a perspective that makes me uneasy, even as I relate to parts of what Mary has to say. I see humanity as one portion of the life on this planet and believe we will do great damage to ourselves or, at the extreme, even destroy our own race if we do not pay attention to how we treat the whole of the world around us. In some ways, Mary is saying something similar to those who speak of being the body of Christ, only rather than using the human body as the template, she uses the globe we live on and all living beings as part of Christ.

More than anything, this image of the mushroom emphasizes the reality that the structures and roots that support life are often hidden, unseen. The Spirit is similarly hidden—an invisible energy that shapes how we interact with the world.

The images of the body and the environment both express interdependence and stress relationship. Both images value aspects of the whole that seem small or almost irrelevant, be they a little finger or an amoeba. As the earlier quotations of Joe Snyder and Lloyd Lee Wilson demonstrate, both images can fit with Christianity. The place where they speak to me of different dimensions of relationships is in their placement of humanity. The one image places humanity as central and the human body as a metaphor for Christ present among us. The other image visualizes the entirety of life on earth as the measuring point. In this latter metaphor, the body of

Christ includes animals, plants, and other life forms as well as humanity. It sets us in a different relationship to the world and brings to the fore a concept of stewardship that recognizes our responsibility to all living things, which have value in themselves, rather than seeing all other life as being put on earth for the purpose of sustaining humanity. Few people would advocate either extreme. My tendency is to look for the ways each is useful.

In researching this book, I did not ask Friends to address this question of how to describe our mutual relationships and responsibilities, The Friends I know best would tend to say that we have to step back from seeing humans as having total dominance and other species as existing only for our benefit.

Being Part of an Ecosystem

The tensions of spiritual life and death and of rebirth and renewal after loss define the shifting balance points for my faith. A thread marking such balance points runs through the Bible. I treasure the thread that begins with the glory of creation and the awareness that humanity holds a unique place to do good or ill, meaning that we should take the needs of the whole of creation into consideration. This thread runs through the glorious visions of Isaiah and the life and words of Jesus to the beauty of the city of God in Revelation, and it runs through all the world and all forms of faith. I see this beauty permeating Quaker ministry and linking together the various forms it takes. The tensions between justice and compassion and humility and boldness challenge all of us as we respond to the interdependence and the freedom that are dimensions of the ecosystem of ministry. The prophets help hold us to account both by being living examples of love visible here in the messiness of human existence and by pointing out when we have forgotten to drink of the living waters or weed the kudzu that has engulfed the fields.

Queries for Reflection and/or Discussion

1. How do Friends in your church or meeting relate to one another? Is there a sense of mutual support and interconnection? What helps that thrive?

2. How might you describe the ecosystem in which you live and love and have your being? Where is the nourishment? What are the threats? Where is the balance point, the place of equilibrium?

3. What metaphor best helps you find language to speak about the nature of Friends meetings and churches and our mutual relationships? How do you respond to the idea of the meeting or church as being like an ecosystem? How do you respond to the idea of it being like a body (as Paul states in Corinthians)?

4. Can you see characteristics of a healthy ecosystem in your community? What does that look like? What is missing? What might you act to change?

5. What are the implications of using metaphors? How do they help you understand your relation to your church or meeting community? Do they help you better relate to people or situations you find difficult?

CHAPTER 21
DISCERNMENT IN COMMUNITY

When God taps a person on the shoulder and says, "Do this," a natural response—and perhaps the only appropriate response—seems to be, "Who, me? I am not adequate." In contrast to the fishermen who left their nets when Jesus said, "Follow me," many are the stories of prophets who need to hear the words "Fear not, for I am with you." The great prophets whose stories have come down to us over the centuries did not seek out this calling. In fact, like Jonah, running away from God's call seems to be good common sense. With all our human frailties, finding ways to stand with those who have felt a leading to take up a concern or a call to ministry is a blessing to the community and to the individual who benefits from the practical moral and spiritual care of the group.

Discernment and the call to prophetic ministry are in many ways intensely individual. The call may come in direct words or in visions. Isaiah, Jeremiah, Daniel, and many other Hebrew prophets had such an experience. They also had the clarity that God was speaking to them even if no one around them could hear the words they heard or see what they saw.

However, while acknowledging that the primary discernment is for the individual to know, Friends have always placed great weight on testing individual discernment in community, particularly with others who are known to be aware of the movement of the Spirit. As I will cover in more detail in the next chapter, at times this discernment may involve checking with a few others informally. Or, when the individual has a strong call to ministry or a leading to speak on behalf of Friends in the wider world, there is an expectation that either the entire meeting or a committee acting on its behalf will test the leading and also determine in what ways the community should actively support this work.

The Alternative Community

Walter Brueggemann's book *The Prophetic Imagination* places the prophetic ministry of the Hebraic tradition squarely in the hands of alternative communities that can step back critically from the dominant culture and hear and acknowledge pain as well as articulate hope. His view of the prophet is of one who is attentive enough to see the reality of society, offer a critique based on what has been heard, mourn the ways it falls short, and energize those who would change. In this way, the prophet provides an alternative vision of a way we might live.[1]

As noted earlier, lamentation and vision are both central functions for Hebrew prophets. Woven through the prophetic stories is a sense of apartness, of being apart from the mainstream, feeling a223ware of what seems obvious but no one else sees. This apartness also points to a major threat to prophecy—if the prophet is believed and accepted, how does the prophet avoid being part of creating or perpetuating the next round of growing control and injustice? Every human system carries such seeds.

"I Saw That I Had No Partner"

Being alone has always had an allure for me. In part, this arises from my introversion—I do need time alone to refocus myself, to settle in prayer, to be refreshed. In part, being alone has been a haven from the threats of the world. If no one else is present, I don't have to always watch my back, expecting to hear derisive comments or face hostility. Thus, the lure of aloneness has been a way of addressing my fears, but being alone also means there is nothing to counter imaginary fears that can build without contradiction. Having a community that would help sustain me spiritually was once outside my imagination.

Tom Gates (Philadelphia Yearly Meeting) reflects on the connections developing among Friends around him and gives a glimpse of what it is like to discover a community of support.

> Each case . . . where I had seen people centered in a prophetic activity, where they had experienced a change . . . and were continually living into that changed consciousness, I found commonalities. The thing that stood out . . . was that they all had partners in their activity . . . [or] had a community to whom they submitted in all humility and tenderness in order to remain in good order themselves.

Entering a prophetic community, for Tom, meant finding other everyday prophets. The lives of these people made visible practical actions in the world to relieve suffering and help others support themselves, gain education, and otherwise thrive. The people whose lives touched Tom's showed him what it is to be grounded in God. They were spiritually centered, and the community around them helped them hold that center.

> I saw that I had no partner and hadn't done the internal work of being in a spiritually based partnership. It was also clear that I found myself continually unwilling to submit to anyone else's spiritual guidance, even to the point of being proud of this fact. I saw that my desire to serve was itself prideful. I more or less wanted to be able to look at myself as being a heroic warrior for peace but hadn't done the preparation.

Tom then reflects on the preparation that is part of the prophetic motion. Being in an alternative community, a community that sees its core guide as the Eternal Light, provides a place to experience what it means to be obedient to divine leading. In the very everyday interactions within such a community, we can see our own arrogance. These people quietly make visible our weaknesses and point to a surer Guide than human ego. Tom came to see that the goal was not to be seen as the heroic warrior but to be faithful.

"Unclear If I Was Faithful"

The discipline of listening is a concept that arises again and again. Can we hear or sense the call to act justly? Can we feel the movement of the Holy Spirit within? Just as with the balance of species needed for a healthy ecosystem, such listening is the responsibility of both the speaker and the one who is hearing the words.

The Spirit can also be felt guiding the community as a whole, be it during meeting for worship, in conducting the business of the meeting, or whenever we focus on what is holy. Jan Hoffman (New England Yearly Meeting) describes her experience as a plenary speaker at New York Yearly Meeting and how this blend of individual and group discernment affected the message she had to give to the gathered community:

> When I arrived, nothing was set up, and I felt very alone. I began opening windows, moving the clerks' table and chairs off the stage, finding the podium.
> Once we were settled into worship, I realized . . . I was alone on the stage, and felt this keenly, which increased my sense of unease. I prayed to feel God's presence and tried to remember the elders in the body of the meeting holding me in that Presence.
> During the talk, it seemed to me that I looked at my paper more than usual yet didn't see things. I seemed not to discern from a centered or grounded place [or reach] the rhythm God had given me for the talk. At this point, I said to those gathered, "I need your help. I realize I could go on talking about meeting for business and not go on to fear and authority because I think I'm afraid of what I might be given to say." I was not able to feel such help forthcoming.
> At the conclusion of my talk, I burst into tears. I felt . . . unclear if I was faithful. . . . One

elder then asked, "But who in that room was more faithful than you? Those who listen need to be faithful, too. You can take some responsibility, but not all of it."

For Jan, a Friend who doubted her own faithfulness, the presence of others who specifically had been asked to uphold her and of a community willing to hear her message was essential to freeing the truth she was given to speak. She experienced the two-way nature of ministry. Even when an individual knows the words they are supposed to say, if the listener is not there, be it emotionally or physically, the message has no life.

True and False Prophets

Allison Randall raises a very logical question for Friends: "If the definition of a prophet is someone who communicates with God and passes on the communication to others, isn't anyone who speaks in meeting by the guidelines we have a prophet?" Yes is my immediate answer, but I would emphasize Allison's mention of the "guidelines we have." In other words, simply being a Quaker or naming oneself as a prophet or as having a prophetic ministry is not sufficient (nor do Quakers have any special claim on the prophetic).

Stories abound of occasions when someone has proclaimed a ministry only to experience rejection or disbelief by the community. Sorting out such differences is an important role of the community, holding open the possibility that the least likely among us may be speaking the truth and also that the individual has to accept the possibility of being wrong.

Our meetings include individuals who do not accept any community authority over their actions. Some meetings are strong enough to hold a wide array of views on who we are and what we as a community are called to do. My meeting came close to being broken apart by those who believed every person must be welcomed into worship and those who were deeply distressed by the presence of a convicted child sex abuser. Such conflicting views are extremely painful and can take a long time to resolve and even longer to heal.

Another danger in community discernment is the tendency to approve work that feels familiar or reinforces group expectations. The history of Friends is replete with examples up to the present day of people in authority rejecting and even expelling individuals who do not meet their view of what God would have us do or where Love is leading us. The limits of community discernment are real (as is the question of false prophets), and the community needs to have humility.

Some Friends experience the Devil as a force in the world, a spirit that actively works to lead us astray. This is a spirit that can cause us to do evil while giving us the illusion that we are doing God's work. In my liberal, unprogrammed meeting, I know that quite a few people would look rather askance at me if I were to state I believed this, yet I know a few members of this community who have experienced a living force of evil that has done great damage when ignored, and they name this Satan or the Devil.

I also encountered wide differences of experience when I raised the question of evil in the women's group I attend, which is composed equally of evangelical and liberal Friends. A few knew evil as a tangible dangerous spirit; others named it only in institutions. These disagreements were not between liberals and evangelicals but grew from personal experience, most vividly articulated by one person who had been beaten severely as a child.

Similarly, I have found a strong concern about the potential for false prophecy to arise among us from Friends of varied traditions. I've also encountered differing descriptions of the reasons for false prophecy; most attributed it to mental illness, but some named it as the work of Satan.

Discernment

The section titled "Individual Recognition of the Prophetic Call" deals with the broad topic of individual discernment and support. As many people who have felt active calls to a prophetic ministry have found out, community acceptance of individual callings sometimes is an uneasy thing. By its very nature, prophetic ministry may challenge the community as well as unite the community in challenging the world.

It is not unusual for individuals called to such ministry, especially in responding to injustice, to be strong-willed and vocal, at times stirring up anger, skepticism, or resentment in those around them. Esther Mombo (Highland Yearly Meeting) describes the ambiguity and tension that surrounds prophetic ministry among East African Friends.

> In the Kenyan situation, there is tension—there are questions as to whether prophetic ministry is really Quaker. . . . These are the ones who say, we are Quakers, we are people within the tradition, we are quiet, we are a people of order. Things come orderly. I think the prophetic ministers sometimes do question, do shake us.
>
> There is also the tension of the heart of when it is prophetic. Is it when there is a lot of emotion involved? There is a tension between rationalism and emotion, so that those that get into a lot of emotionalism and talk about being prophetic are seen as following the whims of prosperity, some type of American agenda, evangelical, they can't be proper Quakers. So it is not something that is accepted as such, but it is two sides of the coin—both accepted and feared, challenged and shunned.
>
> Prophetic ministry . . . is sometimes confused with Pentecostalism. . . . Then there is

the tension between the older generation and the younger generation. The younger generation wants bang, bang, bang. The older people are those that say even in the silence there can be prophetic ministry. God can speak through silence, and the younger people say you have to hear it.

The tensions are between supporting it and fearing it, not about accepting whether it is there. But for me, fearing it, it is sometimes God saying something for you that you don't want to do.

The tensions Esther mentions are not confined to Africa. The "tension between rationalism and emotion" breaks out into sometimes ugly and certainly less than generous interactions among North American Friends. This seems to be part of the human condition worldwide. When someone in the community criticizes an accepted practice or otherwise shakes things up, some of us withdraw from anything that seems like conflict. Often, it is hard to hear where the truth is when we react in fear or want to protect something we have long found precious. I know how difficult it was for my community to recognize its own prejudice around homosexuality, and we still feel tensions around racial justice issues. Unexpectedly, my meeting was on edge for a while because some individuals found the silence of worship disrupted by the natural restlessness and noise of the children when they joined us.

Recognition of Vocal Ministry

The recording of ministers by Friends is an early example of a community growing prophets. Each meeting, by faithfully listening, makes space for individuals to hear the Spirit and to offer a message when words are given that are to be shared with the whole body.

A few of these everyday prophets had a call to speak not only in their home congregation but to travel to other Quaker meetings to worship and perhaps speak as well as preach to others who had not been convinced. In order to both support these individuals and help identify who had a true calling versus who might be using the name of Friends loosely (in the seventeenth century, these were called "disorderly walkers") and spreading false doctrine, meetings began to formally minute their approval and provide the ministers with a written copy of the minute to carry with them when they traveled away from their homes so as to make known those whose ministerial gifts were recognized by their home meeting.

In the early twentieth century, many of the more liberal unprogrammed meetings dropped the process of formally recognizing gifts of vocal ministry. Then, in the 1980s, these same meetings began to explore ways to support people who had a calling. Lloyd Lee Wilson (North Carolina Yearly Meeting [Conservative]) writes of the time in the 1980s when he was first feeling called to travel in the ministry.

> In the first half of my active vocal ministry, there were no formal elders supporting me, as I did not belong to monthly meetings that appointed Friends to that station. Nor did these meetings recognize gifts of ministry, which meant they were institutionally unprepared to support and sustain an individual like myself who felt called to dedicate a life to ministry. These meetings and the Friends in them were able to support episodic ministry, and in several cases did quite well.
>
> When I felt led to make a series of home visits in my home meeting in the 1980s, for example, there were seasoned Friends in the meeting who were able to perceive and support this leading as a true calling, even though it had an entirely unfamiliar "look and feel" to them. These Friends were able to talk with me

about my leading, exploring my spiritual groundedness and making some very good suggestions about how to structure the visitations so that other Friends would not feel pressured or made uncomfortable by my asking to bring meeting for worship into their homes. These same Friends then took over much of the logistical work of arranging the visits so that I could be free to attend to the spiritual side of the work.

During this time, these same Friends met with me regularly and helped me assess what was happening and what the implications were. Although their understanding of my call to the ministry was different from my own, as was their understanding of the home visits, by their own faithfulness they were enabled to provide just the right oversight for my visits, and they formulated a structure that I would want to use again if I were moved to do another series of home visits.[2]

While many Quaker pastors today do have seminary training and a few have such training from Quaker institutions such as Earlham School of Religion, a significant number of recorded ministers are simply recognized by others in their community as having the gift of spoken ministry. This formal identification is most often initiated by the church elders and not the individual. The late John Punshon (Indiana Yearly Meeting) describes his experience:

A few years ago, when I was invited out to breakfast by my pastor and the clerk of Ministry and Oversight, I had no idea that they were going to suggest that I allow my name to go forward for recording. . . . It was naturally very gratifying to be asked, and very unexpected. Being already in the ministry, the invitation to be recorded involved no change in what I did, but it changed my perspective in a number of significant ways. . . .

Actually, I had to persuade the recording committee of my gift. They were very enthusiastic about my teaching at Earlham School of Religion, but I had gently to explain that, no, that was not my vocation. So they then said how helpful my writing had been to Friends and I had to explain once more that, no, that was not my vocation. In the end, I convinced the committee that what I felt God had called me to was speaking out of the silence, which I originally did in unprogrammed meetings. . . . They accepted my assurances with good grace, though it might have been a century since anybody had come along with my particular gift. In due course, I was recorded. Also, in due course I began to bring the message on Sunday.

. . . The discernment process can be viewed in two ways. One is to ascertain whether there is a message at all, the other whether the message is likely to have come from a God who is understood within a fairly definite frame of reference.[3]

John then states his belief that meetings that do not have a strong sense of identity and common doctrine are not in a position to record individual ministers. In such meetings, there might be little agreement on what constitutes a valuable ministry to the whole community.

The recording process varies from region to region but often includes guided study with a mentor, sometimes for several years. In all cases, the recording is brought before the entire congregation or a regional body for approval. Recording is not a requirement for being accepted as a pastor. Recorded ministers may simply share their gifts as spontaneous ministry in unprogrammed meetings or in messages offered from the pulpit in Friends churches, but some never take on a formal pastoral position. (See my book *Walk Worthy of Your Calling* for a fuller discussion of the ministry among Friends.)[4]

Release by the Monthly Meeting for a Ministry of Service

Many Friends meetings that do not formally record the gift of vocal ministry have asked themselves the following questions in recent years. When is it right for an individual to seek the support of the whole community? What does such support mean? How does the community become involved and recognize that it is not only those with specific roles (such as elder) who can actively accompany someone in the ministry?

My yearly meeting does not record ministers. We have agreed not to single out particular individuals for offering messages out of the silent waiting worship. Over the past two decades, however, we have "released" several people for particular ministries. In my case, it was for a ministry of writing and teaching. Other ministries in my monthly meeting have included work towards recognition of gay and lesbian marriage, end-of-life care, opposition to the death penalty, songwriting, and work with the homeless. We developed a process whereby both the individual and the community sought clearness about the individual's ministry and the decision to release the Friend was considered by the entire community at its regular business meeting. As a result, an anchor committee has met with me regularly for over twenty years, providing both support and accountability. This committee also periodically reports to the business meeting about my work (see appendix E).

Some recorded ministers meet regularly with an anchor committee, as I do as a released Friend. Those who serve as pastors work under the care of elders, but my sense is that some are left without a regular place to test ongoing leadings, to receive feedback about their faithfulness, or to brainstorm approaches to complex problems facing them. I have found having an anchor committee (which some meetings refer to as a support, oversight, or spiritual accountability committee) essential because my work puts me in places where I am speaking about the nature of Friends faith.

One surprising piece of this for me was when I learned that the people who have served on my support committee (the membership has rotated over the years) have almost uniformly found that it nourished their souls as well as mine. Their engagement in fundamental issues and their responsibility to take part in discernment of the prophetic message challenges them as well as me to greater obedience. This work then has ripple effects through the rest of the meeting.

Queries for Reflection and/or Discussion

1. When is it right to seek the support of the whole community? What does such support mean? How does the community become involved, or is it only those on the anchor committee who actively accompany the minister?

2. What kind of formal procedures does your meeting or church have for recognition of and support for a call to ministry? How extensive is the process, and how often is it used?

3. Have you ever sought help in discernment or accompaniment in your ministry? What was the response of the community?

CHAPTER 22
WALKING WITH ONE ANOTHER

If we are to be everyday prophets and assert that each one of us has the capacity to hear and share words we receive from the Spirit, then prophecy is not something that sets individuals apart as particularly holy. Rather, it is vital to the well-being and life of the community. Ken and Katharine Jacobsen (Ohio Yearly Meeting) explain it this way:

> We think about the "prophetic process" itself as the primary work of the meeting, that is, just as Bill Taber said, to discover and interpret (and we would add practice) the new covenant, the ever-unfolding "law in the heart," a discovery we make especially in meeting for worship together but in prayerful everyday life as well.
>
> In a Quaker community, each one of us participates in the prophetic process. Community is the unit of prophecy: the vocal minister is the speaking, audible edge of the new covenant, the new creation, a vital role in the prophetic process; but we're also thinking of the vital prophetic role of the elders, who tend to the spiritual conditions within the body that allow for the new creation and allow for the vocal minister to speak its messages (however radical and difficult they may be) and to be heard.

When we gather as a band of everyday prophets with an expectation that anyone in the congregation might offer a message during worship, not just a designated pastor, the usual Christian practice of hiring pastors is not an easy fit. Since some modern Friends communities depend totally on voluntary service and others financially release individuals to take on the tasks of pastor, administrator, and preacher, current practice among Friends stretches wide and is sometimes quite innovative.

Sharing What We Have Learned

The Way of Ministry, a year-long program held in 2008–2009 at Pendle Hill, a retreat center near Philadelphia, delved into the nature of the ministry among Friends and how it is reflected in the world. The leaders wove the participants into a complex of groups in which individuals might find both support and accountability. The peer groups were just that—a gathering of equals charged to call one another back to focusing on God's way. Prayer partners had particular foci appropriate for the topic of each session. Several elders were always present and available to provide a listening ear. In addition, each of us had an anchor committee in our home meeting to bridge the time between residencies and also to make our home meeting aware of the spiritual work each of us was doing. Each of these forms of accompaniment was essential to the experience of the program. They were also part of the gift Friends were given to carry with them into the world. More about the ways Friends accompany one another is included in appendix D.

These different tools help mold individuals into a band of everyday prophets. Each form of accompaniment has its own strengths and potential failings. It is up to each individual to explore them in more depth and ask: What helps me face the darkness? When do I need to call in other resources? How might I best name the resistance I encounter and how might we help one another become unstuck? More and more Friends are gaining experience in these different forms, many of which are new to them. Time spent conversing about our experiences—both as recipients of words and prayer and as people who offer to be a conduit for divine love—stretch the heart. When might each best be used? When is a central resource person or expert most helpful, and when might professional help be detrimental to the calling? What allows the Spirit to move most freely?

Finding Clearness Together

Clearness—being clear whose voice we follow and what is ours to do—informs all Quaker decision-making. In groups, we do not ask what the majority wants or even focus on what one thing most people can agree on. Instead, we look for the Light to guide us—or, as some would say, God's will for us, for this time and this place. It is easy to slip into looking for compromise or trying to score debate points in discussion or any of the other normal dimensions of secular decision-making. But in those times when we can walk alongside each other in seeking that which is just and merciful, we know something of the new creation is being realized. In our business meetings as well as in our worship, individuals catch the desire to listen beneath human words to hear the Guide. Here we can glimpse the power that comes when we learn to take up the cross to the demands of the ego and orient the soul to the source of the prophetic message.

Finding clearness is an individual discipline as well as a group practice. I have already addressed learning how to discern. It is by definition a process of sorting out human desires and needs from the Guidance of the Light. The Quaker tradition has given us a variation on discernment that seems particularly crucial for those called to a public witness, which is that of holding clearness committees in which several Friends listen for divine guidance alongside the individual to test his or her calling.

Clearness committees are ad hoc committees, often used to test callings to the ministry as well as the traditional process of clearness for membership or marriage, in which both the community and the individual seek guidance on their actions. These committees may also be formed to aid an individual in making significant life decisions. Here, I am focusing on clearness in relation to a public ministry, and I can't emphasize too much that such gatherings occur with the intent to focus on the guidance of the Inward

Light rather than to act as practical brainstorming sessions. Appendix D lays out in more detail the expectations for both the community and the individual seeking support for their calling.

The clearness process may be initiated by an experienced Friend who notices that someone is being drawn into a particular work that might benefit from public recognition. Or, an individual might contact their meeting to let them know of a growing sense of the Spirit drawing them to public witness in some form. In my case, when I felt a strong calling to a ministry of writing and teaching about Friends, I wrote my meeting asking them to provide me with ongoing support in the form of an anchor committee who would read much of what I wrote, opportunities to offer courses around my work, and freedom from the expectation of serving on meeting committees.

As most often is the case, one meeting of my clearness committee (appointed by our worship and ministry committee) was sufficient for my request to be brought to the business meeting for consideration by the entire community. At times, a second or third meeting of a clearness committee is valuable. The process is facilitated when the individual seeking clearness can articulate their calling and the support needed, in writing and in advance of the initial meeting. It may well be that the shape of the ministry becomes more clear as the committee meets.

It is not unusual for me to get a strongly negative reaction from non-Quakers when I describe this process. The very idea of letting others be part of personal decisions is almost incomprehensible, even for some Friends. I recall long discussions about discernment and clearness from someone on an early committee that was meeting with me for both support and clearness. He felt that the committee gave people license to be judgmental and to tell me what I should and shouldn't do.

The primary judgment that is asked of participants in a clearness committee is whether the focus person is listening for and following the leadings of the Spirit. The clearness committee is not assigned to fix problems or reach conclusions about specifics. Their primary task is to listen, to listen as deeply as possible using all their senses, and to raise queries from that deep center. They may have a secondary role in asking questions about practicalities, pointing out resources, etc., but that is not at the heart of their task. Those of us who have experienced this process have, with rare exceptions, found the process strengthening and opening.

When an individual is called to a radical witness, an increasing number of meetings are establishing procedures for ongoing support and accountability, which includes what my community has come to call an anchor committee, as a way to sustain the witness and enrich the meeting. The members of my anchor committee have given me the courage to engage with difficult questions and have pointed out times when I have been off course in my writing. They have served as an impromptu clearness committee when I have faced major decisions, made me laugh when I have gotten too caught up in myself, and have suggested (strongly) that I learn the meaning of the word no.

Being Present to One Another

A person called to public witness may have to face their own fears or temptations, such as arrogance. At times, they may encounter hostility from others, complex decisions, or significant risks. Accompanying another person can mean being present in celebratory or in painful circumstances. Knowing when it is right to simply be present and when to draw others close is important. At times, the accompanier must consider what is being asked of the minister, who may be going through inward turmoil or outward resistance. How does the accompanier help name what is happening and provide a steadying presence? What traps might befall the minister? Are they ignoring the Spirt? Outrunning the Guide?

Being present to others can be transforming. At one silent retreat I recall, participants were deeply present to each other. A variety of paraphrases of the Lord's Prayer were virtually the only words spoken during the weekend we were together until we shared our experience at the close. Somehow, the Spirit held us during the weekend so that those who needed to had the courage to face some black and roiling corners of their souls. One person was able to acknowledge severe abuse experienced as a child and release much bitterness, so there was space for healing. Another participant had been tormented by his years as a soldier and the killing that was part of those years. In the intense silence, amid prayer and seeking of the Light, he was able to find forgiveness. I carry these as stories of divine mercy flowing through the group, washing away the pain and guilt so that Life might be present more fully in each one.

Supporting One Another in Attending to the Spirit

Ongoing support is invaluable, yet not all Friends are easy with this work. Tom Gates describes the work of support committees among Friends in Philadelphia Yearly Meeting:

> Interestingly, my [support] committee from the Way of Ministry has now evolved into a peer support group. There are six of us, and we meet every two to three months for two hours. Typically, we all have time for a brief check-in (about five minutes each), and then two of us will share in greater depth how our ministry is growing or changing, with ample time for support, feedback, and even accountability. This has been enormously helpful to me and to the others as well.
>
> I suspect what we have been doing is recreating the old meeting of ministers and

elders (this in a liberal meeting that would never consider recording ministers or recognizing elders). Probably most others in the meeting don't even know we do this; I think most in the meeting would recognize those in the group as having a ministry, but at least some might be uncomfortable that we are meeting as a separate entity.

Tom raises a potentially painful issue regarding the creation of small groups. When are they part of a healthy community and when do they act as cliques or are otherwise detrimental? Establishment of short-term support committees has become an integral part of Quaker educational programs focusing on spiritual development. They also provide support and accountability for individuals who have a strong calling for teaching or public witness. Such groups can play a crucial role in keeping individuals grounded and connected with their meeting.

There is a gray area around peer groups or other such gatherings set up outside normal meeting procedures. I've been most comfortable when someone in the meeting is willing to publicly offer materials on spiritual friendship, peer groups, or other ways of deepening relationships with those around us and with the Eternal and sets up opportunities to create small groups. But I know it can be difficult and that not all such groups go well, even as I have seen the ways they can strengthen the bonds between us and deepen our worship together.

In numerous places in the Quaker world, a shifting is happening as people are reaching for a live, energizing connection with all that is holy. For some Friends churches, this means experimenting with sharing with the pastor the responsibility of bringing a message on Sundays and challenging more people to step forward in this role. For others, it is about building daily spiritual practices. Or, it may be about forming small spiritual friendship groups or prayer circles that build

connections throughout the community. Informing
many of these experiments are glimpses of
seventeenth-century practices and spirituality that still
hold life.

The Communal Nature of Prophetic Ministry

Considering Friends as a band of everyday prophets
begs the question of whether all we do is prophetic in
some way if we are being obedient to the power of love
and truth. Ken and Katharine Jacobsen (Ohio Yearly
Meeting) go a step further than many Friends in
considering the whole of the community as engaged in
the prophetic in some way:

> We think too of the vital prophetic role of the
> meeting and committee clerks, who help us
> discern the new messages into particular
> responses, and of the meeting activists who
> carry these messages into action in the world,
> and also of the overseers who provide the
> practical conditions (building and grounds,
> finances, material support) that allow the
> meeting as a whole to function.
>
> This is new thinking for us, prophecy as
> communal, everyone involved in the sacred
> work, of which the vocal ministry is the
> growing edge.

Ken and Katharine remind us that we can't control this
process and conjure up 'radical' messages. Our most
faithful stance is to pray "that each message we offer
may have something of prophecy, of the new covenant
in it." Yet the human reality is that our "words might
well fall short of this, that we always need to practice a
healthy shyness and caution about speaking at all."

In a foundational sense, Friends worship is built on
the belief that everyone present has the potential to be
the vehicle of messages from the Eternal. There is a
Spirit that can speak directly to the condition of each
person, and each person has the capacity to carry and
offer a message to others gathered in worship. This is

part of what the Bible calls the new covenant in Jeremiah 31:31–34:

> *The days are surely coming, says the Lord, when I will make a new covenant. . . . I will put my law within them, and I will write it in their hearts. . . . No longer shall they teach one another, or say to each other, "Know the Lord," for they shall all know me.*

As we walk together as everyday prophets on this path, a central responsibility is to bolster up our neighbor and remind all around us to listen to the depths of the soul for the guidance that is given within. With this understanding, no one person is essential for worship to happen. If that one person does not have a message, anyone else walking this path may have received it instead and has the duty to stand and speak. Ideally, we also listen in a similar way for the task that is ours to take up and have confidence that the Spirit is at work and that others will step in as they are led.

Queries for Reflection and/or Discussion

1. Have you had opportunity to walk alongside others? Have others walked with you? What form did this take? What did it feel like to you? Might something else have worked better?

2. How do you respond to the idea of testing your leadings with a group? When does such testing seem appropriate? Can you see this as a way of enriching and strengthening the community?

3. What are some of the ways your church or meeting helps individuals develop regular spiritual practices? How does it encourage individuals to find ways to share their spiritual journeys and their struggles with others in the community? What role have you taken in making others aware of both possibilities and needs?

CHAPTER 23
BEING HELD TO ACCOUNT

I tend to be overly optimistic about how much I can do. My anchor committee has been laboring with me about this for the past couple of years. Learning when to say no is a hard lesson, especially when I have to make decisions about giving workshops and talks a year or two in the future. The committee was even more important to me when I was writing what became my book *To Be Broken and Tender*. The committee was very clear that my story about my relationship with God and with my spiritual ancestors had to be woven through it. This pushed hard against my satisfaction with my draft academic treatise on liberal Quakers, a much easier and less threatening task. The book as published would not have been possible if I had not been willing to share my work with the committee and if they had not had the courage to respond honestly, with humor as well as critique.

We took to calling the group that supports me and reports back to the meeting on my calling an anchor committee rather than a support committee. Because I travel widely and often feel disconnected from my meeting, the image of an anchor that keeps me from drifting on the rocks is helpful. Sometimes this image is of a boat held fast through the night or the storm. At other times, it seems to me it is a long, long line that holds the balloon fast, keeping it linked to the ground—not just the physical ground but that deeper grounding that reminds me to turn to God.

From almost the earliest days of Friends, particular individuals were designated as responsible for helping hold the worship in prayer as well as assisting in various practical aspects of gathering. They were also the people who had a gift of recognizing the Spirit and nurturing individuals who spoke during worship to help them better discern the touch of the Spirit and grow in trust of its guidance. When a Friend was called to travel in the ministry, sometimes for months at a time, along with providing a letter of support the meeting would seek someone to travel with him or her as an elder or companion. These companions brought encouragement for the grim times, as the trip might involve walking or horseback riding for long distances and in foul weather. They also were charged to be a sounding board and to let the minister know when they had lost track of the Guide.

For the better part of the last two centuries, the liberal tradition of North American Friends has been leery of elders and rarely has recognized or named them, largely because elders had become focused too often on objecting to outward and seemingly petty behavior such as playing the piano or owning fancy clothing or furniture. The evangelical, programmed tradition of Friends has retained the practice of having elders, often as a board or committee within the meeting community.

Ironically, in the early twenty-first century, the more liberal tradition is testing the possibilities of elders or small committees such as my anchor committee, whereas the evangelical tradition is growing more cautious about this because yearly meetings have split over issues of authority and doctrine. All of us struggle to find ways to hold true to what we believe to be central to our faith and to nurture the community in an age of tremendous individualism.

These tensions between the reluctance to take on the responsibility of offering feedback, especially when disagreements are involved, the reluctance of many of us to ask others to provide perspective or guidance, and the ease with which it is possible to slip into rigidly controlling others mean that I see no wide agreement today about appropriate levels of accountability.

The Reluctance to Support or to Question

In today's individualistic culture, it is no wonder that many American and European Friends are hesitant about (or even reject strongly) community responsibility in personal discernment or in carrying out leadings. How can we hold someone else accountable—aren't each of us accountable only to the Inward Light?

In some Friends churches, be it in the Americas, Asia, or Africa, there is a tendency for the pastor and elders to take the lead in most things and expect not to be questioned in their authority or their interpretation of biblical texts. Members of the congregation are often not fully engaged in holding themselves or the leadership to account. In our responses to authority, Quakers tend to mirror the condition of the wider society and the conflicting desire of people to find ways to control their own lives and to find certainty in an uncertain world.

The reluctance of some Friends to take responsibility either to support or to hold one another to account is widely experienced in non-pastoral meetings such as my own. Diane Randall (New England Yearly Meeting) wrote clearly about this dilemma and some of the reasoning behind a specific case in an unprogrammed meeting:

> My experience as clerk of Hartford Monthly Meeting ten years ago was seeing a reluctance from Friends to play a role of oversight that implied both accountability and responsibility for prophetic ministry from an individual who asked the meeting for both. The meeting was reluctant to have any sense of ownership of the individual's ministry, playing out the tension between community and individualism that Quakers struggle with theologically.

The members of Hartford Monthly Meeting are far from unusual in finding themselves in a bind, uneasy with their own sense of authority. As Diane continues describing the process, it becomes evident that in this situation a clearness process would have been valuable both in helping the individual articulate her calling and in helping the meeting develop greater trust.

> Part of the challenge in our meeting came from the fact that the individual was not well known to people in the meeting and that the ministry she identified seemed inchoate. It seemed that there was a lack of trust of the individual and a lack of trust in the community for recognition of God's grace to know how to provide accountability.

Although the recognition of a ministry in an unprogrammed meeting is quite different from calling someone to be a pastor for the church, all faith communities face in one way or another the hard questions that arise when things go wrong as well as the need to find mechanisms to recognize, support, and nurture the individual who experiences a prophetic call.

I am quite conscious of how painful it can be in an unprogrammed meeting when individuals say harsh things to one another or criticize vocal ministry. When the individual who is criticized keeps it to him or herself, bad feelings fester. I have learned of more than one case, long after the fact, in which a person left the community because someone had criticized their spoken ministry. Since it had happened in private conversation and the individual concerned did not feel able to ask for support, it was not possible to mediate the situation or to address the person who voiced the criticism.

When a community establishes an atmosphere in which people feel free to speak up about things that are wrong and know they will be heard if their words have merit, the whole community functions better. Then there is room to hear when something is truly off base before the situation deteriorates. Moses

Bigirimana of Burundi (Kibimba Yearly Meeting) offers his experience:

> Let people understand that life is not running smoothly every day. . . . We should have an attitude that people can come talk to us. Let them talk to you, not just lock them out. Make space for them to talk to you. . . . We need to be talking to people even before something happens: you are not prophesying what might happen but being ready just in case. If something then happens, the shock is not as heavy as it might be. There is room for somebody just to listen to someone.

Creating an atmosphere of listening can include classes or occasional weekend retreats on how to listen for the Spirit in circumstances ranging from personal conversations to the conduct of business for the entire community. Our ability to know when to stand and speak during unprogrammed worship grows when we have such conversations.

Over the years, more and more of us have become engaged in discussions on ways to listen to words that are uncomfortable. One important lesson is that words spoken during worship can be meant for someone else, in which case we might simply let such words flow over us and into the community. However, the difficult words may be important and may point to old wounds of our own that need healing, and thus they are indicators of internal work to be done if we are to avoid projecting our wounds onto others.

Both as individuals and as a community, we are charged with the hope of creating havens for those who have been battered by life and who may be carrying the consequences of having been traumatized. Our business practices reject debate and its competitive dimensions. We have inherited a structure that seeks to be consistent with a vision of all people being accountable to each other and God. No one is the focus of all the energy, and everyone has the responsibility to listen—and to know that "listening" does not mean doing exactly what another person wants you to do. When someone tells you what to do, you always have a choice. Taking a deep breath and turning inward to the Light helps bring that choice to life.

Criticism as Support

I asked Esther Mombo (Highland Yearly Meeting) whether she found the churches in Kenya good at calling people to account. Her response was to describe the tendency to assume that if a person was called by God, no one could question them:

> There are many things we do not ask—there are no questions about money, there are no questions about prophetic ministry. We are not questioned on issues of money, of issues of violence, on issues of abuse, we are not questioned.

Esther went on to describe her understanding of ways in which a meeting can support those called to the ministry and call them to account. The first is the way we listen and pay attention to one another. If we are listening to the individuals among us, be they experienced Friends or those new to our community, it is important to give them feedback. In a situation in which the pastor is given much authority, any response may be valuable, in Esther's experience:

> Community support can be in the form of this criticism; at least they heard the minister's words. It is a big support that they have heard it and can critique it. They are acknowledging one's existence. Even criticism is support because one can think about it and speak about it. We don't expect people to just say "amen, we have heard it." But by questioning, that is also support.

Not being heard at all is devastating. If no one is paying attention or values what is said enough to respond, even to question what is said or offer alternative ways of looking at a concern, then the person who spoke can be left feeling invisible.

The situation is quite different for unprogrammed Friends. Especially for those new to a meeting, criticism can be devastating. To stand and speak out of the silence takes courage and leaves the speaker feeling tender and often very shaky. The best response is to simply tell them "Thee was faithful" or "Your words resonated with me," if those words feel right. Any criticism needs to come much later and very gently, with some exploration of what might have been meant and the source of the words.

Approaching someone who has offered vocal ministry or otherwise spoken out, however, requires an inner good will towards that person and a willingness to help the individual grow. Recognition that the person whose words seemed wrong might actually be the one who has been more faithful to the Eternal Teacher also is invaluable in such tender conversations.

Community support is also expressed through affirmation. Particularly when an individual is preaching from the pulpit, speaking from the podium at a public meeting, or leading a workshop, approval is often all that is heard. Esther notes,

> It is also support you are given by affirmation. But you are called to be accountable. Why are you saying what you are saying? What evidence do you have? That is accountability. It is difficult when you are called to account.

Often, it is not appropriate for such questioning to happen in the public venue, such as during worship. In order for full and honest feedback to happen, times are needed when the speaker/minister can sit with a small group of people and consider openly but in a quiet way where concerns may have arisen. Esther describes this possibility:

> Sometimes accountability comes when you are one on one, not when you are in the pulpit because there you are six feet above criticism. But it is when you sit with people so that they are able to ask and you are able to defend things you are saying publicly, that is accountability. And I do believe that we need to be accountable in this way.

The specifics vary from meeting to church, but the nature of seeing ourselves as everyday prophets asks that we set no one "six feet above criticism" and also that we be tender and open-hearted in our disagreements and humble when others suggest we might be wrong.

Challenging Outward Authority

Americans do love to challenge authority. We can be so certain we are right. Often we are, but definitely not always. We do not always give the right message or address the right audience. Sometimes we are unable to hear ourselves challenging those who are supporting us or even those we seek to protect.

Mike Huber, pastor of West Hills Friends in Portland, Oregon, spoke about this passion to challenge authority (as transcribed by C. Wess Daniels):

> This is what it feels like being a Quaker to us when we get to use our inward authority to challenge some outward authority. We love it! We want to challenge the outward authority of earthly powers. . . . We feel like Quakers when we confront polluters, corporate criminals, and bullies of every kind. We want to take them down. Not using violence but using the power of our inward authority, we want to confront them and we want to shatter their sense of complacency in their own authority by revealing on a deeper authority that

> undermines the very things that they are saying. We love this as Quakers. This is the script we want to follow.
>
> And it is a pretty good script. We've done some pretty good things with it. But the danger is because we love this script so much we can decide to use it on one another.[1]

One of my worst moments when I was presiding at a business meeting happened when a woman finished her report and I forgot the admonition to have all speakers address me, the clerk. The first person to respond to the report angrily chastised the woman for not having taken all his suggestions during a committee meeting. The angry words were compounded by the fact that the man was strong, tall, and had a loud voice and the woman very shy. The rule about addressing the clerk is aimed at just this circumstance and is a reminder that the decision is the decision of the whole group looking for where the Spirit is leading; it is not about personal preferences or personalities. It is easy to reject rules as simply something to be broken or challenged, but it is harder to pay attention to what they are trying to tell us about how we treat one another and their reminder to listen to that Inward Guide.

"Test All Things"

Margaret Namikoye Musalia (Nairobi Yearly Meeting) has these words for Friends: *"Do not despise prophecies. Test all things; hold fast to what is good* (1 Thessalonians 5:20–21). Every believer should test the prophetic ministry."

Energizing the community in response to the Holy Spirit is at the heart of the prophetic work. Yet any one individual might hear wrongly or might unintentionally distort the message of the Inward Teacher, so the community is encouraged to listen in the context of what the Spirit is telling the whole body. Margaret warns us to test what we hear and not to get caught up in the excitement of one particular charismatic voice that might not truly echo what the Spirit would have us do. In her experience:

> Prophets do not give strong directional words, nor look for darkness or sin in people's lives. They suggest that recipients not make major decisions based on one prophetic word but rather pray for divine confirmation of what is spoken and discard anything to which the Holy Spirit does not bear witness.

Margaret also warns against those who would try to control our actions by fear. Fear permeates much of the discourse of the world; fears are raised constantly by social justice activists. Many of the things they fear may be true, but sliding into grand statements of disaster or comparing legislative initiatives to the work of Hitler brings a desperate hostility and shrillness to our actions rather than grounding our work in the Inward Guide. Similarly, I was present at a Quaker pastors' gathering where the speaker said we must always be alert for the work of Satan in our own congregations and act in other ways from a place of fear. Such an attitude builds mistrust and feeds hostility towards anyone who is "different."

Margaret offers her perspective on what is missing in some of our communities when they go astray and fail to nurture the everyday prophets in their midst:

- There is no teaching.
- There is no nurturing.
- There is no caring for the community.
- There is no spiritual support.
- There is judgment of people who are not Quaker.

The call to speak with integrity applies to all of us. It is very difficult to live up to a strict standard of truth-telling. My husband periodically gives me a hard time whenever I tell a story that stretches the facts to make a point. The fears mentioned above often lead into comparisons that push us apart and demonize people we do not know or do not like. Margaret, like all of my correspondents, comes back to the power and energizing dimension of all that is holy to lift us free from the multiple lures that dangle around us, that pull us into self-satisfaction and cause us to be blind to injustice in our own lives as well as in the lives of those around us. Each step towards the holy moves us further from the greed and violence of the world and closer to the city of God.

Many Friends have experienced being empowered by submitting themselves to the community as they search out their sense of leading and carry it out. In return, the community has found itself strengthened by participation in this work. Simply by coming to know each other more deeply, trust can grow.

The Value of Practical Guidelines

Lack of accountability and guidance is a concern for leaders of Quaker organizations as well as for our worshipping communities. Diane Randall became the executive secretary of Friends Committee on National Legislation about two years prior to offering the following reflections:

> I think of the work I do now with Friends Committee on National Legislation as "stepping into prophetic witness," and I don't have a lot of guidance from Friends for how to carry that personally and professionally. I didn't come to the job because it was prophetic; I came to it because I felt called and prepared to lead the organization, and I discovered both a thriving non-profit that needs to be refreshed by younger visionaries and an organization grounded in the vision of the kingdom and the rich legacy of Friends social witness. . . .
>
> Accountability for my work leading the organization is strong from the governing committee, including care for my spiritual well-being, but I don't have anyone serving as a

guide for the prophetic dimension of the work. Not having accountability for the prophetic witness makes me shy away from it. And I confess to a certain lack of discipline in lining up a spiritual support here.

As Diane admits, there is a dual responsibility involved in seeking accountability. The individual may need to ask for guidance when it is not forthcoming as many meetings have no recent tradition of asking probing questions of a member about the work they feel called to do.

It is also easy to assume we all agree on how Friends behave towards each other. We believe we are honest. We believe we do not resort to violence. We believe we treat one another as equals. The list could go on. We hold this image strongly enough that it can be hard to see when someone is behaving outside these norms. It can also be a surprise to find that not everyone shares our norms or our vision of how a Quaker acts.

Speaking Tenderly

How do we speak to someone who we think might have outrun the Guide? Arthur Roberts (Northwest Yearly Meeting) describes having been approached at a time when he had been speaking in a passionate but arrogant way.

> I recall once when, as a young professor with a newly earned PhD, I was waxing stridently on some topic (which I've forgotten) when an older recorded minister, looking directly at me, asked, quietly but firmly, "Arthur, has it ever occurred to you that you might be wrong?" It was a tender but firm rebuke—a word from the Lord, "fitly spoken." He was right. I was properly rebuked.
>   . . . Another time, two active yearly meeting leaders encouraged me to be steadfast—and calm—when, during the Vietnam era, I was receiving criticism

Being able to both give and receive honest reflection does much to strengthen the ministry among us. There is a reason why most descriptions of discernment speak of patience and the willingness to be questioned. Mutual attention to what the Spirit is saying, not whether one person or another is right, is the aim.

My anchor committee gets a lot of practice in holding me to account. They are regularly given copies of my writing before it is published—not to edit so my language is clear, although I appreciate that—but rather to question when I am not being faithful to the Inward Guide or am speaking beyond the Light I am given. At our monthly gatherings, they sometimes gently probe and sometimes ask hard questions. Their willingness to challenge me when my ego gets in the way nurtures the growth of the Spirit in my heart. They suggest I say no more often when obligations pile too high. Most importantly for me, they hold me in prayer when fear looms over me and causes me to draw back when I should be stepping forward.

Being Accountable for the Resources We Are Given

Depending on where in the world we live, financing prophetic ministry places very different challenges in front of us. In the United States, particularly among liberal Friends, meetings are hesitant to provide any financial support for individuals. They take literally George Fox's admonition against the hireling ministry. In parts of Africa, where it is usual to raise funds to support pastors, there has often been little demand for transparency in how the funds are used.

Esther Mombo is acutely aware of how easy it is to misuse material resources or to think it is not worthwhile to track how funds are spent and report back to others about the work that was done.

If the prophetic ministry involves material things, which it would, we need to be accountable for those material things. Accountability is part of prophetic ministry, to use what is given for what it is given for. Sometimes people use prophetic ministry for enriching themselves. For example, in this era of HIV/AIDS, in the developing world we see the results of HIV, the orphans. So if I am going to raise funding to care for them, I should be able to be open and accountable for that and account for the use of the funds, that they are used for what they were given.

Esther has been a leader in calling for financial accountability and good common-sense tracking of the use of funds. Lack of accountability has been an issue in places where money often comes from overseas, but it is also a concern in North America.

The other challenge of finances is the resistance among unprogrammed Friends in the States to providing financial support for ministry. Some of us learned too well the early Friends belief that all ministry should be offered freely. There were good reasons for our spiritual ancestors to object to a state-supported taxation system that paid for priests and churches.

In our unprogrammed meetings, we have no need to pay a preacher. But when we refuse to financially support individuals in our meetings, even to cover basic expenses when we approve their ministry, we make it difficult for any but the wealthy among us to be faithful. This pattern is shifting slightly as young people are coming forward, sharing their callings, and asking for help in living them out. We are slowly learning that if we want our message and vision for the world to be more visible, financial support can be essential in freeing up individuals to travel in support of their ministry. Some meetings are setting aside money for this and other out-of-pocket expenses.

In addition, programmed meetings and churches "release" individuals from the need to earn a living so they might focus on the needs of the congregation and be available as pastors, but Friends from unprogrammed meetings are more apt to raise funds to pay the salaries of individuals to work for peace and justice through organizations such as the American Friends Service Committee or Friends Committee on National Legislation. These organizations provide a structure within which Friends can work on important issues in a way that is accountable to the boards that oversee their work.

The New Covenant

Our only true accountability is ultimately to God. This is the starting and ending point for me even as I am sure that recognizing this requires wide participation in the community. Yet what does a covenantal relationship mean in reality? Jeremiah's new covenant vision that God's law will be written on the heart of each individual is inherent in the Quaker way. So what, then, is a "covenant"? Biblical scholars Bruce Metzger and Michael Coogan define covenant as follows:

> In general, covenant signifies a relationship based on commitment, which includes both promises and obligations, and which has the quality of reliability and durability. . . . Covenant expresses a novel element of the religion of ancient Israel: the people are bound in relationship to the one God, Yahweh.[2]

This description of covenant expresses to me a sense of accountability, of a lasting relationship that has mutual obligations and is intended for the just treatment and mercy that are so often named as key qualities of God in the Bible.

It is easy to find individuals who resent the questioning of any action they take, others who reject any limits on belief, and still others who feel that certain beliefs are mandatory. Some Friends see our books of faith and practice as prescriptive, and others see them as descriptive. Such distinctions do not necessarily follow yearly meeting boundaries, and in many ways they reflect the human condition.

The stories of religious leaders who cherish hierarchy and authority or focus on purity of belief and practice are easy to find. They are worldwide and are not confined to any religion or to religion at all. It seems there will always be among us humans who insist that everyone believe as they do and act as they alone think proper. Imagine a life governed not by such structures of power but instead by mutual, covenant relationships entered freely. For this to happen, each of us has to turn to the Eternal and at times make difficult decisions. Such is the work of transformation of the heart, moving away from putting personal desires first to honoring our obligations to the infinite power of Love and Truth and to each other.

Queries for Reflection and/or Discussion

1. What does accountability mean to you? If you ask for support from your meeting or church, are you expected to keep them informed? Does the meeting or church have guidelines regarding their expectations?

2. What has been your experience of asking for support from your community? How have you responded to others who have asked for support? Did you experience a spirit of generosity and connection? How might the process have gone better?

3. What might make it more possible for you and your community to embrace the work of individuals among you that reaches out to other Friends and to the world? How might you better sustain the relationships around you and be part of a covenant community?

CHAPTER 24
WHEN THE COMMUNITY RESISTS

I have an image of the individual calling and the meeting's engagement in prophetic work as a seesaw relationship. The community holds up the vision and names what it considers most dear—builds the seesaw, if you will—and thus draws individuals to it. For a while, the community may live faithful to its understanding of early Quaker practice or biblical injunctions, but a time inevitably comes when the world has intruded enough or individual egos have upset the balance and one end of the seesaw lowers to the ground.

Most often, I suspect, the individual with the calling has a clear sense of those raw places where the community's actions grate against the ministry's ideals. One end of the seesaw rubs in the dirt, but because it has done so for a long time, everyone ignores it until the wooden seat splinters. But before that crisis happens, one or more individuals may feel the roughness or notice the bump when the seat hits the ground.

The path to some of our most cherished testimonies was not always smooth or quick. In the nineteenth century, Lucretia Mott recognized that she was being paid less for teaching at a Quaker school than the men, yet equal pay for the same work remains an issue today. Despite small schisms in England, women were always recognized as equals in the ministry with men and often traveled widely to preach. Yet it took a couple of centuries for Friends meetings to shift from delegating only a few select decisions to the women's meeting to providing full equality to women in the work of the community. Friends have spread throughout the world, and the equality of women remains an issue in many countries.

In the seventeenth century, Edward Burrough noticed the painfulness of Friends' ownership of slaves, and in the eighteenth century John Woolman and others took a strong stand against slavery. It took decades after the 1688 statement of Germantown Meeting opposing slavery for Philadelphia Yearly Meeting to declare that slavery was evil and that no Friend in good standing could own slaves. Yet Friends retained the practice of requiring African Americans to sit in the back of the meeting room well into the nineteenth century. Even today, few North American meetings have African American or Hispanic members.

Again and again, in these and other issues of justice, once the community recognized the rightness of the prophets in their midst, it did act, at least in part. Friends who would not give up slaveholding were disowned. The entire structure of meetings in North America and England was changed to make women full participants in the community. But the work is still not fully done.

It is not an easy task to stand up and say to those closest to you, "You are wrong. You have to change." But it is essential to the faithfulness of the whole that those who see the gaps name them. In an age and culture of individualism, even saying we are responsible for the work and well-being of a community can be difficult. This is the starting point. Next is the recognition of the gap where we fall short of what we are called to do. The community's behavior is not in accord with the new creation. At this point, a prophetic voice may be raised. How it is spoken can be critical in the response of the group and whether or not it is heard. The community may make use of some of the tools it has to find clarity and reconciliation when it is open to considering criticism. When it is rigid, it may attempt to silence the prophetic voice. Or, the response may be more ambiguous. Often, there is a need for mutual forgiveness before the community can become whole again.

Bumping into Community

In our unprogrammed meetings, Jesus Christ and the Bible became contentious issues in the twentieth and twenty-first centuries, to the point where mentioning either is effectively banned in some meetings. Friends hostile to Christianity see it as rigid and at times venal or violent, which the church has certainly been. Instead of attributing these behaviors to the church, I see them as part of the human condition to be countered wherever people congregate. The early twenty-first century is certainly full of examples of evils done by Christians, Hindus, Muslims, atheists, and others. One question for liberal Friends is how they are to recover the Life that early Friends encountered—the Life that underpins all being—and to challenge the wrongs done in the name of Christ without condemning all Christians.

Unprogrammed Friends have also been described as being "too nice"—that is, being so concerned not to offend anyone that they are not able to speak Truth, especially within our own communities. Yet Joe Snyder (North Pacific Yearly Meeting) has experienced pushback for being forthright in using biblical language. He describes some of his sense of calling as follows:

> Prophecy is not about gazing into a crystal ball and predicting the future. It may talk about future events, but usually in the sense of warning: "If you continue in this path, these are the consequences of that behavior." Or it may be, as in second Isaiah, the holding up of a divinely promised future that will result from healing our broken relations with God.

Joe mentions the tendency of contemporary liberal Friends to speak of "your truth" and "my truth." I see this as another dimension of the way we often tiptoe around one another in the attempt not to do harm. There is good reason to take care with using language. We know how damaging words can be. Many liberal

Friends have felt battered by people in the churches they grew up in. We cannot and should not ignore this reality. It is important that we be kind to one another. It is even more important that the strong among us act with humility and accept the potential for error in our judgments. Speaking about "your truth" and "my truth" is one way of acknowledging the different ways we are shaped by our experiences. The limits come when we do not act to stop real harm or admit that there is a deeper truth that underpins our community.

Our spiritual ancestors had a strong sense that there was one Truth with a capital 'T,' a truth often expressed in George Fox's life after he heard a voice saying to him, "There is one, even Christ Jesus, that can speak to thy condition."[1] Joe is passionately Christian and sees himself as part of a group bringing this dimension back to our unprogrammed meetings:

> We were part of a small, young group of Quakers within North Pacific Yearly Meeting who were interested in meeting with Jesus Christ present, and that Presence is inherently prophetic. During that time [the 1960s], we also bumped into the Movement for a New Society and the New Foundation Fellowship, both delving into the radical and prophetic roots of our faith. . . .
>
> Through my Quaker lifetime, this prophetic awareness seems to reemerge every generation or so, and I'm very encouraged to witness it growing in a new generation of young Friends discovering their heritage.

Joe is conscious of the need to keep his agenda at bay and calls us to listen to God's agenda for the gathered people. He seeks to find truth that is more than "my truth." Nonetheless, simply using Christian language can generate a negative response, which makes visible the challenge of holding together a community in which individual beliefs vary widely.

Attempting to Control the Ministry

Who gets to say what is right? The human impulse to control others can be strong. We often disagree over actions; group decision-making, especially since the whole community is welcome to participate, can be stressful. Our varied life experiences can mean that even our concepts of support for a particular ministry may differ. David Zarembka (Baltimore Yearly Meeting) describes here some of the misled efforts that can pull us apart when supporting an individual's ministry, often due to a lack of trust.

> Members of the meeting—since they felt that they were supporting the released Friend—felt that they had the right to tell the released Friend what to do and how to do it. Often these directions were wrong and certainly not given in the proper spirit. As a member of the support committee, I saw us spending lots of valuable time, energy, and psychic enthusiasm on these dead ends.
>
> Another problem was the short-sightedness of the members who were only willing to release a person for a year or two, meaning that much time and energy was spent in renewing the release. For those releases that lasted a number of years, some people indicated that the released Friend was just sponging off the Society of Friends as he or she should go out in the real world and work for a living like everyone else. Too many people did not understand that a real prophetic ministry might last years, decades, a lifetime. If I had gone the route of being a released Friend, I am sure that my meeting would not have stuck with me for the fifteen years I have now been at this [peacemaking work in Kenya]. Yet can peace be brought to the world in a few short years? Does not one become better at one's ministry as the years go by, learning from mistakes, emphasizing what works best, developing wisdom and a following?

In contrast to David's sense of the process of periodically renewing a ministry being a drain on time and energy, I have found it to be a valuable way of sustaining contact with my meeting. It also helps the individual and their support committee take time to reflect on the ministry in a deliberate way.

David's words could be misread as saying no one should speak up when they feel something is wrong. I don't believe that is what is meant. What a difference it makes when we can sit with someone and honestly name concerns, listen to the response, and then seek to find new ways forward or acknowledge a misunderstanding.

Open-heartedness from all parties can be felt, as can the harshness with which we sometimes state objections and the obstacles we might place intentionally or unintentionally. As Bill Taber has said, one task of the prophet is to see beneath the surface of things, to be able to sit with apparent contradictions as a Buddhist might sit with a koan until the contradictions open, showing the beauties of the paradoxes that infuse life.

Polarization and Paradox

As Friends, we claim that all may be called to be ministers. Ministry is service and attentiveness to divine guidance. I also believe that as ministers we are each called to hold a wide array of paradoxes in tension.

- Wait patiently for God/act with passion.
- Know God is with us, showing the way/know God is mystery.
- Speak with clarity and authority/speak with humility.
- Balance mercy and justice.
- See Christ as Truth/know Christ as only one name for Truth and Love.

- Be obedient to God/act with holy boldness.
- Take personal responsibility/live out of God's grace.
- Define a clear group identity as Friends/be radically inclusive.

Let me define what I mean by paradox. Paradoxes are two things that seem to be contradictory but are in fact both true. Paradoxes are like Buddhist koans; they break open our preconceptions and take us back to "beginner's mind."

Paradoxes link us to *kairos* rather than *chronos* time. Chronos time is the familiar marking of the days and years. Kairos time is not determined by our concepts of minutes, hours, and seconds; it is the time when God acts. It is the intersection of humanity with the eternal, a moment when we purposefully pay attention to the Spirit acting in our lives. The encounter with the divine mystery may also change our perceptions of time, as in those Sundays when I have sat in worship and the hour seems but an instant yet so full that it is beyond comprehension.

Paradox is part of the shift that happens in business meeting when we are stuck in apparent solid disagreement and someone recognizes (is given) a way to reframe the entire question. At that moment, unexpected answers arise that are clearly right to all present. A simple example is the time when my meeting, Multnomah Monthly Meeting, was struggling to find a new building and kept finding the way blocked as we focused on options to either expand the current building or else buy a new, bigger one. We had set up these two polarities as defining our options. Then, during business meeting, a Friend stood and shared a clear opening that she was to facilitate a gathering of people who might start a new worship group. Soon they had started a second unprogrammed meeting in Portland. Today, Bridge City Friends is a lively, thriving, independent meeting.

Being able to live in a world of paradox challenges us to step outside our patterns of linear thinking. Having been trained in chemistry, I am very conscious of how science and technology can push us into a mode of thought that demands "right" answers and material proofs. In fact, I loved being a scientist because it gave clear answers (at the high school level)—I could always know whether I was right or wrong. But, an important factor I did not realize at the time was my fear. The certainty of science reassured me in my fears and gave me a place to stand. It was only later that I learned that science at its best brings us into a place of paradox. The "uncertainty principle" is literally basic to life.[2]

The constant pressure to polarize is worldwide. In being willing to accept paradox in our lives, rather than insisting that there is always a single right answer, I think our role as Friends is as catalysts; only a few of us are needed. In the right places, by reframing the questions, we can turn polarities into paradox. It is not a question of oil versus alternative energy; all of us have to reshape our lives to use less energy. Friends can be witnesses to the reality that having "less" can lead to a rich, happy life and is not necessarily the way to poverty and violence. Similarly, we participate in peacemaking teams in Iraq and Palestine, living the Truth of compassion and respect that is an alternative to the antagonism of Christian versus Muslim.

Living easily with paradox confounds anyone who wants black-and-white answers. Paradox takes away our sense of absolutes. Paradox offers a way out of seemingly intractable conflict. The conflicts among Friends offer only a minuscule glimpse of the ways people dig in their heels and refuse to acknowledge the humanity and divinity in other people. Intractable conflicts grow out of humanity's infinite range of different values, different self-identities, and different perceptions.

When we attack one another because of our differences, it is easy to be trapped in conflict. But sociologist Elise Boulding also warns us that there is such a thing as "premature universality"—the human tendency to want to solve conflicts by thinking that everyone is just like us, that we share the same values, perceptions, and ways of doing things. This is not the way to address the multitude of polarities that exist in the world or to end conflict at its core; it forces others into a false mold that will only break down.

Finding true peace, the peaceable kingdom, involves hard work and a lot of faith. It requires listening, listening with God's ears as well as our own, and cherishing honest differences while seeking the unity that exists in God. This process includes, in part,

- a continual process of learning;
- respect for the other and for ourselves;
- listening with our whole being and with awareness of God as a party to the conversation;
- being aware of and rooting out our own fears and prejudices—all that is not of God;
- knowing that we may be attacked verbally— and perhaps in other ways—when we are dealing with violence in the world; knowing that God's arms will hold us so we have no need to attack in return; and
- living as Jesus called us to live: *"Be ye perfect* [whole, complete, mature], *even as your Father which is in heaven is perfect"* (Matthew 5:18 KJV); *perfect love casts out fear* (1 John 4:18).

One other way to think about paradox is as a bridge. Friends have made a reputation as international mediators who cross battle lines in order to open communications between enemies; as people willing to feed their enemies as well as their allies in times of war; as neighborhood mediators who deal with local disputes. Knowing the inner peace that allows us to stand in the tensions and be open to truth in unusual forms allows us to listen freely without fear and not be defensive. When not anchored to a certain outcome, we have more capacity to live with unresolved tension. Tension is required if a bridge is to span a waterway, or a road, or two hostile groups of people.

Ministry Is "Gentle and without Arguments"

When the gift of ministry comes to those who are not in leadership or presses for the community to change their ways, the congregation or the elders may block the individual or the actions being advocated.

Always, in all traditions of Friends, questions such as these are important: How do we interact in ways that foster growth and maturity? How do we avoid a harshness and arrogance that can squelch an incipient ministry? Margaret Namikoye Musalia speaks of her difficulties growing into her calling in the Kenyan church:

> In the prophetic ministry you don't command, but it's gentle without arguments. [Prophets] are misunderstood and they also don't understand themselves. There is a lot of resistance from the community, which becomes a roadblock. No nurturing to those who have this prophetic gift; the community creates a problem where there is no discernment of this gift. Fellow Christians are the big blockage. Rudeness—arguments with no meaning or [out of] laziness arise. We must be ready to serve others.

Resistance is a very human reaction to something new. We resist letting go of the familiar, including our ideas about who can be members or in leadership in our communities or what the community is asked to say to the world. Yet sometimes we are ready for change, as happened when a number of transgender and transsexual individuals asked to be treated as full participants in my meeting. Some did not identify as either male or female; others knew that their gender was different from that listed on their birth certificate. All felt that they were treated as less than fully human by much of the world. This time, when we heard these people tell their stories of rejection, we were willing to be educated and to shift our behavior. As human beings, it is not unusual to know pain and react badly when people who we think should be quiet ask for full recognition of the gifts they have been given. Occasionally, we do better.

As we engage with the world, I like to think of us as having a highly portable form of worship—where two or three are gathered, we may easily slip into the expectant silence. Even when we are alone, simple measures such as remembering to breathe, being aware of what our senses are telling us, or recalling a mentor and imagining what they might do are among the techniques we can use to regain the center.

One Tool for Reconciliation

Even when we are not sure what the right path is, we have tools that may open up the way forward for an individual or the community. Anthony Manousos (Pacific Yearly Meeting) describes one path that his meeting used in the face of the serious disagreement generated when he spoke up on a current political issue.

> While I spoke, a woman angrily stormed out of the meeting and never spoke to me again. She felt I was "too political." The clerk of ministry and council emailed me (yes, emailed me) saying I was "a knee-jerk liberal." Others gave me more praise than I deserved. I felt deeply conflicted about my vocal ministry. I spent time in prayer in the desert, asking God's guidance about how to proceed. After a long while, the answer came: I needed to ask for a clearness committee, and I needed to ask the person who called me a "knee-jerk liberal" to clerk it. I told him that I wanted to be sure that

> my ministry was Spirit-led. The committee consisted of several Friends who had different views on these matters. . . . I shared my feelings and my sense of how God was calling me. Questions were asked and insights offered that helped me to gain perspective.

Here, Anthony describes a fairly normal clearness process except that one of the participants was carefully selected. Testing a leading can be more difficult when the members of the clearness committee are skeptical or at least do not all share a single perspective. But this extra probing can strengthen a leading and add substantial dimensions to the work. Here, the addition of a skeptical participant had the added purpose of building a relationship that had been characterized by hostility and doubt. Anthony continues:

> But the most important outcome was that the man who criticized me came to appreciate that I . . . was doing my best to be a good Friend. I came to respect his integrity and genuineness. We continued to disagree on many matters, but we became friends. A year later, when I felt led to go to a military recruitment center to get arrested, I asked for a minute of support from my meeting. My meeting was very supportive except for [the person who had challenged me earlier]. He said he didn't agree with what I was doing, but he felt that I had a genuine leading of the Spirit so he would not stand opposed. I totally respected his integrity in making that statement.

It takes courage to be willing to be vulnerable in the presence of someone who has doubted your actions or motives. The clearness process, with its guidelines to avoid arguing and debate, offers a means of finding a connection that may not be apparent at first. Again and again, our tradition assures us that if a leading is true, it will stand up to questioning and testing if we are patient and keep attending to the heart of the matter.

Forgiveness

Challenging people we love and respect is probably going to lead to feeling lonely. Ugly words may be spoken. Hurt may ricochet throughout the group. We may even be pressured to leave the community. It may be a long time before it becomes clear what the right action should have been (for anyone). Forgiveness may be slow to come, but it is essential for the health and wholeness of the community. Bitterness, clinging to self-righteousness, and resentment eat away at the foundations of relationships.

Forgiveness has a variety of meanings: to grant pardon for an offense; to give up all claim on a debt; to cease feeling resentment towards someone. The Lord's Prayer is a mini-sermon on forgiveness in which we ask God to *forgive us our debts as we also have forgiven our debtors*, a passage I learned using the word "trespasses" rather than "debts" (Matthew 6:12). So there are both practical and theological dimensions to forgiveness. The latter specifically recognized that each of us has done harm and needs forgiveness, but we should not expect forgiveness if we hold on to our resentment of people who have harmed us.

I have heard forgiveness described as "reconciliation with the past as it is," that is, acknowledging that the harm may never be undone but still letting go of the bitterness against the person who did the damage. Forgiveness is complicated, involving release and significant reconciliation within ourselves, but while it opens the way to reconciliation between the victim and the one who did harm, reconciliation is not always the goal. This all plays out differently in a small community than it does in the criminal justice system. Sometimes action is needed (and is possible) to rectify the damage done. Here, I am only touching on one small dimension of a complex dimension of human relationships.

Forgiveness is easier to achieve in a community that values humility. Being able to say "I was wrong" can be powerful. Forgiveness may take time to ripen. Sometimes the correct thing to do is immediately clear or it is recognized that the challenger was lifting up a crucial course correction. When this happens (and the people involved are not too proud or embarrassed to admit this), everyone benefits. Or, it may simply be that time is needed for tempers to cool or for someone to work up the courage to say what is needed to mend any possible tear to the relationship. When this happens, even if some time has passed, hopefully all involved will be gracious and glad for the outcome.

In other cases, it may take a long time for the right course of action to become clear and to determine whether the community is acting rightly or a significant change is needed. Holding steady in a place of uncertainty and unknowing is one of the hardest things for me to do. I suspect I am not alone in this. Seeing ourselves with fresh eyes can be irritating. Hearing someone who reads the Bible or other texts we look to for wisdom in an unfamiliar way can jar and be difficult to comprehend, much less accept.

Through all this, the meeting that hopes to grow prophets needs to be able to hear criticism and take it to heart, listening openly for where the truth is. The meeting may not always take the action suggested, but the more it leaves room for dissent and alternative perspectives, the stronger it is apt to be.

To be a part of a spiritual community, be it two or three or a gathering of hundreds, implies a deep caring. The people of the community become beloved if not always liked. The ways of the community begin to shape one's life. As individuals engage with the whole and cherish it, space is formed for the everyday prophets to bring a message to the world. At times, the prophet may urge the community to address its own hurtful actions. But without this base of love, whatever might be said is *a noisy gong or a clanging cymbal* (1 Corinthians 13:1).

Queries for Reflection and/or Discussion

1. Have you been in a situation where you felt strongly that your own worshipping community was wrong and that you needed to challenge their actions or words? How did you discern that action was needed? What did you do? Would you do something different now?

2. Have you seen others challenge an action of your meeting or church or read the Bible in ways that brought up unfamiliar or unpopular conclusions? Describe the circumstances and your community's response. What was your role in this circumstance?

3. How have you been able to forgive others? What was that like? How were you able to release resentment and bitterness? Is there something you need forgiveness for, from God or from others? Is there something you must do first?

CHAPTER 25
SILENCE IN THE COMMUNITY

Silence is part of the Quaker identity, at least for those Friends who worship in unprogrammed meetings without a pastor. This silence can be deeply renewing when individuals and the gathered group bind together with the Spirit and are restored in the Inward Light. When we stop talking and sink down to the Seed, as so many of our spiritual ancestors advised, the Light can transform hearts and bring words and behavior to a condition in which the fruits of the Spirit are evident and compassion is alive in our midst.

However, silence is oppressive when it bathes the community in inertia and self-satisfaction. The weight of a group of people, even if only a few, can stifle anything that threatens their comfort, even the motions of the Spirit. I can feel this resistance in myself when someone in the meeting starts raising issues that challenge my view of the world or asks (or demands) that I change.

Both the richness of the silence and the harshness of it are nurtured in many subtle and direct ways. My meeting is large enough to do regular (at times irregular) adult education and has a library that serves the many who learn from books. In every meeting, our way of being is shared largely by example and by one-to-one conversation.

Naming the Silence That Deadens

Deadening silence can result from inaction or by simply assuming others will act. One African Friend I spoke with at the 2012 World Conference of Friends told this story:

> In my area we started . . . a medical dispensary, but it is not complete. What has stopped it? People are not committed. They want to do this, then this, but very few committed to do it

to completion. That is what is happening in my
area. It is everywhere. I don't know if you have
it in America, but here it is everywhere.

This Friend's frustration at not being able to complete
a project was most intense when he had physical
health problems of his own and could not do the work
himself. Not enough people came forward to finish the
project. Many people who have set out to work on such
projects have encountered initial enthusiasm followed
by inaction and are challenged to find ways to engage
enough people to turn a vision into reality.

This Friend also spoke of the more subtle pressure of a
group that does not want to hear different perspectives
or the words of newcomers, even if they bring much
experience.

Friends will keep on despising one another,
especially like we people who never stayed in
the countryside, and if you go there with your
opinions and different ideas, the people, they
will not listen to you. So you have to be quiet.
You sit and watch, rather than going in there
with your ideas. We have those types of people
in   church,   and   when   someone   comes
upcountry to help, they discourage it.

I hear such comments at times from young people who
are   chastising   us   old-timers   who   have   gotten
comfortable in our own sense of who we are and how
Friends behave. The Friend who told the above story
identifies a rural-urban divide, which certainly can be
seen in the United States as well. Activists feel
resistance from those who have a more mystical
calling and focus on prayer life, whereas mystics hope
to enable activists to ground their work in a solid sense
of God present. There are many, many ways we as
human beings resist that which is new even as we may
be lured by its shine. It is painful when we turn this
human   response   into   emotions   that   break
relationships. I have seen individuals react negatively
to suggestions as nonthreatening as changing aspects

of social hour or having children in worship. Jean Zaru (Ramallah Friends Meeting in Palestine) has long argued that the willingness to take risks and to change is critical to any people who hope to bring about the new creation here on earth:

> More and more I feel that the people of ill will have used time much more effectively than the people of good will. We will have to repent in this generation not merely for the hateful words and actions of the bad people but for the appalling silence of the good people.[1]

Speaking Up to Appalling Silence

At times it can take strong images to get our attention. These same images are often easily misread and misinterpreted, as Micah Bales (Friends of Jesus Fellowship) found through the responses to a post on his blog.

> I imagined what it might mean for a whole community to respond to Jesus' challenge to us as his disciples: to follow him without reservation and without safety net. I used the image of burning down a meetinghouse as a metaphor for what it might look like for us to surrender to God as a community, to lay down all of those things that get in the way of child-like faith. It turns out that this was really shocking imagery for some of my readers. . . . it seems that many people got so stuck on the image of a burning meetinghouse that they could not see through to the underlying message of renewal.[2]

How does our community respond when someone in its midst says that Friends are not living up to their own ideals, not paying attention to the work of the Inward Light among them, or not following the words of Jesus? I have totally contradictory responses to such criticism. One reflex reaction is to be incensed that someone could say such things when I know my intent has been pure. Another reflex is to feel guilty, aware of ways I have failed in being faithful. Even as I write this, I realize how often I confuse guilt and shame.

Guilt is an appropriate response to having done something wrong and a sign that action is needed to repair relationships or make amends. Shame is about embarrassment, disgrace, and humiliation. To feel shame, one need not have done anything worse than wear unstylish clothes or say something others see as stupid. Shame may result from deliberate actions of others, such as an individual or small group that decides to ignore someone. Shame that elicits feelings of humiliation or is used as a method of control should have no place in our communities.

Breaking Deadening Silence

In 2017, news posts reported that administrators in Florida had tried to block the use of the phrase "climate change" in any state documents. This is only one example of the disbelief and refusal to even name what is happening as sea levels rise, much less attribute any of the damage to human causes. The task of speaking Truth is in part about breaking such silence and naming reality.

Naming what is not right with the organizations one is intimately involved in can be very hard, both to speak and to be heard. Naming what is not right with the world can be hard when a blanket of silence has been imposed on the topic. When we do not or cannot speak of a topic, it is easy to pretend it doesn't exist.

Ashley Wilcox, a past clerk of Freedom Friends Church in Oregon, highlights the importance of naming what is awry. She puts it into the context of how she experiences prophetic ministry:

> My personal definition of prophesying is "telling the truth, all the time." Thomas Merton has a much fancier definition:

> To prophesy is not to predict, but to seize upon reality in its moment of highest expectation and tension toward the new. This tension is discovered not in hypnotic elation, but in the light of everyday experience.[3]

Merton's definition also works for me—I tend to see things both as they are and as they might be, which can be quite painful at times. Perhaps a more palatable way to say it is that I am intuitive and empathetic, with a gift for speaking to the present moment.

Ashley continues:

> One thing I have learned is that prophets are mirrors, not problem-solvers. The prophet's job is to deliver the message; it is up to the people listening to decide what to do with it. In practical terms, that means I usually don't have answers when people ask me, "What are you going to do to fix this problem you have named?"

Being known can be a kind of curse as well as a blessing. Ashley has found that others expect her to name solutions and implement corrective actions if she is serious about naming what is at odds with Jesus' teaching.

Silence has many uses. Each of us experiences times when we are actively silenced by others and made to feel unworthy. But silence can also give space for ideas to grow and for an individual to make use of all their senses to see beneath the surface arguments or emotions swirling around them. Silence allows time for regrouping and stepping out of the control of our own anxieties. Silent prayer can reset our focus and energies.

Creatively ending the silence that descends when something is askew takes courage. It takes the ability to step aside from one's familiar view of the world and see the potential for a newness that can be freeing. It takes discernment to know that one is not simply acting out of personal need and to see the holy force impelling action. Courage need not be dramatic; it may simply be about good people not remaining silent. The prophetic voice may stir up a whirlwind, but it is more often compelling if raised in gentle firmness that cuts through our inertia and comfort.

Both coming to terms with silence and being at ease in the silence take practice. Our spiritual ancestors warned us that in the silence we will find a Light that shows us all the dark corners of the soul and asks us to be transformed. This Light also promises to show us a new way of being, the way of Love and Truth.

Few places in this nation invite a group of people to sit for an hour in silence and be enriched. Those of us who sit in silent worship may find this to be a path to spiritual maturity and wholeness. In the silence, there is space to learn to recognize the voices that push us away from God as well as come to know the sound and taste of the Inward Guide that calls us to the prophetic way.

Queries for Reflection and/or Discussion

1. When have you known a silence that fills the soul with joy or opens possibilities? What was that like for you? Have you spoken of this with others? If so, what was their response?

2. Have you ever found yourself silenced? What did that feel like? What was your response? Have you ever felt a silence that was empty or debilitating? Were you able to name it? If so, how did it change?

3. What is your sense of the conditions that foster deadening silence? What is your sense of the conditions that foster the silence that allows one to sink down to the Seed?

HEADWINDS

The following section on obstacles to following the Inward Light is comprised of six chapters. At times I sense the Spirit we seek to follow as the breath of God. This is the Spirit that moves us like the wind that fills the sails of a small boat. Yet there are other energies, spirits if you will, that create obstacles that block our intentions and hopes. Some of these are EXTERNAL HEADWINDS, such as the opinions of friends and family. Our challenge is to recognize these, see when they are buffeting us off our course, and respond to them with patience, self-control, and generosity.

INTERNAL HEADWINDS can be devastating. Our fears, sense of inadequacy, desire to control the world around us or to accumulate wealth—all these can block our ability to sense the breath of God. It is easy to put ourselves first; we all do it. It is also natural to want someone else to step forward and take the risk. Yet, living in faithfulness to the Light brings courage and reminders of that perfect love that casts out fear.

STRUCTURAL OBSTACLES can, like reefs, also block the work of the everyday prophet. Such headwinds might be economic or cultural, unspoken Quaker "rules," or pressures we encounter in the world.

Even when we act faithfully, there is no guarantee we will be effective in the world's sight. At times, all we can do is cry out, "I COULD NOT STOP THEM." But what is our response when the enemies we hoped to defeat follow the divine call and act justly?

FELT APPREHENSIONS concerning authority, proselytizing, evangelizing, and advocacy have rendered us generally impotent in the eyes of at least a few. Which of these apprehensions are real? How might we identify the subtle shifts of the breezes or the signs of impending storms so we might find ourselves more freely RUNNING BEFORE THE WIND?

CHAPTER 26
EXTERNAL HEADWINDS

If you have ever taken the helm of a sailboat for any length of time, you know viscerally the feel of the wind blowing right in your face that pushes you to a stop or even backwards if you attempt to steer directly into its full force. Tacking—the art of using the energy of that headwind but at an angle so it still propels you ahead—is integral to any sailor's skill set. Done well, it can move the boat swiftly and smoothly in the direction you are headed. Your course will not be a neat, straight line but rather will seem to take you to one side or the other. Learning when to come about and head in another direction is essential in keeping off the rocks.

Headwinds come in many forms. Resistance may be external and invisible, arising, as Ken and Katharine Jacobsen describe below, due to unspoken resistance from those around you. Yet external resistance is frequently active, made visible in sharp words others speak or their refusal to support an individual ministry. These external headwinds can block us from proceeding unless we recognize them and find the right way to engage them.

Opposing Spiritual Energies

In worship, Friends are taught to listen for their own deepest thoughts, hopes, and blocks and beyond these to the message that the Inward Teacher might have for their lives. In the 'gathered' or 'covered' meeting for worship, many of those present experience the movement of the Spirit that holds the entire group in prayer. Even without a strong awareness of the Spirit, people can often feel the embrace of this invisible force of caring and guidance. Such a meeting may feel like a fair wind at the stern that fills the sails and moves the boat forward with stately and sometimes exhilarating speed.

In expectant worship, the Eternal Guide can act in mysterious ways when there is a message that echoes through the community. Over the years, I have heard many examples of the Spirit permeating the group and reaching out in ways that defy rationality. At times, first-time attenders at silent worship will sense what the early Quaker theologian Robert Barclay called "a secret power" and announce to the group that the meeting or church is their spiritual home.

In worship, there are also times when an invisible force exerts pressure to stop the rise of a holy message. Ken and Katharine Jacobsen (Ohio Yearly Meeting) write of this experience (they use 'I' to speak for both of them):

> I do know that sometimes I sense a great deal of resistance, of headwind, to what I am saying or even to what I am about to say, as if someone/something in the room doesn't want to hear it—but, because it seems right to speak, I am given some strength to keep speaking through the emotional headwind, loudly, clear enough to be heard. At such times of resistance (and I could tell many stories here), when the community or members of it are opposing me, I lose the sense of the "prophetic community," a body participating in bearing prophecy to the world.

There is an art to sensing the different currents moving during worship, a skill that can grow with practice. Even as I assert this, I also know how hard it can be to be aware of the spiritual dimensions of silence. For much of my adult life, I was not conscious of this movement that permeates hearts and souls. When I did come to know it, the revelation was that of coming into an entirely new dimension of awareness. The reality is that, as has been the case for much of my life, some of those present in meeting for worship cannot recognize the spiritual wind. As a result, many "deckhands" are operating blind and thus are not conscious of the spiritual winds and tides or of the ways the boat—our bodies—resist this motion.

When too many cannot feel the Spirit shaping a message in worship, Ken and Katharine note, the individual speaking out of the silence can feel quite alone. Yet when the speaker rightly hears a message, that individual is often given the strength to continue speaking despite feeling the opposing winds:

> He/she is alone precisely because his/her faith community has abandoned the new and living way to which God always calls them. And when the Quaker community abandons this new and living way, they make of the faithful vocal minister a "lone prophet" fighting a headwind rather than a member of the prophetic community bringing to all the fresh winds of the Spirit.

This situation was familiar to our spiritual ancestors. For instance, Isaac Penington tells us:

> When the life is at any time lost, the only way of recovery is by retiring to the invisible, and keeping there, and growing up there.[1]

This, to me, is another way of reminding me to learn the feel of the wind in the sails rather than to give in to discouragement or anger.

One task of the everyday prophet is to listen closely in order to accurately sort out the source of energy and words and continue to name the right course for the community. This requires ongoing practice and the willingness to be a student of the Inward Teacher.

Loud and Visible Winds

Opposition can arise in any community no matter how progressive and open we think we are or how true to ethical or biblical teachings we think we are living, even when we see ourselves in a meeting whose beliefs reflect our own. The timing and issues will be distinctive to each situation, but anyone who names flaws or makes visible hurts that have been ignored risks a deadening response. The individual may feel rejected, but ignoring underlying problems can leave the whole group adrift.

Fighting the winds that arise in the face of critique is exhausting and potentially dangerous If a strong headwind pushes the boat towards a reef or if the sails are set wrong, the boat can be tossed around, pushed onto rocks, or overturned.

What Will the Neighbors Say?

Headwinds can arise from any of our various communities—the neighborhood, our families, our workplace. Such winds can readily push any of us towards the rocks and make us hesitant to act. These headwinds may include the potential disapproval of our neighbors, loss of a good job, or alienation from family. Arthur Roberts (Northwest Yearly Meeting) tells this story from his youth.

> While pastor of a Friends church in Kansas City, Missouri, an occasion arose that challenged me to "speak truth to power." In 1950, de facto segregation marked cities, including ours. When a family of color moved into our neighborhood, upset residents held a community meeting, using our meetinghouse, to strategize a response. Should I attend? Should I be silent? Should I speak? I pondered how "block-busting" strategies by realtors [designed to force racial turnover in a neighborhood] would probably lead to the diminishment—even demise—of our meeting.
>
> As a seminary student, my tenure [as pastor] was temporary. Silence seemed prudent. Or should I speak up for racial integration? Nudged by the Spirit, I chose to do so. So in the meeting, nervously, I stood up. "These people are good neighbors" I said, "I

have visited them. The best way to preserve our community is to welcome this family among us and continue to enjoy our homes."

At this point, I was booed, and leaders of the gathering requested that local elders fire me. A few days later, the elders met with me. They were caught between pragmatic considerations and Gospel truth. But, somewhat nervously, they affirmed that I had been faithful to biblical truth. A few days later, a neighbor told me, "After what you said I visited with that new family, and, yes, they are good neighbors." She thanked me for speaking up.

Arthur went on to reflect on this experience from the perspective of decades, knowing that neither his efforts nor those of his church would prevent the white flight that would cause the neighborhood to change completely.

Sometimes it is difficult to take principled action in the face of probable and unwanted pragmatic consequences. But perhaps my faithfulness to truth led to personal choices by others who affirmed Christian principles that in the long run led to greater positive good.

Arthur's words speak both to faithfulness and to the pragmatic, and very human, resistance to faithfulness. Life keeps asking us in various ways what price we are willing to pay to honor and follow our testimonies. It becomes even harder, especially for people like me who have a strong bent towards pragmatism, when there is no obvious benefit from our actions. I know I find it tempting to seek to be effective and miss the opportunity to speak words that need to be said, whether they are practical or not.

The Call to Change Hearts

My meeting, which considers itself open and welcoming, generated many contradictory and shifting winds in the face of the efforts of one member to convince us that prejudice against gays and lesbians was alive and painfully visible among us. She had a message for us and asked in many ways for us to change and to help change the wider society. At times, the truth of her message was recognized. At times, we felt pushed too hard and fought back. We, as a community, could not change at the speed she and others wanted us to.

The engagement was erratic and prolonged. The conflicted feelings resulted in the meeting minuting our support of her ministry to gays, lesbians, and transgender people but refusing to provide direct financial support for her work. Her insistence that we should marry all couples on the same basis without regard to gender caused us to stop marrying anyone for several years. Some people still have not forgiven the meeting for this. The conflicting feelings led to business meetings in which many people spoke out of bitterness and agony, causing more hurt. The process was neither clear nor simple. And our meeting was by no means the only meeting to resist the request of the gays and lesbians among us to be treated as equals in their full selves.

This prophet was often not welcome among us, even as more and more of us came to agree that her message was rightly given. It also raised the dilemma that changing hearts can take time even when injustice calls for immediate response. The beauty and weakness of seeking unity, rather than taking a quick vote with the majority winning, is reflected in this dilemma. Those who disagree can't be ignored and told to shape up. Ideally, all will be brought at least to recognize that the Spirit is at work even if they cannot come to fully agree with the outcome. Yet, a few people found they had to leave the community even though all those present when we made the decision were clear to act.

This work was part of a much larger movement for human rights. This woman was not alone in bringing prophetic messages that shook up the practices of various meetings.

Becky Thomas Ankeny (Sierra-Cascades Yearly Meeting of Friends) speaks to the risk involved in a prophetic ministry:

> There is also the sense of risk involved in a prophetic ministry—maybe a part of the definition, even—is there some risk to you in what you share? There is little risk (I would think) in insisting that God is love, though I have found that, for some, God's wrath is a part of orthodoxy in a way I am surprised by. So there is the risk of being labeled and losing one's voice in the conversation because of not being adequately orthodox.
>
> The prophet seems always to be resisted by someone, and when that someone is influential, the resistance can be lethal to the prophet. The target [of] the prophet seems often to be complacency brought on by defining what God wants as meeting a series of criteria rather than living in dynamic and obedient relationship with God.

This is part of the preparation of the prophet: recognition of the likelihood that they will not be well received, perhaps in their home community and perhaps elsewhere. Each of us benefits by asking, Where do I find support when these headwinds arise? And, What are my own weaknesses that, if not addressed, will cause me to steer off course, to fail in my faithfulness?

Queries for Reflection and/or Discussion

1. How have you been received by your own community? Do other communities respond to you differently? Can you speak to that difference?

2. Have you encountered serious blocks to your own sense of calling? What does that feel like? How do you articulate your concern in ways that might be heard more clearly? How do you discern whether there is truth in the resistance?

3. When has resistance helped you grow and expand your ministry? Have you received words that were hard to hear but were rightly spoken?

CHAPTER 27
INTERNAL HEADWINDS

Headwinds from within can be more daunting than those arising from the world around us. This wisdom is found in many traditions. For instance, the Yoga Sutras describe five obstacles to developing the inner life and surrendering to God. These obstacles (*kleshas* in Sanskrit) are aversion and clinging to bodily life, attachment, ignorance, and egotism.

Here, I am using the Hindu *kleshas* to emphasize my sense that internal headwinds are part of the human condition. I find it too easy to slide into thinking Quakers are unique or have all the answers; I need to remind myself that wisdom arises in many cultures and among all people. There is much in the Quaker literature that echoes other ancient wisdom and that notes the many traps that can arise as we take on the risks of ministry. For instance, Friend and author Lloyd Lee Wilson (North Carolina Yearly Meeting [Conservative]) identifies some of the obstacles to prophetic ministry:

- fear of success
- fear of failure
- complacency
- being a "tall poppy," which tends to get cut off
- outrunning the Guide or lagging behind the Guide
- false humility
- scorn
- embarrassment
- comparing yourself with others
- falling in love with the sound of your own voice
- being the lone voice in the crowd or not being supported by the meeting
- the ripples of changing life circumstances, effects on family, or cost to all involved[1]

Wilson's advice is, above all, don't do it alone. Draw strength from a companion to travel with in the ministry, a supportive family, a spiritual accountability group, or any of a number of other community resources that offer support, perspective, and occasional correction.

Aversion: Resistance and Depletion

Many people who speak in meeting for worship experience times when the message they have to give feels odd, something they don't want to say. Dorsey Green (North Pacific Yearly Meeting) describes such a time.

> I was in meeting for worship and heard Jesus tell me to stand and say, "Someone here is in pain and you need to do something about it because no one else will fix this." I pushed back and asked not to do it because I would sound crazy; I offered to talk to the person with my therapy skills but continued to hear the command to speak. Ultimately, I did say some version of that message and added, "You can ask for a care committee, see a therapist, or talk to friends, but you need to do something." I was too nervous to attribute the message to Jesus. At the rise of meeting, three people told me that the message was for them and thanked me.

Ann Janes (Britain Yearly Meeting) offers her perspective on how difficult it can be to be faithful to the divine call, not just in worship but in every aspect of life.

> I have experienced resistance to exposure of any kind for as long as I can remember, particularly if I perceive it to be imposed without due warning. The only place I have learned to accept the call with some degree of ease has been in vocal ministry. I continue to struggle with maintaining focus and

commitment in all areas of my life and have had to learn to discern carefully when to ride the energy wave to best advantage as I easily become depleted. It can be hard to discern when I am resisting and when I simply need to stand aside and wait for a while.

The resistance and struggle is by no means confined to Friends from unprogrammed meetings in the West. Zablon Malenge (Nairobi Yearly Meeting) shared the difficulty he faced as he became aware that he was to be a pastor.

Yes, initially my calling was to become an evangelist/pastor, but I resisted it. I actually prayed in my heart that God may give me a different gift because sometimes I am too shy to do things that evangelists and pastors do. Well, I thank God, He heard my prayer, but I had to bear the consequences of remaining simple, without pastoral roles or titles.

Friends assert that every one of us may experience a divine calling, such as to work with the dying, to end the threat of nuclear weapons, or to speak of our faith. The source of the calling is the common thread and what can make any work ministry. Any calling may be uncomfortable or ask us to take risks, be they external, such as taking an unpopular action, or internal, such as requiring old, familiar behaviors to change.

Clinging to Bodily Life: Confusion and Terror

Each of us has many conflicting feelings and thoughts colliding within our beings. Arrogance may bump up against insecurity and fear, and resentment may compete with envy. Many are the ways we can trip ourselves up. Offering a ministry of hope is the calling of Kathleen Wooten (New England Yearly Meeting). She has been filled with the joyous sense of being supported, surrounded, and filled with eternal love.

She knows the terror and blessing of the Light's embrace.

> Everywhere I go, I hear it reflected back, and now written as well on my travel minute: "You have brought us hope"; "You have reminded us that we are not alone." To be dropped into those loving arms of Light, to be carried, to be comforted, is a terrifying thing but joyful, always, as well. I can't hide that. I am called to *be* that witness in the world. This is about transformation, living "as if," a continual state of becoming in Love.

Despite her solid knowledge of her call to embody hope in the world, Kathleen still experiences the whirling of internal confusion. When there is no external anchor to point to, an anchor that everyone—even the most skeptical, the most disbelieving of our critics—can see, internal feelings tend to break loose and knock us about. Kathleen reports that this is "overwhelming, and confusing," stating, "I am so fearful (especially now) of outrunning my Guide."

Confidence that the Inward Teacher is not bound by our limitations and fears is an initial step in facing the blanketing confusion.

> In those moments of confusion, of terror, of unfaithfulness—my Guide can keep running too. He can keep up. So when I stumble, as I pray I pray soon and often if that is what it takes.

In addition, Kathleen has been able to know herself and the motions of the Spirit in her heart well enough to not be trapped in a sense of shame or guilt.

> God is still right there beside me. Always comforting, always teaching, always ready to correct in Love. The pain I felt was not a punishment. It was a deep failure to receive, accept, and nurture the gifts that have been given. Always in grace, never in my asking, certainly not in my own will or power.

Ultimately, as she continues to be faithful and listen for the movement that informs her of the next step to take, Kathleen finds:

> And yet that call still comes. And *we* stand at the edge, my Beloved and I, a new invitation, a new way of moving, with so many lessons laid upon my heart. Almost too scared to move, in fear that I might fail again. But Love always wins. It is better to risk, to try again in Love, to attempt to hear that still small voice of Hope. That lesson as well can only be learned by doing, by living into a new way of being. Tentative, fearful, yet so filled with Love I cannot help but stumble forward. That is what it means to me today to say "yes."

Always coming back to the motion of Love is a constant theme I heard from those who contend with the inner headwinds that seek to blow us onto the rocks of self-doubt, distrust, and disbelief. Again and again, people who know the divine call speak of the awareness of the Love that connects deep in the soul embracing or filling them. To know that feeling is something one never forgets, even as it may slip from consciousness when we get distracted, be it by seeking a continual emotional high or by attempting to get off those rocks under our own power.

Attachment: Putting the Self First

A member of Nairobi Yearly Meeting who asked not to be identified writes of some of the ways he has resisted the leadings of the Spirit.

> Yes, I have [resisted] on several occasions. I just focused on self- and life-fulfilling things and thought I needed to seek my own satisfaction first. I remember just leaving without a second thought to pursue my own ambitions as opposed to the call. The consequences included dissatisfaction. I lacked a sense of belongingness, and although I had

part of what I desired to attain, still it was worthless and added no value to my life. There was the feeling of being not complete despite the fact that I was lacking nothing at that very moment.

This Friend names the lure that most if not all of us experience, the desire to pursue personal happiness and success. Writings on self-fulfillment and the right to "be all that you can be" seem to be pervasive in recent decades. Even teachings on spiritual gifts can verge on encouragement to focus on what we can do well and what feels satisfying. Focused on this, one can miss the divine guidance to take up work that is awkward or that uses human weaknesses rather than strengths.

I've often been called to do something that I did not want to do. I'm often embarrassed by my stumbling speech. Others are given a message that is difficult for their listeners to hear. A few are put in harm's way. Seventeenth-century Quakers believed so strongly that leadings were often difficult that at one point a positive sign in discernment was that the individual did not want to act. They soon realized that this was not an adequate way to test the leadings of the Spirit, but in the short term it caused individuals to do such things as literally "walk naked as a sign."

It is hard not to put self before God. I want to enjoy life, be comfortable, have fun, and accomplish something that the world will notice or that at least will give my ego a boost. I don't believe that purposefully seeking self-sacrifice is the answer, either. I agree with the African Friend above that acting solely on the basis of self-satisfaction is ultimately empty. A life in tune with the Inward Guide may or may not be consistent with enjoyment and accomplishment. Our job as part of a prophetic community is to follow where that Guide draws us.

Ignorance: Inadequacy

How often do we look at other people who are following a calling and set up expectations for ourselves? The lure of trying to live up to the image of what a prophetic minister should be is real. When we set the imaginary bar too high, following a calling can seem impossible. Darren Kenworthy (North Pacific Yearly Meeting) writes about a time when he visited Guatemala and felt a calling to stay and work in a school there that had offered him a position.

> I had an authentic prophetic experience. My consciousness of what it meant to live in a wealthy industrialized nation at the expense of the many who didn't live there changed. My way of relating to my material wants and needs was altered. I didn't, however, have the capacity to live that out as a ministry in the way that some other folks I had met might. This insight, framed in different terms at the time, coupled with a clear sense that the technical challenges of the job were at least somewhat outside what I had any reason to think I was capable of at the time, prompted me to tell the people in charge of the school that I would be tempting God to allow me to fail if I were to accept.

Darren experienced a complicated interweaving of desire to follow the Inward Light, wanting to be a pattern and example for others, and seeking to be a vessel for divine love. Here he names what held him back:

> Seeking to show others how to be without allowing oneself to be shown, without acknowledging what comes before us and makes our own light possible in the first place, seems to me a great pitfall of prophetic ministry.

As he revisited his decision to not take up the possible ministry, he felt the pain of not having cultivated a spiritual discipline in his life that would have allowed him to take the radical step of living in a country not his own and taking up a new work and a new life.

> When I find myself beyond my guide, wishing to be or do something I haven't yet earned through practice, I revisit the shame. Given an opportunity to live out a prophetic call, I found myself in the embarrassing position of not having cultivated the spiritual resources needed to actually do so. There is some pretty heavy vanity involved in thinking that a particular externally appealing path is mine to glory in, even if I haven't prepared myself to walk it. As I left Guatemala, I was wallowing in the shame this vanity unleashed

Feelings of inadequacy are the flip side of the desire for self-satisfaction. Both are driven by putting our own personal needs and feelings first. It is virtually impossible to let go of the ego if the ego is so small or tortured that there is nothing to release. One of the paradoxes of ministry is the need to have a clear enough sense of self in order to give up the self so that you might find yourself. To do this may well mean letting go of the illusion of inadequacy and accepting that the divine Teacher will prepare you as need be.

Egoism: Wanting Someone Else to Act

The ego is an odd thing. Blown up and out of proportion, it leads to arrogance. Deflated, it leaves us feeling unable to do work that may be well within our capacity. We might find ourselves telling others to act because either the task is beneath our dignity or we don't want to expose our perceived inability. Tom Gates (Philadelphia Yearly Meeting) describes a time when he was a new member of his yearly meeting's worship and ministry committee.

> Our task was to organize a plenary session on our differences around the use of religious

language. The clerk asked for a member of the committee who might feel led to introduce a panel discussion with a few words of wisdom about how we might approach this potentially divisive subject. I remember immediately thinking to myself, "I wouldn't touch this with a ten-foot pole." No one volunteered, and we were asked to continue to be open to the leadings of the Spirit.

In the days that followed, I found myself thinking, "Here is what a person might say to introduce the topic . . . ," evolving into, "Here is what such a person should say . . ."

. . . Eventually, it hit me that *I* was being led to this task. It took some courage, but eventually I contacted the clerk of the committee to ask if anyone had yet volunteered. He replied that he had been waiting for me to step forward: he expressed much more confidence in me than I felt in myself.

Over the next several weeks, I gave this some thought and wrote down what I thought should be said. In the end, I threw away my text and spoke without notes and set a constructive tone for what turned out to be a very healing panel discussion.[2]

Describing his inward state, the pressures of the winds pushing him backwards and away from obedience, Tom noted:

There was a combination of trepidation, a feeling of not wanting (or even not being able) to put myself forward, balanced by an equally strong feeling of being led, of not being able to say no. This experience was instrumental for me in learning to trust that sense of leading. Nowadays, I think I would not resist so long.

The number of excuses I can find to not act is pretty amazing. Believing that someone better qualified will step forward is certainly one excuse that serves in many instances.

Ignorance: Perfect Love Casts Out Fear

Many, many individuals have stories of how they have been worked on in the deepest places of the soul. All the excuses, all the worries and fears fade under the intense glow of Christ's Light. Carla Coleman (Northwest Yearly Meeting) describes what it feels like when she pays attention to that Light, and she identifies some of the reactions and behaviors that tell her she is moving free of the interior muck.

> I know when I'm out of whack because my perception will be way off. I still have the worst anxieties and fears about what people think of me, like they can only see what I believe are my worst flaws (yeah, He and I are still working on those). When I'm paying attention to the Holy Spirit, or simply praying humbly, then I feel a physical urging/nudge as if I'm being awakened/aroused. It's like a light bulb goes on inside, and my otherwise sleepy brain is suddenly sped up.
>
> I am an introvert, and my thoughts come slowly. . . . I don't like talking in front of a crowd. . . . usually I freeze up and I am essentially brain-dead. But when I am in sync with Him, everything flows and I say things, amazing things that I sense and feel are from His heart. Then I forget most everything I said!
>
> . . . I've noticed that as more healing occurs, more space is made for His love in my heart. Perfect love really casts out fear.

Ignorance comes in many forms. For Carla, it is in part present in the way she freezes up and forgets what she wanted to say or do. Ignorance may also come from our attempts to control the world around us in ways that leave us thinking that our perspective and assumptions will provide the right solution and should dominate. The simple practice of listening to others can often make clear consequences that had not been obvious or reveal other limits to any one person's view of the world.

"If I Deserve Credit for Courage . . ."

Being aware of our internal headwinds is part of the task of the prophetic ministry. Without such knowledge, we can get caught up in our own limitations and never hear the voice of the Light or become stuck in our own fears and desires.

Quakers in Palestine live under stressful conditions even between periods of active violence in the streets. Jean Zaru (Ramallah Friends Meeting) points to the way she has found out of her internal paralysis.

> What is that inner force of regeneration? . . . I believe I have to bear witness to what is happening in my land, to expose the structures of violence and domination, to bring them out into the light, and to undercut their power. If I deserve credit for courage, it is not for anything I do here but to continue in my daily struggle at so many fronts to remain open to love, to the beauty of the earth, and to what it looks like when it is smashed. Struggle changes us; it also gives life depth and vision, insight and understanding, compassion and character. It not only transforms us but also makes us transforming as well.[3]

Reading Jean's words, I see again the interior walls, the inner state I sometimes experience when a place that feels like the source of Light within my heart is totally cut off from my consciousness. Without the awareness of that love that "gives life depth and vision," I cannot go forward. The distress I experienced when entering through the check-point that penetrated the thirty-foot-high walls around Bethlehem was nothing compared to what Jean and so many others experience who live with that reality day after day. But these walls have come to symbolize for me both the inner work as well as the outward actions essential for a renewed world.

Queries for Reflection and/or Discussion

1. What are the impulses that pull on you and draw you away from the prophetic ministry? How do you recognize feelings and pushes to act that are not of the Spirit?

2. When you feel paralyzed or overwhelmed by the work you are called to do or by the distractions of the world, what helps you to break free and be faithful to the leadings of the Light?

CHAPTER 28
STRUCTURAL OBSTACLES:
DEPENDENCE AND FAITH

At times, the strengths of our community become obstacles to the spiritual life of the meeting. Perhaps one or two individuals who speak frequently in worship overwhelm a new, tentative ministry. Or, perhaps, a self-appointed individual decides to criticize someone else's words. Other times, we are simply blind to apparently minor things—the way we set up the chairs, the tendency to speak to old friends or deal with meeting business after worship, or even a lack of religious education—that create blocks to newcomers or to the growth of the regular attenders.

One example of unintentional obstacles to the health of the community occurred when my husband and I were traveling and went to a meeting we had never visited. We were slightly late arriving, and the group was settled into worship. As we looked around the room, we noticed that comfortable chairs were set around the edges of the room. Down the middle were two rows of stiff, straight-backed chairs facing each other. All the comfortable chairs were taken and none of the middle chairs. I was sorely tempted to turn and leave. We did enter and sit, feeling very conspicuous as well as uncomfortable. I can imagine many others who might never come again. Then, as if to make a point, during introductions a woman stood and said that she had been worshipping there for about a year and had never had been told what to do in the silence. This request was greeted with silence. Eventually, I stood and gave some impromptu remarks about ways to enter into listening worship. During the coffee hour afterwards, several people talked to me at length about how they might offer more religious education.

Barriers to Public Ministry

The above story addresses how we nurture the entry of new people into the community, something essential if our meetings are to thrive. An equally critical dimension of our meetings is how we make visible the hope and reality of the divine presence among us and the expectation that at least some of us will be called into public ministry of some form.

Here are a few dimensions of the obstacles our communities can face in nurturing the prophetic ministry among Friends.

- At times, our meetings become a refuge for individuals, making them a place for people to hide rather than to heal and grow.
- We can be too silent, such as when we do not speak about God's work in our lives.
- How the community uses or doesn't use money demonstrates its priorities and can become contentious.
- Cultural and economic factors shape us in many ways without us realizing it, from influencing the messages given in worship to business meeting decisions.

Two other dimensions are important in nurturing the ministry: first, the way in which we do or do not recognize, encourage, and support individuals who experience leadings or callings, and second, the complex question of how we hold people accountable. Many Quaker meetings and churches struggle with one or both of these tasks. These are crucial, so each of these dimensions is addressed in its own chapter (see chapters 21 and 22).

Community as Refuge

It is quite lovely to be cared for, to have someone who sees to our needs and prevents harm. When there are people who have the resources—spiritual, physical, and financial—to keep the lights on, to provide warmth, to offer guidance, and to help navigate the uncaringness of the world, it can be a real blessing. When we are children, such care is necessary. At times, when we are adults, conditions may arise where such care is needed again, perhaps just in one aspect of our lives or perhaps more broadly. This is one thing a loving community can do—provide such care.

If overdone, however, care can be a structural obstacle to being fully who we are as a faith community; it can leave us mute. In the United States, liberal, unprogrammed Friends have frequently referred to their meetings as a refuge, a place where individuals who have been battered by the world can come and find solace.

Knowing how to balance tender care for those among us who are seeking refuge with the need to become more fully whole and to boldly speak out what we know is a place of profound humility for me. Speaking boldly can easily be experienced as arrogance or aggressiveness. Not speaking is seen as being namby-pamby or not standing for anything. Neither should be true when we are ministering from the mystery that is compassion.

Speaking from the Heart

To speak from the heart is to take risks, to become vulnerable. It is not to be done lightly or carelessly. Yet speaking of that which is dear does much to tie people together.

In some meetings, the word 'God' is rarely if ever heard. To many people, the word God represents a patriarchal, hierarchal society, perhaps with many other harsh dimensions. I rejected the image of the controlling old man in the sky by the time I was a teenager. It took decades before I realized that God is a useful concept when it stands for the force of love and truth in the universe and points to justice for the powerless and food for the hungry. Thus, I have come to use this word with ease.

In a healthy meeting, each of us, hopefully, finds words that express what is deepest in our hearts and that strengthen relationships among us. In doing this, we may also help ourselves and others see how we might live out such ideas more fully.

Money, Always Money

One piece of teaching about Quakers that was well embedded in my consciousness growing up in an East Coast unprogrammed meeting was the testimony against the hireling ministry. I was certain that Friends could not have pastors who offered sermons and organized the activities of the meeting and that we were not to pay anyone for anything that might be labeled ministry.

My attitude is slowly shifting a half-century later, but only slowly. My meeting pays a part-time 'hearthkeeper' who manages rental of the building, puts out a weekly bulletin, and does other administrative tasks. This is not unusual for meetings with over a hundred members. Similarly, we hire someone to clean the building and young people to run the nursery during worship and meeting events. These were not particularly controversial decisions beyond figuring out whether we could afford it. It was a much more difficult decision to agree to hire someone to organize and implement a program for the high school students. Gradually, we are also becoming used to the idea of offering an honorarium to Friends who run workshops for us (as long as they are not meeting members).

Although Friends churches believe in releasing individuals for the ministry by paying them so they do not have to hold other jobs, many pastors can attest to the fact that their stipend is minimal and provides a difficult financial base for raising a family. Small churches, in particular, struggle to pay a pastor a decent living. Sometimes the yearly meeting is able to step in and supplement whatever is available locally. Other times, a pastor might serve more than one church or hold down a part-time job. Preparing for worship, leading religious education, working with the children, meeting the spiritual needs of individuals, and providing pastoral care when members are ill or suffering in other ways all require time and energy.

Having a full- or part-time paid pastor relieves some of the burden of care, nurture, and inspiration from community members. Yet a healthy congregation needs many individuals to step forward to take on a variety of responsibilities. This is certainly true if we are to be a band of everyday prophets, especially if, as some argue, the pastoral system does not fit the Quaker way of life and worship.

The non-pastoral tradition depends almost completely on volunteers to step forward and take on all the responsibilities that lie with the pastor elsewhere. This has the great strength of engaging everyone in mutual care. It is much harder to be a passive participant in an unprogrammed meeting. At the same time, meetings struggle with the fact that in industrialized nations both parents often need to work, which places huge burdens on young families. In addition, families are widely separated so that when a member of the community becomes ill, the meeting often needs to step in to facilitate care. Few individuals have the training in counseling, theology, and spiritual practices that is usual for pastors. These and other dynamics of twenty-first-century culture make it challenging for such communities to thrive and grow.

Questions regarding money permeate many discussions of public ministry. It is not unusual for individuals to feel a call to travel in the ministry in some way or to obtain extra training but struggle to be able to finance that work. I am one of the fortunate ones who do not need an honorarium when I speak, but I accept such offerings (and then donate them) because establishing a routine practice of covering both expenses and at least a small stipend makes it possible for young people or those without resources to take up the ministry.

Cultural, Economic, and Biblical Pressures

Esther Mombo (Highland Yearly Meeting) has a clear call to minister to the condition of women in the Friends church and in Kenya despite the resistance she encounters. She has more freedom than some to speak boldly because of her position at the university. Yet she feels the opposition among some Quakers and wonders why she has not been "kicked out" of her yearly meeting. Nonetheless, she continues to carry a strong message of equality.

Our awareness of what is particularly our work to do can free us to be more present to that work and to speak with greater authority. A constant danger is being pulled into addressing every issue that grabs at us. It can be painful to admit we can't do as much as we dream we can. Esther has learned how important it is to be faithful in opening the doors we can and not be thrown around by the guilt that we did not do tasks that were not ours to undertake.

> Since I can't do everything, that is the path I have chosen—to speak about injustices, particularly gender-related injustices—to critique and challenge, to speak boldly against cultural practices that are used to exploit, that are used to marginalize, that are used to justify injustice. There, I have spoken boldly.

The work can be difficult and the structural obstacles may be basic and perhaps invisible. If you are trained to be respectful to your elders, how can you criticize them and tell them they are wrong? If the professional culture of your workplace presents one set of expected behavior, how do you introduce something totally different without being marginalized or fired? Esther knows all these challenges that surround us on a daily basis.

> I pray about it. It is not an easy thing to speak to people who are older than you, who are professionally different from you, to speak to people who are traditionally aware that they are the Quakers and you fellows are just waking up. So it is not easy, but I want to say that with the leading of the Spirit I am able to say, "This is not acceptable." Especially, to exclude or to marginalize is not acceptable. To interpret Scripture to justify injustice is not acceptable. If Jesus was here today, I don't think he would be with the clean, the pure. Jesus would be with the outcasts, with the marginalized.

Esther's response rests in the depths of a message that values the outcasts and raises up those who have been harmed by the system. Having heard her speak and interact with those around her, I know she has found a way to bring Jesus' message without belittling others. She knows how to fiercely and firmly call people to act justly and walk humbly.

Shifting the Structure: Moving Obstacles

Structural obstacles can permeate even the most aware communities that have the best of intentions. Ben Richmond (Indiana Yearly Meeting), describes a time when his self-imposed goal of providing the weekly sermon got in the way of faithfulness and the possibility of a prophetic message.

> I recall my own experience as a pastor at West Branch, Iowa, in the early 1980s. I had striven mightily through the week to prepare my sermon, but I knew that it had not come together well. Nevertheless, I delivered it in a rather halting fashion. It was our practice to have a period of "open worship" following the sermon, and immediately after I sat down, a relatively new attender stood up and said, "Last

night I had a dream, and in it God gave me the message for today. If you had just been quiet, I would have had time to deliver it." She did go on to recount the message she had been given in brief summary form, but I must admit that the only thing I remember was her well-deserved rebuke. That was the word of a prophet to an erring pastor!

This community was fortunate in having an attender who not only had been given a message for the day (although not the space to speak it) but also had the courage to stand before the community and rebuke the pastor for having gone beyond his Light. More often than we want to admit, our meetings need the person who, out of prayer and strong leading, can name what is wrong as well as the corrective action. And we need the individuals such as Ben who can hear the message with humility, know it was rightly spoken, and grow from it.

The desire to live up to the expectations of a particular role or standard is by no means unique to pastoral meetings. Recently, a member of my meeting was extremely upset because the worship at the time of a crisis in Syria around chemical weapons was not devoted to responding to that issue. He felt the lack of ministry on the topic meant that we did not hold this issue to be important and were not acting to stop it. We were not living up to his image of what being a Quaker was all about. Yet others of us present felt that the worship was centered and faithful to what needed to be said that day. This is just one small example of how our structures, and the expectations we bring to them, shift our experience of worship and of how we are to act in the world.

Awareness, the courage to speak up, tenderness in how we speak, the willingness to be criticized, and humility on the part of all involved are all components of living authentically and faithfully so that the Spirit may move freely within the community.

Queries for Reflection and/or Discussion

1. Does your community welcome new people and new ways of seeing themselves and their faith? If not, how might you help them be more open?

2. What are some of the cultural pressures that have bound your community and kept it from being as strong and faithful as it might be? What are some of the steps that might shift the community away from unhealthy cultural pressures and closer to God?

3. Have you experienced, as Ben Richmond did, an unexpected rebuke when it was sorely needed? What was your response?

CHAPTER 29
"I COULD NOT STOP THEM"

Who among us does not want to succeed? To be recognized as having some authority—to be someone who is listened to? To have our words mean something to others? I certainly have strong impulses in that direction, be it to complete a book and see it published or to help someone who is in pain find comfort. Part of the human condition is to feel passionately about aspects of the world around us and want to share that passion with others, along with the frustration and pain that can arise when we are ignored. For some, the second part of this desire is to succeed on our own terms. The story of the prophet Jonah is about a prophet who disagreed with God's aim for him.

In many cultures, women and young people are dismissed as having no authority. In the United States, people are easily dismissed based on many other criteria, including skin color, ethnicity, or income. The following story is about a young woman whose voice was probably discounted due to both her age and gender as well as because she challenged behavior her elders thought was theologically grounded.

Julie Peyton (Sierra-Cascades Yearly Meeting of Friends) tells us a story from her youth of a time when she passionately wanted to make people stop tormenting another young person. She could not make herself be heard. Her voice did not carry the authority sufficient to affect the actions of the adults in charge. She tells the story this way:

> As a young teenager, I was a member of an evangelical, charismatic Lutheran church in southern California. One year, on the bus trip home from our annual summer retreat, we had mechanical difficulties, and the bus was stuck at the side of the road. We kids were mostly oblivious as the leaders went off and held counsel together.

When they returned, they informed us that the bus had broken down because someone among us had sinned. They had even determined who it was. At this point, I became very upset because I was sure which young man they meant.

Despite my best efforts, which were hampered severely by my being in tears, I could not stop my leaders from blaming that kid for causing the bus to break down because of his sin. As far as I could tell, I was the only one concerned about this. All the others seemed content to go along with it. The young man in question . . . left the church and his faith behind, just as I had feared.

Julie was true to what she believed. She alone spoke up when the adults delivered a false message of blame and guilt. She was not heard.

I was devastated. For many years, this was the worst day of my life. I carried with me a sense of failure because I was unable to stop this horrific injustice from happening; if only I had been able to control myself, maybe I could have talked sense into them. Maybe my words could have stopped it. But my words were choked and were not heard.

The lesson from this that guided me for the next twenty years made me very careful to watch for errors by those who spoke publicly and, when I found errors, to speak clearly and not show weakness or vulnerability.

This immediate lesson of seeking errors in others and calling them on it governed her life for years, but, as recounted in chapter 4, she came to learn the falsity of that lesson and how limiting it could be.

One other message Julie took from this incident was to assume some of the blame. She berated herself for having been in tears and inarticulate and as a result tried to change her own being. This is a reaction that may be more common among girls and women than among men, if for no other reason than that women's softer voices can be more readily ignored. In my generation, girls were often trained to believe that they could not effect change—that their job was to support the males around them. However, reading the Hebrew prophets shows us many examples of men who believed they were directed by God but failed to stop the destructive behavior of others. As Julie experienced, attempting to change hearts is not a simple matter, something that early prophets also learned.

A Soul in Pain

The prophet Jeremiah felt to the depths of his soul that his people would not listen to him. As Abraham Heschel writes,

> Jeremiah's soul was in pain, stern with gloom. To his wistful eye the city's walls seemed to reel. The days that were to come would be dreadful. He called, he urged his people to repent—and he failed. He screamed, wept, moaned—and was left with terror in his soul.[1]

In response, Jeremiah screamed and called down heavenly anger on all those who would not listen. He foretold doom. Because of their own weaknesses, people still did not change their ways. Jeremiah's pleadings were in vain. His warnings were ignored. At one point, he was arrested and accused of deserting to the Babylonian enemy; he was only freed when the Babylonians captured Jerusalem. Nebuchadnezzar destroyed the king's palace, scattered the inhabitants of Jerusalem, and tore down its walls, just as Jeremiah had predicted.

Jeremiah's reaction is not very different from my contemporaries who called out loudly against waging war in Vietnam and, more recently, against war in Iraq, Afghanistan, and elsewhere. We yelled and wept and moaned. The ears of those in power were closed.

Our nation has continued on what seems to many of us to be a destructive course. We have not been invaded yet and no one has burned Washington, D.C., since the British did in 1814, but many people foresee long-term animosity and hostility of the world against our nation. It is painful to be part of a powerful nation and not be able to change its actions. In some ways, though, our position is not much different from that of young Julie Peyton when she could not stop the adults from blaming the supposed sins of a young man for the mechanical problems of their bus.

I have come to believe that such deafness on the part of the elite combined with the all-too-human resistance to change are critical problems, but our tendency to yell, criticize, and attack those we disagree with simply makes things worse. I know my own reflex is to dig in my heels and become defensive when someone tells me I am wrong. Quakers such as Gene Knudsen Hoffman (Pacific Yearly Meeting) have developed training programs to teach us how to empathize with strangers. Her method of 'compassionate listening,' an approach similar to Thich Nhat Hanh's 'deep listening,' has been used in many situations around the world. Gene writes:

> Some time ago, I recognized that terrorists were people who had grievances, who thought their grievances would never be heard and certainly never addressed. Later, I saw that all parties to every conflict were wounded, and that at the heart of every act of violence was an unhealed wound. I began to search for ways we peace people might help to heal these violence-causing wounds.[2]

I am active in efforts to build relations between evangelical and liberal Quakers in the Pacific Northwest. We seek to hear what others are saying with a depth that leaves us open to the possibility of being changed in the process. A small group of women in Portland has met monthly since 1985, and the Pacific Northwest Quaker Women's Theology

Conference has been held biennially since 1995. Many of these women are active in the many other convergent gatherings in the region that bring together Friends from different branches. These joint actions include the Way of the Spirit courses on Quakerism, joint support of the young people involved in Quaker Voluntary Service, and monthly convergent worship. This work has healed many wounds caused by misunderstandings and by the rigidity that can sometime arise out of religious faith, but it did not prevent Northwest Yearly Meeting from splitting apart over issues of authority, biblical interpretation, marriage equality, and same-sex relationships.

Modern research keeps finding evidence that rational arguments telling people they are wrong do not change minds or hearts. The use of fear and fear-inducing methods may force someone to verbalize what you want them to say, but in the end it may embed rage and bitterness that can last generations. Creating relationships, sharing common goals, identifying ways we all might change in order to live more freely and fully on this planet—all these seem to be more fruitful than threats. Yet such work takes time and caring and hope and is too easily distracted by the desire to bring about immediate change. While there are times when a strong, immediate response is needed to protect the weak, I keep hoping we can be more creative in our actions rather than turning to violence.

Should we become cynics and say that the powers of the world cannot be moved and that therefore our only role is to keep our own souls clean and weep for all that is wrong? Or are we to be naïve optimists who believe that change will happen no matter what the apparent odds? Can we build relationships with our enemies?

At What Cost?

I do not have to look far to see examples of people trying to stop actions they see as harmful. The actions range widely in seriousness and in motive. Stopping a toddler from running into a busy street is an obvious case of an action both necessary for the health of the child and immediate in its demands. The cost, whether it be a moment's scare and a bit of heavy breathing or real danger from a fast-approaching car, are nothing in light of the life of the child—yet I do not know if I could step into the street.

As I write this chapter in the mid-2010s, the U.S. Congress is in a stalemate between those who are determined to end the health care plan adopted a few years ago and those concerned to protect health care for the poorest among us. Republicans and Democrats are both determined to stop what they see as the destructive actions of the other party. This determination seems at its heart absolutely contrary to the dilemma of protecting the child running into the street or Julie Peyton's efforts to stop the abuse of a teenager. The actions of a Congress that believes people can raise themselves up better without government intervention leave many Americans without food and other basic needs, at least in the short term.

It is hard for me to see how the U.S. Congress "rules for God," an essential criterion Margaret Fell used in naming her support for the English government. How does this wrangling stop, and at what cost? How can I better respect those whose vision is substantially different from my own and seems to be harming people with the least ability to protect themselves? The next obvious question is whether I should respect these views. One lesson of Quaker process is that, at least in some cases, treating two seemingly opposing actions with respect can make visible a completely fresh way of behaving that is more in line with what we know of Truth and Life than either original proposal.

Nonetheless, sometimes it is essential to say no. When I interviewed Moses Bigirimana, the legal representative of both yearly meetings in Burundi, he described to me what it was like to be caught up in the horrid killings that had swept his nation. His responses to the chaotic events were complicated, but ultimately he reached a point when he had to say, "Stop! You cannot do this."

> I was not taught to kill. I was fleeing when I was to be killed. I was teaching at Kwebuka, and somehow I escaped. When I went home, I found that people had been killing each other. I didn't witness the people who were killing, but I still found people who were looking at others and thinking that they could be killed. This is where I had to stand and say, "Killing is not allowed."

Yet not every choice was between kill or be killed. Some people were using the chaos to demand money under threat of death. Moses came to believe it was more important to prevent immediate killing than to worry about the horrible bargain of life and dollars. The value of not taking a life was paramount for him and others in his church at a time when many were making the opposite decision.

> When people were saying "We must kill you unless you pay us," I personally had to pay the rest of the money I had so these people would stop killing. I know many members of my local Friends church at Mutaho were the same way. Even before I returned home, I heard many testimonies. So, we have those values.

Moses named the actions of those who worked to end the killing as prophetic ministry and as essential to being part of a Friends church.

> Being a prophet is being someone who is separated from the earthly practices. You know you are sent for a particular message, for a particular purpose. In our area, they know that Friends members, they don't kill, they don't drink, and they don't venture into sexual immorality. You are in a Friends church, and

you are known for that. So I think being a
prophet is being that.

Moses notes that Friends in Burundi face a different
challenge now that the genocide has ended.

Nowadays the country is in a period of
reconstruction, a period of trying to rebuild, to
cover the old image with a new image for the
country. I think that Burundi Friends are not
doing much now. The values are there, but we
need to reinforce them. . . . We need to be more
active rather than only being people of
theories, of principles.

Yet, speaking informally with others from Burundi and
Rwanda, I know that there are Friends who have
devoted their lives to working in trauma healing and
finding a way to rebuild a society that has been
devastated. Our generation knows more about the
physical and psychological legacy of being immersed
in violence than any past generation. We are beginning
to know something of how we might mitigate or to
some small degree reverse the damage that has been
done. Such work goes hand in hand with teaching
different ways of responding to violence than the old
tendency to seek retribution, be it learning about
alternatives to violence through training via the
American Friends Service Committee or the Africa
Great Lakes Initiative or any of a number of other
options. This too is part of the prophetic stream.

What If They Do Stop?

Jonah is my favorite biblical character. His resistance
to God's call resonates with me. But that is not my
focus here. Jonah did eventually repent of running
away from work he knew was his to do. After coming
out of the belly of the whale, he heeded the call to go to
the wicked city of Nineveh and cry out: *"Forty days
more, and Nineveh shall be overthrown!"* (Jonah 3:4).
The king heard of Jonah's prophetic cry and
commanded, *"All shall turn from their evil ways and*

from the violence that is in their hands" (Jonah 3:8). Their repentance was real and convinced God to be merciful. Jonah had succeeded in his mission.

You would think Jonah would feel satisfaction, but his reaction was otherwise. The fourth chapter of Jonah begins: *But this was very displeasing to Jonah, and he became angry.* Jonah did not want Nineveh to be protected. Nineveh was the enemy, and Jonah could not bear anything but its destruction, which is a very human reaction.

Jonah's story offers an interesting counterpoint to Julie's. Julie tried to be faithful to what she knew of God's way but failed to change other people's actions that she knew to be wrong. Jonah did everything he could to avoid being obedient. He did not agree with what God was asking of him and was quite angry at his success in changing the hearts of the people of Nineveh.

Jonah was aware enough of his own reaction to see that it was counter to all he knew of God. In fact, he argued with God about Nineveh's fate, pointing out that he did not want to be part of this from the start, knowing God would grant mercy to his enemies. In other words, he had originally run away from his prophetic task because he was sure the results would not be what he wanted.

The book of Jonah lays out in an unforgettable way the fact that the peaceable kingdom can be totally at odds with human priorities. Forgiving enemies is one of the hardest things humanity is called to do. It is very difficult to let go of the harm others have done to us and forgive, even more so if we don't accept that they had first suffered more than we ever did. We don't know directly if Jonah ever relented, but the last part of his story shows God's way as beyond human comprehension when a variety of miracles gain Jonah's attention and it is made clear that mercy is essential.

Queries for Reflection and/or Discussion

1. Consider a time when you have been put in a position where you felt (either immediately or in retrospect) that you should have said "Stop!" What caused you to feel you should act or speak? What action did you take?

2. Has there been a time when you had a deep sense that you should act and you did not? What was the inward state that told you to act? Why did you not respond? Have you done anything differently since then?

3. Have you ever experienced a clear call that you did not want to take up? What told you this was a leading of the Spirit? Why did you not want to accept the calling? How did you respond then? How does Jonah's plight resonate with you?

CHAPTER 30
FELT APPREHENSIONS

> The kindling is as plentiful as humanity. But, what is the source of heat? Where is the leadership? These are questions that challenge us. Regrettably, our latter-day "Quaker" apprehensions concerning authority, proselytizing, evangelizing, and courageous advocacy have rendered us generally impotent and nearly irrelevant as the ocean of darkness flows ever beneath. We hardly speak to fellow Friends of this reticence to minister in the world, let alone share the simplest Truths beyond the meetinghouse door.

The above words from Don Badgley (New York Yearly Meeting) are discouraging. Are Friends as lost and fearful as he suggests? He speaks as part of a liberal, unprogrammed meeting and, as such, lists the fears of some Friends about actions that our evangelical siblings would find essential. I suspect, however, that it would not take long to come up with a similar statement from the evangelical perspective. The Religious Society of Friends in the United States is tiny; there are only perhaps one hundred thousand of us nationwide. There is good reason to wonder whether we can make any difference or be heard at all.

Don's apprehensions are for Quakers as a whole. Numerous Friends yearn for the period when, at least as perceived from the distance of centuries, we were full of fire and life. We called people to know the Light in their own hearts and to be transformed by Christ's spirit. We once had a clear, definite message to share: the kingdom of God is among us and we are to live it now in our own day and time as well as know its reality after death. We do not have to wait for some distant millennium for Christ to return. Christ is alive, present, and speaking to each of us now if we will only listen.

How is this fire alive today? Need it be expressed in these words? How do we reconcile those who turn to a force of love and truth that exists in all religions and cultures with those who are certain that Jesus Christ is the only path to salvation? Are we as reticent as some believe? Have we totally lost our way? What will future observers have to say about our actions now?

These questions are real, yet I see people whose hearts are full, people who have been called to work they never imagined doing. I can also sense the resistance and weight of those who seek safety and comfort among us and are threatened by a radical, public witness. Quakers, and every other group that survives beyond an immediate enthusiasm, have to face this resistance. I can feel the tug towards conventionality and safety in myself. For most of us, it is difficult to be out there saying things in opposition to what our family and neighbors believe—or even what those in our meeting believe, for we are by no means in unity about who we are in the twenty-first century.

It is not cool to be religious in the liberal circles that many unprogrammed Friends inhabit. It is not seen as "Christian" to have women ministers, much less to fully accept gays and lesbians and transgender individuals or to speak out against war, in the evangelical circles that encompass many programmed Friends. Yet we in the United States do not have many African Americans or Latinos in our meetings. We are affected by the pressure to fit certain molds, to be who others expect us to be. The varied traditions of Friends have been separated from each other for long enough that many false images of "the other" have developed. In our isolation from each other, our theology and practices have slid closer to those aspects of the broader culture where we feel most at ease and are affirmed.

I have experienced the life and growth that can be present when Friends of contrasting traditions engage with one another, ask hard questions, and are willing to listen to the answers. This process is not what most would consider safe. It requires the willingness to be vulnerable, to speak from the depths, and to risk one's views being rejected or stomped on. It asks us to settle in the place of compassion as we listen, even when what is said threatens what we know. But is this not the reality of prophetic ministry?

Arguing with God

When she is asked to speak at a gathering, Jan Hoffman (New England Yearly Meeting) regularly asks God what message she is to offer. The answers are not always what she wants to hear.

> Quite early on in my prayers, I asked God what message he had for me to offer New York Yearly Meeting. The response: "Tell them to repent."

Calling others to repent is, of course, a very uncomfortable message to have to give. Jan had an immediate response: "Well, you can forget about my giving that message." Even as Jan objected to what she'd heard, she remained in prayer until further guidance came.

> The second message God gave me was, "Tell them God loves every single one of them." I immediately expressed my willingness to deliver that one.

There is a long, well-honored Jewish tradition of arguing with God. Most famously, Moses argued when God called him to lead the Israelites, claiming he could not speak. God listened and told him his brother Aaron could be the actual spokesperson. In fact, prophets often protest that they are inadequate to take on the work God gives them. In the case of Moses, as in the modern situation of Jan Hoffman, the divine response was to make the way easier for them.

Hebrew prophets also are found regularly arguing with God against divine judgment and for mercy on behalf of the people. In Genesis 18, Abraham stood before God and asked, *"Will you indeed sweep away the righteous with the wicked?"* (v. 23). Then ensued a long bargaining session. If I find fifty righteous men, will you save it? Yes. If I find forty-five? Thirty? Twenty? Ten? God responded, *"For the sake of ten I will not destroy it"* (v. 32). In the end, only Lot and his family would listen; they fled and saved their lives when the cities of Sodom and Gomorrah were destroyed.

The Hebrew Testament offers many examples of this constant tension between the compassion and mercy of God and the desire to end idolatry, to end the mistreatment of the weak and poor, to stop the hatred of the stranger in the land. The prophet is at times a voice calling people to stop doing evil to one another. At other moments, the prophet sings out the hope for a land rich with food and comfort, a land that values respect and just treatment for all. The prophet in some ways is the individual caught between the command to speak of the consequences of injustice or hatred—calling down the wrath of the heavens—and enticing people with the promise that the world is and can be a better place if they will only listen.

From this in-between place, the prophet argues with YHWH, calling forth the infinite mercy that is central to the divine nature. Even as the prophet tells the people to stop worshipping idols (a foreign deity, wealth) or harming other people, the prophet begs with the Infinite to withhold punishment.

Jonah's story delineates the huge gap that can exist between what might be asked of us and what we want to do. It is very easy to expand on Jonah's desire for Nineveh's destruction and say we don't want the politicians we dislike or the person who aggravates us most in meeting to thrive. I see Jonah's call as a graphic example of the call to love one's enemies, which is one of Jesus' most ignored commands.

Apprehensions Overcome

Christopher Hill has written a history of early Friends and other nonconforming groups in mid-seventeenth-century England titled *The World Turned Upside Down*. His book describes the time of the English Civil War, an age when the English king was beheaded and society was radically shaken.

For a brief period, mid-century, Oliver Cromwell and his New Model Army lifted up hopes for a totally revamped society and the advent of the kingdom of God on British shores. They thought that it could be brought about by the force of arms. According to G. H. Sabine's work on Gerrard Winstanley, the ranks of men who became some of the earliest Quakers included many who had been soldiers in this prophetic army and who dreamed

> that the bottom might come to the top, that the first might be last and the last first, that [the] 'community . . . called Christ or universal love' might cast out 'property, called the devil or covetousness.'[1]

These former soldiers became thoroughly disillusioned with Cromwell due to his inability to bring the dream alive. But, if anything, they were strengthened in their commitment to God's kingdom on earth even as they turned away from the fallacies of human armed struggle. All too quickly, money and power had reasserted sway after the death of the king had offered hope. Cromwell's skills as ruler of England were not sufficient to build a lasting new structure. The force of arms did not change hearts and minds. Soon the monarchy was restored and groups such as the Quakers were persecuted heavily for refusing to follow the Church of England or to pay the mandatory tithes to support that church.

Even as they were targeted by an act of Parliament that declared their worship a danger to the nation and made their gatherings for worship illegal, Friends grew in numbers and became more visible in their assertions of another way of being and living. They stressed dependence on faithfulness to the Light over obedience to any human ruler. They became convinced that the "weapons of this world" would never make real the new creation. They could only fight with the weapons of the Lamb—of Christ—which were the weapons of nonviolence, truth, patience, and other means by which Jesus worked to change hearts.

Our spiritual ancestors, at their most radical, lived out an absolute nonviolent ethic. They also had an understanding of death that feels alien to those of us brought up in the American culture, which idolizes individual action and doing everything possible to prolong individual life. Seventeenth-century Friends such as Edward Burrough believed that the work they were called to do was not dependent on them alone. Burrough did not cringe from death:

> If you should destroy these vessels [our bodies], yet our principles you can never extinguish, but they will live forever, and enter into other bodies to live and speak.[2]

These men and women knew the Pure Principle so completely that they had confidence that others infused with the vision they carried would step forth and live it out. How do we receive those who hold this confidence today?

Queries for Reflection and/or Discussion

1. Have we lost our way? In what fashion? What might open a way forward?

2. What doubts do you carry that cause you to stumble? Who and what help you to become grounded again?

CHAPTER 31
RUNNING BEFORE THE WIND

I have neither the courage nor the skill to encounter the ocean with only some sails and a tiller. Only rarely do I have the faith to simply speak the words I am given without writing out all that I think I am supposed to say.

I learned to sail on small boats on a warm lake. Part of this learning was to capsize the boat and figure out how to right it again. This practice taught me that boats are inherently unstable. Righting them was fun close to shore and without fear of hypothermia. When, as an adult, I was given the chance to take the tiller in water colder than the body can endure for long, I couldn't shake the expectation that the boat would capsize, just as all my childhood ones had. I imagined disastrous consequences despite a heavy keel that held us upright. My head knew we were safe, but my body would not trust this reality and kept insisting that we were in danger.

Both sailing in a boat without a motor and putting oneself totally in the hands of God ask for an odd mix of trust in our human skills and trust that the winds will not overwhelm us and push us beyond our capacities. Most, if not all of us, put a motor, a dimension of the human will, on the back of our sailboats to move us when there is no wind and to help us navigate complicated winds and tides. I do not know how to put all my trust in God. Just as my fears make me conscious of all that can go wrong, I know more about headwinds that slow my way than about the tailwinds that aid my journey.

Tailwinds

I've only sailed in the open, frigid North Pacific Ocean one time. I recall vividly that moonlit night with no wind stirring. We had motored out the Strait of Juan de Fuca, dodging freighters that were visible only as a moving line of black between the sea and the thick fog. We motored all night along the Washington coast under the full moon and the cover of stars. The light was bright enough to see the coastal hills several miles away.

Come morning, a breeze arose behind us. We shut off the mechanical propeller and sailed silently, with a speed that increased as the day progressed. The wind was directly at our aft—a fine tailwind pushing us towards the mouth of the Columbia River, our destination. The two sails were set 'wing on wing,' with one stretching out from each side of the mast to catch as much wind as possible. The entire day was a glorious sleigh ride running down the long ridge of unbroken waves that carried us forward.

How often I forget that the winds of the Spirit will carry me like that fine tailwind. When the sails are set, it is possible to enter fully into the movement, the awareness that force is not needed. We are carried almost like a hawk on the wing. It is easy to laugh in celebration.

My tendency is to distrust, to wait for the assurance that I am being led by the Inward Guide. I am not a racer who heels (tilts) the boat over, risking tipping it over. I forget the glory of running before the wind.

Others have the opposite tendency, be it delight in heeling the boat far to the side so the sails will catch as much wind as possible or loving and seeking out the exhilaration of sailing wing on wing. The excitement of the ride is contagious but can make it hard to sustain awareness of the nuances of the winds. An unanticipated shift in the wind can cause the boat to rapidly come about—to turn in a way that forces the boom to swing across the boat unexpectedly. Anyone not paying attention can be struck painfully or even knocked overboard. The shift can even capsize the boat. Spiritually, this is a good way to describe the process Isaac Penington called "running ahead of the

Guide"—when we get so entranced in the glory or the excitement of offering a message that we forget to keep our ears attuned to the Spirit.

Many metaphors exist to convey what we can of the spiritual, unseen powers that shape our lives, such as the flight of birds, a nurse log in old-growth forest, or playing a musical instrument. The list can be greatly extended. Such images can give words to convey the work of the Inward Guide—the spiritual North Star—as well as the force, gentle and otherwise, of the spirits that tie us together or press us apart. The Bible is full of such images. They speak of God as a mother hen, of us as a weaned child on our mother's lap, protected by the Holy One, or of our rising up as eagles in our reliance on this power I call God. Jesus loved to use parables; he used the vivid image of sowing seeds to represent communicating his message. With such words, we might help point out the way and aid others to find their sea legs or give them hope.

The flight of the hawk on the winds that are the breath of God is perhaps the most powerful image I carry in my heart of freedom in the Eternal. But I only know that from watching the hawk and sensing what it might have to say. In contrast, I can feel the sea rising and falling under me, the wind cutting across the deck or gently wafting by. I know something of the tiller and how it can turn the boat to fight the winds or let them move us. I am aware that heart, mind, body, and soul contribute to the process. Skill comes over the years in sensing and learning to move with the winds, being respectful of their action while still keeping focused on the guidance of the Inward Light and where it would lead us.

An experienced sailor knows about the angles of the winds and the currents, knows the feel of a steady tailwind and how to move joyfully with the Spirit, attentive to adjusting to the shifts in that wind. The sailor knows that if you head your boat at the correct angle to a headwind and set your sails accordingly, it is also possible to sail quickly and freely. Because headwinds require moving at an angle to where you want to be, attention is needed to readjust the course periodically and reset the sails so that the overall movement is in the right direction. In tight places, when the wind is strong and rocks are nearby, the boat may need to come about quite frequently to adjust to those forces humans do not control.

Thus it can be as we engage one another. Instead of clashing, we can feel when the wind is shifting and move with it, knowing the interplay that brings us all home.

Queries for Reflection and/or Discussion

1. Do you enjoy the exhilaration of running before the wind? How does this express itself in your spiritual life?

2. What helps you recognize and face the headwinds? Have you ever had a time when you faced and overcame something you saw as an obstacle and found that engaging it was a time of growth or moved you closer to where you were supposed to be? What was that like for you?

3. Do you try to run before the wind whenever possible or are you more conscious of the headwinds? Do you resist the divine call or tend to run ahead of the Guide?

4. How might you learn to better move with the winds and keep attentive to the shifts that might cause unexpected or perhaps painful change?

MAKING SPACE FOR
THE PROPHETS AMONG US

This final section offers seven chapters reflecting on Quakers of the past and today. Friends today often delight in telling stories about 'hat honor' or THE SPIRIT OF THE HAT but forget the disagreements on this topic that existed in the early movement. Humans do seem to have some deeply engrained behaviors that can only be shifted by guidance greater than the ego or individual willpower. We can know the Inward Light that illuminates where we have gone wrong and also shows us how to come more fully into wholeness and integrity. Again and again, early Friends insisted that the kingdom of God is within. That is where we must begin.

LISTENING TO OUR SPIRITUAL ANCESTORS reminds us of the ways the early Friends supported one another in times of persecution. They actively defended their actions and their community and created structures that helped sustain them in the face of fines and imprisonment.

DISCERNING STRUCTURES THAT FOSTER INJUSTICE AND VIOLENCE is part of the work of a prophet and part of the task of the prophetic community. Naming where our lives and the lives of others miss the plumb line that demarcates alignment with all that is holy is part of the prophetic task. As we look around us, it behooves us to consider ways of ENGAGING IN TODAY'S WORLD.

Each community is the sum of many individuals who can help each other grow in the Spirit. MOVING WITH THE WIND is one way I express the work of the Infinite in my soul.

Friends have divided many times over the generations. We at times have lost track of who we are and who we might be. REWEAVING THE STORY is one of today's challenges. Who are we amidst our squabbles and disagreements? Can we together be a people who live out the new creation? Do we still have a message for ourselves and the world?

Such a message might grow as we engage in BECOMING A BAND OF EVERYDAY PROPHETS, seeking a common prayer that reaches for that which is deepest in the soul and can unite the world. My hope is that we might become a band of everyday prophets who see Truth and are willing to speak it and who listen inwardly for the Guidance that sets our feet on the path of compassion and justice.

CHAPTER 32
THE SPIRIT OF THE HAT

Early Friends were not without painful disagreements and internal conflicts. Former Quaker William Mucklow published a pamphlet in 1673 titled *The Spirit of the Hat* criticizing George Fox and his supporters. The author of the pamphlet's preface states,

> I hope we shall not suffer our selves to be imposed upon by their nauseous Self-commendations, to believe that they transcend all others, or that their Principles are better than those of other Christians whom they condemn, at least it will not appear from their Practices that they are so.[1]

'Hat honor' was one of the distinctive behaviors of seventeenth-century Friends. Quaker men refused to take off (doff) their hats to men of higher social standing. This practice enraged the aristocracy and caused numerous Friends to be disowned by their families, to lose friends, or to be imprisoned for not honoring judges. In contrast to Mucklow, we look back at hat honor as a sign of how passionately they believed in equality.

Internal disagreements also circled around whether to have fixed times and places to worship, which made it easier for authorities to break up their gatherings, or to recognize women as ministers. Then, as now, disagreement led to separation, although on a much smaller scale than we have experienced over the past two centuries.

I bring up hat honor as an example and as a warning. I find it wonderful that the early Friends happened upon this simple action—not removing your hat in a society that had an elaborate ritual for doffing hats among the wealthy and titled—that created a conspicuous public statement about the inequities of society. I often wonder what the hat honor of today is—a simple, easily recognizable public action that points to one of the major ills of society. This practice also seems to raise the caution that we should not forget how messy and controversial life is, even within a tight-knit society, when we lift up our past.

Remembering That the Kingdom Is Within

Lists of rules are much simpler to deal with than the admonition to listen for a voice that is not audible to our outward ears. *Thou shalt not* . . . begins the classic set of ten commandments established when Moses was given tablets of stone thirty-five hundred years ago. Fifteen hundred years later, the Bible recorded a new relationship between humanity and the Eternal that was based not on rules but on an inward law "written on the heart." Jeremiah brought this message presenting the words of God: *"they shall all know me, from the least of them to the greatest"* (Jeremiah 31:31–34). This inward knowing of those who turn towards the Light underpins Friends worship, decision-making, and prophetic ministry.

The inward knowledge of God and the assurance that human actions can align with the divine call to justice and compassion were articulated by early Friends in terms of the kingdom of God, the city of God, or the new creation. James Nayler wrote:

> You pretend as to the Kingdom of God, but you are not seeking where it is; you have been seeking without, but it is within you, and you must find it, if ever you find it, it is not to be found in Forms and Customs, and outside Observations; but the Kingdom of God is within you, and the way to the kingdom is within you, and the Light that guides into the way and keeps in the way is within . . . and this light is not a Chapter without you, in a Book, but it is that light that revealed that to the Saints in their several measures, which they spoke forth, and which thou readest in the

Chapter; and this light being minded will lead to the perfect day, which declares all things as they are . . . and so will lead up to justice and to peace.[2]

Words similar to these were frequent in the near explosion of pamphlets that accompanied the spoken messages of Friends during their early years. The power of the Light Within that leads up to peace is dependent on the awareness of wrongdoing and the commitment to respond to that same Light when it illuminates error and shows another way to behave, one that is not dictated by the demands of the human ego. Friends often spoke of this commitment in terms of taking up the cross, an act essential to anyone called to the prophetic ministry.

Taking Up the Cross

Margaret Fell, in her 1660 pamphlet *A True Testimony*, writes of obedience to the cross of Christ, which is the power of God."[3] A natural first thought is to see the cross as a place of death, as an instrument of torture. Beyond that, there are many layers of Christian theology that complicate the picture and reveal how confused the church itself can be about what it considers a central event. Yet Margaret Fell was quite sure that this is where the power is, where the life is—the Power and Life that come from the divine source.

What is "obedience to the cross" to me? It is an all-encompassing embrace. It is the clear direction to share that embrace with others and the long process of working out what that looks like in my particular life. It is the gift of words, but they do not come easily. It is the gift of companions and intimacy I received once I was able to let myself be vulnerable. It is the hardest work I've ever done. It is a call to honesty, to seeing with clearer eyes. It is recognizing how wrong I've been about "other Friends." It is the need welling up within me to rectify my wrongs. It is about *forgiveness*, forgiveness of self and of others. Once, I heard internally the clear words, "Your Father forgives you." But it is also about me offering and seeking forgiveness from others in our mutual wounding rather than turning towards retribution and vengeance.

Taking up the cross is learning to attend to the Pure Principle that illumines the soul. It is about learning to notice and recognize the Light at work within me. It includes much sorting out of what needs to drop away. I have had to turn away from being solely driven by my own wants, such as accumulating wealth or pride—being ego-driven is another way to say this—and turn instead to greater awareness of the more that is being asked of me.

Inward Renewal

I sense the cross as being about death in the way that winter is about dying: leaves die only to become the compost that feeds the formation of new leaves in the spring, becoming part of the growth, newness, and generation of fruit and seeds. Without the winter, much of life on this planet could not exist in its current form. Jesus' death is part of this story, but so is his rebirth. Each of us faces many small inward "deaths" throughout our lives by which things that hinder us, behaviors that are damaging, and all that is deadening fall away in the winter storms. The process is not necessarily light or easy, but if we are responding to the Divine Life within and are true to its guidance, we can become more fully part of that eternal cycle of renewal.

This interior renewal is an ongoing part of coming to live more fully the way Jesus showed us. Galatians 5:22 offers the often-repeated list of fruits of the Spirit: *love, joy, peace, patience, kindness, generosity, faithfulness, gentleness, and self-control.* Such are the visible consequences, the new life, in our behavior as we take up that cross to all the "ways of the flesh"

337

listed in Galatians 5:19–21: *fornication, impurity, licentiousness, idolatry, sorcery, enmities, strife, jealousy, anger, quarrels, dissensions, factions, envy, drunkenness, carousing, and things like these.* As we take up the cross to the ego (what William Penn called "that divine grace which crosses the carnal wills of men"[4]), such things fall away. Yet, our memory of having done such things can give us compassion for those still caught up in quarrels, greed, retribution, or envy, helping us grow into new life.

Movement into Life, or seeking Light and Life, knowing periods of darkness and the dying away of the old, is part of finding our place in the wholeness of the community of life on this globe. Can we see ourselves as integral parts of God's new creation? Can we learn to listen to the movement within the heart and soul that makes visible our place therein? This is what taking up the cross is about—knowing what is ours to do as an integral part of the whole rather than seeing the world as being in service to our peculiar needs.

Sorrow and Pain

Even amid the joyousness of rebirth and renewal, taking up the cross also speaks of the pain and sorrow of the world. To take up whatever cross we are given to bear is to stay with the pain rather than to run from it.

To be able to walk alongside those whose lives have been destroyed—in small ways as well as large—is to listen without false sympathy or facile comfort, offering companionship and empathy. It is inviting the Holy One to walk alongside us through the blank hardness life sometimes throws at us.

Sometimes we are asked to give more than we can bear. We feel abandoned, and every bone in our body wants to get us as far away as possible from the pain. Our hope lies in finding the strength that impelled those who have gone before who were able to stand still in the Truth. The cost we bear may be mostly an internal pain or a process of giving up some material good, yet we shift the world around us when we are faithful even in small things. In each generation, however, a few, such as Martin Luther King Jr., Dorothy Day of the Catholic Worker Movement, or Malala Yousafzai, the Pakistani teenager who stood up to the Taliban, are asked to do so much more. Yet each of us needs to support those individuals the best we can and not turn our heads away from injustice and do nothing.

Entering into the Suffering of the World

Much of the Bible tells stories of suffering, both individual and as a community or nation. The Hebrew prophets often name or even predict that suffering. Jewish scholar Walter Brueggemann's book *The Prophetic Imagination* offers a challenge and a road map to any who would take up the prophetic call. In the section on Jesus of Nazareth, he writes:

> The crucifixion articulates God's odd freedom, his strange justice, and his peculiar power. It is this freedom (read religion of God's freedom), justice (read economics of sharing), and power (read politics of justice) that break the power of the old age and bring it to death. Without the cross, prophetic imagination will likely be as strident and as destructive as that which it criticizes. The cross is the assurance that effective prophetic criticism is done not by an outsider but always by one who must embrace the grief, enter into the death, and know the pain of the criticized one.[5]

Brueggemann places a weight on the cross that echoes Margaret Fell's unequivocal statement that obedience to the Light of Christ is obedience to the cross of Christ . . . the power of God. Fell and her contemporaries in the seventeenth century may not have had the word 'ego' to toss around, but they encouraged all to take up the cross daily in words that clearly meant stepping

339

aside from the demands of the ego. In this, they sound much like the Buddhists who advocate self-emptying and connection to the whole of the world.

Queries for Reflection and/or Discussion

1. What might be a 'hat honor' for today? Can you imagine some simple, widely recognized action that points to the heart of why many North Americans reject immigrants and idolize violence or the amassing of wealth?

2. How might you speak of 'taking up the cross'? How do you convey the power and life that comes through when one lets the demands of the ego drop away and depends on inward guidance?

3. Where do you find inward renewal? What helps you let the 'works of the flesh' die away so that the fruits of the Spirit may take firmer hold within you?

4. Have you been asked by the Spirit to take on a task that has been painful or difficult for you? How did you bear the cost? Who walked alongside you?

5. How have you walked alongside others who have taken up the cross, and have you perhaps borne the cross for them for a brief time?

CHAPTER 33
LISTENING TO OUR SPIRITUAL ANCESTORS

In the midst of this century's litany of horrors and threats, most of which affect us in the United States only indirectly, what does it mean to be part of a community founded in a period of direct persecution and civil war? If nothing else, considering these actions encourages me to raise up the need for broader practical thought as well as prayer instead of the frustration that too often characterizes discussions about the future of Friends.

This chapter is an open invitation to Friends to consider what we might do today to reframe the way we see our small community and its place in the world. What might be of service to individuals who honestly are attending to the voice of God and seeking to be faithful yet feel lonely and abandoned?

Quakers are spread around the world, some of us in comfortable, protected circumstances with the luxury of actively disagreeing and deciding to separate into smaller and smaller mini-communities. Others live in places where proclaiming Christ is dangerous or where simply being of the wrong tribe can lead to death or torture.

The Past: What Might Be Alive?

The statistics are grim. By 1655, a significant number of friends were imprisoned. In 1662, the Quaker Act, which asserted that Friends were endangering public peace and safety because of their way of worship, made Quaker worship illegal. Friends listed 3,179 in prison and 32 dead before 1660 and over 5,000 in prison and an additional 22 dead in the following decade.[1] Margaret Fell, George Fox, and many others of the first generation of Friends developed a system of mutual support that bolstered those who might be afraid and provided physical as well as spiritual sustenance to those who suffered for their faith. They also mounted a politically sophisticated campaign to convince the world of their righteousness.

These points are identified by Rosemary Moore in *The Light in Their Consciences: The Early Quakers in Britain, 1646–1666*.[2] As the world shifts around us, I find it helpful to revisit and reconsider some of the treasures that have been handed down from our spiritual ancestors. Some, such as the nature of early Quaker worship with its many differences from that of other Christians in England, are familiar today. Some of the early Quaker practices have not been well known until recent intensive scholarship on the seventeenth century rediscovered them. I, for one, had not realized the wide scope of Friends' support of one another in the face of severe condemnation and persecution. Moore has uncovered valuable patterns in how they reached out to one another. Some are quite useful to consider in this day and age as we attempt to find new vitality and to comprehend how we might enliven our prophetic voice once again.

Not Suffering in Silence

Early Quakers did not suffer in silence. They let their neighbors and everyone possible know when Friends had been thrown in jail, whipped, or otherwise wrongly treated by those in power. The 1655 publication *Saints Testimony Finishing through Sufferings* is an early example of the many publications describing the ill treatment of Quakers by the authorities and proclaiming their innocence. As Moore tells us, this work gave much attention to the cases of Ann Audland, who was charged with blasphemy and eventually acquitted, and of Richard Farnsworth, who was imprisoned for eight months.[3]

Honoring and Supporting Those Who Suffered

By 1654, George Fox and Margaret Fell were both urging Friends to keep track of their sufferings, and Friends were instructed in 1657 to send careful lists of all sufferings—imprisonment, fines, confiscation of household goods, or deaths—so that other Friends might visit those in prison and provide other assistance. Moore notes that the visiting Friends brought food and clean clothes as well as companionship, hope, and news of the world and otherwise helped families survive when they had lost their bed, or their cow, or their printing press and were left without resources.[4]

One of the earliest actions of meetings, as they were organized into more formal monthly meetings and a yearly meeting, was to respond to the query, "What Friends imprisoned for their testimony have died in prison since the last yearly meeting?"[5]

Making Use of the Law

Side by side with the publicity and direct help provided to those who suffered for their faith, Friends undertook intensive lobbying, first with Oliver Cromwell while he served as protector and then with King Charles as well as with the English Parliament. Over the decades, there were successes, such as in 1659 when a radical Parliament was sympathetic to Quakers and other nonconformists. Then, after the restoration of the monarchy, Friends faced great setbacks, such as the passage of the Quaker Act and other harsh laws enacted against all who were not part of the Church of England. Through it all, Quaker leadership was sophisticated in their approach, making use of advice from knowledgeable Friends and also from sympathizers who could help them access the right people.[6]

The early Quakers also quickly learned to use the courts to their advantage and directly challenged both judge and jury to live up to God's truth. The most famous court case, that of William Penn and William Mead, grew out of their arrest for preaching at worship outside a meetinghouse that had been locked by the authorities. They were charged with causing a riot; after hearing the evidence, the jury refused to declare them guilty. The judge then sent the jury to Newgate Prison until they changed their minds, which they did not do. The case was appealed, and the higher court upheld the right of juries to bring a verdict independent of the judge's opinion.

Threatening Disaster to Persecutors

Friends wrote a large number of pamphlets and letters refuting the multitude of charges against them. These writings often used strong, apocalyptic language that accused their attackers of being the spawn of the beast or the anti-Christ and doomed to judgment before God. The early Friends were by no means gentle in their language—something I have yet to come to terms with.

In a 1655 letter to Gabriel Camelford, who had been attacking Quakers, Margaret Fell writes: "Oh thou serves an evil Master. He causes thee to lie thy nakedness and filthiness openly; and the shame of thy abomination appears."[7] She then turns Camelford's own arguments against him and declares that he is

- "a pleader for sin" (as a Calvinist);
- "an enemy of God";
- "an enemy to the light which is the first principle," which reveals the Truth;
- "antichrist and a denyer of Christ come in the flesh"; and
- "a devourer of widow's houses."[8]

Fell concludes by stating that Camelford's portion is in Jeremiah 8:12–14, which says in part, *therefore, shall they fall among them that fall: in the time of their visitation they shall be cast down, saith the Lord* (KJV).[9]

In the seventeenth century, as Moore explains, this kind of language was widely understood and was part of the general discourse.[10] This leaves me with a big question. What is the right way to speak truth today— how do we speak truth solidly and clearly so that it will best be heard?

Today, we know more about how humans think, and we have learned that it is almost impossible to change people's minds by condemning them or berating them. Something else is needed to break through defenses and to open people to perspectives that initially seem alien.

Being open to change has been one of the central tenets of the Pacific Northwest Quaker Women's Theology Conferences. These gatherings have brought together evangelical and theologically liberal women since the early 1990s. When we first gathered, we were virtually terrified of each other. Liberal Friends worried about being evangelized. Christian women were fearful of lesbians. A longing to know something other than hostility among Friends carried us all past the fear and strengthened our desire to know and feel empathy with one another. Change flourished, if slowly. Both the Bible and lesbians became more widely accepted. This is one of the formative experiences that have convinced me that condemning those who do not agree is not part of the Quaker way. Reconciliation seems impossible without trust and openness, no matter how difficult it may be to create the conditions that allow change.

A Theology of Suffering

James Parnell was a young man who in his teens was already viewed as an inspired minister. His death in April 1656 at the age of nineteen from mistreatment in Colchester Prison struck Friends hard. Parnell was among the first of the many Friends who suffered miserably over the course of nearly half a century. Friends were defined by their experience of the Light of Christ in the soul. In the face of their suffering, they came to know that this inward knowledge of Christ that brought them into obedience to God also readily led them to know the reality of Jesus' warning that one consequence of being his friend was that the world would hate them.

As noted earlier, early Friends regularly wrote of "taking up the cross daily." Taking up the cross to the will, to the demands of the self in obedience to God's will, involved actions that ranged from getting rid of the paintings in their homes to refusing to swear an oath, knowing these acts could lead to weeks or even years of living in the dark and filth of an English prison. The cross was a measure of obedience, yet taking up the cross was also a source of joy and power—God's power, the power of absolute love that would defeat all evil. This gave them the strength to sing amidst the bugs and excrement, to convert their jailers, and to not only survive but thrive as a prophetic witness to the kingdom of God.

Becoming a Friend in the early years often meant suffering. In a 1658 pamphlet, Humphrey Smith expressed his confidence in redemption:

> And him that kills the body we fear not, much less those that can but whip or imprison for a few months, for our life you cannot reach, neither can you disturb their rest whom the Lord has crowned with honour.[11]

Fox knew beyond any doubt that he was doing what he was called to do. He, along with most other Friends, identified fully with the words of the Gospel of John in which Jesus said,

> *"This is my commandment, that you love one another as I have loved you. No one has greater love than this, to lay down one's life for one's friends. You are my friends if you do*

346

what I command you. I do not call you servants any longer, because the servant does not know what the master is doing; but I have called you friends, because I have made known to you everything that I have heard from my Father." (15:12–15)

The specific structures that Friends established in the seventeenth century built on their foundational encounter with Jesus Christ alive and guiding people in their present lives. Their worship assumed that anyone present might be given words directly by the Spirit, not just those trained in certain colleges or those of particular status. Similarly, they made decisions that affected the functioning of the community in business meetings open to all members and based on the sense of those present that they were being guided by the Light, not by a few people who could argue most effectively for a particular course of action.

These broad metastructures described above are an indication of how the early Quakers adapted to the particular situations they faced while remaining faithful to their knowledge of God's way for the whole body.[12] Our challenge today is to consider again how the basic structures we have in place now, which carry forward some of the seventeenth-century practices but with a patchwork of other structures mingled in, serve our needs today. How do we need to change in ways that reach inward to that guidance we each seek and outward to awareness of the condition of the world today?

Queries for Reflection and/or Discussion

1. In what ways do the actions of early Friends described in this chapter seem relevant today?

2. Have I experienced or known of actions that are so unconscionable that I cannot simply sit back without taking action? What did that feel like? What action did I take? Who stood by me?

3. What changes do we need within our meetings or churches to create an atmosphere that welcomes prophetic ministry, encourages us all to be everyday prophets, and supports the individuals who are called to public witness?

CHAPTER 34
DISCERNING STRUCTURES THAT FOSTER INJUSTICE AND VIOLENCE

Esther Mombo (Highlands Yearly Meeting), whose words run through this book, carries the vision of prophetic ministry as Friends know it. She has seen the injustice done to the poor by dishonest shopkeepers and has spoken out against weighted scales, just as seventeenth-century Friends advocated fixed prices for goods so that the weakest among them would not be exploited as they spent their pennies for the basics of life.

> The bigger story, that God is a God of justice and that justice will roll like the waters, this is language which I interpret as being involved, not just preaching. . . . I see it as living out what we preach. There is a difference between a shop that is seen as Quaker and a shop run by someone else—this is about tipping the scales, or exploiting the poor.
>
> In the U.S., we should be asking "what are we doing about the payday check cashers who will give out money at exorbitant interest rates?" These are as bad as or worse than the shopkeepers with dishonest scales. The stores that will give you money are only part of a massive system that entwines much of the nation in debt, mostly through the easy availability of credit cards. Again, the interest rates charged are often unconscionable.

Esther critiques Friends, and Christians in general, for not making conditions better for the poor. In Kenya, Friends have not been able to prevent merchants from charging for false weights, and in the United States there has been little action to stop payday loans with exorbitant interest rates. She asks of us, when we are not acting to prevent violence or injustice, "So, where was our voice? Where was our prophetic ministry in such things?" Her assessment is that we have too often failed to step forward and act, and she is right. We have fallen short. Friends are more visible on broad issues. Jay O'Hara, for instance, stopped a coal tanker (temporarily) with a small fishing boat, which raised the issue of climate change when he spoke before the judge on the practical and spiritual dimensions of his witness.

Esther does acknowledge that Friends have done a lot to feed and tend to the victims of violence, but she pushes us to look at the need to change the underlying systems that feed the violence.

> Maybe there is much more we have to do, not just to bind the wounds. . . . What are the systems that enhance the ethnic wars that we had? Where were we when the systems were being developed that allowed it to happen? That for me is the internal critique that we have to give ourselves. We have not really practiced the prophetic ministry in terms of involvement, though we may have spoken to each other about it among ourselves. It is not a clean slate. I am still with this question myself.

Esther's comments apply to Friends around the world, everywhere that people step back and say "this does not concern me directly" or "it is not safe to take a stand." Esther's questions apply to each of us, whether we are concerned about how children are treated in our schools or the proliferation of nuclear weapons.

Familiar Structures and Ways of Being

From the perspective of North America, Friends' criticism of other Friends tends to focus on the degree of comfort that pervades many of our meetings as well as the lifestyles of our members. Martin Kelley (Philadelphia Yearly Meeting) is an active blogger from the liberal tradition who has a concern for the recovery of the evangelical passion of Friends. In a post on his blog *Quaker Ranter*, he named some of the major obstacles to attracting younger people to

Friends and blocks to the vitality and growth of meetings. As a younger Friend, he is very conscious of how far Friends in his tradition have moved away from Quakerism's deep roots in Christianity and sees our meetings to be more often social gatherings than religious ones. He describes a long tradition of birthright membership in his yearly meeting that leads some families to feel ownership of the local meeting and resist change.[1]

This is compounded by the reality that, in many small meetings, everyone knows one another and no one is willing to contradict others or articulate who Friends are. He describes it this way: "Too many Friends are happy with their nice cozy meetings. The meetings serve as family and as a support group, and a real growth would disrupt our established patterns." He believes that, in reality, "Many of us actually yearn for more care, attention and oversight in our religious lives and more connection with others."[2]

Part of the problem Martin (and others) has encountered is the overly busy life of so many people compounded by priorities that tend to allocate only a few specific hours for religion. Martin writes in his blog:

> Religion in America has become yet another consumer choice, an entertainment option for Sunday morning, and this paradigm is true with Friends. We complain [about] how much time our Quaker work takes up. . . . A more involved Quakerism would realize that the hour on First Day morning is in many ways the least important time to our Society. Younger seekers are looking for connections that are deeper and that will require time. We can't build a Society on the cheap. It's not money we need to invest, but our hearts and time.[3]

His final concern is about bigotry and the ways we unconsciously exclude many people from our community while boasting of being open and inclusive:

> The Liberal branch of Friends spends a lot of time congratulating itself on being open, tolerant and self-examining and yet as far as I can tell we're the least ethnically-diverse branch of American Quakers. . . . We need to re-examine and challenge the unwritten norms of Quaker culture that don't arise from faith. When we have something to offer besides upper-class liberalism, we'll find we can talk to a much wider selection of seekers.[4]

Martin's blog is hopeful in that he frames it as a challenge for Friends to pay attention and take on several tasks if we have any wish of reenergizing the Society. He calls for a reexamination of our roots as Christians and as Friends, a desire to grow, a renewal of discipline and oversight, a more personally involved and time-consuming commitment, a renewal of discipline and oversight, and a confrontation of our ethnic and cultural bigotries.

Martin ends with the query, Can we do it?

Helping People or Supporting Ministry?

Julian Beresford, another Philadelphia Friend and blogger, speaks to a question that has been often asked among Friends and elsewhere: Are we trying to fix other people's problems or are we seeking to empower them to address what is wrong in a way that makes sense to them? This question is appropriate in our home communities when we seek to aid someone who is struggling, just as it is in issues of international aid where the wealthy get to decide how their money is spent.

> On the topic of funding (or starving) people's ministries—there are some aid ideas that tend to see people in poor countries (or poor communities) as people to help, rather than people whose ministries we should be

supporting. These aid ideas tend to stifle people's economic and creative abilities rather than encourage them. When I got started in ministry I saw myself more as a "doing ministry" person than a "giving people resources to do their ministry" person.

What I learned is, when we help people outside our own community, we have the chance to live out that old Quaker ideal that everyone's a minister—to give in a way that empowers people and respects their abilities to be problem-solvers for their families and communities.[5]

This desire to do things for others is a worthy human trait. When people are starving, we should be feeding them. When homes are destroyed by typhoons, we should be helping people find shelter and rebuild their lives. Such is the stuff that knits society together and helps define the best of humanity worldwide. It acknowledges the connections among us and begins to weave a larger web of mutual dependence that I see as part of the new creation.

Yet how often do we engage Julian's question by considering whether we are offering assistance as part of a complex chain of mutual support or are being patronizing and determining what is right for others in a way that denies them their full humanity and responsibility? Julian calls out this question in relation to ministry. When are we giving people the tools and encouragement to take on their own ministry and when are we "doing ministry" for them? Such questions are very much alive among those Friends looking at the racism that still exists among us and naming the degree to which many of us have been beneficiaries of white privilege. Quaker schools are proud to be among the best in the nation academically. A few have made a commitment in recent years to racial justice despite a long history of refusal to enroll black students. One example is Germantown Friends School, which rejected the offer of a beautiful suburban property and elected to remain in a largely black neighborhood and raise money for local children to attend. In this, they took a step to counter the social structures that make it difficult for black children to get a good education.

In our churches, this question of the nature of ministry is a dilemma that Quaker pastors face. Pastors are at times expected to take on full responsibility for ministering to the congregation. In some Christian traditions, pastors are given the authority to hear God's will for the whole body. Some Quaker pastors face the pressure of congregational expectations brought from other denominations; these people may not have had models of pastors who wish to encourage members to take up their own ministries. Some Quaker pastors have been innovative in setting up ministerial teams that engage members of the congregation who have particular gifts. Such congregations pay attention to gifts and callings without regard to conventional rules. My sense, observing this as an outsider, is that there is much potential to create vital models of pastoring but that there is also much room for learning and experimentation in this area. Similarly, unprogrammed Friends need to experiment with more ways to offer religious education and pastoral care as a group of volunteers.

Queries for Reflection and/or Discussion

1. What do you see as the cultural biases among Friends? In what ways have we slipped into being like the culture around us, to the detriment of our meetings and churches?

2. What would a Quaker culture be? What would it look like in our church or meeting? What does it mean to lead a Quaker life?

3. How are our structures grounded in faith? Which structures are supported mainly by habit?

CHAPTER 35
ENGAGING IN TODAY'S WORLD

> The gathered people felt living water flowing around them. They were opened to the Truth Who holds us all, the true Liberation and Love always available to each of us. They stood together in the power of an endless Life. Their hearts knew that God is Real.[1]

Noah Merrill (New England Yearly Meeting) offered these words as a young plenary speaker at the 2012 World Conference of Friends. He used the story of Elijah to name what is at the core of Friends faith. He also found in Elijah, who was "zealous for the Lord," a guide to help us see when we have lost this Truth. Noah writes of himself:

> In my life, I have been zealous for the LORD. I have outrun my Guide. I have isolated myself, thinking I was working alone. I have seen how far I am from who God invites me to be. My heart has been broken open. At my most tender and vulnerable, I have felt the Whisperer who waits below the whirlwind, on the other side of the earthquake. Who is not consumed by the fire. And I know from experience that we can be changed.[2]

Noah, who spent seven years building relationships between Iraqi and American people, has found himself at times pushed into being so focused on social justice that he has lost track of guidance from the Giver of Life. He is just one of many in the new generation of leadership among Friends who has questioned the secular approach to peace and justice work that has been so prevalent in my generation.

I find many younger Quaker thinkers and writers seeking the life within our meetings and attempting to articulate a possible way forward. Mostly, I've been looking among those who consider themselves "convergent Friends," as defined by Robin Mohr. Convergent Friends find themselves on "the intersection of theology, practice, and dialogue between evangelical and liberal, programmed and unprogrammed, Christian and non-Christian Friends all being blown in the same direction by the 'winds of the Spirit.'"[3]

Robin states that convergent Friends tend to connect online and to reject dualisms; she notes that their community is formed more by dialogue than by common understanding. My experience of this amorphous group is that deep bonds have formed among them as well as an atmosphere that supports radical experimentation and keeps pressing all to attend to the Inward Guide. What follows is only a small sample of what such Friends have to say.

Finding Common Ground or Radical Change?

Friends today are looking for life in new places, places that echo our heritage in surprising ways. 'Familied monasticism' is a term occasionally used to describe early Friends' call to live uncloistered lives yet practice a daily spiritual discipline similar to that of monks. Young people today from many variations of Christianity have coined the term 'new monasticism' to describe their desire for this kind of life that unifies action and faith. Robin Mohr took on leadership of the American Section of Friends World Committee for Consultation while raising two children. In 2009, she described in her blog *What Canst Thou Say?* what she has learned from the new monasticism movement that she thinks might be valuable for Friends:

> The list of 12 Marks of a New Monasticism is another list of characteristics of a religion I want to be part of. Much like Gibbs/Bolger's nine elements of emerging church or Diana Butler Bass's Ten Signposts of Renewal. Each of these strikes me as a good set of measurements or goals for considering how

> I'm living my own life and how my Meeting is
> connecting our community life.[4]

In this blog, she highlights two actions that she sees as particularly relevant to Friends. The first is to move meetinghouses out of well-to-do neighborhoods and into places where marginalized people live and work. Here she speaks from the experience of her home community in San Francisco, which did exactly this.

> The first is "relocating to the abandoned places of empire." Fifteen years ago, San Francisco Monthly Meeting moved to the South of Market . . . on purpose. It's less abandoned now than it used to be, but it's still a place where we regularly wrestle with our right relationship to our homeless, poor, mentally ill or addicted neighbors. It's hard sometimes, and I wouldn't say we always get it right, but we can't ignore them either.[5]

Yet despite such efforts, even the best intentioned of us find it difficult to sustain such commitments. Robin and her husband used to live in this neighborhood, but "for the last seven years we have lived in quieter, cleaner neighborhoods." This causes her to ask: "How are we modeling our discipleship here? Or have we just backslid and given up? This is a real question for me some days."

The second point from the new monasticism movement that Robin raises up is the concept of intentional community. For much of the history of Friends prior to the twentieth century, most Friends lived within walking or easy horseback-riding distance of the rest of their community. The rhythm of life made for stronger personal connections and care. Robin describes today's situation:

> Another is "nurturing common life among members of intentional community." One of the recurring functions of our Meeting is to set up small groups that meet in each other's

homes for a meal and fellowship. We call them Friendly 8's. . . . We have to be intentional about our community because it's not based on a natural affinity. I mean I like these people, but we didn't all really know each other before. It's not super-time-consuming either; one night a month we meet for an early potluck dinner and worship sharing. But it's a good beginner's laboratory for building community.[6]

Robin admits that these steps towards intentional community are simply baby steps. There is little mutual dependence, but, for many, potluck meals are all they can manage in the press of cultural expectations around jobs and family. This cultural pressure is perhaps one of the major factors that limit our ability to nurture the prophetic ministry in our midst. Often we do not even know each other enough to recognize when someone has a calling or is trying to sense how the Spirit is pushing them. Some people seek out tiny home meetings so they might develop deeper connections, but it is then easy to slide into the comfort of a known group and resist growth in spiritual risk-taking as well as growth in numbers.

Robin recommends the book *Christianity for the Rest of Us: How the Neighborhood Church Is Transforming the Faith* by Diana Butler Bass, which summarizes a study of mainline Protestant churches. Robin writes,

What are the practices that characterize a thriving mainline congregation? Officially what their study looked at was the coherence of spiritual practice in a congregation, the authenticity of their practices, and the degree of transformation through their practices. The main things they found that these churches had in common were shared tradition, practice and wisdom. And a commitment to a transformative form of Christianity. And humility. These were not churches that claimed to know all the answers, but who were working through the questions together.[7]

Bass offers ten "signposts of renewal": hospitality, discernment, healing, contemplation, testimony, diversity, justice, worship, reflection, and beauty. At first glance, I found these signposts too broad because they miss central dimensions such as nonviolence, prophetic witness, and the call to walk with each other in the midst of tragedy and fear. But Bass's list echoes some of the elements from our own tradition.

The Culture of Activism

It is a stretch to define modern Quakers. We do not hold our spiritual ancestors' common vision of the Lamb's War or even of the kingdom of God. Is personal morality most important? What does that look like? Do we have a responsibility to change the culture of American or world society and the institutions that govern us? Among the more liberal Friends with whom I worship, there is disagreement over whether our work is grounded in God or in ethical values and whether it is acceptable to mention God or Jesus Christ. We also disagree on the place of conflict in the context of our testimony to nonviolence. Are verbal argument and bold criticism acceptable? Is reconciliation always the aim?

Movement for a New Society (MNS) was formed in 1971 in Philadelphia, and its founders included Quakers such as George Lakey. They sought a life of radical activism that they could not find within the Religious Society of Friends, which they felt was moribund in many places. MNS generated much excitement and drew in many wishing to change society.

MNS was more secular than religious. For instance, its members used consensus decision-making rather than seeking the 'sense of the meeting' or unity— compromise rather than looking to the guidance of the

Spirit; this was also the practice in some unprogrammed Friends meetings at the time.

In its heavy reliance on secular social justice, MNS epitomized approaches that I and many other Friends took up in the twentieth century in our passion for a better world. Even as I have come to know the power that comes when I've been faithful to the True Guide, I can't help but see a prophetic dimension in MNS because they looked beneath the surface of society and sought to address the root causes of injustice. They expected their own lives to change as they worked to change society. Movement for a New Society as an organization no longer exists, but its influence is still apparent.

Now, over forty years after the founding of MNS, many of us, particularly younger Friends, are looking to respond to our passionate awareness of divine guidance in our speech and actions even amid explorations of such questions as the need to be strategic in protesting injustice.

On Being Strategic

I don't have a simple answer as to whether or not prophets need to be strategic. Certainly that is not their main task, but it has a place. Early Quakers made savvy use of the legal system, and Jesus' example tells us much about how we might face manipulators, liars, and others who tend to blame the poor for their condition and amass great wealth or otherwise perpetrate violence. Jesus' ability to sense when the Pharisees were attempting to trap him was rather amazing. He had a clear sense of what he was doing and the resistance he might experience. Being dependent on the guidance of the Spirit does not necessarily mean being naïve and foolish. Friends in many places are stepping into a life of faith that includes practical lobbying and strategic thinking.

Earth Quaker Action Team (EQAT, pronounced "equate") formed in the twenty-first century with a focus on climate justice. Centered in Philadelphia, more than half of its board members are in their mid-twenties to early thirties. Eileen Flanagan (Philadelphia Yearly Meeting), clerk of the EQAT board, speaks to the spiritual dimension of their activism:

> We are really experimenting with how to bring our spirituality into action while being welcoming and accessible to non-Quakers, including many young people who have found a spiritual home with us, not because we talk about God but because they have experienced a powerful connection to the Divine in action.

Between 2010 and 2015, EQAT organized over three hundred people in thirteen states and the District of Columbia to pressure PNC Bank to stop financing coal mining by mountaintop removal in Appalachia. Eileen wrote a blog in 2015 for the online publication *Grid Magazine* highlighting the strategic approach that she found invaluable in EQAT's success in getting PNC to stop financing coal mining.

1. Choose one campaign.

. . . Many issues need addressing, it's tempting to try to do a little bit on all of them, but history shows that picking one and focusing on it for an extended period of time is the best way to get results.

2. Pick a strategic target.

Was PNC the only bank financing environmental destruction? No, but PNC claims to be a "green" bank, has Quaker roots and as a result, many Quaker customers. . .

3. Don't be boring.

Surprising actions are more likely to attract participants and press. For example, EQAT sang, "Where Have All the Flowers Gone" in front of the PNC pavilion at the 2011 Philadelphia Flower Show. . . .

4. Be willing to take a risk.

Protesting inside a bank or a shareholder meeting is scarier than speeches out on the sidewalk. . . . encourage your members to do something just a little bolder than what they've done before.

5. Create a dilemma.

One way to escalate the pressure on your target is to create a situation where they lose something no matter what. In the case of the shareholder meeting where Earth Quakers sang to the PNC board, the CEO . . . could have [had] the protestors arrested, attracting even more press and disrupting the meeting. Instead, he shut his legally mandated annual meeting down after only seventeen minutes.

By keeping its focus on PNC, EQAT has created an even bigger dilemma for the bank: stop financing companies engaged in mountaintop removal coal mining and risk angering the coal industry, or continue losing customers over this issue.[8]

There is much more to be said here, and books abound on the nature of nonviolence and social justice activism. The tension between faithfulness and effectiveness reflects just one dimension of the multitude of our different faith perspectives. Our history reveals a wide variety of ways individuals have acted out of what they felt they were led to do. In the eighteenth century, John Woolman would patiently speak to slave owners one at a time, sometimes giving a message at business meetings, and then would go home before the discussion had even started, leaving the results in God's hands. About the same time, Benjamin Lay was making dramatic gestures such as stabbing a bladder full of blood to demonstrate the evils of slavery. He became seen as an important voice in anti-slavery work but was disowned by Quakers.

My inclination is to see the value of a variety of approaches even as I cringe at Benjamin Lay's actions. My participation in marches against several wars upset my parents. My work for women's rights pulled me into politics as well as led me to establish a National Organization for Women chapter in southern Virginia. There are seemingly infinite occasions where a clear prophetic voice is needed as well as good strategic thinkers. Yet I also know the reality of being over-reliant on self and without an anchor in the Whisperer who animates Noah Merrill and all of us.

Articulating the Roots of Our Peace Testimony

Martin Kelley decries the lack of attractiveness of Friends for young people today. He asks: "What if we started testifying to one another about that great Power that's taken away occasion for war, what if our testimony became a witness to our faith?"[9] His complaint is about liberal Friends—our unease at sharing our own personal faith, the absence of enunciating the roots of our testimonies in First Day School programs for children, and our tendency to always take the safer, less vulnerable way by only naming the ethical grounds of our actions.

The book of Revelation was a central text for the earliest Friends. This last book of the Christian Testament is full of images of evil and the need to confront and destroy it. These Friends entered into the allegory fully and empathically, drawing forth the image of the Lamb's War. This is a fight against evil, but it is a fight that can only use the weapons that Jesus did, the weapons of love and justice, of generosity and steadfastness and integrity. The early Friends were certain that if we fight evil using violence, hatred, greed, and the desire to control others, we only end up imitating that which we seek to destroy.

Micah Bales helped form meetings in Washington, D.C., and Philadelphia that carry a passion for both Christ and social justice. He wrote a post titled "Burning Down the Meeting House" on his blog *The Lamb's War*:

> Our God is indeed a consuming fire, and all of us—young and old—have dross to be melted away as we wait in that refining Presence. How must we change so that we can wait together as a body, receiving the teaching of the Holy Spirit? . . . And how do we avoid making the tools and gifts our focus, rather than God? How can we live into these questions together, as an intergenerational community?[10]

As noted earlier, the title of this particular post got a strong reaction from those who took it literally. Some felt threatened by young Friends rejecting the iconic buildings that often have become a symbol of who we are. I am simultaneously protective of Friends having places to gather and glad when we recognize that we have made them idols. It is a challenge to speak out when we see ourselves ignoring the call to live out the Lamb's War and instead look for comfort and protection among like-minded people.

A few months later, Micah wrote further reflections about his earlier post. On page 277 of this book, he addresses why he used that provocative title. In the quote below, he talks about the importance of avoiding conflict:

> To begin with, my experiences in several Quaker communities had taught me that being too assertive was dangerous, and that I could get more done through passive influence than direct argument. . . .
> Perhaps a better reason for avoiding conflict has been that as I have grown to love other people more, I am more sensitive to the fact that conflict can be painful. . . . [It] has the potential to severely disrupt our relationships.

> I have been a part of many small, fragile groups, and I haven't wanted to unleash a dispute that would destroy the whole community![11]

Micah's challenge to us to face our discomforts is a real one to me. My natural inclination is to be quiet and to gently make suggestions. I know that significant numbers of people who worship with us have been abused; even strong language can trigger unwanted memories and feelings. We need to be careful regarding the level of conflict in our community and the way it is expressed. But I also have learned that there are times when we have to stand and be clear, both in our own communities and in the world. This is one more piece of the paradox of holy living: to be humble yet bold and to offer a refuge from the world as well as a place that sends out radical prophets.

On Power

Power has a lot of different meanings. In the early twenty-first century, the disagreements over who has authority to interpret the Bible have been felt as a misuse of power in several yearly meetings that have separated in recent years. Among the yearly meetings that have separated in recent years, often the central point of disagreement was the authority of Scripture relative to the Inward Light. This authority was most visibly tested over acceptance of same-gender relationships. The most recent split was in the Pacific Northwest of the United States, resulting in the creation of the Sierra-Cascades Yearly Meeting of Friends in 2017. Its initial co-clerks, Cherice Bock and Eric Muhr, are both articulate bloggers. Cherice writes:

> In an ideal world, Friends would listen to the Spirit and follow its guidance whether or not they agree with its politics. . . . no power struggles would be necessary: no political positioning of individuals in positions of power within the community. . . . In this ideal

world, the importance is not, "What does this person believe?" Rather, the questions are more like, "Is this person someone who I trust to listen well to the Light of Christ?" . . . What I see is not trust; it is fear.[12]

In this, as in so many human disagreements, people have behaved badly and have made fear-filled accusations and assumptions about 'the other.' In this separation, people have cried over broken relationships and have sought to mend them, reaching out in love despite their fears.

Cherice goes on to speak about how we frame disagreements and the importance of avoiding taking sides.

> This means that I can't control the outcome. It means that the way we solve the problem may not be the way I would have liked, or the way I would have done it. In our heads, we know this opens up the process to the potential of the "third way" we like to talk about as Friends, but this act of submission is scary. It makes us feel vulnerable.[13]

She acknowledges the legitimacy of the many fears we face if we accept this path of giving up power and control. She describes the reality that her previous yearly meeting had refused to recognize her as a recorded minister. This led to her asking herself, "Why not just give up? Since I can listen to God on my own, why do I need these people?"

Her response to her own questions reflects her longing for a community she can trust.

Remix and Renewal

Various Friends in the younger generations are testing out new ways to communicate who we are. Noah Merrill gave a lecture titled *Prophets, Midwives and Thieves: Reclaiming the Ministry of the Whole* in which he used fresh words to describe the motion of ministers who give birth to new Life and the elders who serve as midwives to this Life. He renames overseers the "watchers at the wall" who attend to the conditions for faithful living and cites Margaret Fell's usage of the word "thieves" to describe those who speak of the Spirit and know it not in our souls.[14]

C. Wess Daniels, who is now teaching at Guilford College, finds hope in remixing traditional and contemporary culture, pointing to Freedom Friends Church in Oregon as setting a precedent for Quaker meetings seeking participatory renewal. He says that the members of this church

> foster a new contextual theology through the use of remix, authentic resistance and decentralized authority. They remix Quakerism as convergent Friends, pulling together the best that Quakerism has to offer and synthesizing it in new ways.[15]

Their remix of the Bible and traditional Quaker thought creates a new combination that is not afraid of innovation. They reject creedalism and fundamentalism, turning instead to authentic resistance that removes obstacles so that people may "encounter God in powerful ways." And they provide space for all to engage in gospel order and discernment together as a multi-voiced community.

Queries for Reflection and/or Discussion

1. How do you envision the ideal community of faith? What do you long for? Do Robin Mohr's words speak to your condition?

2. How might you help change antiquated but sometimes beloved structures without engaging in violence—be it physical, verbal, emotional, mental, or spiritual?

3. How does the example of EQAT (or other approaches mentioned in this chapter) speak to your heart? What new forms and practices can you envision for supporting one another and all those working for justice?

4. What responsibility does the everyday prophet have to speak in a way that can be heard? Is this in conflict with the call to be faithful and obedient to the Spirit?

5. How might you envision engaging in bringing about the new creation or participating in the Lamb's War? What might be your role? The role of your meeting or church?

CHAPTER 36
MOVING WITH THE WIND

One day the wind was blowing strong. Six of us were on a sailboat headed towards the rocks of the Maine coast at exhilarating speed. We were confident in our ability to steer the boat and have it 'come about,' to turn away from the shore and begin the next leg of the journey we were on. As we approached the rocks, about to make this move that would take us back out to sea, there was a loud ripping sound. The jenny, the large sail on the front of our boat, tore raggedly in two. This turn was not going to happen as we had planned.

Our skipper headed the boat directly into the wind so that the wind was no longer pushing us as hard towards the rocks. The most agile among us clambered over the rigging and took down the shreds of the old sail and rigged a new one.

We can train and practice and hone our skills. We can memorize our most central texts, be they the Bible or the sailing manual. But then there is the moment when the sail rips to shreds. The moment when everything we thought would happen and all our apparent control fails. The moment when all we can do is point the boat directly into the wind, the point where motion stops. In that moment of stillness, we can begin removing the tatters of our expectations and put up the new sail that can once again catch the winds.

The Spiritual North Star

My journey is headed towards the spiritual North Star. At least, that is my intent. This small boat that I call my body has few defenses against the power of the waves, and the power of my muscles and my will are readily overwhelmed by the force of an active storm or even the intensity of day-to-day winds. Much of the time, I do not have the option of powering straight ahead to follow that star unless the wind is with me and the currents aren't too strong.

This image I can feel in my bones from having sailed in the Pacific Northwest among the Gulf Islands, in Desolation Sound, off the coast of Alaska, and in the open ocean. In such territory, there are many narrow places where the wind and current are against you, more than the capacity of the boat to overcome. The only option is to wait for the winds to change or the tide to turn. On other days, it is still and beautiful, but no air is moving to fill the sails. Without a mechanical motor, one can only remain at dock or drift on the currents.

When facing a strong headwind, it is no use to curse it and try to go directly to your destination. You will only be blown backwards, perhaps onto the rocks. This is most evident in the small boats I am familiar with, but even the largest of our human freighters can find themselves caught on a reef or aground in the muck—which is a helpful metaphor for the way humans too often want to engage those they disagree with. We have such an impulse to attack, to contradict, to let others know we have the right answer. We try to bully our way into the headwind and then find the pushback harsh. We can make no headway.

The word for wind—*ruah* in Hebrew—is also how the ancients named the Spirit. This same word designates the breath of the Divine and human breath. It speaks of the invisible moving air that can destroy or transport. It is the central force of life. It is an external force that moves us and cannot be held or controlled by mortal hands. This word offers a profound link between Spirit, the breath of life, and the wind that constantly circles our planet.

The mystery that is God, the incomprehensible power of the tornado, the breath of life, the spirit that enlivens and nourishes our soul—how do we learn to sail such seas, move in the midst of such dynamics? We may steer with confidence amid the rocks that can penetrate the hull of our ship, thinking we know how to avoid them all. Then the sail disintegrates in the wind.

When we have attended to the Spirit over the years and learned something of the nature of that divine breath, we can settle back into the stillness with the prow pointed directly into the wind—towards the Infinite—and discover the way forward. If we panic and flail and get caught up in our own emotions, we may easily be stuck in crisis. The more we know the ship (our body) and are familiar with the nature of that wind that comes from God, the more we are able to right ourselves and find the course that is ours to follow.

Setting the Sails to Move with the Breath of God

If you align your boat—your heart, if you will—at the correct angle to the headwind and set your sails accordingly, it is possible to sail quickly and freely. Because you are moving at an angle to where you want to be, readjusting the course and resetting the sails is essential if the overall movement is to be in the right direction. In tight places, when the wind is strong and rocks are nearby, the boat may need to come about quite frequently to adjust to the forces we humans do not control. Thus it can be as we engage with one another, not by clashing but by feeling where the wind is shifting and engaging with it, knowing that interplay that brings us all home.

The motion of the Inward Teacher is sometimes faint, so slight it is easily ignored. The motion of the Spirit is sometimes overwhelming and powerful beyond knowing. Learning and relying on this motion of mystery is the way Friends have chosen. In this way, the markers are often invisible to the hardened eye. The voice of the Light is not always heard or believed. Books and charts offer rules and clear direction. Yet unless one puts a hand to the tiller in the face of the wind, one cannot recognize when a sharp motion of the tiller will right the boat and when it will spin the craft into the reef.

There may be times when we have done all that is possible and still end up suspended on an uncharted reef or amidst logs floating so low on the surface they can barely be seen. Such are the natural dangers that arise simply from living on this earth. Worse are the human-caused dangers, epitomized by the massive trash vortex in the Pacific Ocean:

> The trash vortex is an area the size of Texas in the North Pacific in which an estimated six kilos of plastic for every kilo of natural plankton, along with other slow[ly] degrading garbage, swirls slowly around like a clock, choked with dead fish, marine mammals, and birds who get snared. Some plastics in the gyre will not break down in the lifetimes of the grandchildren of the people who threw them away.[1]

At times, the foulness of the world rises up in our faces. This huge eddy of plastics that suffocates any fish and mammals that encounter it makes vivid the horror of human actions. The inhumanity of human behavior includes using much we have no need for and tossing material things thoughtlessly into the world. The outward horror makes visible the consequences of ignoring the spiritual life and seeking only after personal pleasure, ignoring the Inward Teacher that shows a way of being sensitive to the needs of others and of the planet.

The waste symbolized by this vortex is only one of many human actions that make me furious. At times I get so angry that I can't think clearly at all and simply want to lash out at whoever is acting in such a way.

Anger on the open sea is a danger to all on the small floating structure that is keeping us alive and whose sails propel us on our journey. We lose track of where the wind is and ignore the gathering, billowing dark clouds. Such inattention can easily result in swamping the boat or someone being washed overboard. This reality does not negate the horror of the trash vortex; it only amplifies the need to take fruitful action.

Attention to the holy demands that we also attend to the health and the safety of the people and the world around us. This is true in multiple dimensions. Jesus was concerned to heal the body and the soul, the heart and the mind. He was regularly questioned by the authorities who sought to discredit him, yet this did not stop him from healing others.

Awareness of the winds of the Spirit tells us much about how we might act in response to our own fury at injustice and evil and how we might do so without causing more harm. Setting the sails with gusto and pressing hard to change what is wrong asks for a balance between our huge energy and the decided calm that lets us read the waves and calculate our course from the stars.

The Vast Openness into Which We Sail

Being out under the night sky in a small boat is one way I experience the infinite. The water and the sky are all there is. Depending on the night, the sky may carry its own brilliance of stars beyond the ability to name. The sea may display a phosphorescent wave trailing in the boat's path. The moon may light up mountains along a barely visible coastline. The absent moon and stars leave a different emptiness. The times when the clouds touch the water make the world infinitely finite yet without boundaries or borders.

This is how it is to be totally centered and grounded in God, to be bound in the unceasing distance of all that gives life and awareness. This is where prophetic ministry begins and where it returns again and again for sustenance and renewal.

In this image is part of the vision carried by Friends, the qualities of visibility and openness. This is part of our work, which is to make Truth visible in our lives. The city of God is the city on the hill that cannot be hidden, the lighted candle that won't be confined under a basket. The story of the children in Reading, England, is often told, but I never tire of it. When early Friends were meeting in Reading for worship, soldiers came and dragged the adults to prison. Other similar groups of religious dissenters experienced imprisonment and continued to meet, but they did so in secret. Friends, however, continued to announce the time and place of their meetings for worship. After all the adults had been imprisoned, the children continued to worship at the appointed time and place.

This true tale seems right for our time and place and speaks to something that may be slipping away from Friends: the willingness to be visible, to not hide. Speaking to the power of God in the world and in individual lives is a witness that challenges the state, any government that wants to control its populace and intimidates in the name of safety. Safety is important. We all need healing at times, but healing implies returning to wholeness and engaging again with life. We carry the heritage of our spiritual ancestors' willingness to rely on the strength and power of the Infinite to carry us back into society and witness to another way of being that is grounded in beauty, not fear.

Coming into Port

We all need a safe harbor where we can rest, restock our supplies, and make repairs. Such stays may be brief, in which case more frequent stops are helpful, or they may be times of prolonged retreat when major repairs are needed. Knowing where our home port is gives us security. In our home port are people who care for us, a community that knows us and can help us sort through confusion or competing demands. Some of us are called to remain in port to be a quiet welcome, to help with repairs and healing. The more such people know the voice of the Inward Teacher, the better they are able to be part of the prophetic community and serve as anchors for those who venture out into the winds.

Leadings, or even callings to prophetic ministry, do not necessarily last forever or even for a person's lifetime. We reach safe harbor, the end of the voyage, or the transition to a new leg of the trip. Attentiveness is needed to know when to lay down such work. The particular work as a whole may be done, or it may be that a given task may be complete. The gift may be withdrawn for some reason. Clear guidance may come that signals release, as it did for John Woolman, who wrote of being released from a task:

> My exercise was heavy, and I was deeply bowed in spirit before the Lord. . . . At length, feeling my mind released from the burden which I had been under, I took my leave of them in a good degree of satisfaction.[2]

In this case, Woolman was referring to his attendance at yearly meeting and the burden he felt to speak about some weighty Friends who were slaveholders. He had private conversations with some of these Friends about their slaves and arranged to meet with all of them after the end of the annual sessions. Woolman then spoke to them all about the concern he carried and why he had brought them together. He reported "a free conference" upon the subject, after which he felt released from the work. His task was only to raise the concern and leave it in the hands of individual Friends to listen to the Inward Guide in their own hearts.

The release from ministry or from a particular task may be sharp and clear, as it was in this instance for Woolman. It may be a niggling sense of completion or the awareness that someone else has taken up the task or that health or other demands of life have made it impossible to continue. At times, a clearness process for laying down a ministry may be as valuable to the individual and the group as was the clearness committee that aided the consideration of taking up the call. It should be honored similarly.

Arrival in port releases us from the demands of skippering the vessel that carries us, whether it is a sailboat, a cruise ship, or simply our skin and bones. In the harbor, we find protection from the heavy winds and seas, the opportunity to find fresh food and water, friends old or new to welcome us, dry clothes, and much more. Awareness of the need to enter the harbor to find renewal, or even to complete the journey and sell the boat, is one of the tasks of the everyday prophet.

Queries for Reflection and/or Discussion

1. Do you feel blocked by headwinds, be they your own fears or the objections of others, or do you tend to run before the wind with such exhilaration that you don't notice the wind has shifted and you are in danger?

2. In what ways have you learned to parry the thrust of opposition or resistance, the 'headwinds'? How do you reset your sails in such a way that the resistance strengthens and frees you to do the work you are called to?

3. What tells you when it is time to step aside from work you have been doing and spend time in the harbor restocking supplies, becoming grounded again, and finding renewal? Have you built times of refreshment into the rhythm of your weeks or years, or do you tend to keep pushing until you are exhausted or disillusioned? How might this pattern change?

4. How do you recognize when a leading has ended? What does it feel like to ask yourself that question?

CHAPTER 37
REWEAVING THE STORY

The tensions among Friends weigh on my heart. Much pulls us apart, even as many of us work to build connections despite the fear and even hostility that are apparent at times. The threads that make up the Quaker tapestry are as many as there are individuals who name themselves Quaker. How might we hone our skills in stitching together the wounds dividing us so that the scar tissue is not disfiguring and wholeness is attained? How might we take this multitude of threads and weave relationships even when the disagreements seem impenetrable? This is a query not just for us but also for the world. The sheer volume of humanity is such that it is nearly impossible to ignore either the neighbors whose view of life is distinct from ours or the way we are reshaping the environment that sustains us—the creation that has been our home.

Awareness of the Changing Planet

Many people today have been engaged in efforts to envision how humans might best live on this planet in harmony with the eternal way and with the natural world that sustains us. I am certain we can't uncritically draw on examples taken from the wild as we seek images of the world as we want it to be, yet many compelling examples exist and can be valuable. Keith Helmuth wrote in 1989 of the intertwining of humanity in relationship to all life on the planet as well as to God:

> The living soil, the place and animal forms—the biosphere—is the larger body of the human community. Each is . . . the Spirit home for the whole realm of life.[1]

This is a view that is not uniformly held by Friends, but it is appearing more and more often. This statement appeared in conjunction with an article by a professor at George Fox University, an evangelical Quaker institution.

Integrating our growing awareness of the human relationship to all life on this globe with our feeling of impending disaster may be our most important task, according to Quaker author and pastor Doug Gwyn, who writes:

> If peace was the dominant theme of Quaker testimony in the twentieth century, the interaction between personal simplicity and work for a sustainable human society on earth will focus much of our imagination and energies in this century. It has to. Anything less will amount to nihilism and massive destruction.[2]

Globally, Friends have voiced their awareness of a changing climate that has the potential to disrupt every individual's life. At the 2012 World Conference of Friends, held at Kabarak University in the Rift Valley of Kenya, there was unity as Friends asked: "Is this how Jesus showed us to live?" They laid out the following concerns:

> We have heard of the disappearing snows of Kilimanjaro and glaciers of Bolivia, from which come life-giving waters. We have heard appeals from peoples of the Arctic, Asia and Pacific. We have heard of forests cut down, seasons disrupted, wildlife dying, of land hunger in Africa, of new diseases, droughts, floods, fires, famine and desperate migrations—this climatic chaos is now worsening. There are wars and rumors of war, job loss, inequality and violence. We fear our neighbors. We waste our children's heritage. All of these are driven by our dominant economic systems—by greed not need, by worship of the market, by Mammon and Caesar.[3]

The statement, approved by the over 850 Friends gathered for the conference, laid out the following:

We are called to see what love can do: to love our neighbor as ourselves, to aid the widow and orphan, to comfort the afflicted and afflict the comfortable, to appeal to consciences and bind the wounds.

We are called to teach our children right relationship, to live in harmony with each other and all living beings in the earth, waters and sky of our Creator, who asks, "Where were you when I laid the foundations of the world?" (Job 38:4)

We are called to do justice to all and walk humbly with our God, to cooperate lovingly with all who share our hopes for the future of the earth.

We are called to be patterns and examples in a 21st century campaign for peace and eco-justice, as difficult and decisive as the 18th and 19th century drive to abolish slavery.

We dedicate ourselves to let the living waters flow through us—where we live, regionally, and in wider world fellowship. We dedicate ourselves to building the peace that passeth all understanding, to the repair of the world, opening our lives to the Light to guide us in each small step.[4]

These words are not a call for just a few people to act but for all of us to nurture our awareness of the Light and Spirit that can guide us and to reorient our lives so that this Inward Guide becomes visible in everyday actions. It lays out a broad hope. The small steps towards that hope are many and often only become obvious once we start on the way. My experience of following a calling has often been one of moving one foot forward in heavy fog and finding that the next paving stone to step on becomes obvious as I take this miniscule action. Occasionally the fog parts enough for me to see the sky, a glimpse of the wholeness towards which I move, but most often I need to act in faith. It is much more challenging for a community, with all its differing desires and perspectives, to move together.

The Prophetic Voice Brings Hope

It is very easy to look at information about climate change, rising sea levels, and extinction of species and give in to hopelessness and despair. The messages of scientists can be grim, and political realities can be frustrating as they seem to push quickly into chaos rather than offer solutions. If we are a community of everyday prophets, what is our role? I don't believe having more people calling out disaster is what is needed, although more sorrow and mourning may be appropriate because expressing the loss we feel may open us to viewing a way forward that draws on imagination and brings us back to hope. Cherice Bock (Sierra-Cascades Yearly Meeting of Friends) holds a similar view:

> What I realized was missing was a full account of the prophetic role. In the Judeo-Christian tradition, the prophet is not only an apocalyptic doomsayer, but also a hope-giver. Though the traditional theologian of the last several centuries, like the traditional scientist, has felt the need to be "objective," stating theory and expecting others to live it out, the issue of climate change has brought many in both fields out into the civic realm with passionate and alarmist cries of warning. These cries, however, have more often than not engendered fear and inertia in the attitudes of the public, or communicated a sense of the inevitability of the apocalyptic conclusion.
>
> It is hope, however, which gives people courage to act faithfully, even in the face of oppression and suffering. The biblical prophet encourages the community of faith to move forward into a hoped-for future world by enabling them to make meaning of the situation.[5]

Hope is an intention, an orientation to the world. Cherice uses the term 'critical hope' to indicate that it is not a passive, wishy-washy expectation that all will be well if only—if only we pray enough, if only we give up our materialism, if only we wash enough oil-soaked birds.

Approaching the issues raised by major threats using the lens of faith mixed with realism and full appreciation of the magnitude of the shifts needed in human behavior has the potential to bring us the energy to act on the root causes of what is askew and to be open to unconventional responses that seek to engage unheard voices as part of the solution. The lens of faith may be, as it is for Cherice, grounded in a fresh reading of the Judeo-Christian tradition, or it may tap into the spirituality of people such as the Aborigines of Australia whose lives are not defined by Western materialism.

Life in the New Creation

How do we live together on this earth? This is not just our question; it is also one for the world. Do we value land that is not constantly tended by humans to serve our purposes? As noted earlier, the prophet Isaiah's image of the new creation has inspired people for thousands of years. Isaiah saw a world where the lion could lie in peace next to the lamb and the child play with the poisonous snake without risk. This is a potent vision filled with hope. Accepting it and living into it informed and shaped the lives of early Friends. Meetinghouses today still hang Edward Hicks's paintings of this vision on their walls.

The Bible, whose stories are interwoven into Quaker lore and hopes, begins with God creating the world and ends by inviting all into the city of God. In Genesis, creation begins with the wind from God sweeping across the waters and God proclaiming, "Let there be light!" In Revelation, the river of the waters of Life flows through the city, and next to this river stands the tree whose leaves are for the healing of the nations. This city needs no physical temple for worship; God is the only temple and its source of light. This light shall guide the nations and the kings of the earth. These visions continue to be part of the Quaker vocabulary and to inform our practices, even if often not explicitly recognized. I cannot ignore them or dismiss them as irrelevant.

The Bible is a complex and difficult book, embraced by many Friends and completely rejected by some. Nonetheless, it was the primary text against which our spiritual ancestors tested their understandings of the leadings of the Spirit.

How are we to understand these visions today? This planet is a vibrant and sometimes terrifying place. Scientific research, ecology, our growing knowledge of the multitude of cultures that inhabit this earth, and much else all expand the ways in which we may read these ancient texts. Looking for what underpins all these teachings and seeking to read all the various texts set before us with the eyes of the Spirit is part of the challenge we face.

Friends only gradually recognized that the Bible did not endorse human slavery; they did not make it a disownable offense until the late eighteenth century. The reality of this came home to me when I found a bill of sale for "one negro woman" dated May 18, 1742, among old family letters. Today we are seeing more explicitly that the creation story in Genesis does not put the earth here for humans to ravage at our whim. The need to reenter into the meaning of stewardship and learn the importance of sustainability is very much alive today.

A Fifty-Thousand-Year-Old Tradition

Traveling among Friends in Australia in 2016 gave me glimpses of the people that have inhabited that beautiful but often harsh land for over fifty thousand years. Quakers James Backhouse and George Walker were among the early European explorers of the continent, and they were affected strongly by the plight of the Aboriginal people. They quite bluntly stated that "the Aborigines have had wholesale robbery of their territory committed upon them by the government" and that "settlers have become the receivers of this stolen property."[6] As social justice reformers, they saw many ills needing action, but they were essentially blind to the value of the spiritual traditions of these people and their dependence upon the land.

Australian Susannah Kay Brindle, in the 2000 Backhouse Lecture, offers a vivid sense of her engagement with the Aboriginal people that can contribute to a real reconciliation with the earth and all the varied parts of humanity that inhabit this planet. I can only hope more and more of us are called to this work. Brindle highlighted the particularity of the Aboriginal people's relationship with the land,

> a relationship which, we incomers must ever remind ourselves, it would be arrogant in the extreme for us to aspire to. We are, however, continually invited by Aboriginal peoples to acknowledge the customary law of this land and to take the first step of honouring its sacredness by asking permission to be here.
>
> "Just don't think you can walk in here and take over. You must ask first—that's the Law!" is something I often hear Aboriginal people say.[7]

Such a view is fundamentally different from the Western approach and the assumption that the needs of humanity outweigh all other demands. The "law" Susannah refers to are Aboriginal customs and culture. I have no illusions about worldwide adoption of Aboriginal practices, yet these people have much to teach us about respect for the land and all the life that abounds on it. They have much to teach us about seeing the sacredness of the world around us.

Susannah sees ecological violence as "an issue that needs every nuance of our Quaker peace testimony" and encourages us to develop "a conscious, ongoing relationship with the More-than-Human world—a relationship that manifests in prayerful understanding of the issues and practical actions of support." She asks us to be present, to pay attention, and to listen "even when what we hear terrifies us" and to have the courage needed to face the pain we have inflicted on other people and the natural world.[8]

These are glimpses of ways Friends are reaching out for new ways to be part of the cycle of life on this planet and to expand our awareness of the wider world that we are part of.

Embedded in Community

In addition to these varied worldviews that underpin or add to our sense of who we are and how we are impelled by the divine voice to embody the new creation, Friends have also created a multitude of organizations, largely in the past century, to aid in making a collective witness. The American Friends Service Committee was founded in the early twentieth century to provide alternative service opportunities for conscientious objectors to war and then became heavily engaged in feeding the hungry in Europe after the end of World War I. Two decades later, the Friends Committee on National Legislation was created in response to the need to support conscientious objectors during World War II. Friends Center Ofafa was created in 1955 in Kenya to aid detainees from detention camps during the government-declared emergency leading up to Kenyan independence from Britain. Today, large numbers of such committees often provide practical help and ways for Friends to act on common concerns, at times providing a prophetic, communal witness and expressions of hope for the future. They are usually called committees to emphasize the nonhierarchical nature of their work.

I do know that being embedded in a larger group teaches us much about how to relate to other human beings and how to see our place on the globe. In community, we learn ways to respond to disagreements and make decisions despite holding differing understandings about issues that affect us deeply. We learn to stand with people when they are overwhelmed by emotion. The vision our community holds about the future, whether we call it the new creation, the kingdom of God, or something else, shapes us and is integral to our witness to the world as well as points to ways we might come closer to being a community of everyday prophets

Friends over the generations have held this vision up as a reality that can be made manifest on earth. Knowing this vision, it becomes easier to see when the world is out of balance. To name that imbalance and to take steps to restore it is also the task of the prophet. Some everyday prophets may be called for a time into public arenas or to make a radical witness to the world. But their call can go astray if they lose touch with the need to walk humbly with God. Essential to this witness is the array of everyday prophets who attend to the Inward Guide as they go about their daily lives in their schools, their homes, and their meetings. In such places they can practice their faith in ways that matter. Without the body of the faithful who listen for the Light and help others to do the same, the witness can leave prophets lost and alone.

Queries for Reflection and/or Discussion

1. How do you envision yourself as part of life on this planet? What questions and fears do you have about the future?

2. Where do you find hope? How might you be part of bringing that hope to your meeting or church? To the world?

3. How does your faith bring you strength to act when needed? Can you bring worship into your work and your everyday life, making space for holy imagination to grow?

CHAPTER 38
BECOMING A BAND OF EVERYDAY PROPHETS: FINDING A COMMON PRAYER

Since 1549, the *Book of Common Prayer* has laid out the expected form and words of the Anglican worship service. This seems fundamentally opposite to the original Friends form of worship, where all simply gathered in the silence. The early Friends waited expectantly for the Spirit to move freely among them. Some came to experience the quaking that meant they were to offer a message for those gathered. A similar distance exists between the printed prayers that are found in many branches of Christianity and the Quaker practice of praying silently and only making prayer vocal as led by the Light. What might it mean to hold a "common prayer" among Friends or among the peoples of the world?

My simple answer is that our common prayer comes in turning to God—to that Spirit of truth and compassion that is available to all people and seems to be present in some form in virtually every religion and culture. I know the reality is not so simple. Continuing examples of separations are present among Buddhists as well as Christians, Muslims, and Hindis, evidence of how strong the human urge is to be among like-minded people. Centering prayer, whether it is Catholic, Buddhist, Quaker, or from another tradition, helps stitch the wounds we inflict on ourselves and each other and provide a path to healing.

A Common Prayer

Friends today are scattered and often hold such conflicting understandings of who we are and what we are about that it sometimes seems we are completely lost. It is easy to bemoan the differences and the loss of our apparent power in the world. It is tempting to hold ourselves apart from those who think or speak in ways we don't understand or agree with. It is a much more difficult yet joyful discipline to place ourselves in the midst of the city of God.

Rational dialogue can only get us so far towards finding wholeness or even towards coming to respect one another. Our tradition is one of listening for the Voice of the Light, which most Friends know as Jesus leading us and some know by other names. I believe that the measure of our unity is visible in our words, hearts, and actions, not in the different names we use for the divine, eternal Power deep within that upholds us all. We find this power to be active, mending and expanding our souls as we submit to it prayerfully.

Emma Churchman (Southern Appalachia Yearly Meeting and Association) sees herself as Christian and has trained with a Celtic shaman. She thus embodies some of the conflicting strains within Quakerism. She offered this poem as her response to my queries about how she understands the prophetic ministry. Her words press me to reach into a deep, inward place where the Spirit moves freely, uniting all and calling all to continue this dance of turning towards God and being reformed in the way of the holy:

common prayer

when the still small voice
settles itself onto my heart
I shall die and be reborn

that I may die a thousand deaths
in order to prepare the way of the Lord
This is my common prayer

that I may be brought to the promised land
with my brothers and sisters

that I may be anointed with the blood of the lamb

that the workings of the Spirit
may be poured into my body

This is my common prayer

that I may stand with my feet
firmly planted on the earth
and my eyes to the world
seeing that which is holy
This is my common prayer

What stands out for me in Emma's prayer is the phrase "that I may stand with my feet firmly planted on the earth . . . seeing that which is holy." This is a more elegant way of stating William Penn's admonition that we be in the world but not of it. The holy is not separate from the planet on which we live and our everyday concerns of finding food and shelter. So often in the Judeo-Christian Scriptures people are chastised for not having cared for the widows and orphans, the task that Jesus announced as his at the start of his ministry. Materializing the new creation interweaves the sacred and the ordinary. The harshness of day-to-day life becomes leavened with hope.

Grounded Hope

While working on this book, the question "What is the Friends vision for today?" arose regularly in my reflections. My best answer so far is "grounded hope."

This hope is for the living out of the new creation on this earth, a variation of Isaiah's image of the lion and the lamb lying down easily at one another's side. In Hicks's painting of this scene, humans (Europeans and Native Americans, in this case) who had so often battled one another to the death treat one another justly and with respect.

This hope is grounded in the knowledge of the power of compassion, the infinite mercy of God. This hope is named by those who have drunk of the river of life that flows through the city of peace whose gates are never closed. This hope comes from the lives of those who have tasted the fruits of the tree that stands by the banks of this river and who have touched the leaves that are for the healing of the nations. This vision, from the end of the book of Revelation, was a living thing for our spiritual ancestors, who knew the Lamb's War as a war that could only be fought with compassion, justice for the least among us, and integrity and Truth.

Hope: An Orientation

It is very easy to see hope as an emotion, a desire for something that will magically happen and cure all ills. Hope gets labeled as unrealistic and dreamy. But what if we see hope as part of the prophetic task? As Walter Brueggemann puts it, "This way of hope is the work of ministry."[1] In my mind, the new creation is the embodiment of hope and the prophet helps identify the steps we might take to enter into this forthcoming way of being on this planet. Christine Betz Hall (North Pacific Yearly Meeting) the founder of the Way of the Spirit program that brings together a wide range of Quakers and others who wish to encounter what is alive in the Friends heritage, sees the concrete experience of hope as the result of six intentions:

1. being filled bodily with the knowledge of God (Isaiah 11:2, 9) and living in holy alignment
2. seeking the growing edge (Howard Thurman): an awareness of God even at the edges of turmoil and destruction
3. actively resisting fear: not falling prey to the fear that shuts down possibilities
4. letting go of attachments: reorienting life from the ego-self to God
5. waiting for YHWH: not pressing through everything following one's self-will
6. being open to unimagined possibilities

One does not have to be a public Friend to live with this kind of intentionality. Hope can arise from places undreamed of. Hope is the intersection of the dreams of ordinary people and the promise of something new that permeates our tradition. Hope can carry a person through fear, past the very real dangers of this world, in ways I don't pretend to understand.

Hope is embodied in the reports of people like Tom Fox, who wrote back to his meeting from Iraq with certainty and sureness in the weeks and months before his capture and death. His witness to the ways our country was harming civilians blended with his work to ease the situation in Iraq. He made concrete the potential that our lives can unfold in a way contrary to the ways of the powerful. Surely he knew what Isaiah meant about being filled with the knowledge of God.

Centering Prayer

My question "How does one prepare to be a prophetic minister?" spoke strongly to Hal Wright (Intermountain Yearly Meeting). His immediate response was, "I believe that one must have a daily spiritual practice to be confident in having an authentic prophetic voice." Hal then went on to explain what he meant:

> I used to wonder what it meant to love God. I could never feel love or emotion for an abstract concept, something that wasn't a physical person. We need a different word for divine connection than love. I learned what loving God is in centering prayer. It is not a feeling like loving someone; God is incomprehensible and one can have no direct sense of a separate entity. Loving God is the yearning and intention to be present and open.
>
> I am what is called an 'apophatic' mystic in theology, also called a dark mystic. It's a hard road, a lonely road, and often a discouraging road. Mother Teresa of Calcutta was a dark mystic. I felt comforted . . . [by her] stunning statement in one letter, "I have come to love

the darkness." Accepting the darkness is the
surrender of self and all desires. God for me is
cosmic awareness and consciousness beyond
all matter and energy and form. God is in the
darkness. God is Darkness to human
consciousness. Your experience may be
different. You may be a light mystic.

Friends encounter God in many ways. Some have
regular conversations with Jesus and even see him
standing by the door or sitting next to them in the car.
Others have no felt sense of Presence at all (these
individuals may be deeply Christian, or they may be
atheists), yet most of these Friends have a lively
confidence in a power that sustains them. Still others
may be mystics, either 'apophatic' (imageless) mystics
as Hal is or 'cataphatic' mystics who experience
periodic visions that help shape their lives. Hal came
to know the love of God in centering prayer. I found,
or rather was found by, an infinite, all-embracing love
in the midst of worship and mourning. We each have
our own path that might be better realized in mutual
support, the sharing of what we know, and regular
spiritual practice.

The inward life is rarely summarized in a few words
and certainly has a different flavor from person to
person. Yet the commonality I see flowing through all
these lives is movement towards a life of integrity,
where action and belief support and sustain each
other, where words and deeds match the intent. Some
name this salvation, and others speak of wholeness.
Hal offers his understanding of a life centered in God,
which includes daily spiritual practice and honest self-
knowledge as well as living in accord with the
testimonies of simplicity, peace, community, integrity,
and equality. These are all manifested in selfless
service and are heard in the prophetic voice:

> The result of centering prayer is an integrated,
> centered life. . . . The process with which one
> begins to be integrated is a daily spiritual
> practice. It is like the process of growing up.

When one turns eighteen years old, one does not suddenly have maturity. Maturity comes as a result of gradual personal growth. Different capabilities emerge in imperfect form at different points in time when one is growing up. In spirituality, immature capabilities will emerge, mature, and perfect, hopefully, along one's spiritual journey. At some point during the process of integration, the prophetic voice emerges. I am not a realized, integrated person yet. But I have been on the path long enough to feel a prophetic voice.

There is a Voice in the silence of centering prayer. It is not an auditory voice. It's more like a realization or intuition, something like what happens when one is reading something and one's mind "hears" the words. Actually, there are two voices, one mine and one not-mine. Sometimes I can tell the difference; sometimes I cannot. I find the Voice sometimes comes in response to a question or personal need. I once asked the Darkness why I couldn't hear the Voice anymore, and the Darkness said, "It won't speak to you unless you are willing to obey it."

Am I willing to obey, to follow? That has been a question I have set aside as I have worked on this book. I have had a clear sense, beginning a few years ago, that this is my work to do—the mix of solitary writing and communal conversation in workshops and other venues that are integral to shaping my books. As I near the end of this task, I can't help but wonder what comes next and whether I will be willing to undertake it. As I age, this becomes more of a concern, and I can't help but ask how much more is mine to do. When do I lay down this work? For some, only death brings an end. For others, there is a time when they can step back from the world and tend more local gardens, physically or metaphorically.

No matter how much time I have left, or whether my tasks are ordinary, everyday ones or continue to take me to many corners of the globe, I know I cannot go forward without remembering to center. If I cannot find that point where love stretches me and draws me, I am lost.

What I call prayer may be simply sitting on the shore of Oregon's Lost Lake and staring at the reflection of Mount Hood in its waters. It may be playing the music of Bartók on my piano. It may be walking alongside a person deep in grief or doubt or pain and holding them in the Light. There are many ways I know this thing I call prayer. Words are not needed. Attention to the power of Love is.

Becoming a Band of Everyday Prophets

The word 'band' brings to mind celebrations, parades, and loud brass instruments that proclaim joy. A band in this sense requires more than just one person. The bass in a jazz band may provide a steady beat that keeps the whole tied together while the saxophone improvises and does some riffs.

Music harmonizes the many voices and instruments, making of them a kind of whole. It is quite obvious when someone can't really enter into the music, hits wrong notes, or loses the beat. In a good band, there is someone who can note this quickly and perhaps take steps to adjust, either by shifting the key or taking time to teach the person how to stay in tune. Each time a jazz band plays, the music is new—maybe just a bit or maybe a lot. We may like the old favorites of the marching band, but what happens if that is all we hear, if we lose the capacity to be excited by a fresh composition?

This interplay of what some call "eternal truths" and the possibility of hearing a fresh rhythm or seeing our environment with new comprehension is part of the work of the alternative community. This band is made up of individuals of many different skill levels, intentions, and degrees of ease with themselves and the world. Often the prophetic work starts with self-knowledge and personal healing, the practice that is part of joining the band. The Light, which is such a powerful conductor, is also relentless in allowing us to see the painful corners of our attitudes and behaviors. Peace is not just about protesting war but is initially felt within each heart and soul.

Then, consider the musicians who delight in Beethoven sonatas and those who are into Def Leppard. Is it possible for them to form one band? Or even necessary? A Def Leppard fan who tries to join a classical orchestra may feel pretty lonely and will likely be ostracized if they attempt to get everyone to play heavy metal.

It is not unusual for two bands to have very different repertoires. They can share a love of music and find ways to cooperate, perhaps alternating venues or reaching out to a much wider audience to share this common love. Both need to learn how to play their instruments—just as Friends need to learn about the ways of the inner life and discernment. Evangelical and liberal Friends expect different pieces of music to be played. They still have to find ways to be present together, to not reject one another or label one another in harsh, divisive ways.

Any group of people faces the challenge that all people face: how do we live together on this planet in a way that is respectful, that does no violence to others, and that makes space for the variety of life that creation has given us? I encourage each of us, as a member of a band of everyday prophets, to pay attention to the Inward Guide and live out our calling no matter how seemingly ordinary it is or how fearful and uncomfortable it may seem.

Universal Mercy and Love

Lloyd Lee Wilson (North Carolina Yearly Meeting [Conservative]) offers us three lessons from the story of the prophet Jonah:

> That God's love and mercy are universal; that God's true intention and desire are reconciliation and conversion, not judgment and punishment; and that running away from our gifts or our calling—or from God—never works out.[2]

These are good things to recall when testing whether a nudge we are given is consistent with living in the new creation. No matter whether one sees God as the active God of the Hebrew Testament interacting with humanity or knows a basic force that shapes the world in its image if we pay attention to it, the movement towards reconciliation, mercy, and love remains essential. When in alignment with these intentions, it is possible to live out of a sense of abundance, hope, and generosity, to be simultaneously humble and bold in our service to humanity and to all life.

Again and again we have the choice to shift our focus from what is "ours" to what is infinite. Early Friends again and again pointed out that the kingdom of God is within and that we will find this new creation in acts of kindness, patience, self-control, simplicity and nonviolence, not in jealousy, revenge, rage, or selfish ambition. The prophetic voice is nurtured by communities that know the reality of the new creation. Such a body is filled with everyday prophets and nurtures the occasional individuals who call the community to account as well as carry their deepest hopes to the wider world.

Is being a band of everyday prophets possible for Friends? I believe so, but it is not an easy task to take up. I believe this is at the core of what we are all about: attention to the Inward Guide that breaks open hearts and remakes them with compassion. People who know the touch of the Light and are willing to follow where it leads knit together our relationships. At the same time, they help make visible when we, and the world around us, fall short of what we might be. Such everyday prophets are at once ordinary and radical, both humble and bold. They act out of a weave of mercy and justice, valuing each being on this earth. May we cherish those among us who are faithful.

Queries for Reflection and/or Discussion

1. What is your daily practice; what keeps you centered and grounded? Is there a "common prayer" that stays with you and guides you? What are the dimensions of that prayer?

2. How do you know hope? How is it present in your life? Would it change you to be intentional about hope? What might that look like?

3. Can you imagine Friends as a band of everyday prophets? What does this look like in your imagination? What are the preconditions that would allow this to happen? What might be your first step in becoming part of this band?

APPENDIX A

Glossary

Advices and Queries. Friends have always rejected creeds and other formal belief systems. Instead, they emphasize the need to link faith with words and actions and regularly pose advices and queries for individuals and meetings to consider.

American Friends Service Committee (AFSC). A Quaker organization founded in 1917 that is dedicated to social justice and peace work.

Books of Discipline (Faith and Practice). These volumes are prepared and adopted by individual yearly meetings to describe the practices and beliefs of each body of Friends. Some are considered descriptive of the practices, others prescriptive.

Church. Traditionally, Friends only used the word "church" to refer to the congregation and not to the building. Today, most Evangelical Friends Church International and Friends United Meeting bodies refer to themselves as churches or use the designation "church" and "meeting" interchangeably.

Consensus. A means of decision-making designed to reflect the will of the entire community and rejecting voting, which reflects majority rule. It is largely a secular practice, different from the Friends practice of seeking unity (God's will).

Conservative. In the Quaker context, 'conservative' refers to conserving early Quaker practices and beliefs. Thus, Conservative Friends practice unprogrammed worship rising out of the silence and are more Christ-centered than many other Friends of the unprogrammed tradition.

Evangelical. A term widely used among Christians. Here, it is generally used to indicate Quakers who are

Christian and have paid pastors and a set order of service with hymns and Bible readings.

Evangelical Friends Church International (EFCI). An umbrella organization comprised exclusively of evangelical Friends churches.

Friends Committee on National Legislation (FCNL). The Quaker lobby for peace and justice based in Washington, D.C.

Friends General Conference (FGC). An umbrella organization that consists of theologically liberal, unprogrammed meetings.

Friends United Meeting (FUM). An umbrella organization that includes both evangelical Friends churches and theologically liberal Quaker meetings.

Independent. Yearly meetings that are not affiliated with Friends United Meeting, Friends General Conference, or Evangelical Friends Church International, the contemporary organizations resulting from various separations. A few monthly meetings are considered independent and have no affiliation with any yearly meeting.

Leading. Perceived guidance from the Spirit to speak, most often used in relation to unprogrammed worship, or to undertake actions in witness to one's faith.

Liberal. Used to refer to Friends with an openness to different theologies and liberal politics. Most often, liberal yearly meetings are affiliated with Friends General Conference or are independent.

Light. Friends initially called themselves "Children of the Light," referring to the Light of Christ that they believe is available to every person (see the first chapter of John), whether that person knows Jesus or not. The Light is both a guide and a monitor. Its transforming work is central to Friends.

Meeting. The word 'meeting' is normally used by all Friends associated with Friends General Conference and by some Friends churches to refer both to the worship on Sunday mornings and to the community that worships together. It is used by some meetings in all branches of Friends but is most common among Friends General Conference yearly meetings.

Meeting for business. The gathering of Friends in worship for the conduct of the business of the congregation. Traditionally, all members of a congregation gathered once a month to consider questions of budget, property, membership, marriage, policy, and more. Their intent was to be open to the leadings of the Spirit for the whole body and seek the sense of the meeting.

Monthly meeting. Used by all Friends General Conference and some Friends United Meeting and Evangelical Friends Church International bodies to refer to the congregation that worships together weekly and to the monthly gathering for the conduct of business out of a sense of worship.

Programmed meeting. A form of Quaker worship in a Friends church that has a pastor and a regular order of worship with designated hymns, Bible readings, and a message prepared in advance.

Release. Individuals are said to be 'released' when they have the affirmation of their meeting to minister in some way to the wider community. Meetings related to Friends General Conference may have a process for formally recognizing a particular ministry such as environmental work, prison reform, or writing and teaching. Friends churches release individuals for service as pastors to the community by providing a salary.

Testimonies. Friends often use the word 'testimonies' to refer to how their lives are a witness to the Light and Truth. Beginning in the twentieth century, unprogrammed Friends often used this word to refer specifically to actions related to simplicity, peace, integrity, community, and equality. Some programmed Friends use the term more often to refer to statements about the way Christ has shaped their lives.

Unity. Unity refers to a deep underlying sense of connection with others and with God. When doing business in the manner of Friends, the group seeks unity (or the sense of the meeting) with God's way for this time and this place.

Unprogrammed meeting. A form of Quaker worship where individuals gather in silence and listen for guidance that may be personal or may be shared with the community in vocal ministry. Often referred to as 'worship' or 'meeting for worship.'

Vocal ministry. The words offered out of the silence during unprogrammed worship.

Yearly meeting. A regional body of Friends that gathers annually for worship, fellowship, and consideration of faith and practice. The term also refers to a voluntary association of monthly meetings or churches that adopts its own book of discipline. Yearly meetings are recognized by other Friends through an exchange of epistles written at annual business sessions.

Note: The contributors to this volume are identified by their yearly meeting. The list of abbreviations here also identifies the umbrella organizations that each yearly meeting is part of.

Alaska Friends Conference (FGC)
Australia Yearly Meeting (Independent)
Baltimore Yearly Meeting (FGC and FUM)
Britain Yearly Meeting (Independent)
Evangelical Friends Church—Mid America Yearly
    Meeting (EFCI)

Great Plains Yearly Meeting (FUM)
Highland Yearly Meeting (FUM)
Holiness Friends Yearly Meeting (EFCI)
Indiana Yearly Meeting (FUM)
Intermountain Yearly Meeting (FGC)
Kibimba Yearly Meeting (EFCI)
Nairobi Yearly Meeting (FUM)
New Association of Friends (FUM)
New England Yearly Meeting (FGC and FUM)
New York Yearly Meeting (FGC and FUM)
North Carolina Yearly Meeting (Conservative)
North Pacific Yearly Meeting (Independent)
Northwest Yearly Meeting (EFCI)
Ohio Yearly Meeting (Conservative)
Ohio Valley Yearly Meeting (FGC)
Pacific Yearly Meeting (Independent)
Philadelphia Yearly Meeting (FGC)
Rwanda Yearly Meeting (EFCI)
Sierra-Cascades Yearly Meeting of Friends
    (Independent)
Southeastern Yearly Meeting (FGC)
Southern Appalachian Yearly Meeting and Association
    (FGC)

APPENDIX B

Letter: Friends, welcome prophets among us in these dark times!

To New England's meetings

Dear Friends,

Many of us are feeling under the weight of grief, fear, and anger in the face of national and world events. Many of us are digging deep, to feel where a prophetic response may be: Is there a word from the Lord that Friends are to carry at this time, in deed or in word? Is our spiritual condition healthy, alert, and clear enough to hear and receive such a word?

Here is one thing I know: A prophetic people is one which welcomes the arising of prophecy. The first motion is, in love, to make room for the leadings, and the people who are led, and give them opportunity to bring what they have been given. This advice comes from the earliest life of the Christian movement. In the ancient book of advice called the "Didache" or "Teaching of the apostles," the little fellowships gathered in Christ's name are admonished to be open to the motion of the Spirit as embodied in traveling ministers: "Let every apostle [one who has been sent] who comes to you be received as the Lord." Knowing that we have this treasure in earthen vessels, we are to "try the spirits" and feel where the divine is present when someone feels moved to act or speak under the guiding influence of the Divine Spirit—but we are warned not to quench the Spirit's motion, but to accept the unexpected activity of that Spirit in our lives as a community as well as individuals: "The spirit blows where it will, and you hear its sound, but don't know whence it comes or whither it goes. So is everyone who is born of the spirit." As a people, we have fallen so far into a comfortable and secular mind, that we think concerns and leadings are somehow a

403

matter personal to the concerned Friend, and our meetings can pick and choose whom to hear, whom to invite and allow to come among us! That is a way to avoid the uncomfortable evidence that the living God is still working through us, preparing individuals and pushing them or drawing them into service. It is a way not to change, not to grow, to keep control of our schedules and our attention; to keep ourselves unfree. We often talk about being "spirit-led," but as a people how available are we really to that experience?

When we make time for the unexpected, when we accept the opportunities that come to us through Friends who are called to travel to us and have the encouragement of their meetings to do so, we enable those Friends, and others not yet arisen, to learn better how to watch for, hear, bear, and accomplish their service. Our meetings are "schools of the prophets"—or can be if we recognize the opportunities that come our way, accept them with joy, and learn from them—both from the message and from our experience of reception and discernment.

I have known many Friends, newly drawn into service, who have been discouraged by the convention that prophets come to meetings only when meetings issue invitations. This turns the matter upside down, Friends: The calling and the service are given through the body, through and out of the common life in the Spirit, and represent an invitation from God to see, to feel, to know, and perhaps to act in fresh ways, in ways renewed by the living water of God's life that brings these leadings and opportunities to us.

It can be inconvenient for a meeting to make room for such an unplanned, "wildcat" experience of the Spirit. It may also be that a Friend's concern, to be brought to a meeting, will require some discernment by the meeting about ways and means. I can assure you, though, that it is pretty inconvenient for a Friend to have such a concern, to set aside other things, and dare to stand forth, dare to speak for God and for us. The sense of unreadiness, of unworthiness, of emptiness, is very sharp in such a Friend, and he or she is only too conscious of difficulties for themselves and for their visitors. Yet the act of faithfulness, however imperfectly accomplished, is a step into greater life, and if it is rooted in love, it is evidence of God's work and life active among us. And Friends, there is such a famine among us, and among people in general, for such evidence!

So if a Friend reaches out to your meeting with an earnest statement that he or she is traveling under concern, with the unity of their meeting (your brothers and sisters!), remember that we can earn a prophet's reward even by offering a cup of water to a prophet. Find a way to entertain this Friend, as we are to entertain strangers sent among us, for thereby we may unexpectedly be visited by an angel—not the traveling Friend, but the beloved Spirit, the Shepherd and Teacher, made available in the giving and receiving of spiritual hospitality. Make room, Friends, light your lamps in welcome, live like people who truly love the Spirit, and who love to see the springs of Life break forth in any!

In Christian love your friend,

Brian Drayton
AMOR VINCAT

Amor Vincat (blog), Dec. 4, 2016, https://amorvincat.wordpress.com/2016/12/04/letter -friends-welcome-prophets-among-us-in-these-dark- times/.

APPENDIX C

Ten Ways We Enter Prophetic Ministry
A Talk by William Taber[1]

I have been asked to open a time of worship sharing about how the call to be prophetic has been emerging among us. As a beginning, I am reminded of Howard Brinton's assertion that all true Quaker ministry is prophetic, "arising spontaneously and unpredictably under a sense of Divine urgency." Even though the context of a given message may be categorized as "teaching ministry" or "pastoral ministry" (giving comfort or inspiration at times like births, funerals, marriages, etc.) or speaking to the condition of one or more people in the meeting, all such ministry is prophetic if it arises from a Divine "inward motion" in the speaker. This use of the word prophetic goes beyond the common understanding that prophecy is only about foretelling the future. Instead, it assumes that prophecy is really about God's yearning for us to shape up now, in the present time! Later in these remarks I'll come back to how Friends have traditionally been able to sense the authenticity or validity of prophetic ministry.

Early Friends saw themselves as part of a living stream going back to the Old Testament prophets. They believed that the same Power that moved the ancient Hebrew prophets moved also in them. Some of them even felt led to act out their prophecy as well as to speak it. Knowing their Bible, these early Friends believed and experienced that Jesus was the super prophet—and much more than prophet—who had been promised by earlier prophets. They also knew that the New Testament mentions female and male prophets functioning in the church. And we can assume from other early sources that traveling prophets may have been as common in the church as were traveling ministers during the first two centuries of Quakerism. I believe that we modern Friends still have access to that Living Stream of which all of the prophets were and are a part.

This dimension of reality—this Living Stream—can seem independent of time—as when we are absorbed in waiting worship—though this dimension can also be acutely aware of what is happening at our moment of history. It is this paradoxical combination of the sublime and the mystical with the painful awareness of contemporary blindness and evil which makes being a prophet no easy matter! Prophecy often calls into question the taken-for-granted practices or institutions of a society. In other words, prophecy can make us question the unquestionable. This can make prophecy irritating, unpopular, and even dangerous.

That last comment was motivated, in part, by my recent rereading about Old Testament prophets, especially Abraham J. Heschel's book *The Prophets*. It is also motivated by the fact that I have often turned down my own sensitivity to the pain, anguish, and blindness of our present world because I do not think I am strong enough to endure its intensity or to do much to change it. Yet the message of Jesus, the example of many great souls—and the presence of the Living Stream—will not allow us (or me) to bury our heads in the sand. We are called to be alert and sensitive to the world's anguish—because there is one who is the Truth, the Way and the Life, who can enable us to bear it, one who can guide us in our small role in healing the world. So, any hope of having a prophetic ministry among us begins with being in touch with the Living Stream which is both independent of time and which is very much aware of what is happening in our time.

As a way of starting our conversation I propose to look at ten ways that people in this room may have been drawn into prophetic ministry. (As we go through this list, you may think of other ways you have experienced—feel free to add them to the list at the appropriate time.)

Quitting Trying to Fix It All

For some souls, this first one may be the most important form of prophecy. It is just to be in this sacred place, the state of consciousness which both lifts us out of time and yet which allows us to be a conduit through which Divine Energy and Divine Harmony can flow to those around us in meeting and those around us in our daily life. I need to repeat that.

As we learn to live ever closer to the center of this Living Stream in public and personal worship as well as in our daily life, we become radiators of God's love. Keeping our consciousness open to this Living Steam gradually—or sometimes suddenly—changes the way we see the world around us, and it changes our attitudes and behavior as well.

As we continually open ourselves to this Living Stream, this Ocean of Light as George Fox experienced it, we also become aware of the incredible disharmony of our planet, which seems to be headed for ecological and social catastrophe. So, like the prophets of old and the early Friends, we are drawn—or driven—back to that Ocean of Light to find the true foundation on which to stand in the midst of swirling change.

As we become more sure of this foundation, we are sometimes moved to quit working so hard at trying to fix the world. We remember that "unless the Lord build the city, they labor in vain who build it" and "unless the Lord keep the city, the watchman watches in vain." This does not mean permanent withdrawal from the world. However, it may signal a time of inward-outward reorganization of our life so that we can work with even more energy at what is truly important.

Changing Lifestyles

So, a second form of prophetic call—at least for some people—can result in dramatic changes in lifestyle and/or occupation. Probably we are all called to at least some degree of prophetic lifestyle changes. These may range from the kind of chocolate we buy (if we even use it at all) to the location and construction of our homes and the way we use transportation. There may be people in this room who have been called prophetically to make dramatic and sometimes costly changes in lifestyle, place of residence, and occupation.

Responding to Urgings

A third kind of prophetic urging usually emerges as we stay close to that Living Stream and Ocean of Light and allow ourselves to be nourished and transformed by it. These urgings come in the midst of our daily lives. Sometimes that urging is only secretly to pray for someone who comes to mind, or it may be secretly to pray for someone on the street or in the store or in the office. Sometimes that urging is more pushy, leading us to speak to that person or to lead the conversation in a certain direction. We probably all know Friends who are given a sense of people's conditions or, as the old Friends would say, their "states." If we are faithful to this gift of the Holy Spirit, we become inconspicuous minor prophets, lovingly speaking to the needs of those we encounter.

"Opportunities"

This sensitivity and this urging may become strong enough to lead into a fourth kind of prophetic activity, which has happened to me now and then. For at least the last 35 years I have occasionally been led to ask someone for an "opportunity" or I have agreed to sit with someone at their request. Sometimes these private meetings for worship were just good times of spiritual refreshment. Sometimes they appeared to come at just the right time for the other person, providing encouragement and insight when they needed it. I encourage all Friends to be open to the nudges for this kind of minor prophetic ministry, for which there is always a continuing need. Some Friends may find this calling may even lead them to seek opportunities with the ill and the dying.

Speaking in Worship

Finally we come to a fifth form of prophecy—speaking in meeting for worship. I assume that most of us here today have had to speak in meeting at least once—or many, many times. Speaking in meeting is almost never easy, though sometimes the message just appears or grows in the mind, and the inward motion to speak is both so delicate and so strong that we have no choice but to stand and let the words flow. A few Friends apparently are called to stand in meeting even before they know what their message is going to be. Sometimes we learn after meeting—or sometimes only many years later—that our words did speak to someone's condition or that we did answer a question in someone's mind.

I, at least, almost never know precisely who in the meeting needs this message, and if I do think I know, I am usually wrong! One simple example was when I was overwhelmed with the sense that someone in the meeting needed to make an important decision today, and I gave that message. After meeting, a man whom we all knew had the gift of ministry told me that my words were meant for him; he decided that he should apply for membership in our local meeting. I later learned that another man in the same meeting felt that he was being told that it was time for him to propose to my daughter, which he did that evening! Sometimes it is very difficult to give in and deliver the message, yet we know we must, like the prophets of old who felt the terrible responsibility of their task. It may literally be a matter of life and death for the message to be delivered faithfully and on time!

But prophetic vocal ministry is always more than words. From the beginning of Quakerism until now, Friends have recognized that when vocal ministry is "in the Life" the spoken words are accompanied with a sense of Presence or "gatheredness" which the meeting can feel. Or we might say, the spoken words take the gathered hearers to a place beyond words, to that deep center in all of us where we can touch the Living Stream.

A story is told of John Crook, a prominent 17th-century Friend who withstood the persecutions of that time and was a powerful preacher. Late in his life some of his friends came to feel that he was no longer preaching from the Spirit, but only from his mind. So, with loving frankness they told him so. He accepted their counsel and consequently did not speak in meeting for a couple of years. Then he gradually began to speak again, and his friends recognized that he was again speaking "in the Life" just as he had done during the earlier years of the Quaker movement. I tell this story as a reminder that, especially if we are called into some of the more urgent or dramatic forms of prophecy, the ego can play tricks on us, and we all need spiritual friends who can keep us both faithful and honest, as was the case with that very weighty Friend John Crook.

It is our faith that every Friends meeting is open to inspired messages which bring to one or more of the hearers the words they need to hear now—and not the words only, but the Spirit to which the words lead. Hopefully each of us is willing to take the risk of being that prophet. And hopefully, each of us has spiritual friends or a clearness committee or a spiritual director who can help us keep the ego from distorting or hijacking the prophetic message.

The Work of Business Meeting

A sixth form of prophetic ministry can occur in the meeting for business or in a committee meeting. One trouble with being a prophet is that sometimes the Lord seems to want us to be very specific! Since most Quaker prophetic work in the world is usually generated or modified in committee or business meetings, it is especially important to stay in touch with the living stream when we are sharing or modifying prophetic concerns in a business meeting. It is not easy for the modern mind to stay in a worshipful state during a busy or contentious business meeting— but it is possible "with a little help from our Friends." Classic Quaker theory holds that every spoken word in a committee or business meeting should come by inspiration or at least by assent of the Spirit. The important prophetic work of a business meeting may, first of all, concern the life and vitality of the meeting community itself.

Most meetings also are concerned with witness and service and contact with wider Quakerism as well as the world around us. One example of prophetic decisions about the meeting community can be found in a recent *Friends Journal* article about how more than one meeting has felt led to have some form of "Sabbath year." Knowing how Quaker process works, we can assume that these decisions were not reached in one easy, quick business meeting!

As I reflect on my own experience in business meeting, I admit that sometimes I had to use great self-discipline to remain centered when I felt a powerful prophetic yes or prophetic no in a lively and contentious business meeting. Sometimes the prophetic yes or no was so strong that I could feel it physically. At such times it is very difficult to distinguish between prophetic pressure and internal emotional pressure. There are times when we must speak to an issue and trust grace to keep us honest and loving and faithful all at the same time! This brings us back to the first manifestation of prophecy on our list: "For some souls this may be the most important form of prophecy—to just be in this place, this state of consciousness which both lifts us out of time and which allows us to be a conduit through which Divine energy and healing can flow . . ." So, in a contentious or wordy business meeting, it is especially important that a good number of Friends present know how to stay in touch with the Stream at such times. Friend, this may be thy most important prophetic work!

Leading Workshops and Retreats

A seventh kind of prophetic nudging may lead some Friends to set up or to teach classes or workshops or to arrange for a meeting retreat. Or we may feel led to accept invitations to give talks or lead workshops or retreats. I imagine many of the people in this circle have been involved in such ministry—or you will be. We are usually given a sense of guidance in this process, and frequently new connections and openings will occur as a result of our faithfulness.

Witness and Service

An eighth form of prophetic call has led Friends throughout our history to prophetic witness and service. Agencies like AFSC [American Friends Service Committee], FWCC [Friends World Committee for Consultation], QUNO [Quaker United Nations Office], FCUN [Friends Committee on Unity with Nature], and Christian Peace Teams developed as the result of specific prophetic callings—sometimes very specific calls for specific purposes. It is important to remember that many such calls are very specific and may be quite independent of existing institutions. No doubt all of us have been involved in public and political witness for peace, justice, and equality. For many of us, our prophetic work may be to support and aid those who have obeyed the profound urgency of a prophetic call to dramatic or costly witness or to a sacrificial change in lifestyle or occupation. At this point I am reminded of an Australian Friend who feels prophetically called to devote his time to the spiritual nurture and spiritual formation of people called to peace activism.

Speaking to the Powerful

A ninth form (or intensity) of the prophetic call is exemplified by the story of Steve Angell's obedience to the command of the Spirit to give a message to President Nixon in 1970. Even though Steve resisted this call as he drove toward Washington, D.C., a series of what appeared to be coincidences led him by surprise to the very gate of Camp David where Nixon was spending the weekend! He didn't get to see Nixon, but a polite official from inside the compound did come out and sit in his car and promised to give the message to the president. Steve later received a very short note apparently signed by Nixon.

Even though most of us will not be called to such high-level prophecy, it is well to remember that an occasional Friend throughout our history has been given such a call and has been faithful to it. For example, in the 19th century an American Friends minister was able to give a message "from the Lord" to the king of England. James Henderson, a Barnesville, Ohio, farmer and Quaker minister of the old style, was allowed to deliver a message to two presidents in the 20th century. He also tried to see President Franklin Roosevelt but could only speak to his religious secretary.

Even though most of us will not be called to speak to the president, we may be called to speak to someone in government or business or in our community or in our yearly meeting—and the call may come with the same intensity. On occasion, such a call has even led a faithful Friend to travel to another place, not knowing why until arriving.

Research and Writing

A few people may experience a tenth type of prophetic call to a specific project of writing or research and writing.

There may be other categories of prophecy you have experienced that are not listed here. If so, let's add them now as we continue our worship sharing about how the prophetic is emerging among us and around us.

Questions for Reflection and Sharing
Prepared by William Taber
Feb. 27–29, 2004

1. Sometimes the prophetic emerges into our life before we have been deeply grounded in the prophetic stream. Did this happen to you?

2. What has been your experience in coming close to the Living Stream? How did it affect you and others through you? Have you known people who appeared to radiate a presence coming from the Living Stream? What changes did it bring into your life?

3. What has been your experience with nudgings for prayer for specific people or nudgings to reach out to them?

4. Has the "opportunity" played a role in your growth and your ministry?

5. Have you experienced an especially powerful leading in meeting to give a message which you knew was not easy to "hear"? When you hear a message in meeting, how to you know or feel that it is especially prophetic? Have you been given help, support (and correction?) for your prophetic ministry? Have you been able to help and support a Friend in the throes of prophetic ministry? Have you had the experience of prophetic ministry being resisted? Have you experienced in your ministry what happened to John Crook? Or do you know someone who did?

6. We have probably all seen times when a prophetic concern was tested, modified, and strengthened in a spirit-guided business or committee meeting. What factors made it possible? Have you seen a prophetic ministry get tangled up and weakened through Quaker process? What factors might have brought about a different outcome? Have you found trusted friends or clearness committees who can help a prophetic concern mature or who can help lay it aside or postpone it if that seems right?

7. The Old Testament speaks of Schools of the Prophets. Have some of us in this circle been part of a network which acts like a school of the prophets—

nurturing and encouraging faithfulness to the prophetic call?

8. Have any of us felt a prophetic call to make major changes in lifestyle, place of residence, occupation? This could include a call to witness and service in dramatic, dangerous, or ordinary ways.

9. Have you had an experience like Steve Angell's— being profoundly compelled to give a message to someone in authority?

10. Have any of us had a prophetic call for a specific writing or research and writing?

APPENDIX D

Forms of Accompaniment

Friends have many tools—specific forms—for accompaniment. We have forms such as clearness and support committees and prayer groups that are based in a local community—these are the first four categories below. The remaining sections describe some of the various names and functions for those who travel together, be they minister and elder (where the minister is clearly accountable to as well as supported by the elder), two companions (both traveling with a gift of ministry), or one who is called and a stranger who feels led to join him or her (this individual usually serves as an elder).

Some of the primary ways support and accountability are given to recorded ministers include pastors' retreats, social media or other ways to communicate with peers, yearly meeting boards of elders, and individual support or anchor committees. Possibly only the individual support committees are unique to Friends; the others, oriented to Friends churches with pastors, are relatively standard in other churches.

1. Prayer partners: Prayer partners may be any number of people who feel called to pray together, whether once or on an ongoing basis. This is much more prevalent among evangelical Friends, who welcome verbal prayer, but it is a valued dimension of the spiritual life of all Friends, including those who find most nourishment in silent prayer. For both evangelical and liberal Friends, in silent worship a person may center using a mantra, a simple internal prayer of a few words that circles round and round within until awareness of God's presence rises up. In verbal prayer, a few familiar spoken prayers may do the same thing as words pile up on each other, taking on a life of their own. For Friends, a deepening sense of Divine presence is the focus, not the words or absence thereof.

2. Missions/evangelism committees: Missions or evangelism committees encourage prayer and financial support for missionaries and evangelists as well as keep the church informed about such work. These are the individuals who pay attention to others in the church who might be called to such service, encourage them, and help them get the training that will facilitate and enrich this work.

3. Clearness committees: Clearness committees were developed in the unprogrammed tradition as a way for members of the community to aid the individual in discerning where God is calling them. At the start of the process, the focus person articulates where they are seeking guidance and what they know of how the Inward Guide might be leading. The primary responsibility of the others present is to listen for the way God is working in the life of that individual and help them articulate that. They are invited to ask open-ended questions (questions that are not leading and to which they cannot know the answer). If the focus person wishes, those present may offer reflections on what they have heard or make suggestions. However, this is not a problem-solving group. Its responsibility is to open space so that the Light of Christ may shine through.

4. Peer groups: A peer group consists of three to five individuals who meet regularly with the intent of encouraging one another in regular spiritual practice and faithful attendance in obedience to the guidance of the Inward Teacher. Everyone present has equal time to speak to about where the Spirit is acting in his or her life and the struggles they are experiencing. The others then may ask open-ended questions and offer reflections if requested. Usually the time together closes by asking each participant, "How may we pray for you?"

5. Anchor/support committees: Committees that offer spiritual and practical support for an individual called to a ministry have a number of names, including anchor or support committees. Such committees also serve to hold the minister to account.

6. Elder and minister: One traditional way for Friends to travel in the ministry is for a recognized elder to accompany the person who has experienced the call. Jan Hoffman and Kenneth Sutton write, "We need first to recognize and affirm the elders among us so that our ministers will be rightly grounded and boldly offer their ministry. . . . A minister alone is not sufficient to sustain the deepest life in our faith communities."[1] They describe some of the gifts of the elder as "praying for the meeting and for the meeting for worship, discerning and encouraging gifts among the members, and conveying the Quaker tradition through example or teaching."[2]

7. Two traveling ministers: At times, individuals traveling in the ministry may each have felt a calling and are able to travel as equals, supporting each other. Peggy Parsons (now Morrison) reports on her travels with Alivia Biko, "Working with [her] made me much more aware of how I did ministry; what was personality, what was habit, and what was belief. . . . I have discovered the centrality of simply being a message bearer for the Spirit."[3]

8. Strangers and close companions: When someone is called to travel long distances, the cost and time involved often mean that no one from their local meeting can accompany them. In this case, someone (perhaps a stranger) who lives near where the visiting is happening may serve as companion.

8. Opportunities: This is an old-fashioned word for a spontaneous time of open, expectant worship wherever two or three are gathered. It most often refers to the visits of individuals traveling in the ministry who meet with families or other small groups. As part of this time of worship, the minister will share as the Spirit guides about the condition of those present.

10. Learning from our spiritual ancestors:
Many Friends cherish the time spent reading excerpts
from the journals or other writings of early Quakers.
First-hand reports are a primary way that Friends pass
down our particular theology. Thus, Quaker theology
is full of stories of individual and group encounters
with God. Their steadfastness and some of the
amazing consequences of total obedience to the cross
of Christ continue to inform the lives of many today.
This is mingled with the practice of Bible reading and
attention to other sacred writings.

11. Travel minutes: When an individual is
recognized by his or her meeting as having a call to
ministry, and in particular a call to speak to or work
with groups outside the home community, they may
ask the meeting to formally approve a minute at their
regular business meeting, starting the meeting's
recognition of this calling. The individual carries this
minute with them as they travel and asks the clerks of
the meetings they visit to add comments of their own.
Nancy Hawkins reports in her essay on ministry in
Walk Worthy of Your Calling:

> When traveling in unfamiliar places, it is
> comforting to know the prayers and support of
> members in my own meeting follow us. The
> minute I carry from my meeting not only
> shows their support, it is a means by which I
> can return with greetings from each meeting
> we visited. The minute also conveys a sense of
> the condition of that meeting. The host
> meeting, according to custom, directs their
> clerk to write and sign a return minute. This
> seemingly small item of business gives the
> sense that my meeting is participating with me.
> When my leading is fulfilled, I return the
> minute, complete with the comments made by
> the clerks of each meeting we attended. I can
> never sufficiently report to the meeting the
> many nuances which Wisdom has used to

guide me in my travels. The returned minutes supply those links for me.[4]

12. Recognition of gifts: Recognition of our gifts means naming them and knowing what is ours to do and what is not ours to do.

What gifts might we recognize today among Friends? What do the gifts of ministry, eldering, and others that we name look like today? How do we know these gifts among us, and what expectations do we have as to how they might be used?

For the large majority of Friends, the first place to look for answers to these questions is in the Christian Testament. First Corinthians 12:4–11 lists gifts given by the Spirit. "All these are activated by one and the same Spirit, who allots to each one individually just as the Spirit chooses." These gifts include:

- utterance of wisdom
- utterance of knowledge
- faith
- healing
- working of miracles
- prophecy
- discernment of spirits
- speaking in tongues
- interpretation of tongues

Wisdom, knowledge, faith, discernment, and prophetic ministry are all firmly welcome if sometimes disturbing gifts. The remainder of this list is problematic for many Friends, as it has been for other churches in the twentieth and twenty-first centuries. Despite their affirmation of a direct relationship with God and reliance on the Light, the Holy Spirit, Friends have not been particularly open to speaking in tongues. In fact, in the United States the Vineyard Church was begun by Quakers who wanted a more charismatic approach to worship. In East Africa, and to a lesser degree in South America, various "Holy Spirit" churches have spun off from Friends churches over this issue. Similarly, modern Friends have been uneasy about the working of miracles. In fact, this unease dates back to the seventeenth century, when reports of miracle-working and healing were removed from George Fox's *Journal* before it was published in 1691. Nonetheless, there have been anecdotal reports of healings among Friends over the centuries.

Expanding on this earlier list, 1 Corinthians 12:27–31 reads:

> Now you are the body of Christ and individually members of it. And God has appointed in the church first apostles, second prophets, third teachers; then deeds of power, then gifts of healing, forms of assistance, forms of leadership, various kinds of tongues. Are all apostles? Are all prophets? Are all teachers? Do all work miracles? Do all possess gifts of healing? Do all speak in tongues? Do all interpret? But strive for the greater gifts. And I will show you a still more excellent way.

Following this statement is a full chapter describing the "still more excellent way," which is to love with the fullness of God's love. Without such love, our gifts are of little use and perhaps even detrimental to others. Thus, whatever gifts others may see in us must be accompanied by patience and kindness. If we are arrogant, rude, or boastful, if we envy others or insist that our way is the only right way, we are off track. Paul understands the human heart enough to warn us against rejoicing in the wrongdoing of others, that temptation to feel superior to people who mess up or give in to greed. Central to love is the convincement that our deepest hopes will not fail us in the end. We can trust in the power of divine love to carry us through suffering as well as success.

In the Christian Testament, prophecy is just one of many ways individuals build up community and embody the new creation here on earth.

APPENDIX E

Multnomah Monthly Meeting's Process for Discerning and Supporting Ministry

MULTNOMAH MEETING PROCEDURES RELATING TO CLEARNESS, SUPPORT, AND ACCOUNTABILITY FOR FRIENDS WHO EXPERIENCE A CALL TO MINISTRY LOCALLY OR TRAVELING OUTSIDE THE REGION

January 16, 2018

CALLINGS

At times, various members of the meeting have experienced a divine call to one of numerous forms of ministry: these have included such things as concerns around the death penalty, music, and writing and speaking about Friends. This may be a particular deep concern to undertake a particular service, a call to travel among Friends, or a call to offer support and counseling. Support of such ministry has taken many different shapes. Multnomah Monthly Meeting has minuted formal support to some Friends. At other times standing committees have worked with individuals, or occasionally a concern has been taken on by the entire meeting, as in the case of Sanctuary. When the individual seeks Meeting support of such a calling, a clearness committee of 3 or 4 persons is normally named by either Worship and Ministry or Oversight Committee to test this leading and explore the rightness and shape of any Meeting support.

Above all, we seek to find a way to uphold one another in prayer and worship, as well as in practical ways which support actions led by God or in response to Friends testimonies, recognizing the many ways we speak about what is holy. The focus of this document is on dual clearness committees, anchor, and support committees for Friends in Ministry, who we name as

Released Friends: those whose calling is formally minuted by the Meeting or individuals who request a minute to travel in the ministry.

The following sections first offer some definitions and then describe several ways the Meeting might formally recognize and support a divine calling. When there is relevant information in North Pacific Yearly Meeting's 2017 *Faith and Practice*, this has been included in the text.

DEFINITIONS

Clearness and Care Committees. Meetings form various kinds of ad hoc committees to assist members and attenders spiritually, physically, and emotionally. Across the country different meetings use different names, but we are proposing some language that seems to work for Multnomah Monthly Meeting relating to aid in finding clearness and to providing support.

No matter what the committee is called, the Meeting seeks to take care to establish any such committee mindfully, state its charge clearly, and name a clerk to convene its meetings and guide its process. Typically either the Worship and Ministry or the Oversight Committee appoints the committee in consultation with the person or group needing clearness, support, or care.

Clearness Committees. Clearness Committees are ad hoc committees appointed by either Worship and Ministry or Oversight Committee.

Clearness may be for assistance in **personal discernment**. When an individual, family, or other group is facing a particularly difficult situation, they may request a Clearness Committee. In this case, our concern is to help the individual(s) find what actions or decisions they might undertake that are consistent with our faith and the guidance of the Spirit. Normally a Clearness Committee only meets once or twice. For more on this practice, see *Faith and Practice*.

Finding clearness is an integral part of the relationship between the Meeting and its members and attenders. We normally seek **dual clearness** in response to requests for membership, marriage, or support of callings. In these instances, *both* the individual making the request and the members of the Clearness Committee need to discern that this is the right action for all involved. Again, the expectation is that this Committee will meet once or twice. See *Faith and Practice* for specific discussion of marriage and membership.

Support Committees. Ad hoc committee acting as elders for a Friend who is filling a responsible position within the meeting or the Society or who has a minute to travel among Friends. The clerk of a meeting, a hospital chaplain, a prison visitor, or an individual with a call to travel among Friends may have a Support Committee to help them discern how their work is unfolding, where the Light is leading, and when they might have outrun the Guide. The Oversight Committee or Worship and Ministry Committee appoints the Support Committee (usually two to five people) and names its clerk in consultation with the Friend concerned. The Support Committee exists for the duration of the Friend's work.

Anchor Committees. An ad hoc committee to provide spiritual support and accountability for Released Friends who have been recognized by the Business Meeting as having a calling, perhaps in response to explore in depth Friends' way in the world or a leading in peace, social justice, the creative arts, or environmental action. The Anchor Committee consists of 2-4 people most often named by the Worship and Ministry Committee. It is expected to meet at least quarterly with this Friend, offering a gentle, strong listening presence to help them stay faithful, grounded, and accountable in their ministry. The Anchor Committee is expected to report biennially to the Business Meeting via the Worship and Ministry Committee. The Anchor Committee continues to meet as long as the ministry is under the care of the Meeting.

Care Committees. Usually consists of 2-4 people who walk alongside individuals or families during times of crisis such as long-term illness or major transitions. The Oversight Committee appoints the committee and names its clerk in consultation with the Friend concerned. The Care Committee responds to the person in need of assistance by arranging for food, prayers, visits, transportation, or other support that can be provided by volunteers. It may make available counsel, information, and support in planning for life transitions. The Care Committee reports regularly to the Oversight Committee and is laid down when the Friend's situation is resolved.

Released Friends/Friends Under a Concern. When a member of the Meeting feels a particular call to service and an imperative to act, they may request recognition of that concern by the Business Meeting.

Traveling Minutes. When a member proposes to travel under the weight of a concern to be shared with other Friends, the matter is first considered by the Committee for Worship and Ministry or by the Oversight Committee, which often names a Clearness Committee to consider the request. Upon recommendation by a committee, the monthly meeting may grant the Friend a traveling minute for that particular concern.

Recorded Ministers. Individuals recognized by the Meeting as having a gift in vocal ministry. North Pacific Yearly Meeting has no history of "recording" gifts of ministry as all Friends once did, and thus our process is inherently different from that of Quaker tradition. Our process recognizes our way of being faithful to the movement of the Spirit among us today.

Letters of Introduction. Fellowship and the spiritual life of the Religious Society of Friends have long been nourished by visitation outside a member's own meeting. Our monthly meeting clerk may write a letter of introduction to certify the person's membership (or affiliation, for a faithful attender who is not a member), describe the person's participation in the meeting, and convey greetings. The visited Friends may write a return greeting on the letter, which is presented to the issuing meeting upon return. Friends who are traveling and wish to visit Friends in other meetings may receive valuable guidance through Friends World Committee for Consultation, Section of the Americas.

Friends in Ministry: Acting under "Concern"

> . . . *That care be taken for the families and goods of such as are called forth into the ministry, or who are imprisoned for the truth's sake* . . .
> Epistle from the Elders at Balby, 1656

"Friends in Ministry" includes Friends with leadings to travel among, write for, and speak to other Friends, as well as Friends whose lives speak in a specific outward witness—for example, visiting prisoners, working among the mentally ill, a ministry drawing upon the creative arts, addressing racism, acting upon concern for the well-being of the planet, or serving at food banks or homeless shelters. In our time, "Friends in Ministry" is expanding among unprogrammed Friends to include, for example, Friends in professions with an explicit pastoral or ministry component, such as chaplains and spiritual directors.

Released Friends with a Concern

Friends endeavor to serve God through their daily lives. However, in some Friends there arises a leading to some specific task. The leading is felt as an imperative claim—it cannot be denied even when the individual experiences deep personal reluctance. This

428

is what Friends call a "concern." It is also possible for a concern to arise spontaneously in a meeting in response to a particular need or opportunity.

From early days the Religious Society of Friends has greatly valued those leadings of the Spirit which result in individual and corporate concerns. However, concerns vary in merit, depending on the validity of the inspiration and the care with which they are considered and carried out. The concerns of even well-known Friends have not always been of equal significance. Some concerns are meant for an individual, others for a wider group. Friends pursue a concern publicly only after they have clearness for themselves and the concern has received the corporate support of their meeting. A person with a concern should have patience and humility in seeking support for it.

When a concern carries sufficient weight that support of the whole Meeting is appropriate, we ask that it first be considered and tested as a true leading of the Spirit. Before bringing a concern to the meeting for business, an individual Friend considers it prayerfully to be sure that it is rightly motivated and of more than personal or passing importance. The Friend then seasons the concern through consultation with a standing committee of the meeting, most often the Worship and Ministry Committee, which will normally convene a Clearness Committee to season the leading and to determine the way forward.

When the seasoning process is complete, the concern comes to the meeting for business in a clear, concise, written statement of its purpose, including the actions proposed and the support needed from the meeting. Until the meeting determines that it will support the concern, Friends avoid statements implying that the meeting has given its support.

Unhurried consideration of the concern by the meeting is important. Consideration may extend over more than one monthly meeting for business. The meeting may unite with and support a Friend to carry out a concern personally—for example, to travel in the ministry, to witness to Friends principles in a given situation, or to do other service living out Friends testimonies or providing spiritual care.

The process of releasing a Friend from meeting to act on a concern involves careful consideration of both merits and methods as well as the qualifications and situation of the Friend to be released. Motivation, character, and family and financial situation need to be considered.

A Released Friend will be given a formal minute of the Business Meeting describing the concern and the nature of the Meeting's support. A meeting's support for a released Friend could include any of the following:

- Release from obligations such as holding meeting offices and serving on committees;
- Appointment of an Anchor Committee to offer advice, encouragement, accountability, and a place to test ideas and leadings;
- Material help as needed;
- Provision of a "traveling minute" outlining the nature of the Friend's concern and stating the meeting's endorsement (see below).

The released Friend's Anchor Committee reports regularly to the meeting on the progress of the ministry. It reviews the concern periodically to see if the help of the meeting should be altered or discontinued.

Britain Yearly Meeting advises that the Meeting which has considered a concern needs to be absolutely clear when it is recognizing a concern carried by an individual or when it is adopting the concern as one it shares as a concern for the whole community. In either case it is valuable to be clear about the support the Meeting is expecting to give.

When the Meeting Unites With a Concern

Sometimes a meeting may find itself so fully in sympathy with the concern that it is laid upon the group as a whole and is carried out by the meeting. If a concern has meaning for more than this monthly meeting, it may be shared directly with other monthly meetings. It may also be forwarded to the quarterly meeting or to a standing committee of North Pacific Yearly Meeting. (See "Bringing Concerns before the Yearly Meeting" in North Pacific Yearly Meeting *Faith and Practice*, Chapter 8, "The Yearly Meeting.") If a meeting fails to unite with a member's concern, the member generally reconsiders it very carefully. Occasionally, an individual who is strongly convinced that the corporate life of the meeting and of the Society will be enriched if it can grow and unite with a particular concern may bring that concern to the meeting repeatedly over an extended period. Many of the Quaker testimonies have evolved because of the patient persistence of a valiant Friend who has perceived the Light with extraordinary clarity. Such persistence has helped some meetings and the Society come to unite with an insight that they could not at first accept. If the meeting still remains unable to unite with the concern, it may be because the Friend is "running ahead of their Guide" or because the concern does not arise from a genuine spiritual leading.

Travel in the Ministry

Friends are relatively few and interspersed widely in our yearly meeting and around the world. Ever since the earliest days of Friends, individuals have felt and acted upon a calling to travel, visiting other Quaker Meetings and at times traveling to speak on behalf of a particular concern. North Pacific Yearly Meeting is spread across the expanse of Oregon, Washington, Idaho, and Montana and many Meetings and Worship

Groups are small, perhaps consisting of a dozen or fewer individuals. Travel among Meetings has been valuable in bringing encouragement to small groups which might struggle in their isolation as well as knitting together the body of Friends. The freshness of a different voice, news of Friends elsewhere, and opportunities for deep sharing on particular topics of interest may all serve to strengthen the community.

Traveling Minutes

When a member proposes to travel under the weight of a concern to be shared with other Friends, the matter is first considered by the Committee for Worship and Ministry or by the Oversight Committee, which often names a clearness committee of 2-4 individuals to consider the request. Upon recommendation by that committee, the monthly meeting may grant the Friend a traveling minute for that particular concern. A Support Committee may be named to provide ongoing assistance and accountability. While individuals from the Clearness Committee may continue on this new Committee, it is not automatically expected.

When a meeting grants a traveling minute, it takes care that, as far as possible, the service of the Friend is not hindered for lack of funds or other resources. This member may already be recognized as a Released Friend or may have a calling for a particular time or purpose.

Traditionally, when possible, Meetings have seen to it that the person traveling with such a Minute has someone—often called an elder or a companion—who might travel with them to provide logistical and spiritual support as well as accountability. Sometimes this individual is a member of Multnomah who has the time and financial resources to provide accompaniment. In other instances, someone at the destination may be available to provide this service. If the travel is extensive, different people may undertake parts of the trip.

The minute of travel should be short enough to be read easily after Meeting, conveying a sense of the individual and the concern they carry as well as greetings from Multnomah. It is helpful if a sense of the duration of the travel in time or distance is identified so all know the extent of the journey.

If the visit will go beyond the yearly meeting, the minute should be forwarded to the presiding clerk for yearly meeting endorsement. Before the yearly meeting endorses the minute, it clarifies that the traveling Friend is aware of and sensitive to differences in theology and practice among the Friends to be visited. Our ministry needs to reach out to others where they are in their diversity lest we not be heard.

Traveling minutes are submitted to and are customarily endorsed by the clerk or other officer of meetings visited by traveling Friends, who are encouraged to offer candid reflections on the visit. The traveler returns the minute and the accompanying endorsements to the clerk of the Meeting within a reasonable time after the visitation has been completed. A copy is archived in the membership file of the traveling Friend. Friends also report to other meetings which have supported the concern and may also find it valuable to reflect on their experience with their support or anchor committee.

What do Friends report back to the Meeting?

- The specifics of travel (where/when) but usually not at length.
- The written endorsements (responses from visited meetings) with the group. If there are additional reflections, these might be shared if appropriate.
- The condition of those visited, shared with loving truthfulness and discretion.
- Lessons the Friend has received in the course of this travel.

What does this report do for the Meeting?

Weighing the experience of the travel certainly benefits the Friend and there is nothing quite like the requirement of reporting to get us to do that weighing.

Hearing the report can knit the Friend's work into the fabric of the meeting. It can open eyes to aspects of travel under a concern or in the ministry that neither individuals nor the body would have thought of simply because the minute was approved.

The report can be a lesson to the Friend and to the Meeting in what it means to travel carrying a minute. It can open the hearts of more in the Meeting to the possibility of travel.

The Work of Clearness, Support, and Anchor Committees

The Clearness, Support, or Anchor Committees all are centered on meeting together in worship with the individual to seek divine Guidance.

Clearness Committees

The focus of a Clearness Committee is a specific question or issue. The process begins with the person or group asking for the committee to help hear what God may be asking of them in a particular area of life. The committee usually consists of two to four trusted individuals (but not necessarily close friends) willing to listen. It is helpful if the person requesting clearness prepares a letter describing what is on their heart and the decisions they see in front of them.

The Clearness Committee's clerk convenes the committee and keeps it focused. Another member may take notes if the individual seeking clearness wishes this resource. Some individuals find that just having a list of the questions asked has been helpful for further reflection.

While the aim of all such committees is to accompany the individual as they seek to be faithful to the Inward Guide, when an individual is seeking formal support from the Meeting, the Committee also has the responsibility to seek clarity as to whether the concern or the request for a Travel Minute should be brought before the Business Meeting, if an ongoing Support or Anchor Committee is needed, or other actions as appropriate.

The basic shape of Clearness Committee meetings
- The committee gathers in silent worship.
- The focus person speaks out of the silence concerning the question weighing on them. Listeners first take time to see if clarification is needed. Then, after further silence, gentle open-ended questions are offered. The focus person responds from the heart without expectation of response.
- The committee's inquiries invite the focus person or group to deeply engage and discern their own truth, rather than offering advice or judgment in the guise of questions.
- All present are committed to attend to the movement of the Spirit, recognizing that this is a time to find the way forward for the individual and the Meeting in accord with the Light, not an opportunity to share stories about similar circumstances or problems.
- The listeners reflect back what they have been hearing. The intent is that all persons present find clarity as to how the Spirit is leading the individual and what the Spirit is asking of the Meeting community in the way of support for this ministry.
- The Meeting closes in worship and gratitude. Further meetings are arranged if desired.

- In all things, the committee remains aware that the process is confidential.

Support and Anchor Committees

Support or Anchor Committees meet in ways similar to Clearness Committee meetings. They gather in worship and close in worship. The focus person articulates how the Spirit is working in their life and what issues, inward or external, they are facing and how they are responding. Committee members have the responsibility to listen for the presence of the Light and raise up queries for the individual, or at times the whole group, to consider.

The process is essentially the same for Support and Anchor Committees, but the Anchor Committee is specifically for Released Friends and may meet for a decade or more, while a Support Committee assists individuals traveling in the ministry, one in service as Clerk of the Meeting, a time of prison visitation, or other specific ministries.

Because these committees meet for extended periods of time, sometimes for years, it is important that all feel a part of the process and come to know each other more deeply. Following the time of worship, the meeting often begins with a brief check-in whereby people share about their spiritual condition. Doing so also aids the process by allowing personal concerns to be acknowledged and set aside.

The released Friend or individual who is the focus of the Anchor Committee then has the responsibility to speak to their own condition and their awareness, or lack of awareness, of the work of the Spirit in their life. The primary need is for the group to listen beyond the words. As the meeting proceeds, if the focus person wishes, the group may attend to particular issues the individual is facing or respond to a request for clearness on a particular dimension of the ministry. The primary focus is on the conduct of the ministry and faithfulness to God's way. All present seek to bring their own wisdom, experience, and Light to bear on the situation and to live up to the trust that has been placed in them to be honest, caring, and willing to set aside the demands of their ego in order to attend to what the Spirit is asking.

As *Baltimore Yearly Meeting Faith and Practice* notes: "Serving on a Support or Anchor Committee can be tough at times. Committee members may be stressed as difficult obstacles present themselves, discouraging news is heard, and hard facts must be accepted." Such challenges call for a continuing awareness of grounding in worship. Anchor Committees also need to be sensitive to changes in the ministry or the possibility that a ministry is coming to an end and consult with the Released Friend and let Worship and Ministry know what is happening.

Special Sensitivity. Support or Anchor Committees exercise sensitivity and discernment around a potential conflict when a ministry may overlap with activities that also provide a livelihood. Examples include times when specific, learned, professional skills such as counseling, spiritual direction, or musicianship can be requested as part of ministry (and assumed to be gratis) when that skill is also inherent in the livelihood of the individual. Support and Anchor Committees can assist in discerning appropriate responses to ambiguous invitations, messaging distinctions to the meeting, and, when needed, assisting the individual to reduce barriers to making a workable living while staying true to the calling.

How Long? It is important for all those involved to be aware of what is being asked of them. Thus, defining the nature of the task, which sometimes is concrete, such as a journey to visit all the Meetings in the Pacific Northwest, but more often is indefinite, such as gaining equality for gays and lesbians, writing a book, or carrying out a ministry around the spiritual and physical dimensions of water, is important. It also should be stated how long committee members are expected to serve.

Reporting Back to the Meeting. The Anchor Committee in particular has a mandate to report every other year to Worship and Ministry, and to the Business Meeting, on the course of the ministry. Such reports should identify the work undertaken, obstacles met, and whether they have been addressed or if assistance is needed. They should also raise up changes that have occurred in the direction of the ministry and whether the ministry is alive and should continue. If major concerns arise in between these reports, the Committee may want to bring this to the attention of Worship and Ministry. Copies of the reports should be filed in the Released Friend's membership file.

It is expected that the Meeting reaffirm their minute for each Released Friend approximately every four years.

When the work of the committee seems awry. Such a committee may also meet without the focus person or group present, to seek Light for its work. The committee may ask:

- What are our appropriate behavioral boundaries? Are we keeping to them?
- Are we helping or are we hindering, for example by fostering dependency?
- Are we allowing the focus person or group to do their own work, or are we being too directive?
- Are we staying within our responsibility and charge?
- Have we gone beyond our ability? (That is, is it time to recommend professional help?)

Multnomah Meeting Ministerial Support Fund (approved May 2016)

The Ministerial Support Fund was established in 2003 with an undesignated bequest. The Meeting accepted a proposal to create the fund to assist individuals with a special call for ministry. The proposal at that time was explicit that the Meeting might in the future decide to use the funds for other purposes and/or merge this fund with Spiritual Life.

"Ministry" is defined as writing and teaching as well as dedicated action outside the Meeting community to advance the just society cherished by Friends. The fund is complementary to the Spiritual Life Fund, supporting outreach for Quaker belief and testimonies, while the Spiritual Life Fund supports activities within and for our worshipping communities.

Fund guidelines include the following:

- Members or attenders are eligible when they can demonstrate a concern or leading that has been seasoned with a Clearness Committee and recognized by their Monthly Meeting, perhaps as a released Friend. It is likely that such individuals will be members or otherwise will have participated for a substantial time in the life of their Meeting or associated worshipping groups.
- Applications may be submitted without concern for a time limit or deadline. Eligible recipients may receive continued assistance on a case-by-case basis over consecutive years, based on the Trustees' consideration.
- If financially possible, grant amounts will be limited to the income earned during the previous year. Otherwise, the Fund trustees will decide how best to allocate funds from this account, based on its sustainability and fund purposes and guidelines.

How to ask for financial assistance: When seeking assistance, please write to the Special Funds Trustees in care of the Clerk. In your request, include information about:

- The nature of your ministry and when it was taken into the care of the Meeting.
- The amount of the request. Be specific about fees, transport, room & board, etc., and include information about other sources of funding, including your own resources.
- If you need full funding, please give an explanation of why this is true.
- If you are attending a conference, it is helpful to include a description of the conference or, at the very least, a website link to that information.
- It will add substance to the request if it is also endorsed by your Support/Anchor Committee.
- Briefly state how you will bring what you learn back to the local community.

Please allow at least 4 weeks for the Trustees to consider a request. This gives time for proper seasoning and potential payments to take advantage of early discounts and travel expenses. Be aware that the Trustees may ask additional questions and/or may want to meet with you as part of their discernment. This is not an onerous process, but the Trustees want to be thorough as they discern the way forward.

BIBLIOGRAPHY

Abbott, Margery Post. *Everyday Prophets*. James Backhouse Lecture. Australia Yearly Meeting of the Religious Society of Friends, 2016.

———. "Prophetic Ministry." *Seeds* [Good News Associates] (August 2012). https://goodnewsassoc. org/wp-content/uploads/2012/08/August-2012-SEEDS.pdf.

Abbott, Margery Post, and Noah Baker Merrill. "Why Do Quakers Care about Politics?" Produced by Jon Watts. January 28, 2016. QuakerSpeak video, 4:41. http://quakerspeak.com/why-do-quakers-care-about-politics/.

Bieber, Nancy L. *Decision Making & Spiritual Discernment: The Sacred Art of Finding Your Way*. Woodstock, VT: Skylight Paths Publishing, 2010.

Boulding, Elise. *One Small Plot of Heaven: Reflections on Family Life by a Quaker Sociologist*. Wallingford, PA: Pendle Hill Publications, 1989.

Bownas, Samuel. *A Description of the Qualifications Necessary to a Gospel Minister*. Wallingford, PA: Pendle Hill Publications and the Tract Association of Friends, 1989.

Brindle, Susannah Kay. *To Learn a New Song: A Quaker Contribution towards Real Reconciliation with the Earth and Its Peoples*. James Backhouse Lecture. Australia Yearly Meeting of the Religious Society of Friends, 2000.

Brinton, Howard. *Prophetic Ministry*. Pendle Hill Pamphlet #54. Wallingford, PA: Pendle Hill Publications, 1950.

Brock, Rita Nakashima, and Rebecca Ann Parker. *Saving Paradise: How Christianity Traded Love of This World for Crucifixion and Empire*. Boston: Beacon Press, 2009.

Brown, Valerie. *Coming to Light: Cultivating Spiritual Discernment through the Quaker Clearness Committee*. Pendle Hill Pamphlet #446. Wallingford, PA: Pendle Hill Publications, 2017.

Brueggemann, Walter. *The Prophetic Imagination*. 2nd ed. Minneapolis: Fortress Press, 2001.

Corbett, Jim. *Goatwalking: A Quest for the Peaceable Kingdom*. New York: Penguin Books, 1991.

Crowe, Avis, and Dyckmann W. Vermilye. *The Ministry of Presence: Without Agenda in South Africa*. Pendle Hill Pamphlet #293. Wallingford, PA: Pendle Hill Publications, 1990.

Dandelion, Pink, and Jackie Leech Scully, eds. *Good and Evil: Quaker Perspectives*. Hampshire, England: Aldergate Publishing, 2007.

Dandelion, Ben Pink. *Open for Transformation: Being Quaker*. Swarthmore Lecture. London: Quaker Books, 2014.

Drayton, Brian. "James Nayler Speaking." Pendle Hill Pamphlet #413. Wallingford, PA: Pendle Hill Publications, 2011.

———. *A Language for the Inward Landscape: Spiritual Wisdom from the Quaker Movement*. Philadelphia: Tract Association of Friends, 2015.

———. *On Living with a Concern for the Gospel Ministry*. Philadelphia: Quaker Press, 2006.

Elam, Jennifer. *Dancing With God through the Storm: Mysticism and Mental Illness*. Pendle Hill Pamphlet #344. Wallingford, PA: Pendle Hill Publications, 1999.

Fendall, Lon, Jan Wood, and Bruce Bishop. *Practicing Discernment Together: Finding God's Way Forward in Decision Making*. Newberg, OR: Barclay Press, 2007.

Fox, George. *The Journal of George Fox*. Edited by John L. Nickalls. Philadelphia: Philadelphia Yearly Meeting, 1985.

Gee, David. *Holding Faith: Creating Peace in a Violent World*. London: Quaker Books, 2011.

Gerona, Carla. *Night Journeys: The Power of Dreams in Transatlantic Culture*. Charlottesville, VA, University of Virginia Press, 2004.

Griswold, Robert. *Quaker Peace Testimony in Times of Terrorism*. Torrance, CA: Friends Bulletin, 2003.

Guiton, Gerard, *What Love Can Do: Following the Way of Peace, Justice and Compassion*. Northcote, Victoria, Australia: Morning Star Publishing, 2016.

———. *The Early Quakers and the Kingdom of God*. San Francisco: Inner Light Press, 2012.

Gwyn, Douglas. *The Anti-War*. San Francisco: Inner Light Books, 2016.

Haines, Pamela. "Waging Peace." Pendle Hill Pamphlet #420. Wallingford, PA: Pendle Hill Publications, 2012.

Heschel, Abraham Joshua. *The Prophets*. 2 vols. New York: Harper Torchbooks, 1962.

Hill, Christopher. *The World Turned Upside Down*. London: Penguin Books, 1972.

Holmes, Scott. "Why I Don't Wear a Tie in Court." Produced by John Watts. August 21, 2014. QuakerSpeak Video, 6:12. https://www.youtube.com/watch?v=n8Szc3vSfCg.

Hyzy, Kathy, ed. *An Inner Strength: Quakers and Leadership*. Torrance, CA: Friends Bulletin Corp., 2013.

Keiser, R. Melvin, and Rosemary Moore. *Knowing the Mystery of Life Within: Selected Writings of Isaac Penington in Their Historical and Theological Context*. London: Quaker Books, 2005.

Lakey, George. "On the Value of Conflict." *Friends Journal* 56 (Nov. 2010): 8–15.

Lampen, John. "Answering the Violence: Encounters with Perpetrators." Pendle Hill Pamphlet #412. Wallingford, PA: Pendle Hill Publications, 2011.

McBee, Patricia. *Grounded in God: Care and Nurture in Friends Meeting*. Philadelphia: Quaker Press, 2002.

McNaughton, Marion. "An Orientation to Prophecy." Philadelphia, PA: Wider Quaker Fellowship, 2008. http://fwccamericas.org/pub/McNaughton2008.pdf.

Moore, Rosemary. *The Light in Their Consciences: The Early Quakers in Britain 1646–1666*. University Park: Pennsylvania State University Press, 2000.

Palmer, Parker J. *Leading from Within: Reflections on Spirituality and Leadership*. Washington, DC: Potter's House Book Service, 1990.

———. *The Promise of Paradox: A Celebration of the Contradictions in the Christian Life*. San Francisco: Jossey-Bass, 1980.

Pearn, Jane. *The Language of Leadings: A Reflection on Faith, Action and Concern*. London: Quaker Books, 2017.

Pitman, Ruth. "On the Vocal Ministry." Philadelphia, PA: Tract Association of Friends, 1979. http://www.tractassociation.org/tracts/vocal-ministry/.

Prete, Anthony. *Shalom: Much More Than Just Peace*. Philadelphia: Wider Quaker Fellowship, 2008.

Punshon, John. *Encounter with Silence: Reflections from the Quaker Tradition*. Richmond, IN: Friends United Press, 1989.

Ratcliffe, Jennie M. *Integrity, Ecology, and Community: The Motion of Love*. Pendle Hill Pamphlet #403. Wallingford, PA: Pendle Hill Publications, 2009.

Richmond, Ben. *Signs of Salvation: A Biblical Meditation*. Richmond, IN: Friends United Press, 2005.

Roe, Lizz. "Finding the Prophetic Voice for Our Time." *Friends Journal* 54 (Oct. 2008): 7–9, 50–51.

Schenck, Patricia. *Answering the Call to Heal the World*. Pendle Hill Pamphlet #383. Wallingford, PA: Pendle Hill Publications, 2006.

School of the Spirit. *The Spiritual Care Committee*. Philadelphia Yearly Meeting, 2012. http://schoolofthespirit.org/wp-content/uploads/2012/04/Spiritual-Care-Committee-booklet3-042412.pdf.

Spencer, Sarah, ed. *Radical Witness: Four Talks on Faith Made Manifest in the World*. Boston: Beacon Hill Friends House, 2009.

Taber, William. "The Prophetic Stream." Pendle Hill Pamphlet #256. Wallingford, PA: Pendle Hill Publications, 1984.

Wallace, Terry S. *A Sincere and Constant Love: An Introduction to the Work of Margaret Fell*. Richmond, IN: Friends United Press, 1992.

Wilson, Lloyd Lee. *Essays on the Quaker Vision of Gospel Order*. Burnsville, NC: Celo Valley Books, 1993.

Wink, Walter. *Engaging the Powers: Discernment and Resistance in a World of Domination.* Minneapolis: Augsberg Fortress, 1992.

Zaru, Jean. *Occupied with Nonviolence: A Palestinian Woman Speaks.* Minneapolis: Fortress Press, 2008.

NOTES

Preface (pp. i–iv)

[1] Conservative Friends seek to conserve the original practices and understandings of early Friends.

[2] William Taber, *The Prophetic Stream*, Pendle Hill Pamphlet #256 (Wallingford, PA: Pendle Hill Publications, 1984).

[3] Taber, *The Prophetic Stream.*

Introduction (pp. 1–17)

[1] *Harper's Bible Dictionary* (San Francisco: HarperSanFrancisco, 1971), 826. See also the *New World Encyclopedia*'s good, basic definition of the word 'prophet':

> A prophet (from the Greek word προφήτης, meaning one who "utters forth") is a person who is believed to speak for God (or the gods) with the purpose of delivering a divinely inspired message. A prophet often operates through means of recitation, divination, or channeling, and the process of receiving a message from the divine is known either as prophecy or as revelation. In popular usage, a prophet is someone who is believed to foretell the future.

Source: http://www.newworldencyclopedia.org/ entry/prophet.

[2] West Richmond Friends, "Who Are the Friends?" 2004, accessed Oct. 10, 2017, http://www.westrichmondfriends.org/ friends.htm.

[3] Søren Kierkegaard calls this the "philosophical irony" in his 1841 dissertation *The Concept of Irony.*

[4] George Fox, *Journal of George Fox*, ed. John L. Nickalls (Philadelphia: Philadelphia Yearly Meeting, 1985), 8, 9.

[5] Marmaduke Stevenson, Letter, in *A Call from Death to Life* (London: Printed for Thomas Simmons, 1660).

Chapter 1 (pp. 19–30)

[1] Samuel Bownas, *A Description of the Qualifications Necessary to a Gospel Minister* (Wallingford, PA: Pendle Hill Publications, 1989), xxviii.

[2] Peggy Parsons, "Catching a Message," *Western Friend* 73 (October 2002), 4–5.

Chapter 2 (pp. 31–41)

[1] Jean Zaru, *Seeking: To Live as Children of God,* Ramallah Friends Meeting, March 10, 2017, http://www.rfmq.org/single-post/2017/03/10/Seeking.

[2] Prete, "Shalom," 7.

[3] Prete, "Shalom," 8.

[4] Prete, "Shalom," 10.

Chapter 3 (pp. 42–52)

[1] Isaac Penington, "Some Directions to the Panting Soul" [1661], in *The Works of Isaac Penington*, vol. 2 (Glenside, PA: Quaker Heritage Press, 1995), 205.

[2] *Harper's Bible Dictionary* (San Francisco: HarperSanFrancisco, 1971), 411.

[3] Seth B. Hinshaw, *The Spoken Ministry among Friends: Three Centuries of Progress and Development* (Davidson, NC: North Carolina Yearly Meeting and North Carolina Friends Historical Society, 1987), 12.

Chapter 4 (pp. 53–62)

[1] "As often as Merton discusses the 'true self,' he returns to the theme of the 'false self' frequently in his writings. It might be helpful here to recall Merton's famous remarks on the false self in *New Seeds of Contemplation*. Merton wrote: '

> Every one of us is shadowed by an illusory person: a false self. This is the man that I want myself to be but who cannot exist because God does not know anything about him. . . . My false and private self is the one who wants to exist outside the reach of God's will and God's love—outside of reality and outside of life. And such a self cannot help but be an illusion.'"

Daniel P. Horan, "Striving toward Authenticity: Merton's 'True Self' and the Millennial Generation's Search for Identity," June 2009, The Thomas Merton Center at Bellarmine University, pp. 84–85, merton.org/ITMS/Annual/23/Horan80-89.pdf,.

[2] Adam Curle, *True Justice: Quaker Peacemakers and Peacemaking* (London: Quaker Home Service, 1981), 66.

[3] Micah Bales, "Holy Anger," November 12, 2012, *Religion is Easy. Discipleship is Hard* (blog), http://www.micahbales.com/tag/occupyhomes/.

4 Curle, *True Justice*, 92.

5 John Lampen, *Answering the Violence—Encounters with Perpetrators*, Pendle Hill Pamphlet #412 (Wallingford, PA: Pendle Hill Publications, 2011), 26.

Chapter 5 (pp. 64–75)

1 "A Journey towards Peace and Justice: A Conference for Young Friends in Burundi, Congo, and Rwanda, August 4–19, 2013," accessed Aug. 28, 2013, Northwest Yearly Meeting of Friends, http://nwfriends.org/a-journey-toward-peace-and-justice/.

2 Walter Brueggemann, *The Prophetic Imagination*, 2nd ed. (Minneapolis: Augsburg Fortress, 2001), 14, 15.

3 Brueggemann, *Prophetic Imagination*, 16.

4 Merriam-Webster, *Merriam-Webster's Collegiate Dictionary*, 11th ed. (Springfield, MA: Merriam-Webster, 2014).

5 Brueggemann, *Prophetic Imagination*, 60.

6 Brueggemann, *Prophetic Imagination*, 18.

Chapter 6 (pp. 76–85)

1 William Dewsbury, *True Prophecy* . . . (London: Giles Calvert, 1655), 1.

2 Jean Zaru, *Occupied with Nonviolence: A Palestinian Woman Speaks* (Minneapolis: Fortress Press, 2008), 125.

3 As quoted in Marcelle Martin "Standing Rock: Hope and a Call to Action," Dec. 17, 2016, *A Whole Heart* (blog), https://awholeheart.com/2016/12/17/standing-rock-hope-and-a-call-to-action/.

Chapter 7 (pp. 86–92)

1 Brueggemann, *Prophetic Imagination*, 88.

2 Mary Howgill, *Vision of the Lord of Hosts* [1662], Digital Quaker Collection, Earlham School of Religion, http://esr.earlham.edu/dqc/.

3 Brueggemann, *Prophetic Imagination*, 11.

4 Brian Drayton, *A Language for the Inward Landscape: Spiritual Wisdom from the Quaker Movement* (Philadelphia: Tract Association of Friends, 2015), 58.

5 Drayton, *Inward Landscape*, 63.

6 Jean Zaru, "A Journey towards Transformation," Brussels, Oct. 30, 2010, p. 4, accessed Nov. 20, 2017, http://www.qcea.org/wp-content/uploads/2011/04/conf-jean-zaru-nov-2010.pdf.

7 Nancy Gibbs Richard, *A Small Steadying Sail of Love* (Santa Rosa, CA: Angela Center Press, 2007), 33.

8 Anne Morrow Lindbergh, *Hour of Gold, Hour of Lead* (New York: Harcourt Brace Jovanovich, 1973), 179–80.

Chapter 8 (pp. 93–99)

1 Fox, *Journal of George Fox,* 103–4.

2 Carla Gerona, *Night Journeys: The Power of Dreams in Transatlantic Quaker Culture* (Charlotte: University of Virginia Press, 2004), 29.

3 Gerona, *Night Journeys,* 7.

Chapter 9 (pp. 100–8)

1 Brueggemann, *Prophetic Imagination,* 11.

2 Henry Nouwen, as quoted in Avis Crowe and Dyckman W. Vermilye, *The Ministry of Presence: Without Agenda in South Africa,* Pendle Hill Pamphlet #293 (Wallingford, PA: Pendle Hill Publications, 1990), 10.

3 For examples, see Taber, *The Prophetic Stream,* 36.

4 Howard H. Brinton, *Prophetic Ministry,* Pendle Hill Pamphlet #54 (Wallingford, PA: Pendle Hill Publications), 4–5.

5 Bill Taber, opening remarks, School of the Spirit Reunion and Retreat on Prophetic Ministry, February 28, 2004. Used with permission.

Chapter 12 (pp. 120–32)

1 Zaru, "A Journey towards Transformation," 6.

2 Isaac Penington, *Some Directions to the Panting Soul* [1661], in *The Works of Isaac Penington: A Minister of the Gospel in the Society of Friends,* vol. 2 (D. Heston, 1861), p. 222.

3 Fox, *Journal of George Fox,* 14, 15.

4 Fox, *Journal of George Fox,* 11.

5 Yrma Halarión Escobar, in *From Encounter to Ministry: The Life and Faith of Latin American Friends,* ed. Nancy Thomas (Philadelphia: Friends World Committee for Consultation Section of the Americas, 2014), 4–5.

6 Escobar, "From Encounter to Ministry," 5.

Chapter 13 (pp. 133–41)

1 Isaac Penington, *Knowing the Mystery of Life Within: Selected Writings of Isaac Penington in Their Historical and Theological Context,* ed. R. Melvin Keiser and Rosemary Moore (London: Quaker Books, 2005), 181.

[2] Penington, *Knowing the Mystery of Life Within*, 189.

[3] Penington, *Works of Isaac Penington*, vol. 1 (D. Heston, 1861), 242.

Chapter 15 (pp. 149–57)

[1] "Live Up to the Light That Thou Hast," words by Caroline Fox (1841), music by Susan Stark (1982).

Chapter 16 (pp. 158–65)

[1] C. Wess Daniels, "No! Yes and . . . (Matthew 3)," *Gathering in Light* (blog), February 20, 2014, http://gatheringinlight.com/ 2014/02/20/no-yes-and-matthew-3/#more-5140.

[2] Daniels, "No! Yes and . . . (Matthew 3)."

Chapter 18 (pp. 172–87)

[1] Fox, *Journal of George Fox*, 19.

[2] Fox, *Journal of George Fox*, 19.

[3] Jennifer Elam, *Dancing With God through the Storm: Mysticism and Mental Illness*, Pendle Hill Pamphlet #344 (Wallingford, PA: Pendle Hill Publications, 1999), 5.

[4] Elam, *Dancing With God*, 5.

[5] Elam*, Dancing With God*, 38.

[6] Elam, *Dancing With God*, 7.

[7] Elam, *Dancing With God*, 9.

[8] Jones, T. Canby, ed., "Epistle X," *The Power of the Lord Is Over All: The Pastoral Letters of George Fox* (Richmond, IN: Friends United Press, 1989), 7.

[9] Mewlana Jalaluddin Rumi, "The Guest House," trans. Coleman Barks, All Poetry, accessed Nov. 29, 2017, https://allpoetry.com/poem/8534703-The-Guest-House-by-Mewlana-Jalaluddin-Rumi.

[10] Kenneth P. Jacobsen, personal communication with author, Feb. 14, 2017.

[11] Milan Rei, "George Lakey: Nonviolent Warrior," *Peace News*, no. 2544 (April 2012), http://peacenews.info/node/6690/george-lakey-nonviolent-warrior.

[12] Rei, "George Lakey."

[13] Elise Boulding, *One Small Plot of Heaven* (Wallingford, PA: Pendle Hill Press, 1989), 210.

14 Boulding, *One Small Plot of Heaven*, 211. The Tao is the divine order, a balance between stillness and action that can be lived out within the family.

15 Boulding, *One Small Plot of Heaven*, 214.

Chapter 19 (pp. 188–200)

1 Patience A. Schenck, "Answering the Call to Heal the World," Pendle Hill Pamphlet #383 (Wallingford, PA: Pendle Hill Press, 2006), 4.

2 American Friends Service Committee, "Do's and Don't's for Bystander Intervention," Dec. 1, 2016, American Friends Service Committee, https://www.afsc.org/ document/handout-dos-and-donts-bystander-intervention-pdf.

3 Rosemary Moore, *The Light in Their Consciences* (University Park: Pennsylvania State University Press, 2000), 82.

4 Micah Bales, "Holy Anger," November 12, 2012, accessed October 10, 2017, http://www.micahbales.com/2012/page/3/.

5 Bales, "Holy Anger."

Chapter 20 (pp. 202–21)

1 Moore, *The Light in Their Consciences,* 160–92.

2 Robert K. Greenleaf, *Servant Leadership: A Journey into the Nature of Legitimate Power and Greatness* (New York: Paulist Press, 2002), 22.

3 Jan Wood, "A Broken and a Contrite Heart," *SEEDS* [Good News Associates], January 2013, http://goodnewsassoc.org/wp-content/uploads/2013/01/SEEDS-January-2013.pdf.

4 Wood, "A Broken and a Contrite Heart."

Chapter 21 (pp. 222–34)

1 Brueggemann, *The Prophetic Imagination*, 4, 19, 115–19.

2 Lloyd Lee Wilson, "Faithful to the Promptings of Love," in Margery Post Abbott and Peggy Senger Parsons, eds., *Walk Worthy of Your Calling: Quakers and the Traveling Ministry* (Richmond, IN: Friends United Press, 2004), 95–111.

3 John Punshon, "The Importance of Corporate Discernment," in Abbott and Parsons, *Walk Worthy of Your Calling*, 121.

4 Abbott and Parsons, *Walk Worthy of Your Calling*.

Chapter 23 (pp. 244–59)

1 Mike Huber, as quoted in C. Weiss Daniels, "Mike Huber on Authority, Conflict, and Love in Quaker Contexts," *Gathering in Light* (blog), March 24, 2017, http://gatheringinlight.com/

2017/03/24/mike-huber-on-authority-conflict-and-love-in-quaker-contexts/.

[2] Bruce M. Metzger and Michael D. Coogan, *Oxford Companion to the Bible* (New York: Oxford University Press, 1993), 138.

Chapter 24 (pp. 260–74)

[1] Fox, *Journal of George Fox*, 11.

[2] A brief definition of the uncertainty principle is provided by *Webster's New Universal Unabridged Dictionary* (New York: Barnes and Noble, 1996):

> The principle of quantum mechanics, formulated by Heisenberg, that the accurate measurement of one of two related, observable quantities, as position and momentum or energy and time, produces uncertainties in the measurement of the other. (p. 2055)

Source: http://schools-wikipedia.org/2006/wp/u/Uncertainty_principle.htm.

Chapter 25 (pp. 275–81)

[1] Zaru, "A Journey towards Transformation," 7.

[2] Micah Bales, "Together in the Truth," *The Lamb's War* (blog), July 9, 2012, www.micahbales.com/together-in-truth.html.

[3] The Merton quote is from Thomas Merton, "Message to Poets," in *The Literary Essays of Thomas Merton*, ed. Patrick Hart (New York: New Directions, 1985), 373.

Chapter 26 (pp. 283–90)

[1] Isaac Penington, *Babylon the Great Described* [1659], in Penington, *Knowing the Mystery of Life*, 139.

Chapter 27 (pp. 291–302)

[1] Lloyd Lee Wilson, "Taking on the Risks of Ministry," in *Essays on the Quaker Vision of Gospel Order* (Burnsville, NC: Celo Valley Books, 1993), 73–89.

[2] Tom Gates notes that both this story and the substance of his introduction of the panel may be found in *Opening the Scriptures: Bible Lessons from the 2005 Annual Gathering of Friends* (Philadelphia: Quaker Press, 2006), 18–22.

[3] Zaru, "A Journey towards Transformation," 3.

Chapter 29 (pp. 312–21)

[1] Abraham J. Heschel, *The Prophets: An Introduction* (New York: Harper, 1962), 105.

[2] Anthony Manousos, ed. *A Western Quaker Reader* (Whittier, CA: Friends Bulletin, 2000), 9.

Chapter 30 (pp. 322–27)

[1] G. H. Sabine, ed., *The Works of Gerrard Winstanley* (Ithaca, NY: Cornell University Press, 1941), as quoted in Christopher Hill, *The World Turned Upside Down: Radical Ideas during the English Revolution* (London: Pelican Books, 1972), 386.

[2] Edward Burrough, as quoted in Hill, *World Turned Upside Down*, 386.

Chapter 32 (pp. 334–40)

[1] "G.I.," preface to William Mucklow, *The spirit of the hat, or, The government of the Quakers . . .* (London: printed for F. Smith, 1673), A3.

[2] James Naylor, *The Power and Glory of the lord, Shining Out of the North or the Day of the Lord Dawning: wherein The true Light is holden forth to all who desire to walk in the Day.* (London: printed for Giles Calvert, 1656), 2–3.

[3] Margaret Fell, *A True Testimony from the People of God* (London: printed for Robert Wilson, 1660).

[4] William Penn, *No Cross, No Crown* (Richmond, IN: Friends United Press, 1981), 19.

[5] Brueggemann, *The Prophetic Imagination*, 99.

Chapter 33 (pp. 341–48)

[1] Moore, *The Light in Their Consciences*, 183.

[2] Moore, *The Light in Their Consciences*, 155–63.

[3] Moore, *The Light in Their Consciences*, 157.

[4] Moore, *The Light in Their Consciences*, 157–59.

[5] Moore, *The Light in Their Consciences*, 159.

[6] Moore, *The Light in Their Consciences*, 183–86.

[7] Margaret Fell, "To Gabriel Camelford, A Minister, 1655," in Elsa F. Glines, *Undaunted Zeal: The Letters of Margaret Fell* (Richmond, IN: Friends United Press, 2003), 143.

[8] Fell, "To Gabriel Camelford," 144.

[9] Fell, "To Gabriel Camelford," 148.

[10] Moore, *The Light in Their Consciences*, 90.

[11] Humphrey Smith, *The True and Everlasting Rule of God Discovered* (London: Simmons, 1658), as quoted in Moore, *The Light in Their Consciences*, 163.

[12] Moore, *The Light in Their Consciences*, 224.

Chapter 34 (pp. 349–54)

1 Martin Kelley, "Emergent Church Movement: The Younger Evangelicals and Quaker Renewal," September 6, 2003, *Quaker Ranter* (blog), accessed March 26, 2015, www.quakerranter.org /2003/09/emergent_church_movement_the_younger evangelicals.

2 Kelley, "Emergent Church Movement."

3 Kelley, "Emergent Church Movement."

4 Kelley, "Emergent Church Movement."

5 Julian Brelsford, Releasing Ministry Alliance, April 2, 2014, Facebook, https://www.facebook.com/groups/releasingministry/ permalink/276680749158291/.

Chapter 35 (pp. 355–68)

1 Noah Baker Merrill, "Where We Are Changed" (Philadelphia: Wider Quaker Fellowship, 2012), 3.

2 Merrill, "Where We Are Changed," 6.

3 Robin Mohr, "Convergent Friends," in Margery Post Abbott et al., eds., *Historical Dictionary of the Friends (Quakers)*, 2nd ed. (Lanham, MD: Scarecrow Press, 2012), 87.

4 Robin Mohr, "The New Monasticism in Print and in Person," *What Canst Thou Say?* (blog), April 9, 2009, http://robinmsf.blogspot.com/2009/04/new-monasticism-in-print-and-in-person.html.

5 Mohr, "The New Monasticism."

6 Mohr, "The New Monasticism."

7 Robin Mohr, "Christianity for the Rest of Us," *What Canst Thou Say?* (blog), January 25, 2008, http://robinmsf.blogspot.com/2008/01/.

8 Eileen Flanagan, "Fight Back," *Grid Magazine* (Feb, 25, 2015), http://www.gridphilly.com/grid-magazine/2015/2/25/fight-back.html.

9 Martin Kelley, "Peace and Twenty-Somethings," *Quaker Ranter* (blog), Oct. 17, 2003, http://www.quakerranter.org/ peace_and_twentysomethings/

10 Micah Bales, "Together in the Truth, *The Lamb's War* (blog), July 9, 2012, http://lambswar.blogspot.com/2012/07/together-in-truth.html.

11 Micah Bales, "Why Conflict Is Good for Us," Red Letter Christians, June 13, 2003, http://www.redletterchristians.org/ why-conflict-is-good-for-us/.

[12] Cherice Bock, "On Power," *Quaker Oats Live* (blog), Jan. 24, 2016, http://quakeroatslive.blogspot.com/2016/01/.

[13] Bock, "On Power."

[14] Noah Baker Merrill, *Prophets, Midwives and Thieves: Reclaiming the Ministry of the Whole* (Winter Park, FL: Southeastern Yearly Meeting Publications, 2013).

[15] C. Wess Daniels, *A Convergent Model of Renewal: Remixing the Quaker Tradition in a Participatory Culture* (Eugene, OR: Pickwick Publications, 2015).

Chapter 36 (pp. 369–76)

[1] "The Trash Vortex," Greenpeace, accessed January 9, 2014, https://www.greenpeace.org/archive-international/en/campaigns/oceans/fit-for-the-future/pollution/trash-vortex/.

[2] John Woolman, *The Journal of John Woolman*, John Greenleaf Whittier Edition Text (New York: Corinth Books, 1961), 118.

Chapter 37 (pp. 377–86)

[1] Keith Helmuth, Testimony, in Canadian Yearly Meeting of the Religious Society of Friends, *Faith and Practice* (1989), 4.69.

[2] Douglas Gwyn, *A Sustainable Life: Quaker Faith and Practice in the Renewal of Creation* (Philadelphia: QuakerPress of FGC, 2014), 129.

[3] "The Kabarak Call for Peace and Ecojustice," April 24, 2012, *Friends World Committee for Consultation*, http://fwcc.world/fwcc-news/the-kabarak-call-for-peace-and-ecojustice.

[4] "The Kabarak Call for Peace and Ecojustice."

[5] Cherice Bock, "Climatologists, Theologians, and Prophets: Toward an Ecotheology of Critical Hope," *Cross Currents* 66 (March 2016): 10.

[6] Susannah Kay Brindle, *To Learn a New Song: A Quaker Contribution towards Real Reconciliation with the Earth and Its Peoples*, James Backhouse Lecture (Australia Yearly Meeting of the Religious Society of Friends, 2000), 10.

[7] Brindle, *To Learn a New Song*, 58.

[8] Brindle, *To Learn a New Song*, 40–41.

Chapter 38 (pp. 387–97)

[1] Walter Brueggemann, *Reality, Grief, Hope: Three Urgent Prophetic Tasks* (Grand Rapids, MI: Eerdmanns, 2014), 128.

[2] Wilson, *Essays on the Quaker Vision of Gospel Order*, 152.

Appendix C (pp. 406–16)

[1] Bill Taber's opening remarks at the School of the Spirit Reunion and Retreat on Prophetic Ministry, February 28, 2004. Used with permission.

Appendix D (pp. 417–23)

[1] Abbott and Parsons, *Walk Worthy of Your Calling*, 169.

[2] Janet Hoffmann and Kenneth Sutton, "A Deeper Service: Ministers and Elders Working Together," in Abbott and Parsons, *Walk Worthy of Your Calling*, 153.

[3] Alivia Biko and Peggy Senger Parsons, "Companions on the Road," in Abbott and Parsons, *Walk Worthy of Your Calling*, 144.

[4] Nancy Hawkins, "How Shall They Preach Except They Be Sent?" in Abbott and Parsons, *Walk Worthy of Your Calling*, 93.

INDEX

459

traveling, 134, 229–
31, 244–45, 419
ministry of being, 103–
5, 408
Mohr, Robin, 355–59
Mombo, Esther, 39–
40, 48–49, 79–80,
228–29, 249–50,
256–57, 308–9,
349–50
monasticism, new,
356–58
Morrison, Norman, 177
Morrison, Peggy. *See*
Parsons, Peggy
Mott, Lucretia, 64, 260
mourning. *See* grief
Movement for a New
Society, 263, 359–60
Muhanji, John, 43–44
Muhr, Eric, 365
Musalia, Margaret
Namikoye, 146–47,
196, 214–15, 252–53
mysticism, 110, 146,
176–77, 178, 276,
391–92
new creation. *See*
creation, new
nonviolence, 58, 89,
159, 359
Nouwen, Henri, 104
nudge. *See* leading (of
the Spirit)
obedience, 13, 130, 158,
159, 177, 336–37,
339
obstacles, structural,
303–10
O'Hara, Jay, 350
oppression, 38, 57, 118,
198

outrunning the Guide.
See Guide, Inward
Pacific Northwest
Quaker Women's
Theology
Conference, 316, 345
pacifism, 95, 184
pain, 38, 90–91, 127–
28, 185, 338–40,
407, *See also*
suffering; trauma
paradox, 8, 48, 60, 69,
89, 125, 185, 265–
69, 298, 365
Parnell, James, 345
Parsons, Peggy, 27–28,
419
pastor. *See* minister
pastoral care. *See*
accompaniment
patience, 57–59, 136,
137–38, 159, 256
peace, 184, 268, 363–
65, 378, 395
peaceable kingdom.
See kingdom of God
peer group, 241, 418
Pendle Hill (England),
93
Penington, Isaac, 42–
43, 124, 137–38, 179,
285, 329–30
Penington, Mary, 94
perfection. *See*
wholeness
Peyton, Julie, 53–55,
312–14, 315, 317
polarization, 265–69
power, 365–66
power (of God), 79,
129, 180–81, 196,
336, 374

463

Also available from Inner Light Books

Primitive Quakerism Revived
by Paul Buckley.

> ISBN 978-0-9998332-2-3(hardcover) $25
> ISBN 978-0-9998332-3-0 (paperback)$15
> ISBN 978-0-9998332-5-4 (eBook)$10

Primitive Christianity Revived
by William Penn
Translated into Modern English by Paul Buckley

> ISBN 978-0-9998332-0-9 (hardcover) $25
> ISBN 978-0-9998332-1-6 (paperback) $15
> ISBN 978-0-9998332-4-7 (eBook)$10

Jesus, Christ and Servant of God
Meditations on the Gospel According to John
By David Johnson

> ISBN 978–0–9970604–6–1 (hardcover) $35
> ISBN 978–0–9970604–7–8 (paperback) $25
> ISBN 978–0–9970604–8–5 (eBook) $12.50

The Anti-War
By Douglas Gwyn

> ISBN 978-0-9970604-3-0, (hardcover)$30
> ISBN 978-0-9970604-4-7, (paperback)$17.50
> ISBN 978-0-9970604-5-4, (eBook) $10

Our Life Is Love, the Quaker Spiritual Journey
By Marcelle Martin

> ISBN 978-0-9970604-0-9, (hardcover)$30
> ISBN 978-0-9970604-1-6, (paperback)$17.50
> ISBN 978-0-9970604-2-5, (eBook) $10

A Quaker Prayer Life
By David Johnson

> ISBN 978-0-9834980-5-6 (hardcover) $20
> ISBN 978-0-9834980-6-3 (paperback) $12.50
> ISBN 978-0-9834980-7-0 (eBook)) $10

The Essential Elias Hicks
By Paul Buckley

> ISBN 978-0-9834980-8-7 (hardcover) $25
> ISBN 978-0-9834980-9-4 (paperback) $15
> ISBN 978-0-9970604-9-2 (eBook)$10

The Journal of Elias Hicks
Edited by Paul Buckley

> ISBN 978-0-9797110-4-6, (hardcover)$50
> ISBN 978-0-9797110-5-3, (paperback)$30

Dear Friend: The Letters and Essays of Elias Hicks
Edited by Paul Buckley

> ISBN 978-0-9834980-0-1 (hardcover) $45
> ISBN 978-0-9834980-1-8 (paperback) $25

The Early Quakers and 'the Kingdom of God'
By Gerard Guiton

> ISBN 978-0-9834980-2-5, (hardcover)$45
> ISBN 978-0-9834980-3-2 , (paperback)$25
> ISBN 978-0-9834980-4-9, (eBook) $12.50

John Woolman and the Affairs of Truth
Edited by James Proud

> ISBN 978-0-9797110-6-0, (hardcover)$45
> ISBN 978-0-9797110-7-7, (paperback)$25

Cousin Ann's Stories for Children by Ann Preston
Edited by Richard Beards
Illustrated by Stevie French

> ISBN 978-0-9797110-8-4, (hardcover)$20,
> ISBN 978-0-9797110-9-1, (paperback)$12

Counsel to the Christian-Traveller: also Meditations and Experiences
By William Shewen

> ISBN 978-0-9797110-0-8 (hardcover) $25
> ISBN 978-0-9797110-1-5 (paperback) $15

CPSIA information can be obtained
at www.ICGtesting.com
Printed in the USA
LVHW09s0904081018
592787LV00006B/949/P